JOURNAL FOR THE STUDY OF THE NEW TESTAMENT SUPPLEMENT SERIES
139

Sheffield Academic Press

Jesus and the Sabbath in Matthew's Gospel

Yong-Eui Yang

Journal for the Study of the New Testament
Supplement Series 139

To my mother, Nam-Soon Shin
and
my wife, Hyun-Ja Park

Copyright © 1997 Sheffield Academic Press

Published by
Sheffield Academic Press Ltd
Mansion House
19 Kingfield Road
Sheffield S11 9AS
England

Typeset by Sheffield Academic Press
and
Printed on acid-free paper in Great Britain
by Bookcraft Ltd
Midsomer Norton, Bath

British Library Cataloguing in Publication Data

A catalogue record for this book is available
from the British Library

ISBN 1-85075-654-6

CONTENTS

PREFACE

It is my privilege to express my deep gratitude to those many persons and institutions without whom this work would never have come to completion. My special thanks go, first of all, to my doctoral supervisor, the Revd Dr R.T. France, who has enabled me to look into the precious world of Matthew's Gospel and to appreciate it. In spite of many other things he must have taken care of as the Principal of Wycliffe Hall, Oxford, he has devoted countless hours to reading and responding to every piece of my work. Without his judicious criticism and timely encouragement the present form of the work could not have existed.

I am also grateful to my second supervisor, Professor G.N. Stanton of King's College, University of London, who has offered valuable suggestions about the overall structure of the thesis, especially regarding Chapters 2 and 7. His comments with encouragement have helped me to carry on my project with some confidence. Dr J.G. McConville kindly offered insightful suggestions for Chapter 1 even before I shaped it, and has read the chapter and given very helpful comments on it. I have been also privileged to discuss my subject with Dr R. Mohrlang; his committed attitude to the study of the Scripture has challenged me a lot. My sincere gratitude also must be extended to Dr M.M.B. Turner of London Bible College and Dr M. Bockmuehl of the University of Cambridge, who, as my external advisors, offered insightful comments on the general structure of my thesis; their comments helped me to shape my thesis in a more balanced way. Special thanks are due to my two examiners, Professor I.H. Marshall of the University of Aberdeen and Dr D. Wenham of Wycliffe Hall, who have offered not only helpful criticisms but also encouragement to seek publication. I am very grateful to Professor S.E. Porter for accepting this work into the *JSNT* Supplement series.

I am financially obliged to a number of Korean churches and a scholarship fund founded by Asian Mission in Seoul. More than one third of the financial resources have been provided by an unknown Christian brother who does not want to reveal himself even to me until I finish this work. He wants to remain secret according to Jesus' instruction in Mt. 6.1-4! Some other friends of mine have also helped my research financially. I am particularly grateful to Mrs Jung-Ran Paek for her regular and substantial support. Along with this financial support, the Revd Nam-Joong Yoon, Professor Man-Yoel Lee, Dr Tae-Woong Lee, Dr Jung-Suk Rhee and my co-workers in the rural churches in Kang-Won Province, Korea, have encouraged me in this research with their whole-hearted prayer and love. I extend my sincere gratitude to them.

My greatest praise and thanks are reserved for my family. My four precious children, Sung-Jin, Kyung-Jin, Hyun-Jin, and Eui-Jin, have been a continuous source of much joy and comfort. Their cheerful ways of behaviour at home have offered a refreshing relief from the heavy demands of research. To my mother, who first guided me into the truth of Christianity and taught me the true rest not only at home but also in Christ, and to my wife, with whom I have experienced the preciousness of the true rest at home in Christ even throughout the hard times of my research—to these two women I dedicate this study with my warmest gratitude and love.

June, 1996

ABBREVIATIONS

AB	Anchor Bible
AnBib	Analecta biblica
ANRW	*Aufstieg und Niedergang der römischen Welt*
ASNU	Acta Seminarii neotestamentici upsaliensis
AUSS	*Andrews University Seminary Studies*
BETL	Bibliotheca ephemeridum theologicarum lovaniensium
BEvT	Beiträge zur evangelischen Theologie
Bib	*Biblica*
BNTC	Black's New Testament Commentaries
BZ	*Biblische Zeitschrift*
BZNW	Beihefte zur *ZNW*
CBQ	*Catholic Biblical Quarterly*
CBQMS	*Catholic Biblical Quarterly*, Monograph Series
CCWJCW	Cambridge Commentaries on Writings of the Jewish and Christian World 200 BC to AD 200
ConBNT	Coniectanea biblica, New Testament
CRINT	Compendia Rerum Iudaicarum ad Novum Testamentum
DJG	Green, J.B., *et al.* (eds.), *Dictionary of Jesus and the Gospels*
EDNT	Balz, H., and G. Schneider (eds.), *Exegetical Dictionary of the New Testament*
EKKNT	Evangelisch-katholischer Kommentar zum Neuen Testament
ETL	*Ephemerides theologicae lovanienses*
EvQ	*Evangelical Quarterly*
EvT	*Evangelische Theologie*
EVV	English Versions
FRLANT	Forschungen zur Religion und Literatur des Alten und Neuen Testaments
GNS	Good News Studies
HAT	Handbuch zum Alten Testament
HNT	Handbuch zum Neuen Testament
HTKNT	Herders theologischer Kommentar zum Neuen Testament
ICC	International Critical Commentary
Int	*Interpretation*
ITC	International Theological Commentary
JBL	*Journal of Biblical Literature*
JETS	*Journal of the Evangelical Theological Society*

JQR	*Jewish Quarterly Review*
JSNT	*Journal for the Study of the New Testament*
JSNTSup	*Journal for the Study of the New Testament*, Supplement Series
JSOTSup	*Journal for the Study of the Old Testament*, Supplement Series
JSPSup	*Journal for the Study of the Pseudepigrapha*, Supplement Series
JTS	*Journal of Theological Studies*
LCC	Library of Christian Classics
LCL	Loeb Classical Library
NAC	New American Commentary
NCB	New Century Bible
NGS	New Gospel Studies
NICNT	New International Commentary on the New Testament
NICOT	New International Commentary on the Old Testament
NIGTC	The New International Greek Testament Commentary
NovT	*Novum Testamentum*
NovTSup	*Novum Testamentum*, Supplements
NTAbh	Neutestamentliche Abhandlungen
NTD	Das Neue Testament Deutsch
NTL	New Testament Library
NTS	*New Testament Studies*
OTL	Old Testament Library
RevQ	*Revue de Qumran*
RNT	Regensburger Neues Testament
ResQ	*Restoration Quarterly*
SBLDS	SBL Dissertation Series
SBS	Stuttgarter Bibelstudien
SBT	Studies in Biblical Theology
SNTSMS	Society for New Testament Studies Monograph Series
SNTU	Studien zum Neuen Testament und seiner Umwelt
SPB	Studia Post Biblica
SJT	*Scottish Journal of Theology*
SupVC	Supplements to *Vigiliae christianae*
TDNT	Kittel, G., and G. Friedrich (eds.), *Theological Dictionary of the New Testament*
THKNT	Theologischer Handkommentar zum Neuen Testament
TNTC	Tyndale New Testament Commentaries
TZ	*Theologische Zeitschrift*
VC	*Vigiliae christianae*
WBC	Word Biblical Commentary
WD	*Wort und Dienst*
ZAW	*Zeitschrift für die alttestamentliche Wissenschaft*
ZKT	*Zeitschrift für katholische Theologie*
ZNW	*Zeitschrift für die neutestamentliche Wissenschaft*
ZTK	*Zeitschrift für Theologie und Kirche*

The sabbath has been a controversial issue throughout church history, especially with regard to how the Old Testament/Jewish sabbath relates to the Christian observance of the Lord's day/Sunday. The sabbath was already a matter of controversy during Jesus' ministry (e.g. Mt. 12.1-14 par.; Lk. 13.10-17; 14.1-6; Jn 5.1-18) and also among the earliest Christians (e.g. Col. 2.16-17; cf. Rom. 14.5-8; Heb. 4.1-11). Well before the mid-second century the Apostolic Fathers linked the Lord's day with the sabbath, but not yet as a day for rest but only as a day for worship. It was not until the Constantinian legislation (321 CE)[1] that the Lord's day could begin to be considered also as a day for rest free from work.[2] It was, however, Thomas Aquinas (1225–74) who firmly established the theological foundation for scholastic sabbatarianism, which regards the Lord's day as the Christian substitute for the sabbath and keeps it as the 'Christian sabbath', mainly on the basis of his scholastic 'Natural Law' theory.[3] But this scholastic sabbatarianism was challenged and abandoned by the Reformers. Calvin, for example, made it clear that the sabbath is fulfilled in Christ and therefore abrogated and that worship on Sunday is a matter of convenience and order only, while rest on Sunday is required only in order to be free to worship.[4] The Reformers'

---

1. *Codex Iustinianus* 3.12.2 (Mar. 3.321) and *Codex Theodosianus* 2.8.1 (Jul. 3.321).

2. The first extant Christian writing which claims that the sabbath has been transferred to Sunday is Eusebius's commentary on Ps. 91 written after 330 CE. Yet even for Eusebius it is the worship dimension of the sabbath that has been transferred to Sunday, and not the rest dimension proper; see R. Bauckham, 'Sabbath and Sunday in the Post-Apostolic Church', in D.A. Carson (ed.), *From Sabbath to Lord's Day: A Biblical, Historical, and Theological Investigation* (Grand Rapids: Zondervan, 1982), pp. 282-85.

3. Thomas Aquinas, *Summa Theologica* (5 vols.; repr.; New York: Benziger Brothers, 1948), 1a 2ae 100.

4. J. Calvin, *Institutes of the Christian Religion* (ed. J.T. McNeill; trans. F.L. Battles; LCC, 20, 21; 2 vols.; Philadelphia: Westminster, 1960), 2.8.28-34. See

breach with scholastic sabbatarianism, however, was not inherited by their successors. Instead, by the seventeenth century, the Puritans, for example, returned to the pre-Reformation sabbatarianism,[5] and such a Puritan sabbatarian view, which finds its classical expression in the Westminster Confession (1647), has been adopted or adapted by the majority of the English, Scottish and American Protestant churches.[6] Along with this sabbatarian tradition, however, there have been, on the one hand, those who have not held or who have opposed a sabbatarian position such as W. Tyndale (1531), P. Heylyn (1635), P. Doddridge (1763), J.A. Hessey (1860), *et al.*,[7] and, on the other hand, seventh-day observance movements such as the Seventh-Day Baptists (since the mid-seventeenth century) and the Seventh-Day Adventists (since the mid-nineteenth century),[8] though the influence of neither movement compares with that of Puritan sabbatarianism.

At the present time there is no clear sign that the gap between the different positions is narrowing, in spite of various attempts at dialogue between those of differing views.[9] There are still four or five distinct positions which may be represented respectively by the following works: (1) the traditional Puritan sabbatarianism is advocated by R.T. Beckwith

R. Bauckham, 'Sabbath and Sunday in the Protestant Tradition', in Carson (ed.), *Lord's Day*, pp. 315-17.

5.   P.K. Jewett, *The Lord's Day: A Theological Guide to the Christian Day of Worship* (Grand Rapids: Eerdmans, 1971), pp. 115-21; Bauckham, 'Protestant Tradition', pp. 317-29; J.H. Primus, 'Sunday: The Lord's Day as a Sabbath —Protestant Perspectives on the Sabbath', in T.C. Eskenazi *et al.* (eds.), *The Sabbath in Jewish and Christian Traditions* (New York: Crossroad, 1991), pp. 108-15; E. Spier, *Der Sabbat* (Das Judentum, 1; Berlin: Institut Kirche und Judentum, 1992), pp. 127-28.

6.   The Lord's Day Observance Society in England and the Lord's Day Alliance in the United States are good illustrations of how Puritan sabbatarianism has exercised its influence in those countries.

7.   See R.T. Beckwith and W. Stott, *This is the Day: The Biblical Doctrine of the Christian Sunday in its Jewish and Early Church Setting* (London: Marshall, Morgan & Scott, 1978), pp. vii-viii; Bauckham, 'Protestant Tradition', pp. 329-32.

8.   See Bauckham, 'Protestant Tradition', pp. 332-34; S. Bacchiocchi, 'Remembering the Sabbath: The Creation-Sabbath in Jewish and Christian History', in Eskenazi *et al.* (eds.), *Sabbath*, pp. 82-83.

9.   Cf., for example, the introductions of Carson, *Lord's Day*, pp. 14-16; S. Bacchiocchi, *The Sabbath in the New Testament* (Berrien Springs: Biblical Perspectives, 2nd edn, 1990 [1985]), pp. 12-25; Eskenazi *et al.* (eds.), *Sabbath*, pp. ix-xvi.

and W. Stott in their joint work *This is The Day* (1978);[10] (2) the Seventh-Day Adventist view is upheld by S. Bacchiocchi in his *From Sabbath to Sunday* (1977);[11] (3) W. Rordorf espouses a radically non/anti-sabbatarian view in his *Sunday* (1968 [1962]);[12] (4) P.K. Jewett in his *The Lord's Day* (1971)[13] attempts to modify the traditional sabbatarian position, but ultimately comes very close to the sabbatarian view; (5) D.A. Carson and six other biblical (and historical) scholars in their symposium *From Sabbath to Lord's Day* (1982)[14] expound a clearly non-sabbatarian but less radical view (than that of Rordorf).

Most of the works named above attempt to establish their own positions on the basis of the data from the Scriptures and the evidence of the post-apostolic period, as their subtitles indicate. Nevertheless, they do not always treat the biblical data in sufficient depth, sometimes failing to provide any exegetical discussion of the biblical texts in question; as a result they fail to carry conviction at certain crucial points. And if their treatment of the biblical data proves unreliable, it is inevitable that their reconstructions of the evidence of the post-apostolic church should also be called in question. Such being the case, I propose here to attempt more thorough and convincing exegetical investigations of some of the biblical texts in question, in order to provide a more reliable foundation for further discussion of the sabbath-related issue. If the exegetical investigation is to be thorough and reliable, however, it is necessary to see each text in question at least in the light of its literary co-text and socio-historical context[15] as well as of the theology and literary genre of the

---

10. Subtitled *The Biblical Doctrine of the Christian Sunday in its Jewish and Early Church Setting*. See also W. Stott, 'The Theology of the Christian Sunday in the Early Church' (DPhil thesis, Oxford, 1966); F.N. Lee, *The Covenantal Sabbath: The Weekly Sabbath Scripturally and Historically Considered* (London: LDOS, 1969).

11. Subtitled *A Historical Investigation of the Rise of Sunday Observance in Early Christianity* (Rome: Pontifical Gregorian University Press). See also his later works, *Divine Rest for Human Restlessness* (Rome: Pontifical Gregorian University Press, 1980); *The Sabbath in the New Testament*.

12. Subtitled *The History of the Day of Rest and Worship in the Earliest Centuries of the Christian Church* (trans. A.A.K. Graham; London: SCM Press, 1968); the German original appeared in 1962 (Zürich: Zwingli Verlag).

13. Subtitled *A Theological Guide to the Christian Day of Worship*.

14. Subtitled *A Biblical, Historical, and Theological Investigation*.

15. I will use the terms *co-text* and *context* with distinct meanings throughout the study. The *co-text* refers to 'the sentences, paragraphs, chapters, surrounding the text

whole book to which the text belongs.[16] Surprisingly enough, there has been no serious attempt to offer such a comprehensive exegetical study of, for example, the evangelists' sabbath texts,[17] which are crucial in discussions of the sabbath issue because most of the scholars mentioned above seek to relate Jesus to the sabbath and/or the Lord's day, and so use these evangelists' texts one way or another in order to demonstrate the credibility of their position.

In this book, therefore, I will attempt to offer a thorough and comprehensive exegetical study of a group of those texts, that is, Matthew's two sabbath controversy pericopes (Mt. 12.1-8, 9-14) together with a further Matthean sabbath saying (Mt. 24.20). I have selected these texts for a number of reasons. First of all, these texts and their synoptic parallels contain key pronouncements on the relations between Jesus and the sabbath (Mt. 12.8[18] par.) and between people and the sabbath (Mk 2.27[19]) as well as on the principles of behaviour on the sabbath (Mt. 12.7,[20] 12[21]). Secondly, in spite of the crucial importance of these texts, they have frequently been neglected or misused in discussions of the sabbath issue throughout church history;[22] without a proper

and related to it', whereas the *context* refers to 'the sociological and historical setting of the text'; I adopt these definitions from P. Cotterell and M. Turner, *Linguistics and Biblical Interpretation* (London: SPCK, 1989), p. 16.

16. On the necessity of such a multi-dimensional approach to the biblical text (esp. the Gospel text), see, for example, G.N. Stanton, *A Gospel for a New People: Studies in Matthew* (Edinburgh: T. & T. Clark, 1992), pp. 23-110; see also below, Chapter 3, section 1a.

17. M.M.B. Turner, 'The Sabbath, Sunday, and the Law in Luke/Acts', in Carson (ed.), *Lord's Day*, pp. 99-157, is a good attempt to investigate the Lukan sabbath texts in their own right, but his exegetical investigation is inevitably far from comprehensive since it forms only one chapter of a much larger project.

18. κύριος γάρ ἐστιν τοῦ σαββάτου ὁ υἱὸς τοῦ ἀνθρώπου.

19. καὶ ἔλεγεν αὐτοῖς· τὸ σάββατον διὰ τὸν ἄνθρωπον ἐγένετο καὶ οὐχ ὁ ἄνθρωπος διὰ τὸ σάββατον.

20. εἰ δὲ ἐγνώκειτε τί ἐστιν· ἔλεος θέλω καὶ οὐ θυσίαν, οὐκ ἂν κατεδικάσατε τοὺς ἀναιτίους.

21. ὥστε ἔξεστιν τοῖς σάββασιν καλῶς ποιεῖν.

22. For example, it is remarkable to note how the compilers of the Westminster Confession 21.8 could manage to use Jesus' anti-casuistic arguments of Mt. 12.1-13 to support their own casuistic (though positive) regulations; even more remarkably this is indeed the only use of any sabbath text from the Gospels in the whole Confession. U. Luz, *Das Evangelium nach Matthäus (Mt. 8–17)* (EKKNT, 1/2; Zürich und Brauschweig: Benziger Verlag, 1990), p. 234, points out that the 'history

exegetical understanding of these texts, no sabbath doctrine can be said to be properly founded. It is remarkable to note how little space was spared for these pericopes even in the works mentioned above. Thirdly, since these controversy pericopes are found in all the synoptic Gospels, a study of them may be expected to illuminate the stance of the historical Jesus towards the sabbath, a theme that is important for many of the scholars mentioned above. Having said this, however, the primary focus of my study is not on the stance of the historical Jesus as such but rather on Matthew's understanding and way of presenting the relation between Jesus and the sabbath. To this end I shall also compare the presentation of the same material by the other synoptists with that of Matthew.

My study can be divided roughly into three parts. The first part (Chapters 1–2) is the background study for the main texts (Mt. 12.1-8, 9-14; 24.20). Since the sabbath is not an institution which suddenly appeared as a controversial issue only in the time of either Jesus or Matthew, but has a long history throughout the Old Testament and the inter-testamental periods, it is necessary to survey the data in the Old Testament and the post-biblical Jewish literature before we enter into the exegetical study of our texts. In the investigation of the Old Testament sabbath materials, the etiology of the sabbath, its covenantal and cultic character, and its humanitarian aspect will be discussed; along with these discussions some specific sabbath regulations will also be viewed. In the investigation of the post-biblical Jewish literature, the sabbath materials of the Apocrypha and Pseudepigrapha, the Qumran writings, Josephus, Philo, the rabbinic literature, and also some Graeco-Roman references will be discussed. In the discussion of these post-biblical Jewish materials, the main focus will be on the specific sabbath regulations, which noticeably developed during this period. Through this introductory investigation I will aim to establish the background within which Jesus' sabbath controversies and Matthew's presentation of them were formed and, therefore, against which they need to be understood.

The second part (Chapters 3–6) then is devoted to the main exegetical investigation. As I have pointed out above, in order to provide a reliable

of effect' (*Wirkungsgeschichte*) of our texts is surprisingly insignificant, especially until the Reformation period. Even since the Reformation our texts have played a comparatively insignificant role in discussions of the sabbath issue, compared with that played by, for example, Col. 2.16-17 and Heb. 3.7-4.11, let alone the Old Testament sabbath materials (e.g. Gen. 2.2-3; Exod. 20.8-11; Isa. 58.13; Neh. 13.15-22; etc.).

exegesis of the texts, it is necessary to see them in the light of the theology and the literary characteristics of the whole Gospel as well as their immediate co-texts. Therefore, before I commence the exegetical investigation proper, I will first of all state the basic working assumptions regarding the issues which will inevitably be involved in the exegetical discussions—that is, the synoptic problem, the methodology for this exegetical study, the author, date and provenance of the Gospel, Matthew's community, and the literary character and structure of the Gospel. These initial working assumptions, however, will need to be evaluated, extended, or further elaborated throughout the exegetical investigation, whenever it is deemed appropriate and/or necessary (especially in the case of the synoptic problem). In view of the fact that the sabbath controversy pericopes in Mt. 12.1-14 appear to be closely related to Matthew's overall understanding of the law in relation to Jesus, we also need to consider this overall understanding in the whole Gospel prior to the main exegetical investigation of the texts. From this overall consideration, I will conclude that for Matthew the Old Testament law (in all its aspects) is fulfilled by Jesus and that this fulfilment involves an eschatological tension in that it contains elements of both 'continuity' and 'discontinuity'.

In the light of these background and preliminary investigations, the main exegetical investigation will begin with the study of the co-text, since seeing the texts in the light of their literary co-texts is indispensable for the proper understanding of texts like these. I will argue that the two sabbath pericopes in Matthew (12.1-8, 9-14) are inter-related and that the immediately neighbouring pericopes (11.25-30; 12.15-21) are thematically related to the texts. On the basis of these arguments, I will include not only these texts but also the neighbouring pericopes as the objects of the main exegetical investigation. In this exegetical study, rather than focusing primarily on traditio-critical issues, I will concentrate more on the meaning and significance of the texts as they stand, with a view to clarifying the relation between Jesus and the sabbath as it appears in Matthew. From this exegetical study, I will quite confidently draw a conclusion that for Matthew the sabbath, like the law in general, is fulfilled by Jesus—that is to say, Jesus' redemption has fulfilled the ultimate goal for the sabbath, that is, the eschatological rest—and that this fulfilment of the sabbath, like that of other laws, also has elements of 'continuity' and 'discontinuity'. The Christological and eschatological character of these sabbath controversy pericopes is apparent to any careful reader. I will suggest that this characteristic emphasis on Christology and eschatology over against the Pharisees' casuistic concerns in relation to the sabbath betrays Matthew's concern about the danger of a legalistic tendency in sabbath observance among his community. At the final stage of the exegetical study, I will investigate another Matthean sabbath reference (24.20) which is very short but raises some crucial questions. In the light of our understanding of the other two sabbath pericopes and other law-related passages in Matthew, I will conclude that the phrase μηδὲ σαββάτῳ indicates not that flight on the sabbath was wrong in itself, but that it would be practically difficult.

Considering the fact that Matthew's Gospel does not stand alone but is related to the other synoptic Gospels one way or another, my investigation cannot be complete without discussing the non-Matthean synoptic sabbath-related passages (Mk 1.21-34 par.; Lk. 4.16-30; 13.10-17; 14.1-6; 23.56). I will therefore investigate those passages and attempt to explain why they are missing or present in different form in Matthew. From this investigation it will be argued that Matthew is certainly not more conservative than Mark or Luke in respect of the sabbath, and that Matthew is much more careful in presenting the sabbath material than Mark or Luke. I shall thus conclude that the sabbath was still a live and sensitive issue for Matthew's community. With this synoptic comparative study the second part of my study comes to a close.

In the third part (Chapters 7–8), I will firstly attempt to evaluate how Matthew's treatment of the sabbath was adopted, adapted or overlooked by the Apostolic Fathers,[23] the earliest extant non-canonical writings. This aspect of the study is of special interest because it is frequently argued that the influence of Matthew's Gospel on the Apostolic Fathers was greater than that of the other Gospels. The most significant point noted will be the outright rejection of sabbath observance by those post-apostolic writers, and their putting the Lord's (or eighth) day in opposition to the sabbath, both of which have exercised a long-lasting influence on the whole of Christianity (apart from the Seventh-Day Baptists and the Seventh-Day Adventists).

At the very end of this study I will draw out the theological significance and practical implication of Jesus' fulfilment of the sabbath for Matthew and his community.

The scope of this book is limited in many respects, and it is obvious

23. There are relevant passages in Ignatius's *Letter to the Magnesians*, the *Letter of Barnabas*, the *Didache*, and the *Letter to Diognetus*.

that it alone can not resolve all the long-standing problems regarding the sabbath and/or the Lord's day in today's church. Nevertheless, it is my hope that this study may offer a fresh stimulus for further studies not only of these Matthean texts but also of other sabbath-related texts, together with reflections on those exegetical results on the dangers and needs of today's church in relation to the sabbath commandment and institution.

Chapter 1

THE SABBATH IN THE OLD TESTAMENT:
BACKGROUNDS (I)

Before we enter into the main discussion, I need to make some preliminary statements clearly as they will be reflected in the subsequent investigations.

1) The passages related to the sabbath in the Old Testament and the issues involved in them are so numerous that it is beyond the scope of the background investigation to cover all of them. This chapter, therefore, will be limited to the key passages[1] and will discuss only some central issues which are more relevant to the main discussion in the following chapters.[2] Even for the selected passages detailed exegesis will not be offered in view of the scope of this chapter.

2) In dealing with the materials in the Pentateuch I will not depend on source-critical theories very much, not only because the discussion is to be brief and such theories would not change the result of the discussion significantly, but because the dates and the reconstructions of the texts continue to be the subject of scholarly debate.[3] In the following

---

1.   I will limit myself to the weekly sabbath passages; though some passages like Lev. 25.2-7; 26.34-35 regarding the sabbatical year, or Lev. 16.31; 23.32 regarding the Day of Atonement which is called a 'sabbath', are interesting, they are only indirectly related to the weekly sabbath institution, my immediate subject, and I will therefore leave them aside in the present background study.

2.   For full-scale discussions on the Old Testament sabbath in recent decades, see N.-E.A. Andreasen, *The Old Testament Sabbath: A Tradition-Historical Investigation* (SBLDS, 7; Missoula, MT: Society of Biblical Literature, 1972) and E. Jenni, *Die theologische Begründung des Sabbatgebotes im Alten Testament* (Theologische Studien, 46; Zollikon-Zürich: Evangelischer Verlag, 1956); see also F. Pettirsch, 'Das Verbot der opera servilia in der Heiligen Schrift und in der altkirchlichen Exegese', *ZKT* 69 (1947), pp. 257-301.

3.   For example, the various attempts to reconstruct Exod. 20.8-11, one of the key passages dealt with in this chapter, have produced widely differing suggestions;

investigations, I will mostly concentrate on the final form of the texts.[4]

3) Detailed discussion of the origin of the sabbath, which Old Testament scholars once had investigated very enthusiastically, is beyond the scope of this chapter. In the light of more recent investigations,[5] however, it may be suggested with some confidence that the seventh-day sabbath is very old,[6] and that in the existing extra-biblical sources it has not been found but in the ancient Hebrew literature (e.g. Exod. 34.21; Amos 8.4-10) it is clearly mentioned.

1. *Pentateuch*

a. *Etiology of the Sabbath*

In the Old Testament there are three passages which relate the etiology of the sabbath to God's creation activity—Gen. 2.1-3; Exod. 20.11; 31.17. Since the first one, however, seems to be the key passage as regards this issue, I will here concentrate on it with some references to the others.

Gen. 2.1-3, the description of the seventh day in God's creation, makes a conclusion to the creation account. It is, however, significantly different from what has gone before in form and content. Verse 1 serves as a final summing up of ch. 1. And concerning verse 2a, ויכל אלהים ביום השביעי מלאכתו אשר עשה, two points can be discussed here. First of all, the first part of this statement does not necessarily imply that God completed his unfinished work on the seventh day. Elsewhere in the Pentateuch (Gen. 17.22; 49.33; Exod. 40.33; cf. Gen. 24.19; Lev. 16.20; Num. 4.15; etc.), the phrase ויכל indicates that 'the action in question is past', and a pluperfect is to be used in English translations.[7] Hence the

---

cf. B.S. Childs, *Exodus* (OTL; London: SCM Press, 1974), pp. 388-401, 412-17. For the problems of source criticism, see R. Rendtorff, *The Old Testament: An Introduction* (trans. J. Bowden; London: SCM Press, 1985), pp. 157-64.

4.   However, when it is necessary and where some concrete consensus has been reached among Old Testament scholars throughout the history of criticisms, I will simply follow the classical view without discussing it.

5.   Cf. Andreasen, *Sabbath*, pp. 1-9; Childs, *Exodus*, pp. 413-14; H.H.P. Dressler, 'The Sabbath in the Old Testament', in Carson (ed.), *Lord's Day*, pp. 22-24, 37 n. 31.

6.   Andreasen dates it back 'to premonarchical, and undoubtedly to Mosaic times'; he even suggests that it may well be a pre-Mosaic tradition; cf. *Sabbath*, pp. 8, 117-21, 261-65. Cf. E. Lohse, 'σάββατον', *TDNT*, VII, pp. 2-3.

7.   G. Wenham, *Genesis 1–15* (WBC, 1; Waco, TX: Word Books, 1987),

first part can be translated: 'God had completed...on the seventh day'. Secondly, מלאכה is used three times in vv. 2-3 to describe God's creation activity. Since it is the normal word for 'human work' (cf. Gen. 39.11; Exod. 20.9), it is striking that such a unique divine activity should be so described. As C. Westermann suggests, however, the writer must have deliberately chosen this word to *hint* that 'the conclusion of creation' created 'a rhythm which will effect [*sic*] the whole of creation'.[8]

Those who see the sabbath as a 'creation ordinance' might expect to find in vv. 2b-3 the appearance of the noun שַׁבָּת, but actually we only have the phrase ביום השביעי ('the seventh day')—three times in vv. 2-3. It seems to show that the main concern of the biblical writer here is not with the sabbath institution but with God's rest from his creation activity. Therefore we cannot easily assume that the sabbath is seen here as the so-called 'creation ordinance'.[9] Nevertheless, we cannot deny the strong implication of the relationship between God's rest on the seventh day and human rest on the sabbath, since Exod. 20.8-11 explicitly appeals for the institution of the sabbath to the pattern of God's rest on the seventh day. This implication is further supported by the use of מלאכה (here, once again), as I have observed above. In God's rest the sabbath rest of all his creation has been anticipated.[10] To this extent, God's rest in creation provides the etiology of the sabbath. However, the meaning and scope of his rest on the seventh day is not limited to the sabbath institution at all. In fact, the verb שבת means 'to cease from

p. 35; cf. U. Cassuto, *A Commentary on the Book of Genesis*. I. *From Adam to Noah* (Jerusalem: Magnes Press, 1961), pp. 61-62; C. Westermann, *Genesis 1–11* (trans. J.J. Scullion; London: SPCK, 1984), pp. 169-70; V.P. Hamilton, *The Book of Genesis: Chapters 1–17* (NICOT; Grand Rapids: Eerdmans, 1990), pp. 141-42. For different ways of interpretation, see Andreasen, *Sabbath*, pp. 63-64 n. 2.

8.   Westermann, *Genesis 1–11*, p. 170. Compare Exod. 20.9-10 with 20.11 and 31.15 with 31.17—in both cases God's creation scheme is used as the pattern for the rhythm of human work (מלאכה) and rest. See below, section bii. For a different view, however, see G. von Rad, *The Problem of the Hexateuch and Other Essays* (trans. E. Dicken; Edinburgh: Oliver & Boyd, 1965), pp. 101-102 n. 9.

9.   The etymological argument that the noun שַׁבָּת derives from the verb שבת cannot be a real support for the creation ordinance theory, because the etymology of שַׁבָּת still remains an open question. See below, Excursus 1.

10.   The fact that in Exod. 31.17 God's rest is described in anthropomorphic terms ('was refreshed') further betrays this aspect. Cf. Dressler, 'Sabbath', pp. 29, 39 n. 62.

(work)', not 'to rest'.[11] This does not imply, of course, that God's rest from the work of his creation has simply the negative sense of the end of the creation process. Rather, it means that 'the world is no longer in process of being created', but had been 'completed' by God.[12] The seventh day, then, can be seen as representing the completion of the whole creation, the goal of creation.[13] This day is thus distinct from the other six. This distinctiveness can be further highlighted when we pay attention to the fact that the seventh day does not have the same framework of the first six days.[14] This may imply that the seventh day has no boundaries or no end, and this implication is well expounded eschatologically by a New Testament writer (cf. Heb. 4).[15]

The distinctiveness of the seventh day, however, comes to its culmination when it is declared that 'God blessed the seventh day and hallowed it'. At first sight the meaning of the first clause is not quite clear. As Westermann and many others suggest, however, considering the other two blessings in the creation event (1.22, 28), it seems to be 'not the day in itself that is blessed, but rather the day in its significance for the community'.[16] What is the meaning of the second clause, then? Here the focus seems to shift from humankind to God himself. By sanctifying the seventh day, God set it apart from the other six days. The seventh day, the goal of creation, is not a part of the six ordinary days of work, but a solemn, holy day of rest, the Lord of which is the holy God himself.[17]

---

11.   G. Robinson, 'The Idea of Rest in the Old Testament and the Search for the Basic Character of Sabbath', *ZAW* 92 (1980), pp. 37-42; Westermann, *Genesis 1–11*, p. 173. Cf. Gen. 8.22; Lam. 5.15. Westermann points out that 'the meaning "to rest" derives from a particular use of the word'—e.g. Exod. 16.30; 31.17; Lev. 26.34-35; Neh. 6.3; etc.

12.   G. von Rad, *Genesis* (trans. J.H. Marks and J. Bowden; OTL; London: SCM Press, 1972), p. 62. Here we can notice that the idea of 'completion' and that of 'rest' go together.

13.   A.T. Lincoln, 'From Sabbath to Lord's Day: A Biblical and Theological Perspective', in Carson (ed.), *Lord's Day*, p. 348.

14.   That is, the 'there was evening and there was morning...' formula.

15.   Cf. von Rad, *Genesis*, p. 63.

16.   *Genesis 1–11*, p. 172; cf. von Rad, *Genesis*, p. 62; Wenham, *Genesis 1–15*, p. 36. If the sabbath institution was a reflection of the seventh day in creation, Jesus' declaration that 'The sabbath was made for humankind, and not humankind for the sabbath' (Mk 2.27) seems to support this interpretation very strongly.

17.   Westermann, *Genesis 1–11*, pp. 171-72. This idea of Lordship seems to be well reflected in another of Jesus' declarations as regards the sabbath: 'the Son of Man is lord of the sabbath' (Mt. 12.8 par.).

But even this sanctification seems to have a specific purpose for human-kind, and this purpose is well reflected in the sabbath institution (cf. Exod. 20.8, 11; 31.14, 17). The purpose, however, is not to be limited only to the sabbath. As I have implied above, the seventh day appears to have 'an eschatological, proleptic' aspect, and, therefore, the sanctifica-tion and the blessing of the seventh day may also be understood 'in terms of the ultimate rest for the people of God'.[18]

Excursus 1
The Etymology of שַׁבָּת

As regards the etymology of the term שַׁבָּת, which frequently has been discussed in relation to the question of the origin of the sabbath, a number of suggestions have been put forward.[19]

(1) Some suggest that the term was derived from the Arabic *thabat*, a noun related to the interval between the moon phases.[20] This suggestion has won little support, 'partly because a strong cultic influence on Ancient Israel from Arabia has not been demonstrated, and partly because it now appears very doubtful that the Sabbath can be directly related to the phases of the moon'.[21]

(2) Others suggest that שַׁבָּת and the Akkadian *sapattu* (the day of full moon, or the fifteenth day of a lunar month) are related and the latter is primary.[22] Though we cannot deny the striking similarity of the two terms,[23] this theory is still untenable for several reasons: i) There is little concrete evidence for the hypothesis that the Israelite שַׁבָּת originated from or was influenced by the Babylonian *sapattu*. ii) *Sapattu* can only refer to a monthly day (i.e. the day of the full moon), while שַׁבָּת refers exclu-sively to a weekly day; furthermore, the Hebrew has a separate word for the day of the full moon, that is, כֶּסֶה (Ps. 81.4) and not שַׁבָּת. iii) More importantly, there seems to be a general agreement that the weekly sabbath existed already in pre-exilic times, earlier than Israel's probable encounter with the Babylonian *sapattu*.[24]

---

18. Dressler, 'Sabbath', p. 29. Cf. von Rad, *Hexateuch*, pp. 100-102.

19. Andreasen presents four major etymological explanations in his *Sabbath*, pp. 100-104. In this excursus I will mainly follow his presentation. See also R. North, 'The Derivation of Sabbath', *Bib* 36 (1955), pp. 182-201.

20. Cf. D. Nielsen, *Die altarabische Mondreligion und die mosaische Über-lieferung* (Strassburg: Trübner, 1904), pp. 52-88; *et al.*

21. Andreasen, *Sabbath*, p. 101.

22. Cf. J. Meinhold, *Sabbat und Sonntag* (Leipzig: Quelle & Meyer, 1909); *et al.* More recently Hamilton supports this view in his *Genesis*, p. 142.

23. This might suggest the possibility that 'a common West Semitic root lay behind both words'; Childs, *Exodus*, p. 413. See also Robinson, 'Rest', pp. 40-42.

24. Rordorf, *Sunday*, p. 23; Andreasen, *Sabbath*, pp. 4-5, 9, 101-102; Childs, *Exodus*, p. 413; *et al.*

(3) A classical view derives שַׁבָּת from שֶׁבַע (seven).[25] Considering that the sabbath is so closely related with the number seven, this view seems more plausible. Nevertheless, there is 'still no satisfactory explanation' for the disappearance of the radical ע 'which, incidentally, is a pronounced and forceful consonant in Hebrew'.[26] Therefore, this view is still waiting for a further demonstration of a definite link between שַׁבָּת and שֶׁבַע.

(4) Finally, there have been attempts to derive the noun שַׁבָּת from the common verbal root שׁבת (to cease). Though this seems to be the most plausible solution to the etymological question,[27] the fact that the verb שׁבת occurs only in *qal, niph'al,* and *hiph'il,* but not in *pi'el* still betrays a difficulty in explaining the double middle radical ב of the noun.[28] This view, then, is also not conclusive at all.

Thus, the question of the etymology of שַׁבָּת remains unsettled, and it does not seem advisable to rely heavily on any of the above etymological hypotheses in our discussion of the sabbath.[29]

b. *Commandments*

In the Pentateuch most of the sabbath materials occur in the form of commandments. Here I will classify the materials into five categories mainly according to their contents.

i. *Primitive forms—Exod. 34.21; 23.12.* These two verses are generally considered as revealing the older forms of the sabbath tradition,[30] and

25.   This view was already proposed by Theophilus Antiochenus (c. 180 CE) and Lactantius (c. 300 CE), and has been repeated in recent times by H. Hirschfeld (1896) and C.C. Torrey (1916/7); see Andreasen, *Sabbath*, pp. 102-103 n. 3, and p. 103 n. 1.

26.   Andreasen, *Sabbath*, p. 103, esp. n. 2—in this note he briefly quotes Hirschfeld's explanation in his 'Remarks on the Etymology of Sabbath', *Journal of the Royal Asiatic Society of Great Britain and Ireland* 53 (1896), p. 356, and provides his criticism on it.

27.   Cf. North, 'Derivation', p. 187; E. Kutsch, 'Sabbat', in K. Galling *et al.* (eds.), *Die Religion in Geschichte und Gegenwart*, V (Tübingen: Mohr, 3rd edn, 1958), pp. 1258-60; *et al.*

28.   Cf. Andreasen, *Sabbath*, pp. 104-105. The fact that the verb שׁבת is often used in connection with the sabbath (e.g. Exod. 16.30; 23.12; 31.17; 34.21; Lev. 23.32; 25.2; cf. Gen. 2.2-3), however, may suggest that this view constitutes the 'folk-etymology' whether or not the verb is the historical root of the word; perhaps, this 'folk-etymology' is presupposed in Gen. 2.2-3.

29.   For the dangers and limits of etymological approaches in general in biblical studies, see J. Barr, *The Semantics of Biblical Language* (Oxford: Oxford University Press, 1961), pp. 107-60.

30.   Cf. Andreasen, *Sabbath*, pp. 89-91 (esp. p. 90 n. 2), 264-65.

this general conviction may be supported by their striking similarities which are not common in the other sabbath commandments.[31] In their second parts, however, they are quite distinctive. In 34.21b, the seventh day rest is enjoined even in ploughing time and in harvest time,[32] that is, in the busiest seasons of the agricultural year.[33] This may show that the sabbath commandment, from its primitive form, was strict in its application. Considering the co-text of this verse, that strictness might come from God's ownership of the seventh day (cf. vv. 19-20). In 23.12b, the seventh day rest is linked with the concern for the domestic animals and the slaves. This appears to reveal the humanitarian orientation of the sabbath institution from its early stage.[34] Nevertheless, the inclusion of the domestic animals (i.e. part of God's creation) as well as the slaves might suggest that the foundation of this commandment is not just humanitarian concern but more importantly God's ownership again of his whole creation[35] and perhaps also his rest on the seventh day.[36]

ii. *Decalogue (1)—Exod. 20.8-11; cf. 31.12-17.* Exod. 20.8-11 constitutes the fourth commandment which is the longest in the Decalogue. We have here an elaborate structure. The opening command (v. 8) and the conclusion (v. 11b) constitute the outer brackets of the commandment by providing a parallelism between what Israel is commanded and what God has done. Both speak of the 'sabbath day' not the 'seventh day' (cf. vv. 9-11a) and relate the day to the concept of 'holiness'. The basic regulation (vv. 9-10a) and the motivation clause (v. 11a) also

31.   A simple two-part structure—regulations for the six days and regulations for the seventh day; no identification of the seventh day as 'sabbath'; the positive forms of regulations for the seventh day.

32.   This clause is understood by Jews as prohibiting ploughing and harvest on the sabbath, and *m. Šab.* 7.2 makes these prohibitions clear. See below, Chapter 4, section 3b.

33.   M. Noth, *Exodus* (trans. J. Bowden; OTL; London: SCM Press, 1962), p. 264.

34.   Cf. Exod. 20.9-10; Deut. 5.13-14. Rordorf, *Sunday*, p. 12, argues that 'In the oldest stratum of the Pentateuch the sabbath is, therefore, to be understood as a *social institution*'.

35.   Cf. also the concern even for the land and the wild animal as well as the poor in the sabbath year regulations in vv. 9-11.

36.   Cf. a more developed form of the commandment in Exod. 20.8-11; cf. also Exod. 31.17—the term וַיִּנָּפַשׁ in 23.12b seems to show certain relation to the anthropomorphic terms here, i.e. וַיִּנָּפַשׁ.

roughly correspond to each other, once again by providing a parallelism between what Israel is to do and what God has done in creation. Verse 10b is an expansion to qualify the basic regulation.[37]

This structural observation seems to show that the main thrust of the commandment falls on the verb קרש (vv. 8b, 11b).[38] Israel is commanded to keep the sabbath holy (v. 8b; cf. Deut. 5.12; Exod. 31.14), because God consecrated it (v. 11b; cf. Gen. 2.3). Thus the holiness of the sabbath is attributed to God's sanctifying activity in creation. Verse 10a further qualifies the nature of the sabbath—'the seventh day is a sabbath (belonging) to YHWH your God'.[39] Here we may suggest that the holiness of the sabbath and God's ownership of the day are two sides of the same coin (cf. Exod. 16.23, 25; 31.15; 35.2). The sabbath is holy, because the holy God himself originally consecrated it in his creation and, therefore, he is the Lord of it (cf. Mt. 12.8 par.). What, then, is the implication of the holiness of the sabbath and God's ownership of it to Israel? Verses 9, 10b, 11a provide the answer for this question. As N.-E.A. Andreasen suggests, it seems 'generally assumed that the Sabbath is kept holy when Israel refrains from working on it, and conversely, Israel desists from work on that day in order to keep it holy'.[40] As I suggested above, in God's rest on the seventh day in creation the sabbath rest of all his creation has been anticipated. Thus Israel's rest on the sabbath is a reflection of the pattern which God himself instituted for all his creation by his own rest. Then the long list in v. 10b is not to be understood simply as an expression of humanitarian concern (cf. Exod. 23.12; Deut. 5.14-15); rather it is to be understood as a reflection of the Lordship and holiness of the sabbath for the benefit of all his creation.[41]

The holiness of the sabbath is further explicated in Exod. 31.12-17 when it is explained in terms of a perpetual covenant. Here the sabbath is called a 'sign' (אות) of the covenant (cf. Ezek. 20.12, 20). The sabbath institution, of course, is not an ultimate purpose of God's rest on the

37.   Andreasen, *Sabbath*, p. 170; Childs, *Exodus*, pp. 414-15.
38.   Childs, *Exodus*, p. 415.
39.   Cf. the expression 'my sabbath' in Lev. 19.3, 30; 26.2.
40.   *Sabbath*, p. 205. Childs, *Exodus*, pp. 415-16, points out that 'The command to hallow is not identified simply with not working or resting, but over and above both of these is the positive action of making holy'.
41.   Andreasen, *Sabbath*, pp. 205-206; cf. J.I. Durham, *Exodus* (WBC, 3; Waco, TX: Word Books, 1987), p. 289.

seventh day in creation and his sanctification of it. The ultimate purpose is to sanctify his people (v. 13b) and, perhaps, as I have provisionally suggested above, to provide them the ultimate eschatological rest.[42] Nevertheless, as a sign of the perpetual covenant between the holy God and his people to be sanctified, the sabbath is also holy. Therefore, it is not strange at all when even the death penalty is sanctioned against anyone who violates the sanctity of the sabbath (vv. 14-15; cf. Num. 15.32-36). By keeping it holy, however, Israel will know, generation after generation, the eternal covenantal relationship between God and them (vv. 13, 16-17), which will ultimately sanctify them.[43]

iii. *Decalogue (2)—Deut. 5.12-15*. Another version of the fourth commandment in the Decalogue appears in Deut. 5.12-15. The opening command (v. 12) and the conclusion (v. 15b) are, as in the previous version in Exodus, strikingly similar and form the outer brackets of the commandment; and these outer brackets clarify that the basic reason for observing the sabbath is that God commanded it.[44] But, unlike the version in Exodus, vv. 13-14a do not correspond to v. 15a at all. Verse 15a constitutes a motivation clause, which might have certain relation with the preceding expansion clause in v. 14b. As a number of scholars have detected, this motivation clause appears to reflect a strong humanitarian or social concern.[45] However, considering the fact that Deuteronomy consistently uses the theme of 'the deliverance from Egypt and the rest which Israel must enter' as a theological horizon in the law-giving context,[46] v. 15a is not simply reflecting a humanitarian concern but primarily providing a theological horizon for the commandment.[47] Perhaps, the Exodus motive in the Deuteronomy version may complement

42. Compare close relations between Gen. 2.2-3 and Exod. 31.17. It is significant that the sign of the perpetual covenant is closely related with God's creation activity and his rest on the seventh day in Exod. 31.16-17.

43. Cf. Ezek. 20.12 and the discussion of it in section 3bi.

44. Perhaps this may refer back to the first giving of the commandment at Sinai. Cf. P.C. Craigie, *The Book of Deuteronomy* (NICOT; Grand Rapids: Eerdmans, 1976), p. 156.

45. Cf. G.J. Botterweck, 'Der Sabbat im Alten Testament', *Theologische Quartalschrift* 134 (1954), pp. 138-41; G. von Rad, *Deuteronomy* (trans. D. Barton; OTL; London: SCM Press, 1966), p. 58; Rordorf, *Sunday*, p. 15; *et al.*

46. Andreasen, *Sabbath*, pp. 134, 221-25.

47. Cf. Jenni, *Begründung*, pp. 15-19; Andreasen, *Sabbath*, pp. 130-34; *et al.*

the creation motive in the Exodus version (or *vice versa*).[48] God's deliverance of the Israelites from the slavery of Egypt was a kind of creation, that is, the creation of God's people as a nation, and the memory of that event functioned as a reminder to Israel of God's absolute initiative and their total dependence on God for their redemption.[49] For Israel, keeping the sabbath, then, is a testimony of their election as a nation and redemption from slavery. To make this testimony meaningful, the Israelites must extend their sabbath rest even to their 'male and female slave' whose status they experienced in Egypt. Then, v. 14b is a necessary extension, which, therefore, reflects theological implications as well as social or humanitarian concerns.

iv. *Cultic regulations—Lev. 23.3; Num. 28.9-10; cf. Lev. 24.5-9.* Although most Pentateuch materials on the sabbath are characterized by their regulations on abstention from work, there are at least two places in the Pentateuch (Lev. 23.3; Num. 28.9-10) where the sabbath is clearly associated with cultic elements.

First, Lev. 23.3 calls the sabbath (alongside the annual festivals) מקרא־קדש.[50] As Andreasen suggests, considering all the occurrences of this phrase and other usages of מקרא especially in Isa. 1.13, this phrase should not be translated simply as 'holy assembly' but as 'holy festival'[51] which, perhaps, was 'a national gathering for public worship'.[52] The legislation on the annual festivals (Lev. ch. 23) also shows that the מקרא־קדש was an occasion for the offering of sacrifices. We may suggest, then, that the sabbath was an occasion on which a kind of festal assembly was held at the sacred centre(s) (cf. 2 Kgs 4.23-25) and naturally some sacrifices were offered.

As regards the sabbath sacrifices, we have at least one concrete regulation in the Pentateuch (Num. 28.9-10; cf. Lev. 24.5-9). According

---

48.   Cf. Craigie, *Deuteronomy*, p. 157; D.L. Christensen, *Deuteronomy 1–11*, (WBC, 6a; Dallas: Word Books, 1991), p. 118.

49.   Craigie, *Deuteronomy*, p. 157, esp. n. 18.

50.   This is a characteristic phrase of Lev. 23 (eleven times); it also appears six times in Num. 28–29, twice in Exod. 12.16, and nowhere else. I owe these statistics to G. Wenham, *The Book of Leviticus* (NICOT; Grand Rapids: Eerdmans, 1979), p. 301.

51.   Andreasen, *Sabbath*, p. 59 n. 2, pp. 146-47.

52.   Wenham, *Leviticus*, p. 301; cf. Andreasen, *Sabbath*, p. 147.

to Num. 28.9-10,[53] the sabbath offering is specified as twice the normal daily quantity (cf. Ezek. 46.4-5). Lev. 24.5-9 also shows that the sabbath ritual involved the exchange of bread of the Presence.

As we have seen, the materials on the cultic elements of the sabbath in the Pentateuch[54] are scanty. Considering the holy character and God's ownership of the sabbath, however, it would be natural that the sabbath provided an occasion for gathering of the Israelites at the sacred centre(s) to present them before the Lord with special offering, so that they may remember and celebrate God's creation of the world and his deliverance from Egypt, and express their gratitude for and faithfulness to the Lord of the whole creation and of Israel who gave them the sabbath and, therefore, is also the Lord of the sabbath.

v. *Specific prohibitions—Exod. 16.22-30; 35.3; Num. 15.32-36.* Finally, we have three passages which provide specific regulations or applications of the general principle of the sabbath.

Exod. 16.22-30, which is basically narrative in form, provides a case of application of the general sabbath law in relation to gathering manna (cf. also v. 5). According to the narrative, the writer appears to assume that the sabbath had already existed in some form before the issue was raised.[55] The solution to the leaders' inquiry mostly reflects the basic characters of the sabbath law.[56] There are, however, two significant

53. Num. 28 regulates the sacrifices for various festivals which were already listed in Lev. 23.

54. Scholars are not sure how old the cultic regulations and practices of the sabbath in these materials are. Andreasen, *Sabbath*, pp. 144, 149 (cf. also pp. 142-43), however, suggests that they may go back to the earliest stage of the Old Testament sabbath traditions.

55. Otherwise, we are to suppose that the writer regarded the sabbath institution as derived from its relation to the giving of manna, which is very unlikely (note that nowhere in the Pentateuch apart from here is the manna event related to the sabbath institution; cf. motive clauses in Exod. 20.11; 31.17b; Deut. 5.15). See Childs, *Exodus*, p. 290. Andreasen, *Sabbath*, p. 130, however, interestingly suggests that the priestly writer here presents the narrative in a way that 'the Sabbath is not commonly known to the people, and they now have to learn to regulate their work according to its regulations', before its proper introduction at Sinai. Cf. Neh. 9.13-14, where Nehemiah states that the holy sabbath was made known to Israel on Mount Sinai; then, an indirect reference to the manna is significantly following in v. 15. Cf. also Ezek. 20.11-12.

56. The abstention from ordinary work (in this case, gathering manna), the distinctiveness from the other six days (no manna on the sabbath), and the holiness

elements which are not found in the main group of the sabbath laws. First, the Israelites are encouraged to be prepared for the sabbath. Secondly, they are instructed not to leave their place but to stay where they are. These two specific regulations (especially the latter) are developed further in later writings (e.g. Jer. 17.19-27; Neh. 13.15-22; but most strikingly in the Mishnah).

Exod. 35.3 provides another but more specific type of sabbath regulation—'You shall kindle no fire in all your dwellings on the sabbath day'. Perhaps this regulation may have to do with the preparation of food.[57] The unconditional demand without punishment, however, still characterizes it not as a casuistic but as an apodeictic type law. As Andreasen suggests, however, this passage may demonstrate 'the passage from apodeictic to casuistic law'.[58]

Num. 15.32-36 is probably related to Exod. 35.3.[59] Sabbath violation was already regulated as a capital offence (Exod. 31.12-17; 35.2-3). The only question now is whether gathering sticks constitutes sabbath violation or not. This story, thus, clearly shows that the application of a general principle of the sabbath is bound to raise questions as to what precisely constitutes work. This story seems, as P.J. Budd points out, to act as a reminder that 'confidence in God's good purpose is no ground for indifference to his commandments'.[60]

Having said this, however, this kind of specific regulation is very rare in the Pentateuch, and it suggests a very different sense of proportion compared with later preoccupation with exceedingly detailed casuistic regulations demonstrated, for example, in the Mishnah (especially, *Šabbat* and *'Erubin*).[61]

c. *Conclusions*
I can now draw some conclusions from discussions so far. The etiology study suggests that God's rest on the seventh day created a rhythm

and God's ownership of the sabbath (cf. vv. 23, 25, 26). Cf. Childs, *Exodus*, p. 290.

57.   Durham, *Exodus*, p. 475; cf. Num. 15.32-36.

58.   *Sabbath*, p. 153.

59.   M. Noth, *Numbers* (trans. J.D. Martin; OTL; London: SCM Press, 1968), p. 117; P.J. Budd, *Numbers* (WBC, 5; Waco, TX: Word Books, 1984), p. 175.

60.   *Numbers*, p. 176.

61.   Even the rabbis seem to recognize the extremely unbalanced proportion of the casuistic regulations on the sabbath. See *m. Ḥag.* 1.8: 'the rules about the Sabbath...are as mountains hanging by a hair, for [teaching of] Scripture [thereon] is scanty and the rules many'.

which will affect the whole creation and, thus, his rest does provide the etiology of the sabbath. Having said this, however, the meaning and scope of his rest on the seventh day is not to be limited to the sabbath institution. On the basis of the meaning of the שבת in Gen. 2.1-3 and the distinctive framework of the seventh day, I have cautiously suggested that the seventh day has an eschatological aspect. The seventh day is also characterized as 'blessed' and 'holy'; and we have observed that these characteristics are clearly reflected in the sabbath day, though I have also suggested that the ultimate purpose of the blessing and sanctification of the seventh day is beyond the scope of the sabbath.

My investigation of the sabbath commandments in the Pentateuch has demonstrated some characteristics of the commandments. (1) Most commandments presuppose the holiness of the sabbath, and sometimes explicitly command that it be kept holy (cf. especially, Exod. 20.8-11; 31.12-17; Deut. 5.12-15). (2) Most commandments also presuppose God's Lordship of the sabbath, and sometimes explicitly use the phrase 'my sabbath' (cf. especially Exod. 31.12-17; Lev. 19.3, 30; 26.2). (3) Most commandments follow the pattern of God's creation in six days and his rest on the seventh day, and in two cases the creation motive is clearly stated (Exod. 20.8-11; 31.12-17). (4) In one place (Deut. 5.12-15) the Exodus event is used as a motive for the sabbath keeping. (5) In one place (Exod. 31.12-17) the sabbath is described as the sign of the eternal covenant; by keeping the sabbath holy, Israel will know throughout generations the eternal covenantal relationship be tween God and them, which relationship will ultimately sanctify them. (6) Though there are some signs of humanitarian concern (e.g. Exod. 23.12; Deut. 5.12-15), we have observed that in all cases the primary concern is not humanitarian or social but rather theological. (7) In most cases the holiness and God's ownership of the sabbath are expressed by the Israelites in their rest on the sabbath; in three places (Lev. 23.3; 24.5-9; Num. 28.9-10), however, we can trace another form of such expression, that is, in the form of worship by gathering together as a festal assembly and offering special sacrifices to express their thanks and faith to the Lord who created the whole world, delivered them from Egypt and gave the sabbath as a sign of covenant. (8) Finally, three passages seem to demonstrate 'the passage from apodeictic to casuistic law' (Exod. 16.22-30; 35.3; Num. 15.32-36); I have pointed out, however, that these rare cases suggest a very different sense of proportion

compared with the later preoccupation with exceedingly detailed casuistic regulations.

2. *Historical Books*[62]

In the historical books the sabbath materials appear in 2 Kings, 1 and 2
Chronicles and Nehemiah. In contrast to those in the Pentateuch, most
of these materials do not occur in the typical form of sabbath commandments,[63] and many of them reveal the character of the sabbath
only implicitly. Here I will classify the materials into three categories
mainly according to their contents.

a. *Assemblies*
i. *2 Kgs 4.23*. The brief conversation between a Shunammite woman
and her husband implies that 'when the account was formed it was
customary to visit a prophet on a Sabbath and on a new moon, but not
at other times'.[64] Though we do not have any conclusive evidence for
the date of the formation of the account, a number of scholars assume
that this account, with many other accounts in 2 Kgs 2–13, was formed
during or shortly after the prophet's life time, that is, in the first half of
the eighth century BCE.[65] One may suggest, then, that by the time of
Elisha it was customary for at least some people to leave their homes on
a sabbath to visit a prophet (cf. Isa. 1.13).

---

62.   Under this heading we will cover the books of Joshua to Kings (the so-
called 'Deuteronomistic History'), and the books of Chronicles, Ezra and Nehemiah
(the so-called 'Chronistic History'). Though in Jewish tradition, the former group
belong to נביאים (the 'Prophets'—many Old Testament scholars, therefore, call them
the 'Former Prophets'), and the latter belong to כתובים (the 'Writings'), considering
their content, the term 'historical books' seems to represent the general character of
these books best; cf. W.H. Schmidt, *Introduction to the Old Testament* (trans. M.J.
O'Connell; London: SCM Press, 1984), pp. v-vii, 136-70; cf. also Rendtorff,
Introduction, pp. 164, 183-85.

63.   Perhaps, Neh. 13.22 may be an exception.

64.   Andreasen, *Sabbath*, p. 48. Cf. T.R. Hobbs, *2 Kings* (WBC, 13; Waco, TX:
Word Books, 1985), pp. 51-52—he suggests three possible ways of understanding
this conversation in relation to the sabbath visit.

65.   Cf. G. Fohrer, *Introduction to the Old Testament* (trans. D. Green; London:
SPCK, 1968), pp. 233-34; Andreasen, *Sabbath*, p. 48; G.H. Jones, *1 and 2 Kings*, I
(2 vols.; NCB; London: Marshall, Morgan & Scott, 1984), pp. 68-73; J.A. Soggin,
Introduction to the Old Testament (trans. J. Bowden; London: SCM Press, 1989),
p. 23; *et al.*

ii. *2 Kgs 11.4-12; 2 Chron. 23.1-11; cf. 2 Kgs 16.18*. The rather obscure account of the accession of Joash appears both in 2 Kgs 11.4-12 and 2 Chron. 23.1-11. Since the books of Kings are often considered as representing reliable historical sources, it is possible that we have here a very old (i.e. around the end of the ninth century BCE) sabbath material.[66] Though it is difficult to reconstruct what actually happened on that particular day, we may put forward two probable suggestions regarding the sabbath from our two passages: (i) on the sabbath the changing of the guard was taking place; (ii) on the sabbath, or at least on this particular sabbath, a large group of people were present in the temple.

2 Kgs 16.18 at least shows us that there was a kind of structure (מיסך)[67] in the temple (or between the temple and palace) which was used by the king on the sabbath. This strongly suggests that the king was present in the temple on the sabbath.[68]

From the above discussions one can suggest with some confidence that, by the end of ninth or early eighth century BCE, it may have been customary for the people and also for the king to visit a holy place (i.e. the temple or the residence of a man of God) on the sabbath. Then, we may further draw a probable conclusion that by that time the sabbath was regularly observed[69] by the people and the king by assembling in a holy place, perhaps in order to celebrate it together by offering sacrifices.

b. *Offerings*
i. *1 Chron. 9.32; 23.28-31*. According to 1 Chron. 9.32, the Levites were responsible for the preparation of the shewbread[70] every sabbath. Though we do not know how old this regulation is,[71] we can at least

---

66. Fohrer, *Introduction*, pp. 236-37; B.S. Childs, *Introduction to the Old Testament as Scripture* (OTL; London: SCM Press, 1979), pp. 288ff.; Jones, *Kings*, I, p. 76.

67. The translation of this term is extremely difficult as is well demonstrated by the various attempts at translation by the various English versions and commentators: NEB, Hobbs—'structure'; RSV—'covered way'; NIV—'canopy'; NRSV—'covered portal'; J. Gray—'barrier'. Cf. Andreasen, *Sabbath*, pp. 52-53 n. 3; J. Gray, *1 & 2 Kings* (OTL; London: SCM Press, 3rd edn, 1977), p. 635 n. a.

68. Andreasen, *Sabbath*, p. 147; cf. Ezek. 46.1-2.

69. Gray, *Kings*, p. 572.

70. This (Heb. לֶחֶם הַמַּעֲרֶכֶת) is a typical post-exilic term for 'the bread of the Presence'; cf. 1 Chron. 23.29; 2 Chron. 13.11; Neh. 10.34.

71. We do, however, have good reason to suggest that the institution of

affirm that, by the time our passage was written,[72] the Levites assisted the priests by preparing the shewbread every sabbath. In 1 Chron. 23.28-31, which is ascribed to Davidic decree,[73] the Levites are presented as the assistants of the priests (cf. v. 28) in executing the sabbath offerings (v. 31) as well as with the shewbread (v. 29).

ii. *2 Chron. 2.3; 8.13; 31.3; cf. Neh. 10.34.* 2 Chron. 2.3 (EVV v. 4), which appears in the Chronicler's account of Solomon's construction of the temple, informs us that Solomon intended to build the temple for the regular offerings of shewbread and for burnt offerings on the sabbaths along with other offerings on other occasions.

In 2 Chron. 8.13, the Chronicler describes Solomon as offering offerings on the sabbaths, the new moons and the three annual festivals, according to the commandment of Moses (cf. Num. 28–29). The parallel account in 1 Kgs 9.25, however, refers to only the (presumably) three major festival offerings. Probably the Chronicler spells out other occasions, lest the readers should have misunderstood Kings' description to mean that these three were the only occasions on which Solomon offered. Considering its relation to 2 Chron. 2.3, however, this verse, as H.G.M. Williamson observes, also 'signifies the fulfilment of a major part of Solomon's purpose in building the temple, as set out at 2:4'.[74] In

shewbread is ancient; cf. 1 Sam. 21.3-6. The fact that in the Old Testament the exchange of shewbread is never explicitly joined to any other days but only to the sabbath (cf. Lev. 24.5-9) might imply that the institution of shewbread had close relation with the sabbath from its earliest stage. Cf. Andreasen, *Sabbath*, pp. 54-55, 78-79.

72. There is no final agreement as regards the date of the books of Chronicles (the earlier date suggested—immediately after the rebuilding of the temple in 515 BCE; the later date suggested—the Hellenistic period); we may, therefore, simply leave the issue unsettled. See Andreasen, *Sabbath*, pp. 53-54, esp. nn. 3, 4; Rendtorff, *Introduction*, pp. 283-87; cf. M. Noth, *The Chronicler's History* (JSOTSup, 50; Sheffield: JSOT Press, 1987), pp. 69-73; R. Braun, *1 Chronicles* (WBC, 14; Waco, TX: Word Books, 1986), pp. xxviii-xxix—Braun prefers some time between 350-300 BCE.

73. As regards the composition of 1 Chron. 23–27, see H.G.M. Williamson, 'The Origins of the Twenty-Four Priestly Courses: a Study of 1 Chronicles xxiii-xxvii', in J.A. Emerton (ed.), *Studies in the Historical Books of the Old Testament* (VTSup, 30; Leiden: Brill, 1979), pp. 251-68; for the summary of the results of his investigation, see his *1 and 2 Chronicles* (London: Marshall, Morgan & Scott, 1982), pp. 158-59.

74. *Chronicles*, p. 232.

2 Chron. 31.3 we are informed that Hezekiah also, just like Solomon, provided offerings at the same occasions 'as it is written in the law of the Lord'. The law here (cf. Num. 28–29) does not refer to the king's duty to provide the offerings, but only to the offerings themselves.[75] However, as Andreasen suggests, it is highly probable 'that the king, or prince (Ezek. 45:17), could not escape the performance of such an expensive service'.[76]

When the monarchy ceased to exist, this expensive service in the temple could not be continued without an alternative financial source;[77] now Neh. 10.33-34 (EVV v. 32-33) informs us that in the time of Nehemiah an annual levy (one third of a shekel yearly) was regulated to meet the expenses of the temple service, including the shewbread and burnt offerings on the sabbaths.

According to the Chronistic presentation, then, the sabbath offering was offered as early as Solomon's time according to the law of Moses. The main constituents of the offering were the shewbread (cf. Lev. 24.5-9) and the burnt offerings (cf. Num. 28.9-10). This priestly service was assisted by the Levites. The expenses of the service were to be supported by the kings in the monarchy (e.g. Solomon and Hezekiah), but in the post-exilic period (or at least in Nehemiah's time) a temple tax was levied to meet the expenses. Though we are not able to demonstrate the historicity of all these accounts,[78] it is at least clear that, by the time of the Chronicler, the sabbath offering was settled as an essential part of the temple service, and that, at least for the Chronicler himself, the sabbath offering was taken for granted as part of sabbath observance.

---

75. Andreasen, *Sabbath*, pp. 56-57; Williamson, *Chronicles*, p. 374; R.B. Dillard, *2 Chronicles* (WBC, 15; Waco, TX: Word Books, 1987), p. 250.

76. *Sabbath*, p. 57.

77. Before the time of Nehemiah, Darius (cf. Ezra 6.9-10) and Artaxerxes (cf. Ezra 7.21-22) supported a certain provision for the temple. Cf. D.J.A. Clines, *Ezra, Nehemiah, Esther* (London: Marshall, Morgan & Scott, 1984), pp. 92-93, 104, and 207; H.G.M. Williamson, *Ezra, Nehemiah* (WBC, 16; Waco, TX: Word Books, 1985), p. 335.

78. Considering the king's probable presence in the temple on the sabbath as early as the eighth century BCE (see the conclusion of section bi), we might suggest that the king was there in relation to his duty for the sabbath offerings. Andreasen, *Sabbath*, p. 144, cautiously reserves the possibility that 'some sacrifices, and perhaps the presentation of holy bread, were performed on the Sabbath in much earlier times'.

c. *Specific Regulations*

In the book of Nehemiah we have two separate but (presumably) related passages (10.32 [EVV v. 31]; 13.15-22)[79] which provide specific sabbath regulations. The historical situation reflected in these passages is generally assumed as that of the latter part of the fifth century BCE, that is, during Nehemiah's time.

In the present form of the book, ch. 10, which describes a covenant renewal, is firmly connected to ch. 9 as the sequel to the day of confession (cf. וּבְכָל־זֹאת, 'because of all this' in 9.38).[80] The Chronicler,[81] however, might well have included the sabbath item in 10.32 because of the incidents of 13.15-22.[82] The sabbath law in the Pentateuch, as we have observed, enjoins rest from work, but does not explicitly define buying merchandise or grain as work.[83] Amos 8.5, however, shows that the pre-exilic Israelites already understood this law as forbidding trade.

79.   Cf. Andreasen, *Sabbath*, pp. 26-27, 126; F.C. Fensham, *The Books of Ezra and Nehemiah* (NICOT; Grand Rapids: Eerdmans, 1982), p. 234; Clines, *Ezra*, pp. 199-200, 238; Williamson, *Ezra*, pp. 330-31, 393-94.

80.   There is a strong tendency among commentators to argue that chronologically this chapter follows ch. 13 and has virtually nothing to do with Ezra. Cf. Clines, *Ezra*, pp. 199-200; Williamson, *Ezra*, pp. 330-31. Though I cannot deny that their argument is very attractive, it is by no means conclusive. Cf. Andreasen, *Sabbath*, p. 255. As L.H. Brockington (ed.), *Ezra, Nehemiah and Esther* (London: Nelson, 1969), p. 177, says, 'it is not inconceivable that Ezra did feel it necessary to make a covenant with the people after the marriage question was disposed of, and this verse [10.31] could be regarded as a relic of the original introduction to that covenant'; see also Fensham, *Ezra*, p. 234. The issues of the structural relationship and the chronological order, however, are not crucial to the present discussion; therefore I will simply take the passages as they now stand in the book.

81.   The issue of the composition of Ezra–Nehemiah is complex, and, once again, there is a wide range of different views among scholars. Cf. Rendtorff, *Introduction*, pp. 282-83; H.G.M. Williamson, *Ezra and Nehemiah* (Old Testament Guides; Sheffield: JSOT Press, 1987), pp. 14-47; P.R. Ackroyd, *The Chronicler in his Age* (JSOTSup, 101; Sheffield: JSOT Press, 1991), pp. 344-59. I will, however, adopt the conventional term 'Chronicler', and use it in the sense of 'the final composer(s)' of the Chronistic books, but not necessarily referring to the writer of the books of Chronicles.

82.   We need to note, however, that already in 9.14 a reference to 'your holy sabbath' appears. This reference may also have been in the Chronicler's mind when he included the sabbath item here. For the Chronicler the revelation of the sabbath institution was one of the key works done by YHWH himself on Mount Sinai through Moses.

83.   Cf., however, Exod. 16.22-30; Num. 15.32-36.

Nevertheless, the presence of non-Jewish merchants in Jerusalem might have raised a new question, at least to some Jews, whether it was forbidden to buy even from a non-Jew; and perhaps a public definition was desirable. The present passage implies that the new definition was clear enough, and the people pledged to keep the sabbath according to the new definition. Thus the extended definition of the sabbath law is codified to cover the unforeseen circumstances.

In 13.15-22, an actual case of the sabbath trading problem and Nehemiah's treatment of it is described. In spite of their pledge, many Israelites in the time of Nehemiah (perhaps when the memory of their pledge faded away) must have felt that such restriction imposed 'an unfair commercial disadvantage' on them, especially when Gentiles living among them could freely trade on that day.[84] Naturally some Israelites were tempted to break the pledge and began to take part in the trade with Gentiles as well as to be involved in other works (vv. 15-16); perhaps this abuse was getting worse during Nehemiah's absence between his two terms (cf. 13.6-7). Confronted with such abuse, Nehemiah was determined to prevent it. For Nehemiah, buying on the sabbath was a definite act of profaning the sabbath, and profaning the sabbath was one of the major causes of the destruction of Jerusalem (v. 18; cf. 10.32; cf. also Ezek. 20.23). As a governor, Nehemiah delivered some practical measures (vv. 19-22a).[85] Perhaps, as D.J.A. Clines asserts, 'Nehemiah's measure is an excellent example of the Jewish tendency to make "a hedge about the Torah": lest the sabbath law of burden-carrying should be broken...he removes as far as possible any opportunity for breaking the law'.[86] His concluding prayer, however, might betray his conviction that keeping the sabbath holy cannot be brought about by regulations alone apart from the wholehearted dependence on God's love for his people (v. 22b). Probably the Levites' involvement in the keeping of the city gates on the sabbath demonstrates Nehemiah's high view of the holiness of the sabbath. The command that they should purify themselves first for the task further supports this suggestion (v. 22a).

From these two passages, one can make three observations: (1) In the time of Nehemiah, there were serious problems as regards the sabbath,

84. Williamson, *Ezra*, p. 395.
85. He seems to take his cue from Jer. 17.19-27, where bringing loads into Jerusalem on the sabbath is explicitly forbidden with a threat of destruction of the city; see Clines, *Ezra*, p. 244. See below, section 3biii.
86. Clines, *Ezra*, p. 245.

and Nehemiah treated the problems decisively by extending the definition of the sabbath law (i.e. defining trade as work forbidden on the
sabbath) to cover the unforeseen circumstances, and by delivering some
detailed regulations (e.g. banning the bringing of loads into Jerusalem,
closing the gates, and guarding the gates) to make the extended definition effective in the life of the people in Jerusalem. Some may suggest
that we have here a good example of rabbinic casuistic development of
the sabbath law, though Nehemiah's measures do not compare with the
meticulous details covered by the Mishnaic legislation. (2) For Nehemiah
and perhaps for Israelites in general in his time, profaning the sabbath
was one of the major factors which brought and would bring again the
destruction of Jerusalem. (3) Thus Nehemiah had a deep recognition of
the holiness of the sabbath.

3. *Prophets*

a. *The Sabbath and Cultic Activities*
In the prophetic books there are a few passages from which we can
glimpse the cultic characteristics of the sabbath in various times.

i. *Assemblies—Isa. 1.13; cf. Hos. 2.13; Isa. 66.23.* As H. Wildberger
and others suggest, Isa. 1.13 may come from Isaiah's early period of
activity (i.e. *c*. 730 BCE).[87] Then, considering the picture of people's
trampling the temple court in v. 12, we may assume that some form of
assembly (מקרא; cf. ומועדיכם in v. 14) took place on the sabbath as early
as the second half of the eighth century BCE. The co-text of the verse
also tells us that YHWH hates such institutionalized sabbath assemblies
(along with other cultic activities) because they are vain. Here we can
detect a sign of legalistic observance of the sabbath without full recognition of the original purpose and character of that institution which
should be demonstrated in Israel's holy life.[88]

Hos. 2.13 (EVV v. 11), another eighth century BCE passage,[89]

---

87. H. Wildberger, *Isaiah 1–12* (trans. T.H. Trapp; Minneapolis, MN: Fortress
Press, 1991), pp. 38-39. Similarly Soggin, *Introduction*, p. 304. Cf. Fohrer, *Introduction*, p. 336; J.N. Oswalt, *The Book of Isaiah Chapters 1–39* (NICOT; Grand
Rapids: Eerdmans, 1986), pp. 94-95; *et al.* For a different position, however, see O.
Kaiser, *Isaiah 1–12* (trans. J. Bowden; OTL; London: SCM Press, 1983), pp. 24-28.
88. Cf. Kaiser, *Isaiah 1–12*, pp. 31-33.
89. We have still another eighth-century sabbath passage in Amos 8.5; though it

presupposes the sabbath as one of the well-settled feasts which include the (presumably) three annual festivals and the new moon alongside the sabbath.[90] Interestingly, Hosea also implies that his contemporaries did not recognize a main characteristic of the sabbath, that is, YHWH's ownership of the sabbath[91] in spite of their recognition of the day as a feast.

If we accept some form of the literary unity of the book of Isaiah,[92] it is interesting to note that the problem raised in the beginning of the book (i.e. the vain cultic activities) is solved in the very end of the book by YHWH's promise to recover the true cultic activities (Isa. 66.23). According to his promise, all people shall come to worship before YHWH every sabbath.[93] This promise seems to show that the sabbath assembly and worship had a great significance in Israel's religion at the time when the book was written.[94]

---

does not explicitly talk about the sabbath assemblies, it, at least, suggests that the sabbath was regularly (and, perhaps, strictly) kept by the eighth-century Israelites.

90.   Cf. J.L. Mays, *Hosea* (OTL; London: SCM Press, 1969), p. 42—he suggests that 'Long before the eighth century all these festivals and days had been established as times to worship Yahweh'.

91.   Cf. v. 15: 'the festival days of the Baals'. Note '*her* sabbaths' rather than '*my* sabbaths'; cf. Isa. 56.4, 6; 58.13; Ezek. 20.12, 16, 20ff.; etc.

92.   Since J.C. Döderlein's suggestion (1775) that chs. 40–66 were written in the Exile period and, then, B. Duhm's suggestion (1892) that chs. 56–66 constitute a separate third body, most commentators have treated the two or three individual parts of the book quite separately, 'hardly discussing the reasons which led to the addition of chs. 40ff. and whether there are connections between the two [or three] parts', as Rendtorff, *Introduction*, p. 190, properly points out. It is only in more recent years that scholars begin to pay more serious attention to the question of the composition of the book of Isaiah as a whole. For more detailed discussion of the close literary and thematic connections (or even unity) between the two (or three) parts, see Rendtorff, *Introduction*, pp. 190-200; J.D.W. Watts, *Isaiah 1–33* (WBC, 24; Waco, TX: Word Books, 1985), pp. xxiii-lvii.

93.   וּמִדֵּי שַׁבָּת בְּשַׁבַּתּוֹ—literally 'from sabbath to sabbath'. See R.N. Whybray, *Isaiah 40–66* (NCB; London: Marshall, Morgan & Scott, 1975), p. 293; C. Westermann, *Isaiah 40–66* (trans. D.M.G. Stalker; OTL; London: SCM Press, 1969), p. 428; cf. J.D.W. Watts, *Isaiah 34–66* (WBC, 25; Waco, TX: Word Books, 1987), p. 365.

94.   For some recent discussions of the date(s) of the book of Isaiah, which is largely dependent on the issue of the composition of the book, see Rendtorff, *Introduction*, pp. 190-200; Watts, *Isaiah 1–33*, pp. xxvi-xxiv; Soggin, *Introduction*, pp. 300-302, 365-67, 393-94.

ii. *Offerings—Ezek. 45.16-17; 46.1-12.* According to Ezek. 45.16-17, the people are obliged to pay the religious tax to the prince (נשׂיא) and the prince, as the representative of the people, is obliged to provide the sabbath offerings along with other offerings in the new temple. Significantly the prince alongside the priests played an active role in restoring the true cultic offerings by way of the renewal of right relations with Yahweh (cf. vv. 8b-9).

Ezek. 46.1-12 describes the roles of the prince and the people in the sabbath ritual procedure in the new temple. Here the prince once again, as the representative, enjoys the privilege of going through the vestibule (אולם) of the east gate of the inner court of the temple, which was not given to the people. As L.C. Allen suggests, the closure and the limited access of the gate may have been regulated 'so that the holiness of the temple should not be infringed'.[95] Leaving the gate open until evening, however, may have allowed the people outside the gate to participate in the offering worship (v. 3).[96] This clearly shows that, for Ezekiel, not only the priests and the prince but also the people were expected to be present in the temple on the sabbath, and the sabbath offering (vv. 4-5)[97] was taken for granted as a part of sabbath observance. Even here, however, where the cultic significance of the sabbath is described, its characteristic as a day without work is implied (v. 1).

b. *The Sabbath and the Covenant*
In the prophetic books most of the sabbath materials appear in relation to, or in terms of, Israel's covenant relationship with YHWH. My classification of the materials will, once again, depend on their contents.

i. *Profaning the/my sabbath: punishment—Ezek. 20.10-26; 22.8, 26; 23.38.* According to Ezek. 20.10-26,[98] which appears in Ezekiel's

---

95. L.C. Allen, *Ezekiel 20–48* (WBC, 29; Dallas: Word Books, 1990), p. 267.

96. W. Zimmerli, *Ezekiel*, II (trans. J.D. Martin; Hermeneia; Philadelphia: Fortress Press, 1983), p. 490.

97. Cf. Num. 28.9-10. As regards the discrepancy between the amount of offerings mentioned here and in Numbers, see Andreasen, *Sabbath*, pp. 47, 142-43; Zimmerli, *Ezekiel*, II, p. 491; cf. W. Eichrodt, *Ezekiel* (trans. C. Quin; OTL; London: SCM Press, 1970), p. 476.

98. Though Eichrodt argues that most of the sabbath materials in chs. 20–23 are secondary, Andreasen properly refutes his argument in his *Sabbath*, pp. 40-45. Cf. Zimmerli, *Ezekiel*, I, pp. 406, 410; Allen, *Ezekiel 20–48*, pp. 5-7—both scholars

description of the sinful history of the people of Israel, YHWH's sabbath was given to the two generations of Israel in the wilderness as a sign (אות) of the covenant between YHWH and Israel, so that they may know that YHWH himself marked them out from the nations and consecrated them as his own people (v. 12) and therefore he is their God (v. 20).[99] Both generations, however, rebelled against YHWH and profaned YHWH's sabbath (vv. 13, 16, 21, 24). By despising this sign of the covenant they were naturally under the threat of punishment. Though YHWH repeatedly restrains himself 'for the sake of his name' (vv. 14, and 17, 22; cf. v. 9), this restraint is increasingly elaborated with stronger threats of punishment (a single threat in v. 15, double threats in vv. 23, 25; cf. none in v. 9).[100] According to v. 24, Israel's profaning the sabbath (i.e. the despising of the sign of the covenant) is seen as a crucial cause of the exile (cf. Neh. 13.18).

Ezek. 22.8 forms a part of a judgment oracle addressed to Jerusalem (vv. 1-16). One of the detailed accusations against the city (vv. 6-12) is that they profaned YHWH's sabbaths, which are one of YHWH's holy things. Therefore a sentence is passed upon them (vv. 13-15); YHWH is going to strike the city and disperse its inhabitants. Once again, profaning the sabbath is seen as one of the major causes of the destruction of Jerusalem. Verse 26 similarly forms a part of a judgment oracle, but this time addressed to all classes in the land (vv. 23-31). Among its three representative classes,[101] the priests, who are called to keep and practise Israel's sacred traditions, are accused of betraying their calling. The distinction between the holy and the profane, and between the clean and the unclean, was ignored; and 'A particularly important case of disregard for the distinction...is found in the disregard for the law of the

---

argue that the chronological setting of 20.1-31 is 591 BCE and its geographical setting is the exile in Babylon.

99.   Cf. Exod. 31.12-17. For explanations of the similarity between v. 12 and Exod. 31.13, cf. G. Fohrer, *Die Hauptprobleme des Buches Ezechiel* (Berlin: Töpelmann, 1952), pp. 151-52; Zimmerli, *Ezekiel*, I, p. 410—Zimmerli explains the similarity by referring to 'Ezekiel's origin in the priestly legal tradition with its fixed language'. Cf. also Andreasen, *Sabbath*, p. 42—according to him, the similarity 'can best be explained by assuming that the prophet did not copy his information from other literature, but shared the traditions of Israel's historians and priests'.

100.   Zimmerli, *Ezekiel*, I, p. 407; Allen, *Ezekiel 20–48*, p. 11.

101.   That is, its princes in v. 25 (cf. v. 27—its officers), its priests in v. 26, and its prophets in v. 28; cf. the people of the land in general in v. 29.

sabbath'.[102] YHWH, therefore, brings punishment upon the land. The description of punishment here (esp. v. 31) looks back to the past event, probably, the fall of Jerusalem in 587 BCE.[103]

In Ezek. 23.38 we find another brief sabbath material, which states that the two sisters, who represent the divided kingdom of Judah and Israel respectively,[104] have profaned YHWH's sabbaths alongside other abominable doings. As in the previous passages a pronouncement of punishment follows in vv. 46-49.

All these recurrent sabbath passages in Ezekiel 20–23 show that, for Ezekiel, profaning the sabbath is an act of breaking the covenant relationship between YHWH and his people, and therefore it is one of the crucial causes of the exile of Judah and, perhaps, even of Israel.

ii. *Keeping the/my sabbath (holy): blessing—Isa. 56.1-8; 58.13-14; Ezek. 44.24.* Isa. 56.1-8 is primarily concerned with the status of eunuchs and foreigners in the worshipping community. In v. 2b the awkward parallelism between a concrete and particular demand (i.e. the keeping of the sabbath) and a warning against evil-doing in general may disclose the particular emphasis upon sabbath keeping.[105] Its relation to v. 1 betrays that, for the author, the only real sign of whether a person truly maintains justice and righteousness is the observance of the sabbath. The subsequent verses also show that the most conspicuous sign of the true covenant relationship with YHWH is keeping YHWH's sabbath. Sabbath keeping is the most obvious condition for eunuchs (v. 4a) and foreigners (v. 6b) to be accepted into the worshipping community in the new temple. To those who keep YHWH's sabbath the unexpected promise (cf. Deut. 23.2-9[106]) is made. When they are accepted into the worshipping

102. Zimmerli, *Ezekiel*, I, pp. 468-69. In this connection 44.24 may set out the renewed obligation of the priests as regards the sabbath; see below, section 3bii.

103. On the ground of this fact and the literary dependence of this oracle on Zeph. 3.3-4, 8, most scholars seem to consider that vv. 23-31 is secondary. Cf. Fohrer, *Hauptprobleme*, pp. 99-100, 130; Eichrodt, *Ezekiel*, p. 316. Allen, *Ezekiel 20–48*, p. 35, however, properly points out that 'there is no intrinsic reason why Ezekiel himself did not make use of it, assuming that he had a hand in the literary adaptation of his oral oracles'; see also Andreasen, *Sabbath*, p. 45; cf. Zimmerli, *Ezekiel*, I, p. 467.

104. Cf. vv. 1-4; see Allen, *Ezekiel 20–48*, p. 48. For a different view, however, see Zimmerli, *Ezekiel*, I, pp. 481-84.

105. Westermann, *Isaiah 40–66*, p. 310. Cf. Whybray, *Isaiah 40–66*, p. 197.

106. In this passage the two sets of people are explicitly excluded from the

community, they will rejoice in YHWH's house and their sacrifices will be accepted; they will be given an everlasting name, a name better than sons and daughters (vv. 5, 7-8; compare with Isa. 1.12-15). This promise strongly implies that God's covenant relationship no longer depends on one's national (or social) identity but on one's individual decision and devotion to YHWH, which is to be demonstrated by one's keeping the sabbath. Having said this, however, sabbath keeping is not a sole condition or criterion for one's acceptance into the worshipping community. In both instances the admonition to keep the sabbath is followed by another admonition to hold fast my covenant (vv. 4b, 6b). The vain sabbath keeping which lacked a recognition of the covenantal relationship with God was already rejected in Isa. 1.13. Sabbath keeping is meaningful and important only when it is based on one's covenant relationship with God. The sabbath is, then, only a sign of the covenant (cf. Exod. 31.12-17; Ezek. 20.10-26).

In Isa. 58.13-14, two characteristics of the sabbath are distinctively put forward, that is, the holiness and God's ownership of the sabbath. The conditional part (v. 13) emphatically attaches holiness to the sabbath ('my *holy* day', 'the *holy* day of YHWH') and makes the day 'honourable'. Though the threat of the death penalty against anyone who violates the sanctity of the sabbath (cf. Exod. 31.15) may, as Westermann suggests, have had become a dead letter at this stage,[107] its sanctity is still emphasized by the accompanying promise of the rewards for keeping the sabbath holy (v. 14—taking delight in YHWH). In relation to its holiness, the sabbath is also seen as YHWH's day in the conditional part ('*my* holy day', 'the holy day *of YHWH*'). When the people of YHWH were admonished not to seek their own will, their own pleasure, nor to speak their own words, the issue is not joy or mourning, as J.D.W. Watts properly points out, but 'rather Yahweh's day or our day, Yahweh's will or our will'.[108] The sabbath, then, cannot be an excuse for not doing good for others.[109]

As W. Zimmerli and others suggest, Ezek. 44.24 reflects the problem in Ezek. 22.26, where the priests profaned YHWH's holy sabbath.[110] Here the priests are commanded to keep 'my sabbaths' holy; for

---

worshipping community. Cf. also Ezra 4.1-3; chs. 9–10.

107. *Isaiah 40–66*, p. 341.

108. *Isaiah 34–66*, p. 276.

109. Cf. Mt. 12.9-12, esp. v. 12b. See below Chapter 4, section 4b.

110. Zimmerli, *Ezekiel*, II, p. 460. Cf. Allen, *Ezekiel 20–48*, p. 264.

Ezekiel, the sabbath is the *holy* time, because it is 'the time special to Yahweh'.[111]

iii. *Specific regulations—Jer. 17.19-27; Amos 8.5; cf. Isa. 58.13-14.* Jer. 17.19-27, which is Deuteronomic in style,[112] can be divided into four parts: (i) vv. 19-22—the sabbath law stated; (ii) v. 23—the disobedience of the ancestors; (iii) vv. 24-26—obedience and the covenant blessings; (iv) v. 27—disobedience and the breach of covenant. Thus the whole passage is concerned with the keeping of the sabbath commandment. In vv. 21-22 some specific regulations (i.e. not bearing a burden or bringing it into Jerusalem or carrying it out of one's house on the sabbath) are added to the characteristic sabbath commandment (i.e. do no work but keep the sabbath day holy; cf. Exod. 20.8-10; Deut. 5.12-14).[113] The prophet probably introduces these regulations in order to make the sabbath commandment effective in the life situation in Jerusalem.[114] This

111. Zimmerli, *Ezekiel*, II, p. 460.

112. Most scholars argue, mainly on the ground of its Deuteronomic style, that this passage does not come from Jeremiah himself and belongs to a later time (e.g. the time of Nehemiah; cf. Neh. 13.15-22). See S. Mowinckel, *Zur Komposition des Buches Jeremia* (Kristiania: Jacob Dybwad, 1914), p. 49; W. Rudolph, *Jeremia* (HAT; Tübingen: Mohr, 1958), p. 109; W. McKane, *A Critical and Exegetical Commentary on Jeremiah*, I (ICC; Edinburgh: T. & T. Clark, 1986), pp. 416-19; for further references, see Andreasen, *Sabbath*, p. 31 n. 1. Cf. R.P. Carroll, *Jeremiah 1–25* (OTL; London: SCM Press, 1986), pp. 368-69. Andreasen, *Sabbath*, p. 32 n. 1, however, properly points out that the Deuteronomic character of this passage 'does not necessarily make the passage late and unauthentic'. J.A. Thompson, *The Book of Jeremiah* (NICOT; Grand Rapids: Eerdmans, 1980), pp. 427-28, further argues that this passage depends on Jeremiah's own comments on sabbath keeping. A similar view is taken by D.R. Jones, *Jeremiah* (NCB; London: Marshall Pickering, 1992), pp. 248-49—he suggests that this passage comes from the preachers who 'operated within the Jeremiah tradition'. It seems possible, then, that the basic material of this passage originated from Jeremiah himself. See Andreasen, *Sabbath*, p. 34. When I use the conventional term 'the prophet' in the present discussion, however, it will simply refer to the person who is responsible for this passage.

113. According to v. 22, however, all these regulations were already known to their ancestors. Perhaps Exod. 16.22-30 and Num. 15.32-36 were in the prophet's mind.

114. A similar specific regulation is found in Neh. 13.15-22. McKane, *Jeremiah*, I, p. 417, argues, simply on the ground of this fact, that this passage belongs to Nehemiah's time. His argument, however, is far from conclusive. As Jones, *Jeremiah*, p. 250, points out, 'there is no reason to assume that the practice [forbidden in vv. 21-22] was not common in early post-exilic times' or, perhaps, even

passage, then, may be a sermon showing the applied meaning of the sabbath commandment in a particular context in which the commercial activities on the sabbath may be a key issue (cf. Amos 8.5; Neh. 10.32 [EVV v. 31]; 13.15-22). If they, unlike their ancestors, keep the sabbath holy (of course, by observing the specific regulations—v. 24), the 'covenant blessings' (i.e. the restoration of Jerusalem and of the cities of Judah, and of the temple with its rituals—vv. 25-26)[115] are promised. The basic character of the promise is Davidic and/or messianic; an eschatological consummation of the Davidic/messianic kingdom is looked for (cf. v. 25—'forever').[116] If they fail to keep the sabbath holy, however, YHWH will bring a divinely kindled unquenchable fire to devour the city and its palaces. Here, once again, the prophet sees profaning the sabbath as a crucial factor which will bring the destruction of Jerusalem (cf. Ezek. 20.23; Neh. 13.18; etc.). The future stability and welfare of Jerusalem and Judah, royal house and people, hangs then on the faithful observance of the sabbath. Thus the sabbath is seen, at least in this passage, as representative of the whole covenant.

Amos 8.5 presents a quotation of the very words of the Israelite merchants, from which we can get a rare glimpse into the religious practice on the sabbath in northern Israel during the mid-eighth century.[117] According to the quotation, it is implied that general trade or commercial activities were not allowed on the sabbath, and that the merchants whose words are quoted here observed the outward regulation(s) well and, perhaps, showed how devout they were in keeping the sabbath.[118] But inwardly they were restlessly impatient because they were so eager to resume their corrupt business practices (vv. 5c-6). Therefore the indictment is brought in against those whose religious observance of the sabbath lacked inward devotion to YHWH and was combined with daily activities of dishonesty (v. 10). The legalistic sabbath observance which

earlier (cf. Amos 8.5); see Andreasen, *Sabbath*, p. 34.

115. Thompson, *Jeremiah*, p. 430, suggests that these blessings may represent 'the blessings of the covenant bestowed by Yahweh on his obedient people'. Cf. Deut. 28.1-14; etc.

116. McKane, *Jeremiah*, I, p. 419.

117. Most scholars agree that this passage originated from Amos during the mid-eighth century BCE. See J.L. Mays, *Amos* (OTL; London: SCM Press, 1969), pp. 142-43; D. Stuart, *Hosea–Jonah* (WBC, 31; Waco, TX: Word Books, 1987), p. 383; S.M. Paul, *Amos* (Hermeneia; Minneapolis, MN: Fortress Press, 1991), p. 257; *et al.*

118. Mays, *Amos*, p. 144; Andreasen, *Sabbath*, p. 62; Paul, *Amos*, p. 257.

lacks appreciation of the covenantal relationship with YHWH is thus rejected (cf. Isa. 1.13).

In Isa. 58.13-14, we might also detect one or two specific regulations of the sabbath: (i) restrictions on travel on the sabbath (תשיב משבת רגלך—) '[If] you restrain your foot from the sabbath'; cf. Exod. 16.29; etc.);[119] (ii) restrictions on pursuing one's own interests ('your own ways, interests and words [or affairs]'; cf. Amos 8.5; Neh. 13.15-22). These regulations are far from clear; one thing clear, however, is that the real concern here is not identifying the regulations forbidden but recognizing YHWH's ownership of the sabbath.

iv. The sabbath itself as the focus of blessing or punishment—Hos. 2.13; Isa. 66.23. Hos. 2.13 forms part of an announcement of judgment against Israel's infidelity (vv. 9-13; cf. vv. 6-7 and vv. 14-15).[120] The verse may imply that long before the eighth century the sabbath along with the new moon had been well established 'as times to worship Yahweh'.[121] In Hosea's time, however, these religious festivals including the sabbath became a scandal because on these occasions Israel, the people of YHWH, celebrated and sought not YHWH but the Baals. Therefore, YHWH announces his judgment upon Israel that *her* sabbaths (not YHWH's)[122] will come to an end. This seems to show that in the time of Hosea the sabbath was one of the feast days which brought joy to Israel; therefore, the cessation[123] of the sabbath[124] constitutes a grave covenantal curse.

119. Watts, *Isaiah 34–66*, p. 276. For a different understanding of the clause, however, see Whybray, *Isaiah 40–66*, p. 218.

120. The sayings in vv. 2-15 are generally attributed to Hosea and dated around 750 BCE, during the final 'golden' years of Jeroboam II. See Mays, *Hosea*, p. 36; H.W. Wolff, *Hosea* (trans. G. Stansell; Hermeneia; Philadelphia: Fortress Press, 1974), p. 33; Stuart, *Hosea–Jonah*, p. 46.

121. Mays, *Hosea*, p. 42.

122. The recurring possessive ending ה, ('her') after each festival appears to emphasize that, as Mays, *Hosea*, p. 42, suggests, 'they now belonged, not to Yahweh, but to Israel in her own mad pursuit of the gods of fertility'.

123. Note the verb שבת which may be 'a denominative of שָׁבַת'; Wolff, *Hosea*, p. 38; cf. North, 'Derivation', pp. 182-201.

124. Undoubtedly this is to be understood by Israel as equivalent to the end of their nation as a sovereign state (cf. Lev. 26.31). See Stuart, *Hosea–Jonah*, p. 51. Cf. Lam. 2.6, in which the cessation of the sabbath occurs alongside other covenantal curses including destruction of the temple and the kingdom.

In Isa. 66.23 the sabbath (and new moon) gathering and worship is presented as the concluding promise of the new creation. Here YHWH himself promises the eschatological consummation of the worship on the sabbath by all humankind (כל־בשר—'all flesh').[125] This is significant when we look back to 1.10-17 where Israel's cultic activities on the sabbath were rejected by YHWH. The broken covenant relationship is promised to be restored eschatologically and a concrete sign of it is the eternal and universal worship on the sabbath.

c. *Conclusion*

In the study of the prophetic sabbath materials I have considered two major aspects of the sabbath: the cultic activities on the sabbath and the covenantal significance of the sabbath.

The materials on the cultic activities suggest that by the eighth century BCE the sabbath was settled as one of the national feasts and some form of assembly took place on the day (Isa. 1.13; Hos. 2.13). At least by the time of Ezekiel (probably early sixth century BCE) not only the priests and the prince but also the people were expected to be present in the temple on the sabbath (Ezek. 46.1-3). These materials also show that by the early sixth century BCE (or as early as the eighth century BCE; cf. Isa. 1.12-13) the sabbath offerings were taken for granted as part of sabbath observance (Ezek. 45.16-17; 46.4-5). The people were expected to pay the religious tax to the prince to meet the expenses of the offerings and the prince was obliged to provide the offerings (Ezek. 45.16-17). Finally it would be worth noticing that as early as the eighth century BCE there were signs of danger of vain observance of the sabbath without recognizing the true covenantal character of the institution (Isa. 1.13; Hos. 2.13; cf. Amos 8.5).

From the investigation above we cannot fail to note that many of the sabbath materials in the prophetic books betray covenantal overtones. For Ezekiel and perhaps for others, the sabbath is understood as a sign of the covenant relationship between YHWH and his people (Ezek. 20.12; cf. Exod. 31.13). In some cases the sabbath is seen as a representative of the whole covenant (e.g. Isa. 56.1-8; Jer. 17.19-27; cf. Ezek. 22.26). In such a covenantal understanding, the observance of the sabbath often constitutes the condition for the various covenantal blessings (e.g. acceptance into the community worshipping YHWH—Isa. 56.1-8; taking delight in YHWH—Isa. 58.13-14; eschatological consummation of the

---

125. Whybray, *Isaiah 40–66*, p. 293; Watts, *Isaiah 34–66*, p. 365.

messianic kingdom—Jer. 17.25-26; cf. Isa. 66.23—universal and eternal [i.e. eschatological consummation of] worship of YHWH every sabbath). On the contrary, profaning the sabbath is usually regarded as breaking the covenant relationship, and therefore frequently constitutes the cause for the various covenantal punishments (e.g. most characteristically the exile or the destruction of Jerusalem—Jer. 17.27; Ezek. 20.23; 22.13-15, 31; 23.46-49; exclusion from entering the promised land—Ezek. 20.15; etc.). Having said this, we need to note that observing the sabbath is not the sole condition for the blessings. In some passages superficial or legalistic observance of the sabbath without recognition or appreciation of the covenantal character of the institution is rejected by YHWH (Isa. 1.13; Hos. 2.13; Amos 8.5; cf. Isa. 56.1-8). Therefore even specific regulations of the sabbath are to be understood not as a mere legalistic attachment to the sabbath commandment but on the basis of the covenant relationship (Isa. 58.13-14; Jer. 17.19-27). This covenantal character of the sabbath can be further detected in the consistent recurrence of the two characteristic adjectives used for the sabbath—'holy' (Isa. 58.13; Jer. 17.22, 24, 27; Ezek. 20.20; 22.8, 26; 44.24; etc.) and 'my' (Isa. 56.4; 58.13; Ezek. 20.12, 13, 16, 20, 21, 24; 22.8, 26; 23.38; 44.24; etc.; cf. 'her' in Hos. 2.13). It may be possible then to suppose that the holiness and YHWH's ownership of the sabbath provided the ground for the covenantal orientation of the sabbath in the books of the prophets.

4. *Summary*

I will now attempt to draw together the various discussions in the previous sections and summarize the conclusions reached in the course of those discussions.

1) The etiology study above suggests that God's rest on the seventh day in creation creates a rhythm which is to affect the whole creation and in this sense his rest does provide the etiology of the sabbath. This suggestion may be further supported by the observation that a number of the sabbath commandments appear to follow the pattern of God's creation in six days and his rest on the seventh day (cf. especially, Exod. 20.8-11; 31.12-17). Nevertheless, the meaning and scope of his rest in creation is not to be limited to the sabbath institution only. The ultimate purpose of the seventh day which was blessed and sanctified by God himself is beyond the scope of the sabbath. In this context I have cautiously suggested that his rest on the seventh day may have an eschatological significance.

2) Most of the sabbath references in the Old Testament presuppose the holiness of the sabbath, and sometimes explicitly define it as holy or command it to be kept holy (Exod. 20.8-11; 31.12-17; Deut. 5.12-15; Neh. 13.22; Isa. 58.13-14; Jer. 17.19-27; Ezek. 20.20; 22.26; 44.24). It is on this basis that the death penalty is sanctioned against anyone who violates the sanctity of the sabbath (Exod. 31.14-15; Num. 15.32-36).

3) A great number of Old Testament sabbath references also presuppose God's Lordship of the sabbath (cf. such expressions as 'to/for YHWH'—Exod. 16.23, 25; 20.10; 31.15; 35.2; Lev. 23.3; Deut. 5.14), and sometimes explicitly use the phrase 'my/your sabbath' (Exod. 31.13; Lev. 19.3, 30; 26.2; Neh. 9.14; Isa. 56.4; 58.13; Ezek. 20.12ff.; 22.8, 26; 23.38; 44.24).

4) A number of sabbath references in the Old Testament (and especially in the prophetic books) betray covenantal overtones. In two places the sabbath is called the sign of the eternal covenant relationship between YHWH and his people (Exod. 31.13; Ezek. 20.12). In many sabbath references (especially in the prophetic books) sabbath keeping or breaking constitutes the ground for the covenantal blessings or punishments (Isa. 56.1-8; 58.13-14; Jer. 17.25-27; Ezek. 20.15, 23; 22.13-15, 31; 23.46-49; Neh. 13.18). It is noteworthy that at least in one case the blessing is related to the eschatological consummation of the messianic kingdom (Jer. 17.25-26; cf. Isa. 66.23). Having said this, however, observing the sabbath is not seen as the sole condition for blessing. In some passages legalistic observance of the sabbath without recognition or appreciation of the covenantal character of the institution is rejected by YHWH (Isa. 1.13; Hos. 2.13; Amos 8.5). The creation and Exodus motive clauses in the sabbath commandments (Exod. 20.11; Deut. 5.15; cf. Exod. 31.17) may emphasize the fundamental importance of the recognition of the covenantal relationship in keeping the sabbath.

5) Though we can detect some signs of humanitarian concern especially in the sabbath commandments (e.g. Exod. 23.12; Deut. 5.12-15), we have observed that in every case the primary concern is not humanitarian or social as such but rather theological.

6) Though there are a few specific regulations of the sabbath in the Old Testament (Exod. 16.21-30; 35.3; Num. 15.32-36; Neh. 10.32; 13.15-22; Jer. 17.19-27; Amos 8.5), their proportion within the whole of the sabbath materials in the Old Testament suggests a very different perspective as compared with the later preoccupation with exceedingly detailed casuistic regulations (especially, in the Mishnah). Furthermore,

the measures in Nehemiah and Jeremiah do not compare with the meticulous details covered by the rabbinic legislation. Considering the centrality of the covenant relationship in the sabbath institution, even specific regulations are to be understood not as legalistic attachments to the sabbath commandment but on the basis of the covenant relationship.

7) Finally, in a significant number of sabbath references the sabbath is clearly (and sometimes implicitly) associated with cultic elements. According to the investigations above, by the eighth century BCE (and perhaps as early as the end of the ninth century) the sabbath was settled as one of the national feasts on which not only the priests and the king but probably also the people were expected to be present in the temple (2 Kgs 4.23; 11.4-14; 2 Chron. 23.1-3; Isa. 1.13; Hos. 2.13; etc.; cf. Lev. 23.3; Ezek. 46.1-3). My investigations also show that by the early sixth century (and probably as early as the eighth century) the sabbath offerings were taken for granted as part of sabbath observance (Ezek. 45.16-17; 46.4-5; cf. Isa. 1.12-13; cf. also Lev. 24.5-9; Num. 28.9-10). According to the Chronicler, the sabbath offering was offered as early as Solomon's time (2 Chron. 8.13; cf. 31.3). The main constituents of the sabbath offering were the shewbread (cf. Lev. 24.5-9) and the burnt offerings (cf. Num. 28.9-10). This priestly service was assisted by the Levites (1 Chron. 9.32; 23.28-31); the offerings were to be provided by the kings or princes (2 Chron. 8.13; 31.3; cf. Ezek. 45.17), but in the post-exilic period the people were expected to pay the temple tax to meet these expenses (Neh. 10.33-34; cf. Ezek. 45.16). Considering the holiness and God's Lordship of the sabbath, it would be natural that the sabbath, even from its earliest stage, provided an occasion for festal gathering at the sacred centre(s) to celebrate it with special offerings in remembrance of their covenantal relationship with God who created the whole world and delivered them from Egypt (and later from Babylon).

Chapter 2

THE SABBATH IN JUDAISM TO THE FIRST CENTURY CE: BACKGROUNDS (II)

Before we enter into the main investigation, certain preliminary statements should be made so that they may be reflected in the subsequent discussions.

1) The sea of Jewish literature of the so-called intertestamental period is so vast in its genres as well as in its historical and geographical settings that detailed discussion of these issues, which are sometimes crucial for interpreting the ancient texts in question, is beyond the scope of this chapter.[1] I will try, however, to discuss them briefly when I think it is necessary.

2) In dealing with the literature of early Judaism, I will not aim to present all the materials in chronological order, since this is not always possible to determine.

3) The passages related to the sabbath in the literature of early Judaism are so numerous that it obviously lies beyond the scope of this background investigation to cover all of them. Thus the discussion has to be concentrated on more important passages, though I will try not to disregard minor references completely. Even for the major passages, my exegesis must be selective.

1. *Apocrypha and Pseudepigrapha*[2]

In the Old Testament Apocrypha and Pseudepigrapha the sabbath materials appear in a number of books. But the major passages are found in the four books[3] on which I will focus the discussion here.

1. For an introductory discussion of these issues, see G.W.E. Nickelsburg, *Jewish Literature between the Bible and the Mishnah—A Historical and Literary Introduction* (Philadelphia: Fortress Press, 1981).

2. The terms 'apocrypha' and 'pseudepigrapha', both of which, if they are understood etymologically, can be easily misleading, have signified different things

a. *Jubilees*[4]

i. *Jub. 2.17-33*. In retelling the creation narrative, the author here extends the sabbath material at great length,[5] in order to explain the significance of the sabbath (vv. 17-24) and to illustrate some regulations for keeping the sabbath (vv. 25-33). The narrators of the story are 'all of the angels of the presence and all of the angels of sanctification' (v. 18).[6] The central human figure in the story is Jacob, as in the book as a whole (cf. vv. 20, 23-24, 26-29).

First of all, the author describes the sabbath as a great sign of God's election of 'the seed of Jacob' as his people (vv. 17-24). God who

---

to different people throughout the centuries, and any distinction between the two categories of literature is far from definite. In this section, therefore, I will discuss both categories of literature together without any attempt to draw a line between the two. As a matter of convenience, however, under the heading of 'Apocrypha and Pseudepigrapha', I will cover the documents of the conventional Old Testament Apocrypha which consists of fifteen books or parts of books as given in the Revised English Bible (1989) and the sixty-five Old Testament pseudepigraphal documents which are contained in J.H. Charlesworth (ed.), *The Old Testament Pseudepigrapha* (2 vols.; Garden City, NY: Doubleday, 1983, 1985). Unless otherwise stated, pseudepigraphal quotations are from Charlesworth's edition.

    3.   That is, *Jubilees*, 1 & 2 Maccabees, and Aristobulus. If we include *Hellenistic Synagogal Prayers* in this category, the number will become five. However, since the date of composition is normally set after 150 CE and the final redactor must be a Christian, these documents can provide information for this background study only indirectly, and therefore I will not discuss them here.

    4.   Despite some efforts to date *Jubilees* back to as early as the fifth century BCE (cf. S. Zeitlin, 'The Book of Jubilees, its Character and Significance', *JQR* 30 [1939/40], pp. 8-16; S.B. Hoenig, 'The Designated Number of Kinds of Labor Prohibited on the Sabbath', *JQR* 68 [1977], p. 200), most scholars prefer a date about 100 BCE or slightly earlier; cf. J.C. VanderKam, *Textual and Historical Studies in the Book of Jubilees* (Missoula, MT: Scholars Press, 1977), pp. 214-85, esp. pp. 283-84. Most scholars agree that the author was a Jew who lived in Palestine; cf. H.F.D. Sparks (ed.), *The Apocryphal Old Testament* (Oxford: Oxford University Press, 1984), p. 5; Charlesworth, *Pseudepigrapha*, II, pp. 43-45; D.E. Gowan, *Bridge between the Testaments* (Allison Park, PA: Pickwick, 1986), p. 274; *et al.*

    5.   Cf. Gen. 2.2-3. In extending this material, he freely uses other materials in the Old Testament, e.g. Exod. 31.13ff.; Num. 15.32-36; Neh. 13.19; Isa. 56.1-8; Jer. 17.21ff.; Ezek. 20.12; etc.

    6.   The effectiveness of using the angels as the narrators is impressive in v. 30 when the author demonstrates the antiquity (or eternity) of the sabbath by saying that 'we kept the sabbath in heaven before it was made known to any human...upon the earth'.

sanctified and blessed the sabbath singled out the children of Jacob alone as his people and he blessed and sanctified them for himself so that they may keep the sabbath (v. 21).[7] The children of Israel, therefore, are to keep the sabbath as a sign of their unique relationship to God (cf. vv. 25-33).

In v. 25 the author declares that the sabbath is holy, because it was made holy in God's creation activity. He, then, repeatedly pronounces the sanction that anyone who pollutes it must be put to death.[8] In v. 28, however, he briefly announces the promise to everyone who keeps the sabbath from all work that he will become holy and blessed always like the angels.

Now the author brings forward a more precise description of prohibited work. On the sabbath the children of Israel are not allowed to prepare anything to be eaten or drunk,[9] to draw water, to bring in or out of their gates any work (vv. 29-30; cf. 50.6-13).

According to vv. 31-32, since the sabbath has been given solely to the Israelites to be kept (cf. v. 20), they are to celebrate it by eating and drinking and blessing the one who created all things and sanctified the sabbath and his people (cf. vv. 21, 29). The author finally declares that the sabbath law is eternal (v. 33).

ii. *Jub. 6.32-38*. In the middle of the story of Noah, the author describes a situation in which there is a danger of keeping sacred feasts on unclean days. It was important for him that the sacred days should fall on the

---

7.   Whereas in Exod. 31.12-17 the focus is clearly on Israel's unique covenant relationship with God and the sabbath is merely a sign of it (cf. Ezek. 20.12), here the focus is shifted from the covenant relationship to the sabbath itself. The sentence structure of this verse, however, is quite complicated. Compare Charlesworth's translation with that of R.H. Charles in his *The Book of Jubilees* (London: A. & C. Black, 1902), p. 17; cf. Charles's note on this verse—'*And that they...with us.* This seems a dittography of the second clause of this verse.'

8.   Four times in three verses (vv. 25-27); cf. also the threat 'be uprooted from the land' in v. 27. Cf. Exod. 31.14-15; 35.2; Num. 15.32-36. At this point the Damascus Document is milder than *Jubilees* in the sabbath regulations; according to CD 12.3-6, the person who desecrates the sabbath can be received back into the community after seven years. See Lohse, 'σάββατον', p. 11, esp. n. 71. See below, section 2a.

9.   Cf. 50.9; CD 10.22; Exod. 16.23. The primary reason for preparing the food on the day before may be to avoid kindling a fire on the sabbath; see Josephus, *War* 2.147; cf. Exod. 35.3.

same day of the week year after year (cf. 1QS 1.14-15; 1QH 12.8-9). He therefore emphasizes the importance of guarding the calendar of 364 days which is divisible by seven and makes the above scheme possible.[10] The sabbath which falls regularly on the seventh day of every week is, then, the key to the whole calendar scheme, and, therefore, must have had particular significance for the author.

iii. *Jub. 50.1-13.* At the end of the Moses story which closes the whole book, the author presents a collection of laws concerning the sabbath (vv. 1, 6-13). In v. 1 the author clearly mentions that the sabbath was made known to Israel in the wilderness of Sin.[11] After giving a brief history of jubilees (vv. 2-4) and a forecast of the messianic kingdom (v. 5), the author begins to comment on the commandment of the sabbath. He begins his comments by quoting the middle portion of the fourth commandment in the decalogue (v. 7; cf. Exod. 20.9-10; Deut. 5.13-14). Significantly, the subsequent comments both begin and end with the death penalty sanctioned against the one who does 'anything' (v. 8) / 'any of these [things]' (v. 13) on the sabbath.[12] This literary structure seems to suggest that the author's concern in listing the prohibited works between the two sanctions is to show what kind of works deserve the death penalty. On pain of death, on the sabbath an Israelite is forbidden to lie with his wife, to talk about business, to draw water, to take up any burden to carry it out of his residence, to go on a journey,[13]

---

10.   This calendar may have been adopted by the community to which the author belonged. Cf. *1 En.* 74.10, 12; 75.2; *2 En.* 48.1; 4Q394-398 (part 1). For further discussion of the 364 day calendar, see Charles, *Jubilees*, pp. 56-57; VanderKam, *Jubilees*, pp. 270-77. Cf. J. Maier, *The Temple Scroll: An Introduction, Translation and Commentary* (JSOTSup, 34; Sheffield: JSOT Press, 1985), pp. 70-76; Maier presents a complete reconstruction of the Qumran community's calendar of 364 days based on 'The Temple Scroll' cols. 13-29. It is noteworthy that the author opposes the lunar calendar outspokenly (vv. 36-37), which suggests that it was observed in the society which surrounded his community. Cf. Charles, *Jubilees*, p. 58; E.P. Sanders, *Judaism: Practice and Belief 63 BCE–66 CE* (London: SCM Press, 1992), pp. 360-61.

11.   Exod. 16.1-30. However, cf. Neh. 9.13-14; Ezek. 20.11-12.

12.   Note another appearance of the death penalty at the end of v. 8. Such repeated appearances of the death penalty strongly imply that the author took the sabbath commandment very seriously. Cf. 2.25-27.

13.   This regulation derives from Exod. 16.29. Whereas CD and rabbinic rules regulate the distance of journey (1000 and 2000 cubits respectively), *Jubilees* does not do so. From this C. Rabin, *Qumran Studies* (Oxford: Oxford University Press,

to plough a field, to kindle a fire, to ride on any animal, to travel the sea in a boat, to slaughter anything, to catch any beast or bird or fish, to fast, or to make war,[14] etc. (vv. 8-12). The only exception to the sabbath commandment is offering incense and bringing gifts and sacrifices before the Lord for the days and the sabbaths (vv. 10-11).[15] This is the oldest list of activities prohibited on the sabbath.[16] Here (and in 2.29-30) we can detect the first clear and substantial indication of the later meticulous rabbinic development of the sabbath regulations as in the Mishnah.

For the author, however, the sabbath was not a gloomy day. In vv. 9-10 he points out that the sabbath is a festival day to be celebrated by eating and drinking, resting, and blessing the Lord who gave them the holy day of festival. Fasting is, therefore, clearly forbidden (cf. v. 12; 2.21, 29).[17]

b. *1 and 2 Maccabees*[18]

i. *No war on the sabbath—1 Macc. 2.32-38; 2 Macc. 5.25.* According to 2 Macc. 5.25, in *c.* 168 BCE Apollonius, the captain of the Mysians

1957), p. 90, concludes that the author here forbids leaving the house at all on the sabbath.

14.　Cf. 1 Macc. 2.31-38; 2 Macc. 6.11; Josephus, *Ant.* 12.4; *Mek. Šab.* 1. See Charles, *Jubilees*, p. 261. For further discussions, see below.

15.　Cf. Num. 28.9-10; 1 Esdr. 5.52. For some different views, cf. CD 11.17-18; *m. Pes.* 6.1-2. For general discussions of the issue in brief, see Lohse, 'σάββατον', p. 14; E. Schürer, *The History of the Jewish People in the Age of Jesus Christ* II (3 vols.; ed. G. Vermes, F. Millar and M. Goodman; Edinburgh: T. & T. Clark, rev. edn, 1973–87), p. 473, esp. n. 49. Cf. also Mt. 12.5.

16.　Lohse, 'σάββατον', p. 11. H. Braun, *Spätjüdisch-häretischer und früh-christlicher Radikalismus*, I (2 vols.; Tübingen: Mohr, 1957), p. 120, rightly points out that 'die Jubiläen sind weniger spezialisiert als die Dam[askusschrift]; hinsichtlich der Zerlegung in einzelne Fälle steht die Dam den Rabbinen näher, die Jubiläen sind also offenbar älter als die Dam'. Cf. CD 16.2-4.

17.　According to Jdt. 8.6, this regulation was observed by Judith. This story probably belongs to the same period as *Jubilees*, i.e. the Hasmonean era. See Lohse, 'σάββατον', pp. 15-16; Schürer, *History*, II, pp. 469-70, esp. n. 30. Greek and Roman writers are mistaken, therefore, when they regard the sabbath as a fast day: e.g. Strabo, *Geographica* 16.2.40; Suetonius, *Divus Augustus* 76; *et al.*; see below.

18.　The date of 1 Maccabees, a straightforward historical narrative over the period of mid-second century (*c.* 170–134) BCE, is most probably about 100 BCE (cf. 16.23-24). The author appears to be 'a staunch supporter of the Hasmoneans'; Gowan, *Bridge*, p. 294. Cf. Nickelsburg, *Literature*, pp. 114-17. Though the final form of 2 Maccabees may have been produced about 50 BCE, its original five-

sent by Antiochus, waited until the holy sabbath day, then, finding the Jews not at work, attacked the city with his troops and killed great numbers of people.[19] But Judas Maccabeus, without fighting against them, withdrew himself into the wilderness. According to 1 Macc. 2.32-38, in *c.* 167 BCE, after the above incident, the king's officers and their troops pursued a group of pious Jews in the wilderness and attacked them on the sabbath, but the Jews refused to fight against them and gave themselves up to massacre. On the day a thousand persons were killed (cf. Josephus, *Ant.* 12.274-75). These two independent reports of separate incidents[20] seem to suggest strongly that at the time of these incidents there were a number of devout Jews with genuine enthusiasm to keep the sabbath strictly.

ii. *War on the sabbath—1 Macc. 2.39-41; 9.43-49; 2 Macc. 8.26-28; 15.3.* After the latter incident, Mattathias and his followers resolved to take up the sword for defence on the sabbath also (1 Macc. 2.39-41).[21] This resolution was put into effect when Bacchides with his army in *c.* 160 BCE attacked Jonathan and his followers on the sabbath. Jonathan exhorted his followers to defend their lives against Bacchides' attack, and they killed one thousand[22] of Bacchides' men (1 Macc. 9.43-49).[23]

volume history, i.e. the work of Jason of Cyrene, was probably written about the same time as 1 Maccabees. The period which is covered by 2 Maccabees is slightly earlier than that of 1 Maccabees, i.e. approximately 180–161 BCE. Cf. Nickelsburg, *Literature*, pp. 118-21; Gowan, *Bridge*, pp. 294-95. The period which is covered by our sabbath materials from 1 Maccabees (i.e. *c.* 168–152 BCE) is mostly overlapped by that of 2 Maccabees (i.e. *c.* 168–161 BCE). Therefore, I will deal with the materials from both books together, though they are separate works with distinctive character.

19.   According to 1 Macc. 1.39-45 and 2 Macc. 6.1-6, not long after this (*c.* 168/7 BCE), Antiochus compelled the Jews to forsake the laws of God including the sabbath; hence people could not keep the sabbath and many Jews profaned the sabbath.

20.   We have another report of this kind in Josephus, *Apion* 1.209-11; cf. *Ant.* 12.4. Cf. *Jub.* 50.12.

21.   Cf. Josephus, *Ant.* 12.276-77. Such a pragmatic decision may have fed the later formulation of the rabbinic rule that the saving of life takes precedence over the sabbath; cf. *m. Yom.* 8.6-7; *m. Šab.* 16.1-7; cf. also CD 11.16-17; see Schürer, *History*, II, p. 474; E.P. Sanders, *Jewish Law from Jesus to the Mishnah: Five Studies* (London: SCM Press, 1990), p. 13.

22.   Cf. 'two thousand' men in Josephus, *Ant.* 13.14.

23.   Cf. Josephus, *Ant.* 13.12-14. Cf. also *Ant.* 18.319-24. This resolution,

This resolution, however, did not extend to offensive attack. According to 2 Macc. 8.26-28, in *c.* 166 BCE Judas and his brothers and followers defeated Nicanor's army and pursued them. But when the sabbath was approaching they stopped their pursuit and kept the sabbath.[24] In 2 Macc. 15.1-5 we have a very interesting conversation between Nicanor and the Jews in his army. When Nicanor in *c.* 161 BCE ordered the Jews to take up arms on the sabbath, the Jews refused to do so by answering, Ἔστιν ὁ κύριος ζῶν αὐτὸς ἐν οὐρανῷ δυνάστης ὁ κελεύσας ἀσκεῖν τὴν ἑβδομάδα. Therefore he did not succeed in carrying out his attack against Judas.[25]

c. *Aristobulus*[26]

In Fragment 5 the Jewish observance of the sabbath is discussed 'by means of a Pythagorean-like exposition'.[27] First of all Aristobulus affirms that the seventh day was given by God, the creator of the whole cosmos, as a rest day, because life is laborious for all (F. 5.9; cf. Gen. 2.2-3; Exod. 20.8-11). After identifying the first day of creation with the seventh, he mentions that God himself rested on the seventh day in his creation.[28] For Aristobulus, however, the resting of God on the seventh day does not mean the end of his activity but the ordering of all things

however, seems to have been applied to situations of extreme distress, so that the Gentiles were still able to take advantage of the Jewish sabbath for their battle. See Josephus, *Ant.* 14.63.

24.   Another similar story is found in 2 Macc. 12.38. Cf. however, *t. 'Erub.* 3.7; see below, section 6a.

25.   In later times the Romans felt obliged to exempt the Jews from military service because they did not bear arms or march on the sabbath; cf. Josephus, *Ant.*, 14.223-40. See Schürer, *History*, II, pp. 474-75.

26.   The five fragments of Aristobulus's work, which are normally dated around the middle of the second century BCE (M. Hengel: 175–170 BCE; J.H. Charlesworth: 155–145 BCE), seem to be part of an extended attempt to combine his own Jewish tradition with the ideas of Greek philosophy. Those who accept the authenticity of the fragments think Aristobulus an Alexandrian Jew; M. Hengel, *Judaism and Hellenism*, I (2 vols.; trans. J. Bowden; London: SCM Press, 1974), pp. 163-64; Charlesworth, *Pseudepigrapha*, II, pp. 831-33.

27.   Schürer, *History*, III, p. 583; cf. N. Walter, *Der Thoraausleger Aristobulus* (Berlin: Akademie-Verlag, 1964), pp. 73, 150-77; Hengel, *Judaism*, I, p. 166.

28.   Hengel, *Judaism*, I, p. 166, observes here 'a unique combination of the resting of God on the seventh day and the creation of light on the first day with the pretemporal being of wisdom according to Prov. 8.22 and certain philosophical notions'; cf. *Judaism*, II, p. 108 n. 389.

for all time (F. 5.11; cf. Jn 5.17), and God's work in six days is to be understood as the establishment of the order of time (F. 5.12). 'In this way', as M. Hengel suggests, 'Aristobulus attempted to bring the Old Testament conception of the creation of God in time in accord with the Greek idea of the timeless activity of God.'[29] Aristobulus then goes further and argues that the Jewish sabbath has universal significance by showing that Greeks such as Homer, Hesiod and Linus also considered the seventh day holy (F. 5.13-16). In doing all this he makes use of Pythagorean reflections on the number seven as a prime number and the Stoic definition of wisdom.[30] By using these ideas, which in his view can be reconciled with Jewish thought, in an eclectic manner, he has attempted to interpret the Jewish conception of the sabbath in terms of Greek philosophical cosmology and epistemology without giving up its original character.[31]

d. *Conclusions*

From this investigation into the sabbath passages in these four apocryphal and pseudepigraphal books dating between the second and the first century BCE, the following conclusions may be drawn.

In *Jubilees* we find the oldest list of activities prohibited on the sabbath (*Jub.* 2.29-30; 50.8-12; cf. 2.23[32]), and we can here detect the first clear and substantial indication of the later meticulous rabbinic

29.   Hengel, *Judaism*, I, p. 166; cf. II, p. 108 n. 390; cf. P. Borgen, 'Philo of Alexandria', in M.E. Stone (ed.), *The Literature of the Jewish People in the Period of the Second Temple and the Talmud*. II. *Jewish Writings of the Second Temple Period* (CRINT, 2; Assen: Van Gorcum, 1984), p. 276.

30.   Hengel, *Judaism*, I, pp. 166-67; Charlesworth, *Pseudepigrapha*, II, p. 834.

31.   For his role as the forerunner of Philo, see Hengel, *Judaism*, I, pp. 165-66 and II, p. 108 nn. 387, 389; Charlesworth, *Pseudepigrapha*, II, p. 836; Borgen, 'Philo', pp. 274-79.

32.   On the basis of this verse, scholars assume that there were 22 kinds of works prohibited in *Jubilees*; cf. Hoenig, 'Designated Number', pp. 199-200; M. Casey, 'Culture and Historicity: The Plucking of the Grain (Mark 2.23-28)', *NTS* 34 (1988), p. 5. This verse, however, seems to refer rather to the creation work before the sabbath than to the prohibited works; in fact, I could detect only 14 kinds of works prohibited in *Jubilees* rather than 22. Cf. P. Sigal, *The Halakah of Jesus of Nazareth according to the Gospel of Matthew* (Lanham, MD: University Press of America, 1986), pp. 145-46—he presents 16 items rather than 14; his first item, however, is not to be counted as work prohibited but rather as a parallel expression of 'to do work'; again, in my judgment, his fourth and fifth items are not referring to different kinds of works but to the same kind.

development of the sabbath regulations. In 1 and 2 Maccabees we find examples of strict observance of one particular sabbath regulation, 'do not make war' (1 Macc. 2.32-38; 2 Macc. 5.25; 8.26-28; 15.1-5; cf. *Jub.* 50.12). We can, however, detect two exceptions to the sabbath commandment: (i) offering sacrifices before the Lord for the days and the sabbaths (*Jub.* 50.10-11); (ii) taking up the sword for defence (1 Macc. 2.39-41; 9.43-49)[33]—the decision in favour of this exception may have fed later rabbinic formulation of the rule that the saving of life takes precedence over the sabbath.

Many of the passages I have investigated show concern for the authority of the sabbath in various ways. In *Jub.* 2.17-33 the author emphasizes the authority of the day by demonstrating its antiquity and eternity. In doing this the author also points out its role as a sign of Israel's unique covenantal relationship to God.[34] In Aristobulus, however, its authority is demonstrated rather by its cosmic and universal character. These two quite opposite approaches for similar purposes reflect their different (i.e. Palestinian and Alexandrian) contexts. The authority of the sabbath is still further enhanced when the holiness of the sabbath is emphasized. In the Maccabean passages the holiness of the sabbath is presupposed and sometimes impressively expressed (e.g. 1 Macc. 2.34, 37; 2 Macc. 5.25-26). In *Jub.* 6.32-38 the sanctity of the sabbath is once again presupposed when the importance of the calendar of 364 days is emphasized. In *Jubilees* 2 and 50 the author is quite fanatically obsessed with his concern for the holiness of the sabbath, and the death penalty is repeatedly sanctioned against those who profane the sabbath.

Finally, according to *Jubilees* the sabbath is, in principle, not a gloomy day but a festival day to be celebrated by having good food and blessing the Lord of the day, and therefore fasting is forbidden (2.21, 29; 50.9-10, 12; cf. Jdt. 8.6; 2 Macc. 8.27).[35]

33.   We have here one concrete case that a specific but still broad regulation (here, 'do not make war') is to be further developed in the direction of an increasingly precise case law corresponding to the conditions and needs of a certain group. Cf. Schürer, *History*, II, pp. 467-68.

34.   As we have observed, however, whereas in Exod. 31.12-17 the focus is clearly on Israel's unique covenant relationship with God, here the focus is rather on the sabbath itself than on the covenant relationship.

35.   It may be necessary, perhaps, to make brief mention of other sabbath references in the Old Testament Apocrypha and Pseudepigrapha which have not been discussed so far. Most of them are very brief and they do not particularly add

2. *The Qumran Scrolls*

Though sabbath references appear in several documents in the Qumran Scrolls[36] (apart, of course, from the biblical, apocryphal and pseudepigraphal manuscripts), substantially significant materials are found in the Damascus Document (CD) and in 4Q251, each of which presents a list of specific regulations. I will, therefore, concentrate the discussion on these two documents. The other materials some of which are by and large related to the 364 day calendar will be discussed only very briefly.

a. *Specific Regulations*
i. *CD 10.14–11.18; 12.3-6.* According to Josephus the Essenes[37] were 'stricter than all Jews in abstaining from work on the seventh day' (*War*

---

any significant information for this background study except confirming that some features of the sabbath in the Old Testament have been taken for granted by their authors—e.g. God's blessing of and his rest on the sabbath in his creation in *2 En.* 32.1-2 (cf. *Jub.* 2.19, 24, 25, 31-33; Aristobulus F. 5.9, 11); the sabbath offering in 1 Esdr. 5.52 (cf. *Jub.* 50.10-11); regular sabbath keeping in Jdt. 8.6; 10.2. In *2 Apoc. Bar.* 84.8 the sabbath commandment is interestingly but perhaps not very significantly presented in the negative form 'do not forget...the sabbath' (cf. Exod. 20.8). Pseudo-Philo 25.13 and 44.6-7 show that the author considers sabbath profaning as one of the serious sins, but no more than that.

36.   The Qumran literature except the biblical, apocryphal and pseudepigraphal manuscripts is widely and, in my view, rightly identified with some types of the Essenes, and these sectarian writings will be our primary concern in this section; cf. A. Dupont-Sommer, *The Essene Writings from Qumran* (trans. G. Vermes; Oxford: Blackwell, 1961), pp. 39-67; M.A. Knibb, *The Qumran Community* (CCWJCW, 2; Cambridge: Cambridge University Press, 1987), p. 1; J.H. Charlesworth, *Jesus within Judaism: New Light from Exciting Archaeological Discoveries* (London: SPCK, 1988), p. 63; *et al.* For a different but unlikely view, see N. Golb, 'Who Hid the Dead Sea Scrolls?', *Biblical Archaeologist* 48 (1985), pp. 68-82.

37.   In this section I will simply adopt the recently predominant view that the Essenes are a party composed of at least two branches, one a monastic sect that did not marry and lived near the Dead Sea (i.e. the so-called 'Qumran community'), the other a town-dwelling group that married and lived in communities in Palestine other than at Qumran; CD is best identified with the latter, whereas the Community Rule (1QS) with the former. See Knibb, *Qumran*, pp. 14-15; Charlesworth, *Judaism*, pp. 63-64—he suggests four sub-groups; Sanders, *Practice*, pp. 341-49; N.T. Wright, *Christian Origins and the Question of God*. I. *The New Testament and the People of God* (London: SPCK, 1992), pp. 203-204; cf. G. Vermes, *The Dead Sea Scrolls: Qumran in Perspective* (Philadelphia: Fortress Press, 1981), pp. 87-130. However,

2.147). CD,[38] which is one of several writings of a legislative character among the Scrolls, contains a long list of 28 sabbath regulations in 10.14–11.18[39] and a separate regulation on the sabbath-breaking punishment in 12.3-6; these regulations are on the whole distinguished by a greater severity especially compared with the rabbinic sabbath rules,[40] and thus may show that Josephus's observation was quite right.

The list begins by determining when the sabbath begins (10.15-16); this issue is not discussed in the previous sabbath materials but, according to Josephus, was already a matter of interest for the Jews during that time.[41] The following prohibitions of speaking 'a lewd or villainous word' (10.17-18) and speaking about as well as conduct of business (10.18-20; 11.2, 15) were also not innovations of the Essenes (cf. Isa. 58.13; *Jub.* 50.8; cf. also Neh. 10.31; 13.15-22; Amos 8.5), but the more specific character of these prohibitions cannot be overlooked; the repetitive enumeration of these prohibitions may show that the sect was specially concerned to guard against doing business on the sabbath. In

for a view which rejects the idea of relating the Qumran community with the Essenes, see G.R. Driver, *The Judaean Scrolls: The Problem and a Solution* (Oxford: Blackwell, 1965), pp. 100-21.

38.   The document is divided into an exhortation (1.1–8.21; 19.1–20.34) and a list of statutes (9.1–16.19); the sabbath materials are mainly found in the latter. Though there is no final agreement as regards the date of composition of the document, most scholars seem to agree that it was written after *Jubilees* but before the first half of the first century BCE (there is a scholarly consensus as regards the acquaintance of CD's author with *Jubilees*; cf. esp. CD 16.3-4, which may undoubtedly refer to *Jubilees*); cf. P.R. Davies, *The Damascus Covenant* (JSOTSup, 25; Sheffield: JSOT Press, 1982), p. 203; G. Vermes, *The Dead Sea Scrolls in English* (Sheffield: JSOT Press, 3rd edn, 1987), p. 81. The best text available in English at present and perhaps until the fragments from Cave 4 are eventually published seems to be still that of C. Rabin in his *The Zadokite Documents. I. The Admonition. II. The Laws. Edited with a Translation and Notes* (Oxford: Oxford University Press, 2nd edn, 1958) which is mostly based on Cairo manuscripts A and B, and it is the translation which I will use but with frequent references to other translations whenever it is required. Though the Hebrew text is here cited from the same book, E. Lohse's *Die Texte aus Qumran* (Munich: Kösel-Verlag, 1964) (especially its vowels) will be also referred to.

39.   For a form-analytical observation of this passage, see T. Zahavy, 'The Sabbath Code of Damascus Document X.14-XI.18: Form Analytical and Redaction Critical Observations', *RevQ* 10 (1981), pp. 589-91.

40.   See below, section 6.

41.   *War* 4.582. Cf. B. Sharvit, 'The Sabbath of the Judean Desert Sect', *Immanuel* 9 (1979), p. 44.

10.21 CD states that 'Let him not walk about "outside his town above" one thousand cubits'. Exod. 16.29 and *Jub.* 50.12 restrict travel on the sabbath, but neither of them specify a limit; CD, in contrast, does define the sabbath limit as 1000 cubits. This is another example of the tendency towards becoming more specific probably in order to cater to the needs of the group. Many scholars point out that this sabbath limit is much stricter than that of the rabbis who accepted a limit of 2000 cubits.[42] In 11.5-6, however, 2000 cubits are allowed for bringing an animal to pasture (cf. Lk. 13.15). In 10.22–11.2 it is forbidden to prepare food, as in *Jub.* 50.9, or drink water[43] outside the camp; but if one was bathing on one's journey outside the camp, one could drink where one stood. It is also forbidden to pick and eat anything lying in the field, a prohibition not found in any previous sabbath materials.[44] Another new regulation is also found in 11.9 where opening a pitch-sealed vessel is forbidden (cf. *m. Šab.* 17.8; 22.3; *b. Šab.* 23). In 11.3-4 people are required to wear freshly cleaned clothing; in 11.14-15 it is forbidden to 'spend the Sabbath in a place near Gentiles'. These two regulations may reflect the Essenes' concern for preserving the sanctity of the sabbath.[45] As in *Jub.* 50.12 fasting (11.4-5) and striking one's beast (11.5-6; cf. *m. Šab.* 14.1)

---

42.   Dupont-Sommer, *Writings*, p. 152 n. 4; Sharvit, 'Sabbath', p. 45; Sanders, *Practice*, p. 367; cf. J. Rosenthal, 'The Sabbath Laws of the Qumranites or the Damascus Covenanters', *Biblical Research* 6 (1961), pp. 10-17. The sabbath limits come from Num. 35.4-5. The rabbinic sabbath limit is 'historically attested at Gezer, where one group of "boundary" stones is roughly 2,000 cubits from the nearest point of the wall' (Rabin, *Documents*, p. 53 n. 21.5); cf. Acts 1.12.

43.   (כִּי אִם הָיָה בְמַחֲנֶה) יִשְׁתֶּה (וְאַל)—Rabin, *Documents*, p. 53 n. 23.3, mistakenly understands this as drawing water and says, 'by allowing it anywhere inside the camp, our sect is, for once, more liberal than Rabb'. Dupont-Sommer, *Writings*, p. 152 n. 6, rightly understands that 'the sectaries could therefore drink only in the camp, where the water *had been prepared the day before*' (italics mine); cf. *Jub.* 50.8-9. *M. 'Erub.* 8.6-8, in contrast, explicitly permits drawing water from a well inside the house. So far, there does not seem to be any factor from CD sabbath materials which is more liberal than rabbinic materials.

44.   Perhaps Exod. 16.22-30 may provide an indirect ground for this regulation; otherwise we have no direct precedent for it. For a later example, however, see *m. Pes.* 4.8: 'they [the men of Jericho] ate on the Sabbath fruit that lay fallen under the tree...and the Sages reproved them'. Cf. also Philo, *Spec. Leg.* 66-70; Mt. 12.1-2 par.; see below, Chapter 4, section 3a-b.

45.   Sharvit, 'Sabbath', p. 47. Cf. the clause 'Let no man profane the Sabbath...' (11.15) straight after the latter regulation above.

are forbidden. Perhaps 11.2, 12[46] are more specific clarification of the stipulation in Deut. 5.14 ('your male or female slave...or the resident alien in your town') in accordance with current issues. In 11.7-11 a list of prohibitions as regards bringing in or taking out something appears; we have here outstanding examples of the tendency to develop a general (though specific) regulation in the Scripture (Neh. 10.32; 13.15-22; Jer. 17.19-27) in the direction of increasingly more specific regulations probably corresponding to the current circumstances. Scholars once again notice that CD's regulation here, 'Let no man carry upon himself medicaments to go out and to go in' (11.9-10), is stricter than that of the rabbis who permit 'a spice-box or a perfume-flask' (*t. Šab.* 4.11; etc.).[47] A more significant contrast between CD and the rabbis, however, is found in 11.13-14 where assisting a beast to give birth or taking her new-born offspring out of a cistern or a pit is clearly forbidden, whereas the rabbis permit both.[48] There are two clear exceptions to the prohibition of work on the sabbath: one is saving human life (11.16-17);[49] another is offerings on the sabbath. CD is, however, once again stricter than the rabbis (and, perhaps, *Jubilees*) as regards offerings; in 11.17-18 no sacrifice is permitted except the sabbath burnt offering,[50] while the rabbis require Passover sacrifices even on the sabbath when the days overlap (e.g. *m. Pes.* 6.1).

At the end of this long list of regulations CD adds after a short break a sanction against the one who has profaned the sabbath. We have here

---

46.   11.2—'Let him not send a proselyte (or: Gentile) [בֶּן הַנֵּכָר] "to do what he requires"'; 11.12—'Let no man urge on [יָמְרֵא] his (Jewish) slave...'

47.   Sharvit, 'Sabbath', p. 45; cf. Rabin, *Documents*, p. 56 n. 10.2.

48.   *M. Šab.* 18.3 permits the former and *b. Šab.* 128 permits the latter; cf. *t. Šab.* 15.1-3. Mt. 12.11 shows that popular practice was more liberal than that of CD, and these two passages appear to reflect such liberal practice in the first century CE. Cf. Rabin, *Documents*, p. 57 n. 14.1.

49.   The text is partly corrupt. Here I have adopted the corrected translation by Rabin which is also adopted by Dupont-Sommer and Vermes in their translations. For a different reading, however, see Sharvit, 'Sabbath', p. 46; he reads 'let no man bring him up' instead of 'let any man bring him up'. Rabin rejects such a reading on the ground that 'no ancient sect is known to have denied the right of *piqquah nefesh*' (*Documents*, p. 57 n. 17.3). Rabin's correction is further supported by a recently published document, 4Q251 2.6-7; see below, section 2aii. *Contra* Sigal, *Halakah*, p. 150.

50.   This regulation is based on Lev. 23.38, though 'the biblical text is given an entirely forced meaning' (Dupont-Sommer, *Writings*, p. 153 n. 6).

a striking contrast between *Jubilees* and CD; whereas *Jubilees* obsessively puts emphasis on the death penalty, CD 12.3-6 explicitly forbids the death penalty[51] and allows the recovery of community membership after seven years' custody. Perhaps S.T. Kimbrough's suggestion is quite right when he says that 'there was a movement toward leniency already begun in Sabbath Halakah at Qumran'.[52]

From the above investigations one can make the following observations: (i) There are a few regulations which simply repeat the previously existing prohibitions, especially those of *Jubilees*, with minor change or addition (10.22—preparing food; 11.4-6—fasting and striking a beast; 11.15—profaning). (ii) There are some regulations which are not new but more specific and precise compared with that of *Jubilees* (10.18-20; 11.2, 15—speaking and business; 10.21—travel; 10.23–11.2—drinking water; 11.2, 12—slaves and beasts; 11.16-17—saving life; 11.17-18—offerings).[53] (iii) There are some new specific regulations which do not appear in the previous sabbath materials and may therefore reflect the Essenes' particular concern in their circumstances (10.15-16—when the sabbath begins; 10.22-23—fruits in the fields; 11.9—opening vessels; 11.3-4—clothing; 11.14-15—proximity to Gentiles; 11.13-14—helping a beast). (iv) There are some regulations which are clearly stricter than those of the rabbis (10.21—sabbath limit; 11.9-10—carrying; 11.13-14—assisting a beast; 11.17-18—offerings). Here one may add a comment on the sanction against sabbath breaking (12.3-6); in this section we have one concrete instance which is clearly milder than that of *Jubilees*, though it is not about prohibited works.[54]

From the above observations one may draw the following conclusions. The first two observations show that in many cases CD reflects and develops *Jubilees*' sabbath materials. Observations (ii) and (iii) and the long list of regulations in CD as a whole[55] clearly show the

51.   Rabin, *Documents*, p. 60 n. 3.3; Sanders, *Practice*, p. 350. For a different position, however, see Dupont-Sommer, *Writings*, p. 154 n. 6. For a rabbinic view on this issue, see *m. Sanh.* 7.8; *m. Šab.* 7.1.

52.   'The Concept of Sabbath at Qumran', *RevQ* 5 (1962), p. 486.

53.   Of course, some of these regulations also have equivalents in the Old Testament.

54.   Cf. 10.21: defining the sabbath limit here might be seen as more lenient than *Jub.* 50.12 which simply prohibits travelling.

55.   The numbers of the prohibited works in the three books (i.e. *Jubilees*, 14; CD, 25; Mishnah, 39 categories of prohibited acts which in turn summarize a massive corpus of more detailed regulations) may possibly reflect such a movement.

tendency to develop the previously existing more general regulations in an increasingly more specific and precise direction[56] corresponding to current circumstances, but without emphasizing the sanctity,[57] ownership or covenantal significance[58] of the sabbath compared with the previous sabbath materials. Considering the above two conclusions, we can now affirm with confidence that the list of CD betrays a definite step toward the later more meticulous development of the sabbath regulations by the rabbis. Finally, observation (iv) shows that the prohibitions of CD are on the whole much stricter than those of the rabbis.

ii. *4Q251 2.1-3.6.* 4Q251, which is titled 'A Pleasing Fragrance' in the edition of R. Eisenman and M. Wise,[59] is a typical collection of 'legal minutiae' found at Qumran. It includes a number of parallels to both 1QS and CD;[60] especially in 2.1–3.6, to which we will now turn, we have a significant number of precise parallels to the sabbath materials in CD 10.14–11.18.

According to the reconstruction of Eisenman and Wise, 4Q251 2.2-4 substantially repeats the prohibition in CD 11.3-4 of wearing unclean garments (cf. 4Q274 1.1.3; 2.1.2-4). In 2.4-5 we have a prohibition against moving things into or out of one's residence which is also found in CD 11.7-9; here the former is briefer than the latter but specifies 'anything' as 'any vessel or food'. In 2.5-8 we have strikingly similar regulations about lifting out a beast or a man from a pit to those of CD (11.13-17). From this parallel we may conclude more confidently that

56.   Cf. CD 6.18: 'to keep the Sabbath day according to its exact rules'.

57.   In 3.14 we have one passing statement which describes the sabbath as 'holy'; perhaps the co-text of 6.18 might reflect the sanctity of the sabbath. Cf. also 11.3-4, 14-15. CD's clear ban on the death penalty which is repeatedly emphasized in *Jubilees* may suggest that the writer of CD was not so much concerned with the sanctity of the sabbath as that of *Jubilees*.

58.   1Q22 1.8-9 might reflect such an idea, but only in a passing way.

59.   *The Dead Sea Scrolls Uncovered: The First Complete Translation and Interpretation of 50 Key Documents Withheld for Over 35 Years* (Shaftesbury: Element, 1992), pp. 200-205; the texts and translations of the 4Q documents used here and section 2 come from this edition. Cf., however, F.G. Martínez, *The Dead Sea Scrolls Translated: The Qumran Texts in English* (trans. W.G.E. Watson; Leiden: Brill, 1994), p. 87—it presents a quite different text of 4Q251, which does not include any reference to the sabbath.

60.   As Eisenman and Wise, *Uncovered*, pp. 200-201, suggest, this document may be a 'more or less rationalized' presentation of the legal chapters of 1QS and CD.

the Essenes did allow the saving of human life in peril, but not animal life. In 3.5-6 we have other regulations about sabbath limits[61] which are strikingly similar to those found in CD 10.21 and 11.5-6 separately and in reverse order.[62]

4Q251 2.1–3.6 on the whole, thus, simply strengthens the observations and conclusions made above, without adding any particular information about the Essene attitude to the sabbath.

As a final thought, one may raise the question why 1QS does not have a word about the sabbath. One may argue that the Qumran sect did not care for the sabbath, therefore they did not spare a single line for it. But such an argument cannot stand when we consider the fanatical character of 1QS in general. The group behind 1QS was the Qumran sect proper which was much stricter in keeping the law than the town-dwelling Essene groups represented by CD. E.P. Sanders here presents a convincing suggestion that 1QS deals with 'extremely fine points and their punishments' and it simply presupposes the entirety of the biblical law and takes for granted a whole Qumran library of laws,[63] probably including CD.

b. *The 364 Day Calendar*

In the remaining Qumran Scrolls so far published, we have a few sabbath materials some of which are in some way related to the 364 day calendar. In 'The First Letter on Works Reckoned as Righteousness' (4Q394-398) part 1 we have a complete calendrical list of sabbaths of one full year. The list represents the 364 day calendar which is guarded against the lunar calendar in *Jub.* 6.32-38.[64] This 364 day calendar is further attested in 11QTemple 13–29 when the cycle of festivals and their offerings are regulated.[65] 4Q325 records the priestly courses for

---

61.   2000 cubits when one takes his cattle; and [when one simply walks] 30 stadia which is approximately equivalent to 1200 cubits, but note '[from the Te]mple' (מן ה[מק]דש). The second half of 3.5 is badly damaged, and I have simply followed the reconstruction of Eisenman and Wise.

62.   2.8–3.4 are so badly damaged that it may not be possible to recover the meaning of those lines properly; therefore, I do not discuss them here, though there might have been some interesting regulations about, for example, battle, priests, fasting, etc.

63.   Sanders, *Law*, pp. 15-16.

64.   This may once again show that *Jubilees* played a significant role among the Essenes at least in relation to sabbath observance; cf. Sanders, *Practice*, pp. 360-61.

65.   Cf. Maier, *Temple*, pp. 70-87; on pp. 71-76 he provides a complete

each sabbath and festival which are also based on the 364 day calendar (cf. 4Q323-324A-B; 1QM 2.1-4). All these documents may show that for the Essenes the sabbath was a matter of crucial importance as the key to their calendar.[66]

3. *Josephus*

Josephus's four extant works[67] provide sabbath references in abundance, and many of them are related to the issue of war on the sabbath, to which we will turn first.

a. *War on the Sabbath*
Considering the fact that one of the main themes of his two major works (*The Jewish War* and *The Jewish Antiquities*) is the Jewish strife against the foreign powers, it is not surprising that the majority of the sabbath references in those works deal with the Jewish principle of no war on the sabbath and its consequences.

According to *Ant.* 12.274-75, in *c.* 167 BCE, Antiochus Epiphanes' soldiers attacked Jews on the sabbath and burned them in their caves without resistance, as they were unwilling to violate the dignity of the sabbath even in the face of death. On that day about a thousand with their wives and children died (cf. 1 Macc. 2.32-38). Josephus seems to have this event in mind when he talks about the Jewish heroism demonstrated in their willing obedience to the law even in the face of death in

reconstruction of the Essene cycle of festivals in the 364 day calendar.

66.   The remaining materials are brief and passing references and do not provide any significant information about Essene thoughts on the sabbath, and therefore I will not discuss them here. Perhaps two more references may be mentioned. According to Maier's reconstruction of 11QTemple 17.15-16, the Essenes considered the sabbath as '[a holy convocation for YH]WH' (*Temple*, p. 25); cf. Vermes, *Scrolls (English)*, p. 133—'[(there shall be) an assembly] for [YHWH]'. 1Q22 1.8-9 may show that the Essenes thought Israel's violation of 'the Sabbath of the Covenant' to be one of the crucial grounds for God's punishment upon them.

67.   For recent discussions of Josephus's life and his works, see H.W. Attridge, 'Josephus and his Works', in Stone (ed.), *Second Temple*, pp. 185-232; and P. Bilde, *Flavius Josephus between Jerusalem and Rome* (JSPSup, 2; Sheffield: JSOT Press, 1988) among others. The dates of the works of Josephus (36/37–*c.* 100 CE) according to the above two scholars are as follows: *War*, 75–79; *Antiquities* and *Life*, 93/94; *Apion*, after 93/94. The texts and translations come from H.St.J. Thackeray *et al.*, *Josephus* (10 vols.; LCL; London: Heinemann, 1926–65).

Apion 2.235. *Ant.* 12.4 may show an older case of Jewish non-resistance on the sabbath when Ptolemy Soter, in *c.* 320 BCE, seized Jerusalem on the sabbath, in a deceitful way.[68]

After the former event, Mattathias and his followers resolved to fight even on the sabbath εἴ ποτε δεήσειε (*Ant.* 12.276-77; cf. 1 Macc. 2.40-41). This resolution came into effect when Bacchides in *c.* 160 BCE attacked Jonathan on the sabbath. Jonathan, after exhorting his companions, joined battle with the enemy and killed about two thousand[69] of Bacchides' army (*Ant.* 13.12-14; cf. 1 Macc. 9.43-49). In *Ant.* 18.319-24 we have another report of a battle fought in self-defence on the sabbath by the Jews under Asinaeus against a Parthian army early in the first century CE. This resolution, however, seems to have been applied only to direct attack from an enemy. According to *Ant.* 14.63-64, Pompey in *c.* 63 BCE took advantage of this rule in capturing Jerusalem by raising earthworks and towers for the use of his catapults without engaging in hand to hand combat on the sabbath.[70]

The resolution above, however, does not seem always to be adopted. According to *War* 7.361-62, the Jews of Caesarea did not resist at all when the Caesarean rabble, in 66 CE, rushed upon and massacred them on the sabbath (*War* 2.457). In *Life* 161, we have a clear statement by Josephus in relation to his own experience that 'it would have been impossible for them to bear arms on the morrow [i.e. the sabbath], such

---

68.   This suggestion is supported by Agatharchides' description of the event as quoted in *Ant.* 12.6: ταύτην [= Ἱεροσόλυμα] περιεῖδον ὑπὸ Πτολεμαίῳ γενομένην, ὅπλα λαβεῖν οὐ θελήσαντες; cf. *Apion* 1.209. Perhaps *Ant.* 13.337 might imply another but much later case of Jewish non-resistance on the sabbath.

69.   Cf. 'one thousand' in 1 Macc. 9.49.

70.   In *Ant.* 14.63 Josephus comments thus: ἄρχοντας μὲν γὰρ μάχης καὶ τύπτοντας ἀμύνασθαι δίδωσιν ὁ νόμος, ἄλλο δέ τι δρῶντας τοὺς πολεμίους οὐκ ἐᾷ. Cf. *Ant.* 12.277. This rule, however, may not have been followed by every Jew. According to *War* 2.449-56, in 66 CE, Eleazar's party attacked Romans in Jerusalem and massacred them on the sabbath. A slightly different case is found in *Ant.* 18.354, according to which Anilaeus, in the mid-first century CE, fell upon Mithridates' army on the sabbath as they slept. In the latter case, there was a direct threat of attack next morning, whereas in the former there was no direct threat at all. These two cases seem to be far from a general tendency of the contemporary Jews (note Josephus's strongly negative comment in *War* 2.456: καὶ γὰρ δὴ σαββάτῳ συνέβη πραχθῆναι τὸν φόνον). Apart from these two exceptions, other references betray a stricter tendency towards keeping the rule of no offensive attacks on the sabbath.

action being forbidden by our laws,[71] *however urgent the apparent necessity*.[72]

The rule of no offensive attack (or no war at all) on the sabbath was kept even by Jews serving in a foreign army. In *Ant.* 13.251-52 Josephus quotes Nicolas's testimony which shows that Antiochus, after defeating Indates in *c.* 130 BCE, remained at the Lycus river two days at the request of Hyrcanus because of the festival of Pentecost followed by the sabbath on which Jews were not permitted to march (cf. 2 Macc. 15.1-5). Probably as a result of this strict adherence of Jewish soldiers to the law of the sabbath, 'the Romans felt obliged to exempt Jews from military duties'; otherwise the Jewish sabbath and Roman discipline were to be opposed irreconcilably.[73] Interestingly enough, we find that among the various petitions, letters and decrees from the 50s BCE which Josephus quotes in *Ant.* 14.223-40, there are seven which mention or declare the exemption of the Jews who are Roman citizens from military service.[74] The ground for the exemption is clearly mentioned in 14.226 that διὰ τὸ μήτε ὅπλα βαστάζειν δύνασθαι μήτε ὁδοιπορεῖν αὐτοὺς ἐν ταῖς ἡμέραις τῶν σαββάτων.

b. *Gentile Attitudes to the Sabbath*
Another central issue reflected in Josephus's sabbath material is that of Gentile attitudes to the sabbath. First of all, Josephus shows how widely the sabbath was spread and observed throughout the Gentile world. In *Apion* 2.282 Josephus says that 'there is not one city, Greek or barbarian, nor a single nation, to which our custom of abstaining from work on the seventh day has not spread...'[75] In his earlier work (*War* 4.97-105)

71.   τῶν νόμων, here, may refer to the oral law; cf. *Ant.* 12.274; 1 Macc. 2.34, 37.

72.   Italics mine; in Greek, κἂν μεγάλη τις ἐπείγειν ἀνάγκη δοκῇ. Cf. *War* 2.634.

73.   Schürer, *History*, II, pp. 474-75, esp. n. 62; see also *idem, History*, III, pp. 120-21. Cf. *Ant.* 14.225-27.

74.   They are as follows: a request of Hyrcanus's envoy to Dolabella (14.223-24); Dolabella's letter to Ephesus (14.225-27); Lucius Lentulus's decree to Ephesus (14.228-29); Titus Ampius Balbus's letter to Ephesus (14.230); decree of the people of Delos (14.231-32); a petition of Publius and Marcus to Lentulus (14.236-37); Lentulus's decree to Ephesus (14.237-40). Cf. also Caesar's edict in 14.202-10.

75.   Cf. *Apion* 2.123. Cf. Schürer, *History*, III, pp. 161-62, esp. n. 50. Cf. also *Ant.* 12.257-259, which shows Samaritan observance of the sabbath; cf. *m. Ned.* 3.10.

he implies that Titus showed his respect to the sabbath when he attacked Gischala in 67 CE (cf. *War* 7.96-99).

In *Ant.* 14.241-64; 16.162-68 Josephus quotes letters and decrees to show how the Jews obtained their right to observe the sabbath from the Romans.[76] One of the specific rights allowed to the Jews is that they need not appear in court on the sabbath (*Ant.* 16.163; cf. 16.27). The Gentiles, however, do not seem to have been always in favour of the Jewish sabbath. In spite of the Roman laws which allowed the Jews to keep the sabbath, according to *Ant.* 16.27-30, the people of Ionia mistreated the Jews by forcing them to appear in court on the sabbath and to participate in military service. Other decrees and letters above also imply such mistreatment in other places (cf. 14.244-46, 256-58, 262-64). Such a hostile attitude to the sabbath is further demonstrated by Josephus's quotation of Apion's view of the etymology of σάββατον. In *Apion* 2.21, Apion says that the word σάββατον was derived from the Egyptian word *sabbo* which means a disease causing tumours in the groin. Against such an idea, in 2.22-27, Josephus ridicules its nonsense and points out the wide difference between *sabbo* and σάββατον which in the Jewish language denotes ἀνάπαυσις...ἀπὸ παντὸς ἔργου.[77] Thus, according to Josephus, there was a tension between the favourable and the hostile attitudes to the Jewish sabbath in the Roman world.

c. *Jewish Practices on the Sabbath*

Josephus provides some passing accounts of the various practices of the Jews on the sabbath. According to *War* 4.582, it was the custom that a priest stood and gave notice of the hours of the beginning and closing of the sabbath with trumpet sounds from the temple roof.[78] According to *War* 5.230, every sabbath sacrifice was ministered by the high priest.[79]

---

76.   They are as follows: letter of magistrates of Laodicea to Gaius Rabirius (14.241-43); letter of Publius Servilius Galba to Miletus (14.244-46); decree of Halicarnassus (14.256-58); decree of Ephesus (14.262-64); Augustus's decree (16.162-65); Agrippa's letter to the Ephesians (16.167-68).

77.   Cf. *Ant.* 12.5-6: Josephus here mentions the reproach of Agatharchides of Cnidus who regarded the Jewish sabbath as a 'superstition' (δεισιδαιμονία); for a longer version of the quotation, see *Apion* 1.209.

78.   Cf. CD 10.15-16; cf. also *m. Suk.* 5.5. For a different use of the trumpet on the sabbath, however, see 4Q493 M^c.

79.   According to Josephus, the high priest also sacrificed on the other festive occasions, whereas, by law, he was obliged to do so only on the day of atonement (cf. Lev. 16). Cf. Schürer, *History*, II, p. 276, esp. n. 4.

In *Ant.* 3.237, and *Ant.* 3.143, 255-56, the sabbath sacrifice and the shewbread, which were to be provided at the public expense, are prescribed respectively. According to *Life* 277, it seems to have been customary to have a meeting in the prayer-house (ἡ προσευχή).[80] From *Apion* 2.175, it can be assumed that the Jews regularly listened to and learnt the law every sabbath when they assembled probably at the synagogues. In *Life* 279, Josephus clearly states that it was the Jewish custom on the sabbath to take the midday meal at the sixth hour. In *War* 2.147, as I mentioned above, Josephus provides an interesting report of the Essenes who kept the sabbath in an extremely strict way.[81]

Josephus also presents a couple of interesting comments on the theological ground of sabbath keeping. In *Ant.* 1.33 Josephus makes two points clear in his retelling of Gen. 2.1-3: (i) He assumes that God's rest on the seventh day in creation provides the etiology of the sabbath; here, however, he simply equates the seventh day with the sabbath, which, as we saw in Chapter 1, does not seem to be a correct understanding of the seventh day in the Genesis narrative. (ii) He defines the meaning of σάββατον in the Hebrew language as 'rest'; he seems here to be definite in deriving the noun שַׁבָּת from the verb שׁבת, which, in the recent discussion of the etymology, is not conclusive, though most probable. In *Ant.* 3.91 and *Apion* 2.174 he affirms that the sabbath law with other laws was prescribed by Moses.

d. *Conclusions*
First, Josephus's sabbath materials[82] reveal various attitudes to the no-war principle on the sabbath among the Jews: for example (i) the pre-167 BCE no war extremists (*Ant.* 12.4, 274-75); (ii) the post-167 BCE compromising conservatives (*Ant.* 12.276-77; 13.12-14; 18.319-24); (iii) the post-167 BCE non-compromising extremists (*War* 7.361-62); (iv) the post-167 BCE liberals (*War* 2.449-56; *Ant.* 18.354).

Secondly, Josephus's sabbath materials suggest some points about the sabbath in the Gentile world: (i) The sabbath was widely spread and

---

80.   Probably another name for synagogue; see Thackeray, *et al.*, *Josephus*, I, p. 103 n. b.

81.   'They...are stricter than all Jews in abstaining from work on the seventh day; for not only do they prepare their food on the day before, to avoid kindling a fire on that one, but they do not venture to remove any vessel or even to go to stool'.

82.   As regards the historical reliability of Josephus's materials, see an extended discussion in Bilde, *Josephus*, pp. 191-200—in opposition to the classical negative conception, he argues for the historical reliability of Josephus.

known as a Jewish custom throughout the Gentile world (*Apion* 2.282; cf. the decrees and letters in *Ant.* 14.223-64 and 16.162-68 which exempt the Jews from military service or allow them to keep the sabbath). (ii) There were Gentiles who were in favour of and even observed the sabbath (the decrees and letters above; *Apion* 2.282). (iii) There were Gentiles who were hostile to the sabbath (*Apion* 2.21-27; *Ant.* 16.27-30). (iv) Thus, there was a tension between the favourable and the hostile attitudes to the sabbath among the Gentiles.

Thirdly, though he provides some significant information of Jewish understanding of and practices on the sabbath of his time (e.g. trumpet blasts, sabbath sacrifice, sabbath meeting, learning the law, midday meal, etiology and etymology of the sabbath, etc.), Josephus interestingly provides nearly no information about the current specific regulations as regards prohibited works on the sabbath (of course, apart from those of the Essenes), probably because of the nature and purpose of his writings rather than because of his lack of interest in them.

4. Philo

Philo of Alexandria (*c.* 20 BCE–45 CE) shows a great interest in the sabbath throughout his works.[83] Particularly noteworthy are his allegorical interpretations, especially in relation to the number seven.

a. The Significance of the Sabbath

Philo's general concern for making Jewish law and tradition acceptable to the Greeks and probably also for transmitting Greek philosophy to the Jews made allegorical interpretation an inevitable method for him to adopt,[84] and there was no exception in the case of the sabbath.

---

83. More than half of his extant works (approximately 42 books) include discussion of the issue, many at significant length. For general discussions of Philo's life, works and thought, see H.A. Wolfson, *Philo: Foundations of Religious Philosophy in Judaism, Christianity, and Islam* (2 vols.; Cambridge, MA: Harvard University Press, 1947); Borgen, 'Philo', pp. 233-82; Schürer, *History*, III.2, pp. 813-89; R. Williamson, *Jews in the Hellenistic World: Philo* (CCWJCW, 1/2; Cambridge: Cambridge University Press, 1989) among others. The texts and translations come from F.H. Colson *et al.*, *Philo* (10 vols.; LCL; London: Heinemann, 1929–62).

84. For this two-fold concern and its relation to allegorical interpretation, see Schürer, *History*, III.2, pp. 876-78; cf. Borgen, 'Philo', p. 233. For a fuller discussion of Philo's allegorical exegesis, see Williamson, *Philo*, pp. 144-200.

In *Op. Mund.* 89-128, Philo tries to demonstrate the characteristics of the sabbath by expounding the properties (φύσις) of the number seven. The ground for relating the sabbath to the number seven is provided by the creation account in Gen. 2.1-3.[85] He first of all states the dignity and holiness of the seventh day[86] pronounced by 'the Father' himself, then proceeds to announce its universal character by calling it 'the festival of the universe', 'public' (πάνδημος) and 'the birthday of the world' (τοῦ κόσμου γενέθλιον; cf. *Vit. Mos.* 1.207; *Spec. Leg.* 1.170; 2.59). In order to demonstrate the universal character further, he introduces some popular understandings of the number seven in his day,[87] and shows that the significance of the number seven is generally recognized by the various investigators[88] throughout the world (i.e. by Greeks and other peoples) from numerous phenomena in the universe.[89] From these observations Philo brings out some characteristic properties of the number—for example, harmony (*Op. Mund.* 96, 107ff.; cf. *Deus Imm.* 11; *Vit. Mos.* 2.210), motherless origin/ever virgin/chief/sovereign (100; cf. *Leg. All.* 1.15; *Spec. Leg.* 2.56; etc.), motionlessness (100), perfection/completeness (102, 106; cf. *Vit. Mos.* 1.207; *Spec. Leg.* 2.58), heavenliness (127)—and applies them to the seventh day. His conclusion is that Moses, the lover of virtue, also recognized the high honour of '*the number seven*' and 'inscribed its [*the seventh day*] beauty on the most holy tables of the Law, and impressed it on the minds of all who were set under him' (*Op. Mund.* 128).

In some other places, he further expounds the characteristics of the sabbath thus: 'Peace' (εἰρήνη) and 'seven' are identical according to the 'Legislator' (νομοθέτης), 'for on the seventh day creation puts away its seeming activity and takes rest' (*Fug.* 173). Since to God alone the true

85.   Philo does not, in fact, use the term τὸ σάββατον here, but he simply equates the seventh day with the sabbath in other places; most expressively, see *Abr.* 28; *Spec. Leg.* 2.41, 86, 194; see also *Cher.* 87-91; *Mut. Nom.* 260; etc.

86.   The sacred dignity and holiness of the sabbath is repeatedly emphasized by Philo in many places, e.g. *Op. Mund.* 128; *Vit. Mos.* 2.209, 218ff., 263ff.; *Dec.* 51, 96ff.; *Spec. Leg.* 2.86, 214, 224, 249.

87.   In his speculations on the number seven he is heavily influenced by the Pythagoreans. Cf. Borgen, 'Philo', p. 256; Schürer, *History*, III.2, p. 872.

88.   For example, mathematicians, physicians, philosophers, scientists, astronomers, linguists, musicians.

89.   For example, the circuits of the moon, the stages of men's growth, seven zones of heaven, the Great Bear, the sun, human body, sounds, movements, dancing, the formation of the embryo, women's pregnancy, sciences, grammar, music.

peace and rest is given, he alone in the true sense keeps the sabbath and, therefore, Moses often calls the sabbath 'God's sabbath' (*Cher.* 86-90). God's rest, however, does not mean mere inactivity, because God, by nature, never ceases to work—his rest is rather 'a working with absolute ease, without toil and without suffering' (*Cher.* 87). When God ceases moulding the mortal things, he does not actually cease making, but begins the creating of other divine things (*Leg. All.* 1.16-18).[90] Those who live virtuous lives and only those can participate in God's rest, the rest which does not mean the idleness of inactivity but rather the active exercise of the higher activities such as studying philosophy[91] (*Spec. Leg.* 2.46-51, 60-62). While the body is working for practical benefits for six days, the soul enjoys a respite, but when the body takes its rest on the seventh day, the soul resumes its work for theoretical/contemplative benefits such as knowledge and perfection of the mind (*Spec. Leg.* 2.64; cf. *Leg. All.* 1.18; *Dec.* 98-101).[92] The sabbath has double aims, that is, what is seen (or the literal/outer sense of the laws) and what is not seen (or the allegorical/inner aim of the laws) of which the latter is more valuable, though the former is not to be neglected (*Migr. Abr.* 89-93).

b. *Gentile Attitudes to the Sabbath*

As I have mentioned above, one of Philo's main concerns is making Jewish law and tradition acceptable to the Greeks. We may glimpse a reason for such concern from his accounts of Gentile attitudes to the sabbath. According to *Somn.* 2.123-32, one of the ruling class attempted to do away with the law of the sabbath in Egypt, thinking that its removal would lead the Jews to a general backsliding,[93] but his attempt turned out a failure because of the devout attitude to the sabbath among the Jews. He then argued against them that their devotion to the sabbath

90.   Cf. Aristobulus, F. 5.11; Jn. 5.17.

91.   Philo's understanding of philosophy strongly reflects the Stoic view which defines philosophy as 'the practice (ἐπιτήδευσιν) of wisdom' (Sextus, *Adversus Physicos* 1.13). Cf. Wolfson, *Philo*, II, pp. 211-12; Borgen, 'Philo', p. 256; Williamson, *Philo*, pp. 203-207, 228.

92.   This is a clear example of Platonic body–soul dualism in Philo's thought. Cf. Borgen, 'Philo', p. 256. For the dualistic approach to the practical-contemplative life in Philo, see Wolfson, *Philo*, II, pp. 262-66.

93.   This may betray the key role of the sabbath law in the Jewish religion which might have been correctly detected by the ruler.

in practice could not be consistent in certain calamity situations[94] and asserted that he himself can bring such calamities upon them. Against such an argument Philo counter-argues that his claim cannot be true but rather shows his evil character and, therefore, his argument loses its ground.

In *Vit. Mos.* 2.211-12, *Spec. Leg.* 2.60-70 and *Hyp.* 7.11-16 Philo indicates that some Gentiles blamed the Jews for being idle or wasting time by their sabbath keeping, and responds to the blame by showing the real aims of and practices on the sabbath. He first of all points out that the Jews do not waste time on that day but rather diligently study their holy law, the true philosophy.[95] He also points out the practical benefits of sabbath keeping which refreshes and strengthens the body for the coming six days. He develops this idea further and opens his humanitarian interpretation of the sabbath rest.[96] Its object is to give relief from the yoke of unending toil not only to freemen but also to slaves and even to the cattle. Perhaps Philo's allegorical interpretations of the sabbath law as a whole may be a response to such Gentile criticism.

Philo, however, does not fail to point out in *Hyp.* 7.20 that the significance and benefits of the seventh day for the whole of humankind as well as the Jews are already recognized by many physicians, scientists and philosophers. In *Leg. All.* 155-58 he mentions the recognition of the sabbath by Augustus, the Roman emperor. After pointing out the general tendency in the Roman empire that the Jews 'were not forced to violate any of their native institutions' (155), he provides an outstanding case as regards the sabbath that 'even if the distributions happened to come during the sabbath...he [the emperor] ordered the dispensers to reserve for the Jews till the morrow the charity which fell to all' (158).

c. *Jewish Practices on the Sabbath and Philo's View on the Literal Observance*
Considering the allegorical character of Philo's work in general, we may need to be cautious in using his materials as historical sources for the

---

94.   For example, a sudden attack by the enemy, immediate dangers caused by a river rising, a broken dam, a thunderbolt, famine, plague or earthquake or 'any other trouble either of human or divine agency'.

95.   For some references, among many others, see above, section 4a.

96.   See Pettirsch, 'Verbot', p. 310.

Jewish sabbath practices of his time.[97] According to *Somn.* 2.123-24, the Jews regarded the sabbath 'with most reverence and awe', and in Alexandria they were devout enough to keep it in spite of the ruler's orders not to observe it.[98] In *Migr. Abr.* 89-93, however, Philo indicates that there were some who neglected the literal sense of the sabbath because of their over-emphasis on its symbolic meaning. Against such a tendency Philo strongly asserts that they should not abrogate 'the laws laid down for its observance' for the sake of their symbolic meaning; rather they must look on the outward observances of the laws for the body, as they do on their inner meaning for the soul (cf. *Spec. Leg.* 2.260). As concrete examples, Philo mentions lighting fire, tilling the ground, carrying loads, instituting proceedings in court, acting as jurors, demanding the restoration of deposits, recovering loans. In the case of lighting fire, Philo provides ample discussions in other places (*Vit. Mos.* 2.213-20; *Spec. Leg.* 2.65, 249-51), especially in relation to the incident in Num. 15.32-36, and gives support to the death penalty against the sabbath breaker. In *Vit. Mos.* 2.21-22, Philo restates the sabbath law in an extremely casuistic way whereby the sabbath rest extends not only to himself and his neighbours, freemen and slaves and also his beasts, but to all creatures, even to every kind of tree and plant; he further states that 'it is not permitted to cut any shoot or branch, or even a leaf, or to pluck any fruit whatsoever' (cf. *Spec. Leg.* 2.66-70; cf. also CD 10.22-23; *m. Pes.* 4.8; Mt. 12.1-2 par.). All these may indicate, as Borgen insists, the influence of rabbinic Judaism on Philo.[99]

According to *Spec. Leg.* 2.61-64, *Hyp.* 12-13 and so on, the Jews assembled in the synagogues on the sabbath and spent most of the day in studying the holy laws. In *Omn. Prob. Lib.* 81-82 and *Vit. Cont.* 30-37, Philo describes the ways of keeping the sabbath by the Essenes and Therapeutae respectively; according to him, both groups assembled in their synagogues on the sabbath to study the laws, and the Therapeutae quitted their usual fast and participated in the communal

---

97.   For a negative view of Philo's material as historical sources, see Pettirsch, 'Verbot', pp. 307-308: 'So kommt Philo weniger als geschichtliche Quelle für die Sabbatpraxis seiner Zeit in Betracht' (p. 307). For an affirmative view, see Borgen, 'Philo', pp. 257-59. Even though I give some historical value to Philo's materials, we need to keep in mind that his context is Alexandrian and his witness to Palestinian Judaism may be indirect.

98.   Here Philo describes the sabbath τὸ καθεστὼς ἔθος; cf. *Dec.* 96.

99.   Borgen, 'Philo', pp. 257-59; cf. Wolfson, *Philo*, I, pp. 90-93.

meal. In *Spec. Leg.* 1.168-76, Philo restates the Mosaic regulations of the sabbath sacrifices and shewbread; it is possible that this restatement reflects current practices in the Jerusalem temple.

d. *Conclusions*

As I have suggested above, Philo's allegorical interpretations of the sabbath laws may be the inevitable fruit of his two-fold concern for making Jewish law and tradition acceptable to the Greeks and for transmitting Greek philosophy to the Jews. Considering such concerns, on the one hand his adoption of Platonic, Stoic and Pythagorean ideas in his allegorical interpretations is not surprising, and on the other neither is it surprising that he pays heed to the literal observance of the sabbath regulations and adopts some rabbinic casuistic traditions.[100] All this indicates that he does take his context seriously and tries to contextualize the texts in question in a relevant way.

In his allegorical interpretations he tries to emphasize the holiness and ownership of the sabbath, which, as we have seen in Chapter 1, the Old Testament itself stresses very much; but the covenant relationship which is the basis of these two concepts in the Old Testament is not clearly detected in Philo. His concern is rather to demonstrate the universal relevance of the sabbath for the whole world, and in doing that he attaches to it such characteristics as peace, harmony, motherless origin, motionlessness, perfection and so on, and calls it 'the festival of the universe' or 'the birthday of the world'. In order to adapt the Jewish concept of God's working in time and space to the Greek idea of the timeless activity of God, he develops the idea of God who works ceaselessly but without toil or suffering. Though his exegetical methods are often questionable for modern readers, this is nonetheless a serious attempt to approach the issues in a meaningful way.

As I have pointed out above, the historical value of Philo's materials is limited. From his materials we gain some insight into Gentile attitudes to the sabbath and Jewish practices on it. According to him, as we have seen in Josephus, the sabbath was widely spread and recognized as a Jewish custom throughout the Gentile world, and such popularity sometimes caused hostile attitudes to it and ridicule of it. Perhaps such attitudes and ridicule may have provided him with a motive for his

---

100. Here, it may be noteworthy that he reflects the existence of a halakhah which specifically prohibits cutting or plucking any shoot or fruit from a plant (cf. *Spec. Leg.* 2.66-70). See below, Chapter 4, section 3b.

allegorization. Philo's witness to the Jewish practices on the sabbath adds little to what we have already found apart from a general characterization that they regarded the sabbath 'with most reverence and awe', and an implication that there were some who showed an antinomian tendency against which Philo strongly reacts.

5. References to Judaism in Graeco-Roman Literature

Some interesting references regarding the Jewish sabbath[101] are found in the writings of a number of Graeco-Roman Gentile authors of this period.

a. The Sabbath as the Day of Rest

Most references to the Jewish sabbath pay attention to its character as a day of rest. In his *Remedia Amoris* 217-20 Ovid (43 BCE–17/18 CE) remarks the possibility that the departure of a non-Jew can be delayed by 'foreign sabbath' which he mentions in another place as being held 'sacred' by the Syrian Jews (cf. *Ars Amatoria* 1.75-76). In *Ars Amatoria* 1.413-16 he depicts the seventh day feast, which the Palestinian Syrian observes, as 'less fit for business'. These passages plainly show that Ovid recognizes the Jewish sabbath as a rest day which can affect even the life of a non-Jew.[102]

Sometimes the sabbath as the day of rest is called the day of Saturn.[103] In his *Strategemata* 2.1.17 Frontinus (*c.* 30–104 CE) says, 'the day of Saturn, a day on which it is sinful for them [i.e. the Jews] to do any business'. When Tibullus (second half of the first century BCE), *Carmina* 1.3.15-18, says that 'the accursed day of Saturn'[104] held him back (and

---

101. The references which will be discussed in this section are selected from two useful collections—M. Stern, *Greek and Latin Authors on Jews and Judaism* (3 vols.; Jerusalem: Israel Academy of Sciences and Humanities, 1976–84); M. Whittaker, *Jews and Christians: Graeco-Roman Views* (CCWJCW, 6; Cambridge: Cambridge University Press, 1984). The texts and translations come from the former but with frequent references to the translations of the latter whenever it is necessary.

102. Cf. Tacitus, *Historiae* 5.4.3—here he asserts that the Jews 'first chose to rest on the seventh day because that day ended their toils'; cf. also Strabo, *Geographica* 16.2.40: 'when the Judaeans were abstaining from all work'. Cf. also Horace, *Sermones* 1.9.69-74.

103. For brief comments on and relevant references regarding the relationship between the sabbath and the day of Saturn, see Stern, *Jews and Judaism*, I, p. 319.

104. Or 'the day sacred to Saturn' (Whittaker)—'Saturni sacram...diem'.

delayed his departure), it seems clear that he has a similar understanding of the sabbath to that of Ovid above.[105]

The seeming inactivity on the sabbath is frequently ridiculed or criticized by many authors. Seneca (4 BCE/1 CE–65 CE), for example, asserts that the sabbath is unprofitable, 'because by introducing one day of rest in every seven they lose in idleness almost a seventh of their life...' (*De Superstitione*). Tacitus (56 CE–112/113 CE) also criticizes the sabbath rest as 'the pleasures of idleness'[106] in his *Historiae* 5.4.3. Such inactivity is further ridiculed in relation to the prohibition of war on the sabbath. For Plutarch the lack of self-defence against the attacking enemy is no more than an expression of 'superstition' (ἡ δεισιδαιμονία).[107] According to Josephus, *Apion* 1.210, Agatharchides (second century BCE) deems such lack of self-defence simply 'their folly'.[108]

The rest on the sabbath, however, is not always criticized. Juvenal (c. 60–130 CE), *Saturae* 14.96-106, implies that the sabbath was revered by some non-Jews and kept apart from all their concerns of life.[109]

b. *Misunderstandings of the Sabbath*
Knowledge of the sabbath on the part of Graeco-Roman authors is often garbled by various misunderstandings (and sometimes by prejudice). According to a quotation from Apion's *Aegyptiaca* by Josephus, *Apion* 1.21, Apion (first half of the first century CE) attributes the origin of the sabbath to the Jews' experience of having tumours in the groin in the wilderness; while Pompeius Trogus, *Historiae Philippicae* 36,[110] defines the sabbath as a fast day which was intended to commemorate their experience of fasting and wandering in the wilderness for seven days. Such a mistaken association of the sabbath with fasting is strikingly common among Graeco-Roman authors—for example Petronius (first

---

105.   Further references calling the sabbath the day of Saturn are also found in Tacitus, *Historiae* 5.4.3; Cassius Dio, *Historia Romana* 37.16.2-4; 37.17.3; *Epitome* 65.7.2; etc. Cassius's references are late (150–235 CE) but deal with events of our period.

106.   Whittaker's translation.

107.   *De Superstitione* 8. Cf. Persius, *Saturae* 5.176-84—he presents the sabbath as his first example that superstition enslaves man.

108.   Cf. Frontinus, *Strategemata* 2.1.17.

109.   Juvenal himself, however, criticizes the sabbath rest by depicting it as 'idleness'.

110.   Quoted by Justinus, *Epitoma* 2.14.

century CE), *Fragmenta* 37; Martial, *Epigrammata* 4.4; Suetonius (*c.* 69 CE–?), *Divus Augustus* 76.2; cf. Strabo, *Geographica* 16.2.40; Tacitus, *Historiae* 5.4.3. Sometimes the sabbath is also wrongly associated with some other days. In Horace (65–8 BCE), *Sermones* 1.9.69 we have a problematic phrase[111] which may suggest an identification of the thirtieth day with the sabbath. In Persius (34–62 CE), *Saturae* 5.179-84 an enigmatic phrase, 'the day of Herod', is associated with the sabbath. In his *Questiones Convivales* 4.6.2, Plutarch (born before 50 CE, died after 120) asserts that the sabbath is related to Dionysus and is an occasion for drunkenness.[112] We also have some miscellaneous misunderstandings like Pliny's (23/24–79 CE) report of 'a stream that dries up every Sabbath' in Judaea (*Naturalis Historia* 31.24) and Juvenal's comment that in Judaea 'kings celebrate festal sabbaths with bare feet' (*Saturae* 6.159).[113]

c. *The Sabbath Lamps*
Two passages refer to the Jewish custom of lighting of the sabbath lamps. Persius, *Saturae* 5.179-80, mentions that on the sabbath the violet-wreathed lamps are set in the greasy window. According to Josephus, *Apion* 2.282, this custom was widely taken over from the Jews by other peoples. Such a widespread impact may be testified by Seneca's attack on (or ridicule of) this custom in his *Epistulae Morales* 95.47.[114] A related but rather different aspect of the sabbath is implied in Meleager (end of the second century–beginning of the first century BCE), *Anthologia Graeca* 5.160, when he mentions 'cold Sabbaths', probably because Jews were forbidden to light fires on the sabbath.[115]

d. *Conclusions*
The discussions of the sabbath references above from various Graeco-Roman authors seem to show clearly that the Jewish sabbath was spread

---

111. 'hodie tricensima sabbata'; for a brief comment on it, see Stern, *Jews and Judaism*, I, p. 326; see also Whittaker, *Jews and Christians*, p. 65.

112. Whittaker, *Jews and Christians*, p. 73, says, 'The association of drunkenness with the sabbath is pure fantasy'. For a more detailed discussion of the issue, see Stern, *Jews and Judaism*, I, pp. 560-62.

113. Perhaps Juvenal here confuses the practice of the Day of Atonement with that of the sabbath; see Stern, *Jews and Judaism*, II, p. 100.

114. He forbids lamps to be lit on the sabbath, 'since the gods do not need light'.

115. Stern, *Jews and Judaism*, I, p. 140; Whittaker, *Jews and Christians*, p. 71.

widely and well recognized as one of the most characteristic features of Jewish custom. Most references which we have seen mark its character as a day of rest. Not a few references witness that the Jewish sabbath rest could affect even the life of a non-Jew. It becomes also quite clear that the sabbath rest, when it was especially coupled with the no-war principle, caused much ridicule and criticism, though some non-Jews were attracted by it. We have seen that knowledge of the sabbath on the part of Graeco-Roman authors is often garbled by various misunderstandings, probably because of the lack of direct encounter with the custom or materials about it, but also because of their prejudice in some cases (e.g. Apion's argument about its origin). Nevertheless these misunderstandings may still witness its widespread impact on the Gentile world. Such an impact seems to be further witnessed by the references to the sabbath lamps.

6. *Rabbinic Literature*

Rabbinic literature as the source of knowledge about the sabbath in our period poses some complicated problems, especially if we are going to relate it to the first-century Pharisees. The limited scope of this section will not allow a full discussion; nevertheless, it is necessary to state our position clearly on the problems which will be presupposed in the following discussions.

1) Considering the dates of composition, I will mainly focus on the Tannaitic literature[116] (the Mishnah in particular), but without completely ignoring the Talmuds.

2) I will assume that the Mishnah (and also the Tosefta) is not, as

---

116.   That is, the Mishnah, the Tosefta, and the halakhic Midrashim (Mekilta, Sifra, and Sifre). Unless otherwise mentioned, quotations of the above literature (except Sifra and Sifre, the quotations of which come from J. Neusner, *The Rabbinic Traditions about the Pharisees before 70* [3 parts.; Leiden: Brill, 1971]) and the Babylonian Talmud are from the following editions: H. Danby (trans.), *The Mishnah: Translated from the Hebrew with Introduction and Brief Explanatory Notes* (Oxford: Oxford University Press, 1933); J. Neusner *et al.* (trans.), *The Tosefta* (6 vols.; New York, Ktav, 1977–86); J.Z. Lauterbach, *Mekilta de Rabbi Ishmael: A Critical Edition on the Basis of the MSS and Early Editions with an English Translation, Introduction and Notes* (3 vols.; Philadelphia: Jewish Publication Society, 1933–35)—in my references to Mekilta the page number of Lauterbach's edition will also additionally be used in the bracket (e.g. [L. 3.197]); I. Epstein (ed.), *The Babylonian Talmud* (35 vols.; London: Soncino Press, 1935–52).

J. Neusner asserts in his numerous books,[117] a work of timeless systematic philosophy but a collection of legal and semi-legal debates carried on mainly during the first two centuries CE.[118] I will also assume that, though the primary purpose of the Mishnah[119] was the collection of sources,[120] it was also partly intended as 'a law code' or even as 'a teaching manual'.[121]

3) Though the Tannaitic writings reached their final form around or soon after 200 CE, it can reasonably be assumed that the materials attributed to the first-century rabbis broadly represent the discussions of our period.[122] The materials attributed to R. Akiba and R. Ishmael b. Elisha who were most active in the early second century will be occasionally referred to when they are involved in discussion with the first-century rabbis.

4) As regards the relationship between rabbinic literature and the Pharisees, I will neither follow Neusner's extremely sceptical view that the literature, even in its earliest stratum, does not represent the Pharisees at all, nor the rather uncritically positive view of pre-Neusner scholars who simply presume that the literature (and sometimes even the

117. E.g. *Judaism: The Evidence of the Mishnah* (Chicago: University of Chicago Press, 1981), p. 261.

118. Cf. Sanders, *Law*, pp. 15, 312-24.

119. For a brief discussion of the purpose of the Mishnah, see H.L Strack and G. Stemberger, *Introduction to the Talmud and Midrash* (trans. M.N.A. Bockmuehl; Edinburgh: T. & T. Clark, 1991), pp. 151-54; Strack and Stemberger themselves suggest an all-inclusive purpose.

120. Sanders, *Law*, pp. 15, 125-30, 249-50; *idem*, *Practice*, pp. 463-72. Cf. C. Albeck, *Einführung in die Mischna* (Berlin: de Gruyter, 1971), pp. 149-57; H. Maccoby, *Early Rabbinic Writings* (CCWJCW, 3; Cambridge: Cambridge University Press, 1988)—though they agree in the matter of the primary purpose, their views of the ultimate aim of the Mishnah are drastically different from each other's: a purely academic collection (Albeck) and a blueprint for reconstruction of Israel (Maccoby).

121. A. Goldberg, 'The Mishna—A Study Book of Halakha', in S. Safrai (ed.), *The Literature of the Jewish People in the Period of the Second Temple and the Talmud. III. The Literature of the Sages. Midrash, Mishnah, Talmud*, Part I (CRINT, 2; Assen: Van Gorcum, 1987), p. 227.

122. Cf. Albeck, *Einführung*, pp. 149, 157; Strack and Stemberger, *Talmud*, pp. 42-49; Sanders, *Law*, pp. 5, 133, 243; *idem*, *Practice*, pp. 413, 444; *et al*. For a sceptical view, however, cf. Neusner, *Evidence* and his later works; cf. also Wright, *People*, p. 183.

Talmuds) represents earlier Pharisaic thought;[123] I will rather follow the middle track of Sanders who uses the pre-70 materials in his reconstruction of Pharisaic thought with discretion and also admits the continuity between the Pharisees and the Tannaitic rabbis.[124]

a. *Earlier (pre-70) Materials*

i. *Hillel and Shammai.* According to Neusner's investigation in his *The Rabbinic Traditions about the Pharisees before 70*, throughout the whole rabbinic literature only about nine sabbath passages are directly attributed to Hillel or Shammai, the so-called 'fathers of the rabbinic world'.

In *Mekilta de R. Simeon* (= *MRS*) on Exod. 20.8 we have a statement by Shammai, '*Remember it*—before it comes, *and keep it*—when it comes', which is followed by a comment that 'the memory of the Sabbath did not move from his mouth'. Therefore, when he buys something good or new, he first remembers the sabbath and says 'This is for Sabbath'.[125] Shammai's preoccupation with the sabbath is further highlighted in *b. Beṣ.* 16a when his attitude to the sabbath is contrasted with that of Hillel. According to the passage Shammai was always eating 'in honour of the Sabbath'. He, therefore, put aside the best food for the sabbath. Whereas for Hillel 'all his works were for the sake of heaven', because 'Blessed be the Lord, day by day' (Ps. 68.20). Here it seems clear that Shammai's strict observance is surpassed by Hillel's superior understanding and observance of the sabbath, that is, he observed the sabbath every day.[126] Perhaps the reference to the world 'in which there is Sabbath all the time' in *Mek. Šab.* 1 (L. 3.199)[127] may have relation to such an understanding of the sabbath on the part of Hillel.

In *Sifre* Deut. 203, Shammai expounds that 'One does not weigh

---

123. For example, H.L. Strack and P. Billerbeck, *Kommentar zum Neuen Testament aus Talmud und Midrasch* (4 vols.; Munich: Beck, 1922–28); J. Jeremias, *Jerusalem in the Time of Jesus: An Investigation into Economic and Social Conditions during the New Testament Period* (trans. F.H. Cave and C.H. Cave; London: SCM, Press, 1969); Schürer, *History*; *et al.*

124. Sanders, *Law*, esp. pp. 5, 133, 243ff., 309, 328; *idem, Practice*, esp. pp. 10-11, 413-14, 444, 461-62.

125. Quoted from Neusner, *Traditions*, I, pp. 185-86.

126. Neusner, *Traditions*, I, p. 325. Cf. L. Finkelstein, *The Pharisees*, I (2 vols.; Philadelphia: Jewish Publication Society, 1962), pp. 258-59.

127. Cf. *m. Tam.* 7.4: 'a Psalm, a song for the time that is to come, for the day that shall be all Sabbath and rest in the life everlasting'.

anchor [of] a ship to [journey on] the Great Sea less than three days before the Sabbath'.[128] In *t. 'Erub.* 3.7 and *b. Šab.* 19a another casuistic rule is attributed to Shammai: a camp '...does not besiege a Gentile town less than three days before the Sabbath' (*t. 'Erub.* 3.7); if they encircled it, however, the sabbath does not interrupt the war *'until it falls'*.[129] These two casuistic rules once again show Shammai's extreme caution for observing the sabbath flawlessly, but it is interesting to see that he also allows breaking the sabbath if the war has already begun.

Finally, in *t. Pes.* 4.13 (cf. *m. Pes.* 6.1) Hillel brings out a general rule that the Passover overrides the sabbath by using some of his seven 'middot' and by attributing it to his masters (i.e. the tradition).[130]

ii. *The two houses.* The passages attributed to the two houses (i.e. the house of Hillel and the house of Shammai) are substantial enough in number to glimpse their view of the sabbath. Like their founders these two houses often present different views which are usually contradictory. Although Hillelite dominance is apparent in the rabbinic period, not a few scholars suggest that 'up until 70 it was the Shammaites who dominated';[131] and, according to *m. Šab.* 1.4 and *t. Šab.* 1.18-19, this verdict appears especially convincing in the case of the sabbath (cf. *y. Šab.* 1.4; *b. Šab.* 17a; cf. also *m. Miq.* 4.1).

iia. *Finishing work before the sabbath.* According to *m. Šab.* 1.5-9; *MRS* on Exod. 20.9; *t. Šab.* 1.20-22, the Shammaites forbid one to steep something in ink, dyes, and so on; to put bundles of flax in an oven, or meat, onion, and egg on the fire; to spread nets for wild animals, birds, or fishes; or to open a channel to water the gardens, unless all the works involved can be wholly done while it is still day (i.e.

---

128. Quoted from Neusner, *Traditions*, I, p. 187. Cf. *t. Šab.* 13.10, 12-13, without Shammai.

129. Cf. *Sifre* Deut. 203, without direct attribution to Shammai. For comments on these passages, see Neusner, *Traditions* I, p. 205.

130. Cf. *b. Pes.* 66a-b and *y. Pes.* 6.1—both passages identify the masters with Shemaiah and Abtalion. Cf. also *y. Šab.* 19.1. For detailed discussions and synopses of these passages, see Neusner, *Tradition*, 1, pp. 231-57, 286-89.

131. Wright, *People*, p. 194; see also G.F. Moore, *Judaism in the First Centuries of the Christian Era: The Age of the Tannaim*, I (3 vols.; Cambridge, MA: Harvard University Press, 1927–30), p. 81; M. Hengel, *The Zealots: Investigations into the Jewish Freedom Movement in the Period from Herod I until 70 AD* (trans. D. Smith; Edinburgh: T. & T. Clark, 1989), p. 334; Sanders, *Law*, p. 88.

before the sabbath starts); and the Hillelites permit all of them.[132] The Shammaite caution is extended even to the Gentile's involvement in the work on the sabbath when they forbid a Jew to sell anything to a Gentile or help him to bring a burden on Friday 'unless there is time for him to reach a place near by [the same day]', or to give hides or clothes to a Gentile workman unless there is time for completing tanning or washing in the same day, which the Hillelites permit as long as the sun is up (*m. Šab.* 1.7-8).

Behind all this disagreement on the issue of finishing work before the sabbath lies a different interpretation of Exod. 20.9. In *MRS* on Exod. 20.9, the Shammaites say, '*Six days will you work and do all your labor*—that all your work should be finished by the Sabbath eve', whereas the Hillelites say, '*Six days shall you work* [*and do all your labor*]—You labor all six days, and the rest of your work is done of itself on the Sabbath'.[133]

iib. *Acts prohibited on the Sabbath.* Disagreements between the two houses are further demonstrated when we turn to the acts prohibited on the sabbath. In *m. Šab.* 3.1 (cf. *t. Šab.* 2.13) the Shammaites permit one to set hot water but not cooked food on a double stove if it had been heated with peat or wood, whereas the Hillelites permit both; and the Shammaites allow one to remove [it][134] but not to put [it] back, whereas the Hillelites permit both. In *m. Šab.* 21.3, the Shammaites permit one to take up bones and shells from the table, whereas the Hillelites instruct that 'the entire table must be taken and shaken'. In *t. Šab.* 16.7, however, the teachings of the two houses are reversed.[135] According to

132. In the case of laying down the olive-press beams or the winepress rollers, *MRS* differs from the Mishnah (and probably the Tosefta)—in the former the Shammaites forbid it, whereas in the latter they agree with the Hillelites and permit it.

133. Quoted from Neusner, *Tradition*, II, p. 11. Cf. *t. Šab.* 1.21.

134. It is not at all clear what the object of removing is here. In my opinion, considering the previous rule of the Shammaites, it may be 'hot water', though Epstein, *Talmud*, 'Seder Mo'ed' I, p. 170, prefers cooked food, and Danby presumes in his translation that it includes both; Neusner's comment in *Tradition*, II, p. 126 does not address the problem precisely. Even though *b. Šab.* 36b-37a discusses the issue extensively, it is not helpful for identifying it; neither is *t. Šab.* 2.13. One thing clear, however, is the fact that, in any case, the Shammaites are stricter than the Hillelites.

135. Cf. *b. Šab.* 143a. At any rate, these two pairs are not exactly parallelled and it can not be easily judged which one is stricter; however, cf. Epstein, *Talmud*,

t. Šab. 14.1, the rule of moving utensils was well developed towards leniency before the two houses; and the Hillelites aim to remove the restriction on moving utensils for all occasions, whereas the Shammaites try to restrict permission only to when there is a need (cf. *m. Šab.* 17.4; *b. Šab.* 124a-b). In *t. Šab.* 16.21 R. Simeon b. Eleazar says that the Shammaites forbid one to kill a louse, whereas the Hillelites permit it. In *t. Šab.* 16.22 Rabban Simeon b. Gamaliel says that the Shammaites forbid one to distribute charity to the poor in the house of assembly, or even to pray for a sick person,[136] whereas the Hillelites permit all of them (cf. *b. Šab.*12a).

All these passages[137] clearly show that the Shammaites were consistently stricter than the Hillelites, and the Shammaite rules in the last two passages sound too rigorous and even inhuman. One concrete indication in *t. Šab.* 14.1 that the rules of the two houses had been already relaxed significantly (cf. *m. 'Erub.* 5.5) may enable us to suggest, though without final certainty, that the rules of their predecessors (perhaps in the time of Jesus) may have been much more stringent, especially along the Shammaite line which appears influential at that time as I have suggested above.

iic. *Erub*[138] *regulations.* In *m. 'Erub.* 1.2 the Shammaites prescribe both side-post and cross-beam to make a valid alley entry in order to constitute several courtyards into a single domain, whereas the Hillelites prescribe either one of the two (cf. *b. 'Erub.* 6a). In *m. 'Erub.* 6.4 the Shammaites prescribe that the right of access must be given to the man, who forgot to take part in the Erub, 'While it is yet day', whereas the Hillelites permit it [even] 'After it has become dark'.[139] 'If five companies kept the Sabbath in the same eating-hall', according to *m. 'Erub.* 6.6, the Shammaites prescribe an Erub for each company, whereas the Hillelites prescribe one Erub for all. According to *m. 'Erub.* 8.6, the Shammaites prescribe a partition below the surface level for a cistern

---

'Seder Mo'ed' I, p. 723 nn. 12, 13, and p. 724 n. 5, as regards the interdict of *mukzeh.*

136. Cf. *b. Šab.* 12a—here visiting the sick and comforting mourners are prohibited by the Shammaites, whereas the Hillelites permit them. Cf. also *m. Šab.* 14.3-4; *t. Šab.* 12.9-14; Mt. 12.9-14 par.

137. Perhaps with one exception of *m. Šab.* 21.3 regarding cleaning the table.

138. For a definition of the term 'Erub' and its related term 'Shittuf', see Danby, *Mishnah*, p. 793, app. I.8, and p. 796, app. I.39 respectively.

139. Cf. *y. 'Erub.* 6.4—here the teachings of the two houses are reversed.

between two courtyards, whereas the Hillelites prescribe a partition above the surface level; the later general rule, however, allows either one of the two. In *m. 'Erub.* 6.2 Rabban Gamaliel II says that his father (i.e. Rabban Simeon b. Gamaliel I, the grandson or great-grandson of Hillel) said to him, 'Hasten and put out all the [needful] vessels in the alley before he [i.e. a Sadducee living with them] brings out [his vessels] and so restricts you'. This episode shows that Sadducees, who were stricter on the matter of keeping the law in general, did not admit Erub tradition which is 'a relaxation of the law' (cf. *m. 'Erub.* 5.5; cf. also 8.2) invented by the Pharisees to overcome 'the anti-social aspects of sabbath law'.[140]

b. *Later (70–100) Materials*

About ten rabbis of this period[141] are mentioned in the Tannaitic literature in relation to the sabbath. The materials attributed to them are so numerous that we may not aim to cover all of them. The following are some examples which illustrate the sort of concerns they were remembered as addressing.

i. *Finishing work before the sabbath*. In *m. Šab.* 1.9 Rabban Simeon b. Gamaliel II says, 'In my father's house [i.e. Rabban Gamaliel II][142] they used to give white clothes to a Gentile washman *three days before Sabbath*', which seems a reflection of Shammai's cautious rules of journey and war. This may imply that even the Hillelites sometimes adopted Shammai's teaching. In *t. Šab.* 1.22[143] is added a clause, 'and colored ones on the eve of the Sabbath', because colored ones are easier than white ones to wash. In *m. Šab* 1.10, as regards putting cakes upon

---

140. Sanders, *Practice*, pp. 335, 425, 466-67; cf. *m. 'Erub.* 6.1; *b. 'Erub.* 68b; cf. also CD 11.5-9 for the Essene position; see above, section 2ai. However, cf. Neusner, *Traditions*, I, pp. 379-80, who is sceptical about the authenticity of this logion. Cf. also Josephus, *Ant.* 13.294; cf. S. Mason, *Flavius Josephus on the Pharisees* (SPB, 39; Leiden: Brill, 1991), pp. 213-45.

141. R. Johanan *b. Zakkai*, R. Zadok I, R. Nahum *the Mede*, R. Gamaliel II, R. Joshua *b. Hananiah*, R. Eliezer *b. Hyrcanus*, R. Dosa *b. Harkinas*, R. Eleazar *b. Hananiah b. Hezekiah b. Garon*, R. Judah *b. Bathyra*, R. Ben Bathyra; in addition to these, as I have stated above, we may include the sayings of R. Akiba, R. Ishmael *b. Elisha* and some others selectively. The second names in italics will be omitted in the subsequent discussion.

142. The son of Rabban Simeon b. Gamaliel, hence the great-grandson or the great-great-grandson of Hillel.

143. Here the narrator is R. Eleazar b. Zadok.

the coals, R. Eliezer forbids it unless there is time for 'their bottom surface [only] to form into crust'; whereas a general rule, perhaps agreed by both houses,[144] is more strict and prescribes, 'time for their top surface to form into crust'.

ii. *Acts prohibited on the sabbath.* In *t. Šab.* 4.6, 11 R. Eliezer permits a woman to go out wearing a tiara (= 'a golden city'), a hair-net, a perfume box, and so on, all of which are generally forbidden especially by R. Meir (*c.* 150) in *m. Šab.* 6.1, 3. In *m. Šab.* 9.7 we have an extremely meticulous rule that if a man took out garden-seeds little less than a dried fig's bulk, or two cucumber-seeds, two gourd-seeds, etc., he is liable to sin-offering, and R. Judah makes the rule more exact by defining the amount of garden-seeds as five.

In *m. Šab.* 10.6, if a man removed his finger-nails, hair,[145] etc., and if a woman dressed her hair, painted her eyelids, etc., R. Eliezer declares that such a one is liable to a sin-offering.

M. Šab. 12.4, 6 provides two casuistic rules of writing which clearly belong to our period. In v. 4, if a man scratched letters on his skin, R. Eliezer declares him liable to a sin-offering, whereas R. Joshua declares him not culpable. In v. 6, if a man wrote two letters during two acts of forgetfulness, Rabban Gamaliel II declares him culpable, whereas the sages declare him not culpable.[146]

In *m. Šab.* 13.1 R. Eliezer declares one culpable who weaves three threads at the beginning of the process of weaving, or 'a single thread on to a piece already woven', whereas the sages prescribe two threads for either case (cf. *t. Šab.* 12.1).

iii. *Other specific regulations.* In *m. Šeb.* 10.7 R. Eliezer declares one who scrapes honey from a bee-hive culpable, because he regards it as an immovable property and the act of scraping honey as 'reaping'.[147] According to *m. Šab.* 16.7 R. Johanan is reluctant to allow one to cover

144. Cf. 1.9. If this is the case, R. Eliezer's view may be seen as an example of the development towards leniency.

145. Cf. *t. Šab.* 9.12: 'Even one [hair]'.

146. Cf. *t. Šab.* 11.17, where he concedes to the sages when they declare one not culpable who writes one letter on this sabbath and another one on another sabbath, a festival, or the Day of Atonement.

147. Danby, *Mishnah*, p. 51 n. 9. The sages, however, have an opposite view. Cf. *m. Šab.* 22.1—here the broken honeycombs are no longer immovable property, therefore Eliezer permits one to save honey from it.

a scorpion with a dish for human safety probably because the behaviour may count as hunting a beast.[148] In *m. Šab.* 16.8 Rabban Gamaliel II permits one to use a gangway in order to come down from a ship made by a Gentile (and perhaps also a lamp lighted by a Gentile). In *m. Šab.* 17.7 R. Eliezer allows one to shut up a window with the window-shutter only when it is hung on the window-frame, probably because otherwise such a behaviour may count as building something (cf. *m. 'Erub.* 10.10). In *m. Šab.* 20.4; *t. Šab.* 16.4 R. Dosa permits one to clean out a crib before a fat ox and 'sweep aside [spilt fodder] to protect it from excrement', whereas the sages forbid it. R. Johanan, according to *m. Šab.* 22.3, is reluctant to allow one to put wax on the hole already pierced at the side of a jar, because it may involve smoothing it over which may count as scraping.[149] Debates about various other issues are further found in the following references: *m. Ter.* 8.3—eating a cluster of grapes untithed (R. Eliezer vs. R. Joshua);[150] *m. Šab.* 2.1, 3—materials for the sabbath lamps (R. Nahum vs. sages; R. Eliezer vs. R. Akiba); *m. Šab.* 16.1, 3—to which places Scriptures or food may be taken from fire (R. Ben Bathyra); etc.

iv. *Matters which override the sabbath.* According to the Tannaitic literature, the first-century rabbis made some exceptions to the restrictions of the sabbath: (i) circumcision—*m. Šab.* 19.1, 4; *Mek. Šab.* 1 (L. 3.198, 203-204); (ii) the temple service—*t. Šab.* 15.16; *Mek. Šab.* 1 (L. 3.198); (iii) the Passover—*Pes.* 6.1-2; (iv) saving Scriptures and food from fire—*m. Šab.* 16.1, 3; (v) saving life—*t. Šab.* 15.16; *Mek. Šab.* 1 (L. 3.197-98);[151] (vi) self-defensive war—*Mek. Šab.* 1 (L. 3.200-201).

At the end of the discussion with R. Eliezer on circumcision in *m. Šab.* 19.1, R. Akiba prescribes a general rule that any work that can be

148. Cf. Danby, *Mishnah*, p. 115 n. 2; cf. *b. Šab.* 121b.

149. Danby, *Mishnah*, p. 119 n. 4; Epstein, *Talmud*, 'Seder Mo'ed' I, p. 739 n. 7.

150. Cf. *t. Ter.* 7.10; cf. also *m. Beṣ* 4.7. For brief comments on the complicated issues involved in relation to the tithe, see Danby, *Mishnah*, p. 61 nn. 5, 6; Epstein, *Talmud*, 'Zera'im', p. 231 nn. 8-11, p. 231 nn. 1-3; cf. *m. Šab.* 2.7—on the sabbath tithing is forbidden.

151. At the end of the discussion on the issue, the redactor quotes R. Simon b. Meahsiah's (*c.* 180) interpretation of the meaning of Exod. 31.14, which has a striking similarity with Mk 2.27—'The Sabbath is given to you but you are not surrendered to the Sabbath (לכם שבת מסורה ואין אתם מסורין לשבת)'. Cf. Strack and Billerbeck, *Kommentar*, IV, p. 47, esp. n. a.

done on the day before (or eve of) the sabbath does not override the sabbath, but what cannot be done on the day before (or eve of) the sabbath overrides the sabbath (cf. *m. Men.* 11.3; *t. Men.* 11.5).

v. *Erub regulations*. The rules of the first-century rabbis regarding Erub and the sabbath limit show a picture which is similar to but much more detailed and meticulous than that of the houses. Their debates are largely centred on three issues: (i) Forming various places into private (or neutral) domains: an alley entry—*m. 'Erub.* 1.2 (R. Eliezer vs. the houses);[152] a courtyard with a breach toward the public domain—*m. 'Erub.* 9.2 (R. Eliezer vs. sages); a large field with a fence: its size and shape—*m. 'Erub.* 2.5, 6 (R. Eliezer vs. R. Akiba); etc. (ii) Erub preparation: regulation regarding one of the occupants of the courtyard who forgot to prepare Erub—*m. 'Erub.* 2.6 (R. Eliezer); the kinds and amounts of stuffs for Erub and Shittuf—*m. 'Erub.* 7.10 (R. Eliezer vs. R. Joshua); securing a share in an Erub with a deposit—*m. 'Erub.* 7.11 (R. Eliezer vs. sages); etc. (iii) The sabbath limit: the distance of moving for a man brought to another town or a cattle-fold by Gentiles; the distance of walking on a ship sailing in the sea—*m. 'Erub.* 4.1-2 (Rabban Gamaliel II and R. Eleazar b. Azariah—whole areas vs. R. Joshua and R. Akiba: four cubits);[153] the distance of moving for a man who fell asleep while on a journey and did not know that night had fallen—*m. 'Erub.* 4.5 (R. Johanan b. Nuri [*c.* 110]: 2000 cubits; the sages: four cubits; R. Eliezer—two cubits[154]); regulation for a man who went out beyond the sabbath limit—*m. 'Erub.* 4.11 (R. Eliezer); bringing in phylacteries found in the open field—how many at a time?—*m. Erub.* 10.1 (Rabban Gamaliel II); etc. There seems to be no disagreement as regards the sabbath limit of 2000 cubits, since there is no dispute about it but mostly it is taken for granted.[155]

vi. *The sabbath and the covenant*. In *Mek. Vayassa* 5-6 (L. 2.119-23) we have two sayings as regards the promise for those who keep the

---

152.　Cf. *t. 'Erub.* 1.2. For the views of the two houses, see above.

153.　The episode in *m. 'Erub.* 4.2 implies a rule by Rabban Gamaliel II that, if a ship were within the sabbath limit before nightfall, landing from the ship is permitted.

154.　'Himself being in the middle of them'—for the meaning of this clause, cf. *b. 'Erub.* 45a; Epstein, *Talmud*, 'Seder Mo'ed' II, pp. 313-14 n. 15.

155.　In his exposition of Num. 35.4-5 in *m. Soṭ.* 5.3, R. Akiba explains that 'the one thousand cubits are the outskirts, while the two thousand cubits are the Sabbath limit'. Cf. CD 10.21; 11.5-6.

sabbath. In L. 2.119 R. Joshua says that God will give them three festivals: Passover, Pentecost and Tabernacles.[156] In L. 2.120 R. Eliezer says that they will escape the three visitations: the day of Gog, the suffering preceding the advent of the Messiah, and the Great Judgment Day.[157] In *Mek. Bahodesh* 7 (L. 2.252-53) R. Eleazar provides a rare saying about the holiness of the sabbath by a first-century rabbi: 'Remember the day of the Sabbath to keep it holy'.[158] As far as I have searched, these couple of passages are the only ones throughout the Tannaitic literature which betray, but only indirectly, the Pharisaic and rabbinic thought of the covenantal significance of the sabbath. Bearing in mind Sanders's account of the genre of rabbinic literature,[159] it would be a great mistake to try to discover any direct theological statement about the covenantal significance of the sabbath. Nevertheless we cannot deny that the rarity of even indirect materials regarding the covenantal significance of the sabbath compared to the extreme abundance of the specific regulations is striking.

vii. *The penalties.* As regards the penalties against violation of the sabbath it is not easy to draw a general picture. One thing very clear, according to *m. Ker.* 3.10, 4.2, is that inadvertent violation requires sin-offering (cf. Lev. 4.27-35), though there was no final consensus about how many sin-offerings are required for specific occasions.[160] Though we do not have any direct evidence about the penalty for intentional violation of the sabbath, considering the general tendency towards leniency among the rabbis, we may possibly consider that the view in *m. Sanh.* 7.1, 4, and 8, which clearly pronounces the death penalty by

156. In L. 2.121 he also says that 'he who observes the Sabbath is kept far from sin'. Cf. also L. 2.122.

157. In L. 2.120, 122 R. Eleazar of Modiim (*c.* 110) also says that God will give them six good portions: the Land of Israel, the future world, the new world, the Kingdom of the house of David, the priesthood, the Levites' offices.

158. The following unquoted additional explanation—'keep it in mind from the first day of the week on, so that if something good happens to come your way fix it up for the Sabbath'—may be a reflection of the teaching of Shammai over against that of Hillel in *b. Beṣ* 16a; see above, section 6ai.

159. *Law*, pp. 15, 309-24.

160. Cf. *m. Šab.* 7.1; *m. Sanh.* 7.8. The investigation above also shows that violations of a number of minor rules require only sin-offering, especially in the post-70 rabbinic materials. It is not clear, however, whether this was a common view among the pre-70 Pharisees.

stoning[161] against those who violate the sabbath intentionally even after warning, continues that of the first-century Pharisees and rabbis. Though the Pharisees, as Sanders suggests, may not have been able to enforce their sanction of the death penalty in practice,[162] these indirect evidences drive us to suggest that they may have had enough reason and ground for seeking to impose the death penalty against those who violate the sabbath repeatedly in spite of warning.

c. 39 Categories of Works Prohibited on the Sabbath

Though in *m. Šab.* 7.2 the 39 categories of works are not directly attributed to our period, there are some reasons to regard them as old enough to be related to our period. In *Mek. Šab.* 1 (L. 3.206) Rabbi (Judah) says that 39 categories were given by Moses orally. In L. 3.210, R. Jonathan (*c.* 140) already regards the 39 categories as a fixed rule.[163] Furthermore, a significant number of those categories are already clearly presupposed by the passages which we have discussed above.[164] Then, even though I admit S.B. Hoenig's suggestion that the number 39 was chosen by R. Akiba for the number of the prohibited works,[165] it may be possible to suggest that, if not the complete list, then a considerable number of those categories were already well recognized as forbidden works.[166]

---

161. The second severest among the four kinds of death penalty, according to *m. Sanh.* 7.1. This may show how the significance of the sabbath was highly recognized by rabbis. Cf. *Sifre* on Num. 15.32-36.

162. *Law*, pp. 16-19; *Practice*, p. 426. However, against Sanders's too negative view regarding the Pharisaic influence in the first century, Wright convincingly argues for some significant influence of the Pharisees in his *People*, pp. 189-99.

163. As regards the significance of the number 39 in relation to the sabbath, see Hoenig, 'Designated Number', pp. 193-99, 202-208.

164. At least fifteen—e.g. reaping: *m. Šab.* 10.7; cleaning: *m. Šab.* 20.4; baking: *m. Šab.* 1.5, etc.; washing: *m. Šab.* 1.9; *t. Šab.* 1.22, etc.; dyeing: *m. Šab.* 1.5; *MRS* on Exod. 20.9, etc.; weaving: *m. Šab.* 13.1; *t. Šab.* 12.1, etc.; hunting: *m. Šab.* 16.7, etc.; slaughtering: *t. 'Erub.* 3.7; *t. Šab.* 16.21, etc.; scraping: *m. Šab.* 22.3; cutting: *m. Šab.* 10.6; writing: *m. Šab.* 12.4, 6; *t. Šab* 11.17, etc.; building: *m. Šab* 17.7, etc.; lighting and putting out: *m. Šab.* 2.1, 4; taking out: *m. Šab.* 16.1, etc.

165. 'Designated Number', p. 205.

166. Hoenig, 'Designated Number', p. 207, however, suggests that in Akiba's time 'the laws of Sabbath had already become fully defined rabbinically'. Cf. Sanders, *Practice*, p. 119: 'The social and economic circumstances known by the Mishnaic rabbis cannot have been much different from those that prevailed before the destruction of the temple, and we may take this [i.e. the thirty nine main classes

Even though the 39 categories sound comprehensive enough,[167] for the Pharisees and rabbis who tend to be more meticulous for every situation these categories are still only a general principle; they, therefore, continue exhaustive discussions and add endless casuistic regulations which in many cases are not agreed—an extreme example of such effort is well demonstrated in their Erub discussion.

d. *Conclusions*

The investigation above shows us that Shammai and the Shammaites were consistently more stringent than Hillel and the Hillelites in their regulation of the sabbath; the extreme caution of the former is impressively shown in various areas, and their prohibitions against distributing charity and prayer for the sick sound too rigorous and even inhuman. If the rules of the houses had already been relaxed significantly as *t. Šab.* 14.1 implies, then we may imagine how much more stringent would have been the rules of their predecessors, especially the Shammaite line which appears more influential at that time.

As *m. 'Erub.* 5.5 states Erub tradition was invented by the Pharisees as a relaxation of the sabbath law in order to overcome its anti-social aspects. In spite of such intentions, however, further development of the sabbath regulations towards meticulous casuistry seems to have made those rules rather more inconvenient, time-consuming, and, therefore, probably burdensome.

It seems also quite clear that most of the detailed issues of the debates of the two houses are not directly derived from the Scripture but rather from their tradition, tendency or opinion (e.g. *m. Šab.* 3.1; *m. 'Erub.* 8.6; etc.); therefore their disagreement in details probably could have remained without their blaming each other as unfaithful to the Torah.

The investigation of post-70 materials further confirms the above aspects, and this may support my primary position that the first-century rabbis were in continuity with the Pharisees. Some rabbis still show the Shammaite caution (e.g. *m. Šab.* 1.9; *t. Šab.* 1.22). Most of the specific regulations show the similar tendency towards meticulous casuistry; since more abundant materials than those of the houses are preserved, we have more cases of discussions of extremely detailed and trivial

---

of work in *m. Šab.* 7.2] as an accurate depiction of what "work" was'.

167. Especially compared with the number of categories of work in the Old Testament (less than five), *Jubilees* (14, not 22; *pace* Hoenig) or CD (15 in my count), 39 is an outstandingly high number; see below, section 7.

issues.[168] As more rules are discussed and added, however, we can easily imagine that inconvenience in remembering and keeping all of them may have been increased and therefore the bulk of sabbath regulations may have become more burdensome. The fact that the detailed issues of the debates are not directly derived from Scripture is much clearer here. Unlike the houses, however, individual rabbis do not show any consistent tendency throughout their views,[169] and disagreements among them are more diverse but still coexist.[170] At any rate the abundance of discussions on the sabbath may betray the significance of the sabbath in Pharisaic and rabbinic thought, and such significance seems to be further testified by the death penalty prescribed against sabbath transgressors in *m. Sanh.* 7.1, 4, 8.

The brief discussion of the 39 categories of work suggests that, if not the whole list, then very possibly most of them are very old, and that they reflect the living circumstances of the time as comprehensively as possible. I have pointed out, however, that these comprehensive categories are only a starting point for the more meticulous and casuistic discussions among the Pharisees and the rabbis.[171] Since the 39 categories were already well beyond the level of casuistry of the Old Testament, *Jubilees*, and CD, the whole body of the later and further developed rules of the sabbath among the Pharisees and rabbis cannot be compared to the previous literature in its meticulous casuistry.

This casuistry is by no means an unhealthy thing in itself; it can be the product of a serious attempt to make Scripture meaningful for the current situation.[172] The abundance of casuistic rules for the sabbath in rabbinic literature may, therefore, reflect such a serious attempt by the Pharisees and the rabbis of the time. Nevertheless too many rules which were extremely meticulous regarding trivial areas of everyday life without emphasizing the fundamental significance of the sabbath would

168. E.g., *m. Šab.* 13.1, regarding weaving one, two, or three threads: *m. Šab.* 9.7, regarding the number of seeds to be carried; etc.

169. E.g., compare *m. Šab.* 12.4 (R. Eliezer—stringent; R. Joshua—lenient) with *m. 'Erub.* 2.6 (R. Eliezer—lenient; R. Joshua—stringent).

170. Sometimes even five different views regarding one issue—e.g. *m. 'Erub.* 1.2.

171. For the Pharisaic tendency of precision and strictness on the matters of the law in general, see Josephus, *War* 1.108-109; 2.162; *Life* 191; cf. Mason, *Josephus*, pp. 89-106.

172. Cf. C. Rowland, 'A Summary of Sabbath Observance in Judaism at the Beginning of the Christian Era', in Carson (ed.), *Lord's Day*, p. 54.

have inevitably caused extreme inconvenience, trouble, and sometimes even danger,[173] and become burdensome. We may, therefore, conclude that, in spite of the genuineness of the efforts of the first-century Pharisees and rabbis, their main interest was rather focused on *how* they should keep the sabbath than *why* they should keep it, and as a result of that their abundant production of regulations for the sabbath, which in a sense was intended to lessen the burden of the sabbath, made the sabbath more burdensome in the end.[174]

7. Summary

I am now in a position to draw together the various discussions in the previous sections and summarize the conclusions reached in the course of those discussions.

1) We have noted at least three more or less stipulated lists of (categories of) prohibited works on the sabbath in the early Jewish literature of this period—*Jub.* 50.6-13; CD 10.14-11.18; *m. Šab.* 7.2.[175] Considering the dates[176] and contents[177] of these lists and other related materials, one can confidently suggest that through the centuries up to 100 CE the rather general rules in the Old Testament regarding works prohibited on the sabbath had been developed in the direction of an increasingly more specific and meticulous casuistry, probably in order to render the sabbath law more applicable to the current contexts. On the other hand, comparing the degrees of stringency of certain rules in the different writings, we must conclude that at least some of the sabbath

---

173. E.g. *m. Šab.* 16.7—prohibition against covering a scorpion.

174. For the possibility that Jesus' saying in Mt. 11.28, Δεῦτε πρός με πάντες οἱ κοπιῶντες καὶ πεφορτισμένοι may reflect such a burdensome situation, see below, Chapter 4, section 2b.

175. Cf. also Philo, *Migr. Abr.* 89-93; *Vit. Mos.* 2.21-22, 211-20; *Spec. Leg.* 2.249-51.

176. *Jubilees*—the oldest; the Mishnah—the latest.

177. Especially the numbers of (the categories of) works (*Jubilees*, 14; CD, 25; Mishnah, 39) and the specificity of individual regulations. It is noteworthy that at least five (or even nine) of the 25 kinds of work in the list of CD (cf. CD 10.18-21; 11.2; cf. also 11.4-5, 12, 14-15) are more specific expansions of a rather general rule of 'no business' in CD 11.15, and four of them (cf. CD 11.7-11) are diverse kinds of carrying—the categories of CD may thus be at most 15 rather than 25; such a tendency towards specific expansions of rather general rules is, as we have seen, most fully developed in the rabbinic literature.

regulations[178] had moved towards leniency in the course of the period, probably in order to render the sabbath law more practicable. In spite of such a movement towards leniency, however, the growing number of more specific and meticulous regulations must inevitably have made the sabbath law more inconvenient and burdensome and directed the concern of the people away from *why* they should keep it to *how* they should keep it.

2) The recognition of and emphasis on the covenantal significance of the sabbath in the Qumran Scrolls, Philo and rabbinic literature is strikingly weak as compared with that of *Jubilees* (2.17-33), and still more with that of the Old Testament. The holiness of the sabbath, however, is more widely recognized or emphasized,[179] though in rabbinic literature the concern for that issue is once again not manifestly expressed at all. In Aristobulus and Philo a rather different dimension of the sabbath is demonstrated and emphasized—the universal significance of the sabbath; in doing this they make use of Greek philosophy—for example, Pythagorean reflections on the number seven.

3) A number of references throughout the writings of this period present the sabbath as a festival day to be celebrated by having good food and blessing the Lord of the day (e.g. *Jub.* 2.31-32; 50.9-10; Philo, *Op. Mund.* 89-128); therefore, fasting is forbidden (e.g. *Jub.* 50.9-10; Jdt. 8.6; CD 11.4-5; cf. Erub regulations), though in rabbinic literature (and probably in the Qumran Scrolls) such an emphasis on its festal

---

178. E.g. *sabbath limit*: *Jub.* 50.12—no journey; CD 10.21—1000 cubits; rabbinic literature—2000 cubits (cf. *m. Sot.* 5.3); *offering*: *Jub.* 50.10-11 and CD. 11.17-18—the sabbath offerings only; *t. Šab.* 15.16 and *m. Pes.* 6.1-2, etc.—the sabbath and Passover offerings; *carrying*: *Jub.* 50.8 and CD 11.7-10—anything (perfumes in particular) forbidden; *t. Šab.* 4.11, etc.—a perfume box and many others allowed; *war*: *Jub.* 50.12—no war; *Mek. Šab.* 1, etc.—self-defensive war allowed (cf. relevant references in 1 and 2 Maccabees and Josephus); *penalties*: *Jub.* 2.25-27; 50.8, 13, etc.—death penalty (cf. Philo, *Spec. Leg.* 2.249-51); CD 12.3-6— keeping the breaker in custody; *m. Šab.* 10.6, etc.—a sin-offering (but cf. *m. Sanh.* 7.1, 4, 8—death penalty). The numbers of exceptions permitted may also show this tendency: *Jubilees*—1 exception (sabbath offerings); CD—2 exceptions (sabbath offerings, saving life); rabbinic literature—6 categories of exception (sabbath offerings, saving life, circumcision, etc.). Cf. also *t. Šab.* 14.1.

179. *Jub.* 2.25; Aristobulus, F. 5.13-16; CD 3.14; 10.17; 11.14-15; Philo, *Op. Mund.* 89-128; etc. The emphasis on the 364 day calendar may be a good example of taking the sanctity of the sabbath seriously; see *Jub.* 6.32-38; 4Q394-398; 11QTemple 13-29 (esp. 17.15-16).

character is less pronounced. In many references, offering the sabbath sacrifices in the temple, and gathering in the synagogues in order, for example, to learn the Torah and/or share communal meals, are presupposed or prescribed (e.g. Josephus, *Life* 277-79; *Apion* 2.175; Philo, *Vit. Cont.* 30-37; *Leg. All.* 156).

4) Ample references in Josephus, Philo and Graeco-Roman authors provide the following information about the sabbath in the Gentile world: (i) the sabbath was widely observed throughout the Gentile world, and the Jews obtained their right to observe it from the Romans in the end; (ii) Gentiles, however, were not always in favour of the Jewish sabbath; they were often hostile to it and criticized or ridiculed the Jewish practices on it, especially their prohibition of war on the sabbath; (iii) such hostile criticism or ridicule was sometimes based on various misunderstandings, for example, misunderstanding of the origin of the sabbath or confusion of the sabbath with a fasting day, and so on.

5) All the materials collected and discussed in this chapter may suggest that during this period the sabbath was well established as one of the central characteristics of the Jewish religion; that during the period there were various understandings of, emphases on, and regulations regarding the sabbath, probably because of differing contexts as well as differing theological perspectives; and that the Pharisees and the first-century rabbis, according to the rabbinic literature, are outstanding among those various trends in three respects: (i) their extremely meticulous casuistry; (ii) their movement towards greater leniency (though their preservation of the death penalty may be an exception); (iii) their lack of emphasis on the covenantal significance and festal character of the sabbath—in this matter their tendency may have been shared by the Qumran Scrolls and some other literature.

Chapter 3

JESUS AND THE SABBATH IN MATTHEW'S GOSPEL:
PRELIMINARY CONSIDERATIONS

1. *Working Assumptions*

There are a number of working assumptions underlying the studies in the following chapters.

a. *The Synoptic Problem and Method*

My work is not based on either the two-source hypothesis or the 'two-Gospel hypothesis' (i.e. the Neo-Griesbach hypothesis) or any other particular theory.[1] I assume rather that the literary relationships among the synoptic Gospels are much more complex and indirect than generally supposed, and may have involved various sources (either written or oral) most of which we do not now possess.[2]

1.   Although the two-source hypothesis is still supported by the majority of scholars, it can no longer be taken for granted in the study of the synoptic Gospels. In recent years, it has increasingly come under attack mainly but not solely from the proponents of the 'two-Gospel hypothesis'. For introductory but serious discussions on the issue, see, for example, R.T. France, *Matthew: Evangelist and Teacher* (Exeter: Paternoster, 1989), pp. 24-46; E.P. Sanders and M. Davies, *Studying the Synoptic Gospels* (London: SCM Press, 1989), pp. 51-119; G.N. Stanton, 'Redaction Criticism: the End of an Era?', in *People*, pp. 23-36. For fuller lists of the literature, see W.D. Davies and D.C. Allison, *Matthew*, I (3 vols.; ICC; Edinburgh: T. & T. Clark, 1988 [vol. 1], 1991 [vol. 2]), pp. 97-99 ns. 48-52, p. 115 n. 68.
2.   Though J.M. Rist's suggestion in his monograph *On the Independence of Matthew and Mark* (SNTSMS, 32; Cambridge: Cambridge University Press, 1978) is interesting, he too readily dismisses the significance of the high degree of agreement between the two Gospels in both content and order; cf. G.N. Stanton, 'The Origin and Purpose of Matthew's Gospel: Matthean Scholarship from 1945 to 1980', *ANRW*, II.25/3 (Berlin: de Gruyter, 1985), p. 1901. I assume that there was literary influence between the two which may have been indirect through other unknown sources; given such an indirect influence, Markan priority seems more probable than Matthean priority.

With regard to method, my work uses redaction criticism,[3] socio-historical method and literary criticism interrelatedly whenever they are considered appropriate. As G.N. Stanton properly points out, recognition of the value of all those methods and of their mutual interdependence is 'crucial for scholarly discussion of the gospels'.[4]

b. *Author, Date and Place*

Following the vast majority of recent scholars, I assume that the author of the First Gospel was a Jewish Christian. This assumption is supported not only by the unanimous external evidence but also by the nature of the Gospel itself.[5]

As to date, the universal patristic belief seems to suggest a date not later than the early sixties and not a few modern scholars (though they are still a minority) push the date back before 70 CE, whereas the

---

3.   My redaction criticism will not be the same as the traditional one, because it is not based on the two-source hypothesis or on the conventional view of Markan priority. As regards the possibility of utilizing redaction criticism without assuming the two-source hypothesis, see France, *Evangelist*, pp. 46-49; one of the examples of such an approach may be found in A.F. Segal, 'Matthew's Jewish Voice', in D.L. Balch (ed.), *Social History of the Matthean Community: Cross-Disciplinary Approaches* (Minneapolis, MN: Fortress Press, 1991), pp. 3-37; see esp. p. 4 n. 4: 'I try not to assume either Markan or Matthean priority, only wishing to distinguish between the ways in which the evangelists interpret their stories'.

4.   *People*, pp. 23-110, quotation from p. 108. Realizing the unhealthiness of travelling in parallel lanes between redaction criticism (and socio-historical method) and literary criticism, recently scholars tend to aim to interrelate those methods; see G.N. Stanton, 'The Communities of Matthew', *Int* 46 (1992), pp. 379-82; J.D. Kingsbury, 'Conclusion: Analysis of a Conversation', in Balch (ed.), *Community*, pp. 259-69; D.A. Hagner, *Matthew 1–13* (WBC, 33a; Dallas: Word Books, 1993), pp. xxxix-xliii; cf. also U. Luz, *Matthew in History: Interpretation, Influence, and Effects* (Minneapolis, MN: Fortress Press, 1994), esp. pp. 1-22.

5.   For the three different opinions on the authorship of Matthew, see the chart in Davies and Allison, *Matthew*, I, pp. 10-11. In the chart there are less than a dozen scholars who oppose my assumption; whereas the vast majority of scholars argue for Jewish Christian authorship, and not a few scholars even suggest the apostle Matthew as the author of the Gospel. After a fairly comprehensive discussion on the authorship, Davies and Allison convincingly put forward their observation that, while nothing in the First Gospel demands a Gentile authorship, there are 'several facts that are most easily explained by the supposition that our author was a Jew' (p. 33). As a matter of convenience I will use the name 'Matthew' in the following discussions as a designation of the author of the First Gospel.

majority of modern scholars suggest the final quarter of the first century CE.[6] The majority view in recent scholarship is mainly based on two assumptions: Markan priority and the belief that the reference to the destruction of the city in 22.7 is a reflection of the fall of Jerusalem in 70 CE. Neither point, however, is incontestable.[7] In fact, the present situation does not allow us to reach a firm conclusion; therefore at present I simply acknowledge 90s CE as the *terminus ad quem* without defining the *terminus a quo*.[8]

Many scholars attempt to specify the place of origin of the Gospel. Jerusalem (or Palestine), Caesarea Maritima, Phoenicia, Alexandria, Pella, Syria, and Antioch are among the places proposed.[9] This variety of opinions implies that we are not likely to claim for any specific place a high degree of certainty. The most we can say is that the place of origin was probably somewhere in Syria or Palestine.

c. *Matthew's Community*

It is generally assumed that behind Matthew's Gospel there was a community with which Matthew identifies, and whose setting is reflected in his writing. It is not a simple task, however, to define the identity of the community; it demands a wide range of discussions which go well beyond the bounds of this study.[10] I will, therefore, simply state some of

6. For the spectrum of opinion concerning the date, see Davies and Allison, *Matthew*, I, pp. 127-28.

7. For objections to the second assumption, see J.A.T. Robinson, *Redating the New Testament* (London: SCM Press, 1976), pp. 20-21; B. Reicke, 'Synoptic Prophecies on the Destruction of Jerusalem', in D.E. Aune (ed.), *Studies in New Testament and Early Christian Literature: Essays in Honor of A.P. Wikgren* (Leiden: Brill, 1972), pp. 121-34; France, *Evangelist*, pp. 83-85; among others.

8. Though the date of the Gospel is judged frequently on the basis of the introduction into the synagogue liturgy in about 85 CE of the so-called *birkath ha-minim*, as G.N. Stanton, 'Synagogue and Church', in *idem*, *People*, p. 144, rightly suggests, 'too many uncertainties surround the *birkath ha-minim* to allow us to link it directly to the origin…of Matthew's gospel'; cf. France, *Evangelist*, pp. 85-86.

9. For the various proposals as to the place of origin, see the chart in Davies and Allison, *Matthew*, I, pp. 138-39.

10. For recent extensive studies of Matthew's community, see E. Schweizer, 'Matthew's Church', in G.N. Stanton (ed.), *The Interpretation of Matthew* (London: SPCK, 1983), pp. 129-55; S.H. Brooks, *Matthew's Community: The Evidence of his Special Sayings Material* (JSNTSup, 16; Sheffield: JSOT Press, 1987), especially Introduction and ch. 7; J.A. Overman, *Matthew's Gospel and Formative Judaism: The Social World of the Matthean Community* (Minneapolis, MN: Fortress Press,

the most distinctive characteristics which are apparently shown by the Gospel and/or attested by the majority of modern scholars, and will assume them in the subsequent study.[11]

1. The community was constituted primarily of Jewish Christians but not excluding Gentile converts.[12]

2. Its language was Greek, but its majority (i.e. the Jews) probably understood Hebrew/Aramaic as well.

3. The community was living in the transition period—'late enough for there to be clear distinction and indeed hostility between the Jewish Christian community and unbelieving Judaism, but early enough for the relation between the two communities to be still a live issue'.[13]

4. As Stanton insightfully proposes, though without wide recognition yet, the community was composed of a number of local house groups in and around a city; these groups probably showed some distinctive tendencies of their own as well as the commonalty.[14]

5. The community was struggling mainly against two tendencies

1990); Balch (ed.), *Community*; Stanton, 'Synagogue', pp. 113-281; A.J. Saldarini, *Matthew's Christian-Jewish Community* (Chicago: University of Chicago Press, 1994).

11. It may be important, at this stage, to point out the inevitable circularity (or interdependence) between my working assumptions and the subsequent investigation. On the one hand, my working assumptions by and large depend on the available data most of which are inevitably based on the Gospel materials which I am going to investigate; on the other hand, the assumptions are to be reflected in my subsequent investigation. But certain assumptions must be made, however tentatively; provided that they are used judiciously, this is a proper procedure. For the inevitable circularity of this kind of study and the danger arising out of such a circularity, see France, *Evangelist*, pp. 81-82; Hagner, *Matthew 1–13*, p. xli.

12. Stanton, 'Synagogue', pp. 113-45, presents the four major views on the components of the Matthew's community—(i) pre-70 Jews; (ii) post-70 Jews who were still in Judaism; (iii) post-70 Jews shortly after the parting of the ways and some Gentiles; (iv) Gentiles. Stanton himself supports the third view, and I also adopt it but not necessarily excluding a pre-70 setting. Cf. K. Stendahl, *The School of St Matthew, and its Use of the Old Testament* (ASNU, 20; Lund: Gleerup, 2nd edn, 1968), pp. xiii-xiv.

13. France, *Evangelist*, p. 108; cf. Stanton, 'Synagogue', pp. 124-31; R.H. Gundry, 'A Responsive Evaluation of the Social History of the Matthean Community in Roman Syria', in Balch (ed.), *Community*, pp. 62-67.

14. Stanton, 'Redaction', pp. 50-51.

within and outside the community: within it an antinomian tendency[15] and a Pharisaic influence among others, and outside it 'official Judaism' or 'Pharisaism'.[16] Since these final points are more directly related to this study, I will discuss them a little further in section 2.

d. *Literary Structure of the Gospel*

The structure of Matthew's Gospel has been a centre of controversy and debate for a very long time. In spite of the enormous amount of literature produced on this issue, however, there is no consensus whatsoever on the structure of the Gospel except the general agreement that it is carefully planned and well arranged.[17] Once again, it is beyond the limits of this study to discuss the issue properly, and, therefore, I here present some basic guidelines and my own proposal which is assumed in the subsequent study.

1. There is a definite structural and theological significance of geography in Matthew's Gospel.[18]

2. There is a deliberate constructive relationship between narratives and discourses which is strongly indicated by the five-fold formula καὶ ἐγένετο ὅτε ἐτέλεσεν ὁ Ἰησοῦς... (cf. 7.28; 11.1; 13.53; 19.1; 26.1).[19]

---

15. I am rather reluctant to define it as a definite group. G. Barth's argument for the antinomians (or 'libertines' in his term) as a distinctive opposing group on the basis of Mt. 5.17ff.; 7.15ff.; and 24.11ff. seems to me somewhat forced; cf. G. Barth, 'Matthew's Understanding of the Law', in G. Bornkamm, G. Barth, and H.J. Held, *Tradition and Interpretation in Matthew* (trans. P. Scott; London: SCM Press, 1963), pp. 159-64; cf. also B.W. Bacon, *Studies in Matthew* (London: Constable, 1930), p. 348; R. Hummel, *Die Auseinandersetzung zwischen Kirche und Judentum in Matthäusevangelium* (BEvT, 33; Munich: Chr. Kaiser Verlag, 2nd edn, 1966), p. 165; for more scholars adopting Barth's view, see Stanton, 'Origin', p. 1909 n. 33. For a brief criticism of the view, see Stanton, 'Communities', pp. 387-88.

16. G.N. Stanton, 'The Gospel of Matthew and Judaism', in *idem, People*, pp. 146-68.

17. For a thorough and careful analysis and grouping of various structural approaches, see D.R. Bauer, *The Structure of Matthew's Gospel* (JSNTSup, 31; Sheffield: JSOT Press, 1988), pp. 11-13 and 21-55; for briefer surveys, see Stanton, 'Origin', pp. 1903-1906; France, *Evangelist*, pp. 141-53.

18. Bauer, *Structure*, pp. 22-26, esp. p. 26.

19. Bauer, *Structure*, pp. 27-35; France, *Evangelist*, pp. 142-45; cf. Bacon,

3. The formula ἀπὸ τότε ἤρξατο ὁ Ἰησοῦς at 4.17 and 16.21
    seems to introduce a new phase of the gospel story, but with-
    out interrupting the flow of the immediate narrative.[20]

4. Matthew conceives of the time of Jesus as extending from his
    birth to his parousia.[21]

5. There are certain implications of Matthew's structure for his
    theology, especially in terms of a Christology which presents
    Jesus as the messiah who fulfilled the Old Testament and there-
    fore became the turning point in salvation history.[22]

6. Matthew's Gospel is a coherent narrative and has a plot and
    possibly some subplots.[23] For example, a plot (or dramatic
    flow) of the Gospel story is well manifested by the time line in
    the story. Matthew begins his story with the birth of Jesus,
    which has fulfilled the predictions of the Old Testament, and
    the preparation of John the Baptist who has fulfilled the
    prophecy about Elijah (1.1–4.16). Then he presents the ministry
    of Jesus in words and deeds in Galilee which has fulfilled the

---

Studies. For a list of successors to Bacon's structural approach up to 1972, see J.D. Kingsbury, *Matthew: Structure, Christology, Kingdom* (Philadelphia: Fortress Press, 1975), p. 3 n. 13.

20. Kingsbury, *Structure*, pp. 1-37; *idem, Matthew as Story* (Philadelphia: Fortress Press, 2nd edn, 1988), pp. 2-9, 40-93. For the list of those who adopt this scheme, see Bauer, *Structure*, p. 153 n. 37. Cf. N.B. Stonehouse, *The Witness of Matthew and Mark to Christ* (London: Tyndale Press, 1944), pp. 129-31; E. Krentz, 'The Extent of Matthew's Prologue', *JBL* 83 (1964), pp. 409-14.

21. Kingsbury, *Structure*, p. 31. For the time span reflected in Matthew's struc-ture, see F.J. Matera, 'The Plot of Matthew's Gospel', *CBQ* 49 (1987), pp. 240-43.

22. Bauer, *Structure*, pp. 142-48. However, Stanton's caution in his 'Redaction', pp. 44-45 invites our careful attention—'if we assume that Matthew is primarily a theologian, more questions than answers quickly emerge, for the evangelist does not reshape his sources in the light of a carefully thought-out coherent theology: his gifts and concerns are primarily catechetical and pastoral'.

23. For example, M.A. Powell, 'The Plot and Subplots of Matthew's Gospel', *NTS* 38 (1992), pp. 193-204, suggests a plot which concerns God's saving activity through Jesus and Satan's challenge and two subplots concerning the conflict between Jesus and the religious leaders and the relationship between Jesus and his disciples. For some other suggestions about the plot of the Gospel, see R.A. Edwards, *Matthew's Story of Jesus* (Philadelphia: Fortress Press, 1985); Matera, 'Plot', pp. 233-53; Kingsbury, *Story*; D.B. Howell, *Matthew's Inclusive Story: A Study in the Narrative Rhetoric of the First Gospel* (JSNTSup, 42; Sheffield: JSOT Press, 1990), pp. 93-160; cf. Powell, 'Plot', pp. 187-98.

Old Testament and inaugurated the kingdom of heaven (4.17–
16.20). Finally, Matthew completes his story of Jesus by presenting his movements towards Jerusalem and his suffering,
death, and resurrection, which have fulfilled the will of God,
revealed in the whole Old Testament, and have brought the
kingdom of heaven to Gentiles as well as to Jews (16.21–
28.20).[24] This plot seems to be intensified by the geographical
movements from Bethlehem via Egypt to Nazareth and from
Galilee to Jerusalem which are well indicated by the two turning point formulae at 4.17 and 16.20. Once we accept this plot,
it will follow that a number of literary devices, including the
five-fold formula, the great discourses, the chiasm and the
inclusios among many others[25] as well as the two-fold formula
at 4.17 and 16.20, were used as signalling the development of
the plot of the Gospel. Following R.T. France's conclusion,
'Matthew's account of Jesus is not a static and symmetrical
structure, but a powerful drama with a dynamic force of its
own'.[26]

2. *Jesus and the Law in Matthew's Gospel*

In view of the fact that the sabbath debates in Mt. 12.1-14 appear to be
closely related to Matthew's overall understanding of the law in relation
to Jesus, we need first to consider this overall understanding in his
Gospel before going on to investigate Jesus' attitude to the sabbath as
revealed in Mt. 12.1-14 and 24.20.

a. *Matthew 5.17-20—The Key Text*
The programmatic pericope Mt. 5.17-20 is undoubtedly of crucial
importance for the understanding of the law in Matthew's Gospel. This

24. Matera, 'Plot', p. 241, points out that though the story of Jesus begins with
the birth of Jesus and concludes with a resurrection appearance, a closer examination
shows that Matthew prefaces Jesus' birth with a genealogy (1.1-17) which extends
back to Abraham and that the climax points to the close of the ages (28.20). 'Therefore...it [Matthew's story] encompasses a broader perspective, the time between
Abraham and the parousia. The plot of Matthew's Gospel has something to do with
salvation history.'

25. For the various literary devices used by Matthew, see Bauer, *Structure*,
chs. 3-7.

26. *Evangelist*, p. 153.

pericope, however, poses some of the most perplexing exegetical problems in the Gospel, and numerous treatments of and views about it have been presented in detail.[27] Since the pericope itself is not our prime concern here, I shall merely present briefly some outstanding views regarding certain key issues which are most relevant to this study and then state my own views.[28]

None of the verses in the pericope has any synoptic parallel, except for a partial parallel to 5.18,[29] and there is no scholarly consensus regarding the tradition history lying behind the pericope.[30] In such an unsettled situation, it seems preferable to focus our attention primarily on the pericope as it stands and treat it 'as interpreted tradition', as R. Mohrlang suggests, 'reflecting in its entirety the writer's own understanding and viewpoint'.[31] The pericope no doubt reflects the setting of the Matthean community. There is, however, no inevitable conflict between this hypothesis and the proposal that the origin of this pericope

27. E.g. H. Ljungmann, *Das Gesetz erfüllen: Matth. 5,17ff. und 3,15 untersucht* (Lunds Universitets Årsskrift. NF, 50/6; Lund: Gleerup, 1954), pp. 7-96; W. Trilling, *Das wahre Israel: Studien zur Theologie des Matthäus-evangeliums* (Munich: Kösel-Verlag, 3rd edn, 1964), pp. 167-86; R.S. McConnell, 'Law and Prophecy in Matthew's Gospel: The Authority and Use of the Old Testament in the Gospel of St Matthew' (ThD dissertation; Basel: Friedrich Reinhardt Kommissionsverlag, 1969), pp. 6-58; H. Hübner, *Das Gesetz in der synoptischen Tradition: Studien zur These einer progressiven Qumranisierung und Judaisierung innerhalb der synoptischen Tradition* (Witten: Luther Verlag, 1973), pp. 15-39; R. Banks, *Jesus and the Law in the Synoptic Tradition* (SNTSMS, 28; Cambridge: Cambridge University Press, 1975), pp. 204-26; J.P. Meier, *Law and History in Matthew's Gospel: A Redactional Study of Mt. 5:17-48* (AnBib, 71; Rome: Biblical Institute Press, 1976), pp. 41-124; U. Luz, 'Die Erfüllung des Gesetzes bei Matthäus', *ZTK* 75 (1978), pp. 398-435; I. Broer, *Freiheit vom Gesetz und Radikalisierung des Gesetzes* (SBS, 98; Stuttgart: Verlag Katholisches Bibelwerk, 1980), pp. 9-74; and the appropriate portions of some recent major commentaries on Matthew and on the Sermon on the Mount.

28. For more detailed arguments for my own views, see my unpublished, 'Jesus, Fulfilment and Law in Matthew 5.17-20: A Discussion Focusing on the Eschatological Dimension' (MA dissertation; London Bible College [CNAA], 1992), pp. 23ff.

29. Lk. 16.17; cf. Mk 13.31.

30. A brief list of scholars who present different proposals is found in R. Mohrlang, *Matthew and Paul: A Comparison of Ethical Perspectives* (SNTSMS, 48; Cambridge: Cambridge University Press, 1984), p. 137 n. 17; cf. K.R. Snodgrass, 'Matthew's Understanding of the Law', *Int* 46 (1992), p. 372.

31. *Matthew*, pp. 8-9.

goes back to the pre-Matthean tradition or even to Jesus himself.[32]

i. *Mt. 5.17—Jesus, the fulfiller of the Old Testament.* The introductory formula μὴ νομίσητε may imply the existence of a misunderstanding probably caused either by an antinomian tendency within the Christian community or by Jewish accusers outside it (or by both of them),[33] though it appears clear that the main emphasis of this verse as a whole lies on the positive aspect of it in its latter half.

In the Gospels the term ἦλθον is frequently used to describe 'the mission of the eschatological figure whose action will bring about the startling denouement of salvation-history';[34] and the same may be true in 5.17.

'The Law and/or the Prophets' (τὸν νόμον ἢ τοὺς προφήτας) was a traditional Jewish phrase referring to the entire Old Testament (cf. 2 Macc. 15.9; *4 Macc.* 18.10; Acts 24.14; Rom. 3.21; etc.). In 11.13 Matthew repeats the phrase (in reverse order) with the verb προφητεύειν, which implies that the law as well as the prophets have a prophetic function, pointing forward to 'what Jesus has now brought into being'.[35]

---

32. We may suppose that these sayings were preserved by Matthew or the Matthean community because of their immediate relevance to the setting of the community. A number of recent scholars tend to assign the roots of this pericope, except probably v. 20 (cf., however, H.-T. Wrege, *Die Überlieferungs-geschichte der Bergpredigt* [WUNT, 9; Tübingen: Mohr, 1968], pp. 42-44), to the pre-Matthean tradition; cf. Meier, *Law*, pp. 41-124; R.A. Guelich, *Sermon on the Mount* (Waco, TX: Word Books, 1982), pp. 134-74, esp. pp. 135-36 and 161-72; Hagner, *Matthew 1–13*, p. 104. The comment of D.A. Carson, 'Matthew', in F.E. Gaebelein (ed.), *The Expositor's Bible Commentary*, VIII (12 vols.; Grand Rapids: Zondervan, 1984), p. 141, is worth noting here: 'it must be remembered that Matthew presents these sayings as the teaching of the historical Jesus, not the creation of the church; and we detect no implausibility in his claim'; cf. also D.J. Moo, 'Jesus and the Authority of the Mosaic Law', *JSNT* 20 (1984), p. 29; for a different view, however, cf. U. Luz, *Matthew 1–7* (trans. W.C. Linss; Edinburgh: T. & T. Clark, 1990), pp. 257-59.

33. H.D. Betz, *Essays on the Sermon on the Mount* (Philadelphia: Fortress Press, 1985), p. 40; M.D. Goulder, *Midrash and Lection in Matthew* (London: SPCK, 1974), p. 284; Davies and Allison, *Matthew*, I, pp. 483, 501 n. 54; *et al.*

34. Meier, *Law*, pp. 66-69; quotation from p. 69. Cf. Trilling, *Israel*, pp. 171-72; Banks, *Jesus*, p. 205; Luz, *Matthew 1–7*, p. 265; *et al.*

35. R.T. France, *The Gospel according to Matthew: An Introduction and Commentary* (TNTC; Leicester: IVP, 1985), p. 114.

The crux of v. 17 (and probably of our whole pericope) is undoubtedly the word πληῶσαι. However, interpretation of this word is notoriously difficult, and there are considerable divergences of interpretation. The following are the main ones:

1. To set out the true meaning, spirit, intention or basic principles of the law through Jesus' teaching about the law.[36]

2. To do, obey or carry out the demands of the law, or to realize what is said through doing.[37]

3   To confirm, establish or affirm the lasting validity of the law.[38]

4. 'To fill up' and therefore to complete or fulfil the ultimate goal of the Old Testament.[39]

36.   A widespread interpretation supported by numerous scholars, for example, A. Plummer, *An Exegetical Commentary on the Gospel according to S. Matthew* (London: Robert Scott, 1909); A.H. M'Neile, *The Gospel according to St Matthew: The Greek Text with Introduction, Notes, and Indices* (London: Macmillan, 1915), p. 58; E. Klostermann, *Das Matthäusevangelium* (HNT, 4; Tübingen: Mohr, 2nd edn, 1927), pp. 40-41; M. Dibelius, 'Die Bergpredigt' (1937, 1940), in *Botschaft und Geschichte* (Tübingen: Mohr, 1953), p. 125; M.-J. Lagrange, *Evangile selon Saint Matthieu* (Paris: Gabalda, 7th edn, 1948), pp. 93-94; J.C. Fenton, *The Gospel of St Matthew* (Pelican Gospel Commentaries; London: Penguin Books, 1963), p. 84; H.B. Green, *The Gospel according to Matthew* (New Clarendon Bible; Oxford: Oxford University Press, 1975), pp. 36, 65; J. Lambrecht, *The Sermon on the Mount: Proclamation and Exhortation* (GNS, 14; Wilmington, DE: Michael Glazier, 1985), p. 84; similarly Hagner, *Matthew 1-13*, pp. 105-106.

37.   This interpretation was proposed by T. Zahn, *Das Evangelium des Matthäus* (Leipzig: Deicher, 1903), pp. 210-13, and has been followed by a group of commentators, for example, A. Schlatter, *Der Evangelist Matthäus: Seine Sprache, sein Ziel, Seine Selbständigkeit* (Stuttgart: Calwer Verlag, 1959), pp. 153-54; J. Schniewind, *Das Evangelium nach Matthäus* (NTD, 2; Göttingen: Vandenhoeck & Ruprecht, 12th edn, 1968), pp. 54ff; Luz, *Matthew 1-7*, pp. 264-65.

38.   This interpretation, which is based on the assumption that the verb reflects the Aramaic term קום, has a long history and is supported by a number of scholars, for example, G. Dalman, *Jesus-Jeshua: Studies in the Gospels* (trans. P.L. Levertoff; London: SPCK, 1929), pp. 57-61; B.H. Branscomb, *Jesus and the Law of Moses* (London: Hodder & Stoughton, 1930), pp. 226-28; D. Daube, *The New Testament and Rabbinic Judaism* (London: Athlone Press, 1956), pp. 60-61; D. Hill, *The Gospel of Matthew* (NCB; London: Marshall, Morgan & Scott, 1972), p. 117; D.A.R. Hare, *Matthew* (Interpretation; Louisville, KY: John Knox Press, 1993), p. 47; *et al.* Cf. also D. Wenham, 'Jesus and the Law: an Exegesis on Matthew 5:17-20', *Themelios* 4 (1979), pp. 92-96.

39.   This interpretation is most comprehensively presented by Meier, *Law*, pp. 41-124 (esp. pp. 73-82), pp. 160-61; see also his commentary, *Matthew* (Dublin:

It is, of course, doubtful whether any single interpretation can do full justice to the word πληρῶσαι here, but, in my judgment, the last option seems to point in the right direction for the following reasons:[40] (i) In the LXX πληρῶσαι consistently translates מלא, which has a normal meaning of 'fill up' (to the top), 'fulfil' (the ultimate goal), or 'complete'.[41] (ii) Every other use of the term in Matthew's Gospel is directly[42] or indirectly[43] related to the fulfilment of Scripture, so that πληρῶσαι here should probably also be understood in the same way, that is, 'to fulfil' the Scriptures. (iii) The presence of τοὺς προφήτας as a direct object of πληρῶσαι further supports our option. (iv) As R.A. Guelich properly points out, in Jer. 31.31-34 the 'new covenant' with 'the law written on the heart' (or the 'Zion-Torah' in Guelich's term) is promised over against the 'old covenant' with 'the law written on the tablets of stone' (or the 'Sinai-Torah' in his term);[44] Mt. 5.17 can then be understood as saying that the promise of this 'Zion-Torah' to which the 'Sinai-Torah' pointed forward is fulfilled in Jesus' coming.[45] (v) If Matthew's plot, as I have presupposed, is focused on Jesus as the messiah who fulfilled the will of God revealed in the Old Testament and inaugurated the new age with himself being the turning point of salvation history, it would be most natural to suggest that Matthew's concern here is to present Jesus

Veritas, 1980), pp. 46-48. It is also followed by (with, of course, various modifications) Banks, *Jesus*, pp. 203-26, 229-35; Guelich, *Sermon*, pp. 134-74; Moo, 'Jesus', pp. 3-49; Carson, 'Matthew', pp. 141-47; France, *Matthew*, pp. 113-17; *idem*, *Evangelist*, pp. 191-97; cf. Hagner, *Matthew 1–13*, p. 105. This view, however, was already conceived by C.F.D. Moule, 'Fulfilment-Words in the New Testament: Use and Abuse', *NTS* 14 (1967/68), pp. 293-320; J. Jeremias, *New Testament Theology. I. The Proclamation of Jesus* (trans. J.S. Bowden; London: SCM Press, 1971), pp. 82-85.

40.   For criticism of the other alternatives, see my 'Jesus, Fulfilment and Law', pp. 27-29; cf. McConnell, 'Law', pp. 14-19; Banks, *Jesus*, p. 208; Davies and Allison, *Matthew*, I, pp. 485-86 nn. 8-11, 13-15.

41.   For a full discussion of passages in ancient literature which are relevant to the issue, see Moule, 'Fulfilment-Words', pp. 302-12. Cf. *Pseudo-Clementine Recognitions* 1.39.1; *b. Šab.* 116b.

42.   Twelve out of sixteen Matthean occurrences: 1.22; 2.15, 17, 23; 4.14; 8.17; 12.17; 13.35; 21.4; 26.54, 56; 27.9; cf. Meier, *Law*, p. 80.

43.   13.48; 23.23; and also 3.15 as Meier, *Law*, pp. 76-79, convincingly argues.

44.   Cf. Ezek. 36.25-27; Isa. 2.2-5; 56.1; Mic. 4.1-5; cf. also 2 Cor. 3.3.

45.   Guelich, *Sermon*, p. 140; he owes this insight to H. Gese, 'Das Gesetz', in *Zur biblischen Theologie* (Münich: Kaiser, 1977), pp. 56-84. Cf. Moule, 'Fulfilment-Words', p. 317.

as the messiah who fulfilled the whole of the Scriptures, the law as well as the prophets, as they pointed forward to his person, teachings and actions.

The question of the law in Matthew, then, is 'a question of salvation-history, prophetic fulfilment...eschatology, and high Christology'. For Matthew, Jesus takes the place of the law as 'the center of the Christian's attention, devotion, and obedience'.[46] As R. Banks points out, 'it is not so much *Jesus'* stance towards the Law that he is concerned to depict: it is how the *Law* stands with regard to him, as the one who brings it to fulfilment and to whom all attention must now be directed'.[47] This is not to deny, however, that the normative character of the law still remains in view in the pericope (cf. vv. 18, 19); but even that character is set 'within the broader understanding of Jesus' eschatological coming as the Bringer of the age of salvation to fulfil the Scriptures'.[48] One may suggest, then, that the word πληρῶσαι in v. 17 includes the element of 'continuity' in the sense that Jesus and especially his teaching which fulfils the law are still something to which the law itself pointed forward, as well as the element of 'discontinuity' in the sense that Jesus and his teaching which fulfils the law now transcend the law.[49] This suggestion seems to fit best the plot of the Gospel, the use of ἦλθον in terms of the eschatological mission and the phrase τὸν νόμον ἢ τοὺς προφήτας which shows the prophetic role of the law, and it also makes good sense of the antithesis with καταλῦσαι ('to abolish'); in the subsequent sections we will see that this suggestion best explains the problems raised by the following verses (vv. 18-48) and other law-passages in Matthew.

ii. *Mt. 5.18—The continuing validity of the law.* This verse has a parallel in some of its content in Lk. 16.17 but not in its setting and format; it

46.   Meier, *Law*, pp. 88-89.
47.   *Jesus*, p. 226.
48.   Guelich, *Sermon*, p. 142.
49.   Banks, *Jesus*, p. 210; cf. France, *Evangelist*, p. 196—France suggests a distinction between the 'authority' and the 'function' of the law, and asserts that, though the law continues to have its 'authority' as the revelation of God even after Jesus' coming as messiah, its 'function' has been changed by Jesus' fulfilment. Cf. also Meier, *Law*, p. 87. A brief but interesting observation of the tension between continuity and discontinuity with regard to Scripture (Torah) in Luke's Gospel is found in J.B. Tyson, 'Scripture, Torah, and Sabbath in Luke–Acts', in E.P. Sanders (ed.), *Jesus, the Gospel, and the Church* (Macon, GA: Mercer University Press, 1987), pp. 89-104, esp. pp. 103-104.

does not therefore seem proper to depend too much on the relationship between the two verses in my exegesis of Mt. 5.18.[50]

The referent of τοῦ νόμου seems to be primarily the Mosaic law.[51] Matthew's concern now moves from the whole Scriptures to the law in particular, and this focus is maintained in the following verses (cf. vv. 19 and 21-48). The force of ἰῶτα ἓν ἢ μία κεραία is to emphasize the quantitative wholeness of the law which extends even to the smallest detail. The clause ἰῶτα ἓν ἢ μία κεραία οὐ μὴ παρέλθῃ ἀπὸ τοῦ νόμου as a whole, then, emphatically confirms the indestructible total validity of the law. This emphatic confirmation, however, is qualified by the two ἕως clauses which precede and follow the central clause.

Though the expression ἕως ἂν παρέλθῃ ὁ οὐρανὸς καὶ ἡ γῆ can, by itself, either be a popular hyperbole signifying 'never'[52] or point to the specific time limit,[53] in my judgment, the former seems to be the better option for the present cotext.[54] If this is the case, the whole sentence runs thus: 'The law can *never* pass away even in its smallest detail, ἕως ἂν πάντα γένηται'.

This second qualifying clause, however, poses at least two co-related

50.   For the main discussions on the source and redaction of this verse, see Hübner, *Gesetz*, pp. 15-22; Meier, *Law*, pp. 46-65; among many others.

51.   A. Sand, *Das Gesetz und die Propheten: Untersuchungen zur Theologie des Evangeliums nach Matthäus* (Biblische Untersuchungen, 11; Regensburg: Verlag Friedrich Pustet, 1974), pp. 33-36; Banks, *Jesus*, pp. 214-15; W.H. Gutbrod, 'νόμος', *TDNT*, IV, p. 1059. For the various views on the referent of νόμος, see Banks, *Jesus*, p. 214 n. 2.

52.   W.C. Allen, *A Critical and Exegetical Commentary on the Gospel according to Saint Matthew* (ICC; Edinburgh: T. & T. Clark, 3rd edn, 1912), p. 46; Klostermann, *Matthäusevangelium*, p. 41; for a further list of scholars who understand the phrase here according to this hyperbolic sense, see Meier, *Law*, pp. 49-50 n. 27; more recently, France, *Matthew*, p. 115; Luz, *Matthew 1-7*, pp. 265-66. Cf. Philo, *Vit. Mos.* 2.136.

53.   F.V. Filson, *A Commentary on the Gospel according to St Matthew* (BNTC; London: A. & C. Black, 1960), p. 83; W.D. Davies, 'Matthew 5.17, 18', in *idem, Christian Origins and Judaism* (London: Darton, Longman & Todd, 1962), pp. 60-65; H. Traub, 'οὐρανός', *TDNT*, V, pp. 515-16; Guelich, *Sermon*, p. 144; *et al.* Cf. Mt. 24.35 par., in which Jesus predicts the passing away of 'heaven and earth'.

54.   Even if we take the second option, however, this clause by itself does not seem to clarify the time limit exactly, and it must be further qualified by the second ἕως clause.

problems: first, the meaning of the verb γίνεσθαι; second, the referent of πάντα.[55]

In Matthew's Gospel the verb γίνεσθαι is used frequently in the sense of 'to happen', 'to take place' or 'to come to pass', and in my judgment this should be the meaning here.[56]

As regards the referent of πάντα, there are a few options: (1) The demands of the law.[57] (2) Event(s) which are to come to pass—the event denoted by πάντα being variously identified as: a) the end of this age;[58] b) the death and/or resurrection of Christ;[59] c) Jesus' entire career.[60] Of these four options, the last one seems to point in the right direction mainly for the following reasons:[61] i) it fits best the plot of Matthew's Gospel, which is focused on Jesus who fulfilled 'the will of God' revealed in the whole Scriptures and inaugurated the New Age (cf. option 2a), through his teaching (cf. option 1) and mighty acts as well as his death and resurrection (cf. option 2b), that is, through his entire career; ii) it also fits well into its immediate co-text—first, it fits v. 17, since the whole Scriptures are fulfilled by the events of Jesus' entire career that have come to pass; second, it fits v. 18c (i.e. the main clause), since fulfilling the Scriptures includes Jesus' fulfilment of the law in his person and acts (for the prophetic aspect of the law; cf. 11.13) as well as

55. Its relation to the first ἕως clause would be another problem, if the latter option is taken just above.

56. Meier, *Law*, pp. 53-54, 61-62; Davies and Allison, *Matthew*, I, p. 494; *et al.* Luz's alternative suggestion that γίνεσθαι here means 'to be done' is not convincing; see his *Matthew 1–7*, p. 266—for a brief criticism of this view, see my 'Jesus, Fulfilment and Law', p. 36.

57. Ljungman, *Gesetz*, pp. 45, 47; E. Schweizer, 'Noch Einmal Mt 5,17-20', in *idem*, *Matthäus und seine Gemeinde* (SBS, 71; Stuttgart: Katholisches Bibelwerk, 1974), pp. 82-84; Banks, *Jesus*, p. 217.

58. T.W. Manson, *The Sayings of Jesus* (London: SCM Press, 1949), p. 154; Sand, *Gesetz*, p. 38.

59. Davies, 'Matthew 5:17, 18', pp. 60-65, esp. p. 65—Jesus' death; R.G. Hamerton-Kelly, 'Attitudes to the Law in Matthew's Gospel: a Discussion of Matthew 5.18', *Biblical Research* 17 (1972), p. 30—Jesus' resurrection.

60. Meier, *Law*, pp. 60-64. Guelich, *Sermon*, p. 148, argues for a rather indefinite reference of πάντα here, on the ground of 'the general statement about Jesus' role as the fulfilment of Scripture in 5.17'. Cf. also Moo, 'Jesus', p. 27: he suggests a more inclusive referent, i.e. 'all predicted events, the "whole divine purpose"' (by quoting Plummer, *Matthew*, p. 76), on the basis of a consideration of Mt. 24.34-35.

61. For criticism of other options, see Guelich, *Sermon*, pp. 145-48.

his teaching (for the normative aspect of the law; cf. 5.19, 21-48).[62] In spite of all these strengths, however, this option has a crucial weakness. As I suggested above, Matthew's structure strongly implies that he conceives of the time span of Jesus as extending from his birth to his parousia, not just to his resurrection. If this is the case, we cannot restrict the referent of πάντα only to his first coming but should extend it to his second coming. Then we may cautiously conclude that the time limit of this clause includes not only the 'already' dimension which has been fulfilled in Jesus' first coming but also the 'not yet' dimension which is to be consummated in his second coming.[63] This conclusion partly explains the seemingly unresolved tension between the continuity and discontinuity of the law in the light of Jesus' fulfilment.

According to v. 18, then, for Matthew the law has its validity for a limited period of salvation-history, the end of which has already been inaugurated by Jesus' first eschatological coming; but Matthew is still looking forward to its consummation in his second coming.

iii. *Mt. 5.19—Setting aside/doing the commandments.* This verse is linked with v. 18 by the conjunction οὖν which is almost certainly inferential and links this verse logically to the thought of v. 18.[64]

The verb λύειν seems to mean 'to set aside' an individual commandment rather than 'to disobey' it in view of its cognate verb καταλύειν

---

62.   Even if we take the first ἕως clause as pointing to a specific point of time, this option seems to offer the best explanation of the relation of the second clause to the first one, in that the second clarifies the first by introducing the new idea which is absent from the first, i.e. the explicit eschatological time limit focusing on Jesus Messiah. The second clause is thus neither merely synonymous nor tautologous to the first; it is rather a necessary qualification of the first from the perspective of Matthew's understanding of salvation-history, because the first clause alone, according to current Judaism, could be understood in various ways. Cf. Moo, 'Jesus', p. 27.

63.   The 'not yet' dimension of the time limit, which is to be related to the time factors of the kingdom of God, is indicated in such language as κληθήσεται ἐν τῇ βασιλείᾳ τῶν οὐρανῶν in v. 19 or εἰσέλθητε εἰς τὴν βασιλείαν τῶν οὐρανῶν in v. 20. For comprehensive discussions of the tension between 'already' and 'not yet' dimensions of the kingdom of God and its relation to Jesus' fulfilment as revealed especially in the teaching of Jesus, see, among many others, N. Perrin, *The Kingdom of God in the Teaching of Jesus* (London: SCM Press, 1963), pp. 74-78, 83-89; G.E. Ladd, *The Presence of the Future: The Eschatology of Biblical Realism* (Grand Rapids: Eerdmans, 1974), pp. 45-217, 307-28.

64.   Banks, *Jesus*, p. 20. For a different view, however, see Meier, *Law*, pp. 89—he sees οὖν here as a transitional conjunction.

in v. 17 which clearly means 'to abolish' the whole law.[65]

The key to the interpretation of the verse seems to lie in the phrase τῶν ἐντολῶν τούτων. As regards the referent of this phrase, we have two main options: (1) 'Jesus' commands' or, more definitely, 'the antitheses' in vv. 21-48.[66] (2) 'The Torah' mentioned in v. 18.[67] Considering the general usage of ἐντολή and οὗτος in Matthew,[68] however, it seems almost certain that the phrase τῶν ἐντολῶν τούτων refers back to νόμος in v. 18 (i.e. option 2).[69] Here we may need to identify the character of τῶν ἐντολῶν τούτων more exactly. If my exegesis of v. 18 is correct, in the salvation-history time line the referent of the commandments of v. 19 belongs to the post-fulfilment period,[70] whereas the referent of the law in vv. 17, 18 evidently belongs to the pre-fulfilment period. It seems quite significant here to note the change of the term νόμος in vv. 17, 18 into ἐντολαί in v. 19, which Matthew may have adopted purposively in order to imply such a change of referent.[71] The

---

65. F. Büchsel, 'λύω', *TDNT*, IV, p. 336; K. Kertelge, 'λύω', *EDNT*, II, pp. 368-69. For a different view, however, see Meier, *Law*, p. 89.

66. Banks, *Jesus*, pp. 221-23; E. Schweizer, *The Good News according to Matthew* (trans. D.E. Green; London: SPCK, 1976), pp. 108-109; for the latter view, see C. Carlston, 'The Things that Defile', *NTS* 15 (1968/69), p. 79. Cf. E. Lohmeyer, *Das Evangelium des Matthäus* (ed. W. Schmauch; Kritisch-exegetischer Kommentar über das Neue Testament, 1; Göttingen: Vandenhoeck & Ruprecht, 1956), pp. 111-12.

67. Ljungman, *Gesetz*, pp. 48-55; Meier, *Law*, p. 91. Cf. G. Schrenk, 'ἐντολή', *TDNT*, II, p. 548—Schrenk and some others identify the referent of this phrase as 'the Decalogue', partly on the basis of their understanding of ἐλάχιστος as 'briefest' or 'shortest'; for scholars supporting this view, see Schrenk, 'ἐντολή', p. 548 n. 8. But this suggestion is 'alien to the concerns of the context'; Carson, 'Matthew', p. 146.

68. All the other examples of ἐντολή in Matthew (15.3; 19.17; 22.36, 38, 40) explicitly refer to specific Old Testament commandments; and Moo, 'Jesus', p. 48 n. 197, points out that in Matthew οὗτος is never used prospectively.

69. Banks, *Jesus*, p. 222, finds the antecedent of τῶν ἐντολῶν τούτων in the nearest noun πάντα in v. 18d, which according to his interpretation of the clause refers to Jesus' teaching; cf. Banks, *Jesus*, p. 217. But, since his interpretation of v. 18d is not very persuasive, his suggestion here is not very convincing either.

70. Note that the event of v. 18d (i.e. the second ἕως clause) had already been happening at the point of time of v. 19.

71. It seems, of course, quite true that the change of the term here is mainly because of the change of the object to whom the law/commandments are related, that is, Jesus in vv. 17, 18 and the disciples in v. 19; however, this observation does not

phrase τῶν ἐντολῶν τούτων then refers not to simply 'the νόμος as it was'[72] but rather 'the νόμος as fulfilled'—'the *new* νόμος' which the *old* νόμος pointed forward to; 'the *messianic* νόμος'[73] which now has been fulfilled (or completed) by Jesus' eschatological first coming, and which is still expected to be kept by Jesus' disciples until its consummation by his *parousia*.[74] That is why it is extremely important for the disciples to keep every (even the smallest or most insignificant—cf. μίαν...τῶν ἐλαχίστων) precept of the Torah not only in the light of Jesus' first coming (cf. 5.21-48; 7.12; 11.28-30; 15.19-20; 19.7-9; 22.36-40) but also with the prospect of his second coming (cf. 5.29-30; 18.4, 8-9; 28.20; cf. also 19.17). Matthew then naturally turns his attention to the future aspect of the kingdom of heaven and the status of disciples in it in relation to their attitude and obedience to the law in the following apodoses (ἐλαχίστος/μέγας κληθήσεται ἐν τῇ βασιλείᾳ τῶν οὐρανῶν).

conflict with my suggestion, but rather it may further show why the referent of νόμος/ἐντολαί must be changed.

72.   The referent of νόμος in vv. 17, 18 which belongs to the pre-fulfilment period.

73.   Cf. B. Gerhardsson, *Memory and Manuscript: Oral Tradition and Written Transmission in Rabbinic Judaism and Early Christianity* (trans. E.J. Sharpe; ASNU, 22; Lund: Gleerup, 2nd edn, 1964), p. 327; W.D. Davies, *The Setting of the Sermon on the Mount* (Cambridge: Cambridge University Press, 1964), pp. 94-108; D.C. Allison, *The New Moses: A Matthean Typology* (Edinburgh: T. & T. Clark, 1993), pp. 185-90. Cf. also Guelich, *Sermon*, p. 155; Moo, 'Jesus', p. 28. *Pace* Barth, 'Law', pp. 153-59. On a quite opposite ground from Barth, Banks, *Jesus*, pp. 229-34, is sceptical about the notion of 'new/messianic law'; his scepticism, however, is largely because of his narrow understanding of the concept of the 'law'. In my understanding there is no fundamental difference between my suggestion of 'the new/messianic law' and his notion of 'the teaching of Christ'.

74.   In that case the referent of τῶν ἐντολῶν τούτων suggested by option 1 (i.e. Jesus' commands) can be to some extent assimilated to my view, though the referent of my view is much more comprehensive than that; cf. D.A. Carson, 'Jesus and the Sabbath in the Four Gospels', in *idem* (ed.), *Lord's Day*, p. 78. Cf. also R.F. Collins, 'Matthew's ἐντολαί. Towards an Understanding of the Commandments in the First Gospel', in F. van Segbroeck *et al.* (eds.), *The Four Gospels 1992: Festschrift Frans Neirynck*, II (3 vols.; BETL, 100; Leuven: Leuven University Press, 1992), pp. 1326-48, esp. pp. 1344-48—he properly criticizes Banks's view but improperly limits the ἐντολαί of 5.19 to 'the commandments of the Torah, as these are understood and taught by Jesus' (p. 1346 n. 107); he goes on to clarify the 'least of the commandments' by suggesting that they are 'those other commandments which pale in insignificance beside the two-fold great [love] commandment' in 22.40 (p. 1347).

Finally, the repeated appearance of the phrase ἡ βασιλεία τῶν οὐρανῶν in v. 19 seems to betray Matthew's concern for eschatology in relation to the law issue. In Matthew, as J.P. Meier points out, 'Past, present, and future are all involved in various stages of the Kingdom's coming'.[75] As for 5.19, however, the future tense of the verb κληθήσεται favours the futuristic aspect of the kingdom, the final stage of the kingdom which will be consummated in Jesus' second coming.

The thought and function of the whole verse thus appears as follows. The two pairs of protases and apodoses make it clear that obeying or setting aside the slightest and most insignificant details of the law (i.e. 'the *messianic* νόμος') is the ground on which God will declare 'a status in the final stage of the kingdom' for the one judged. Thus this verse explicates 'the continuing validity of the law' understood in the light of Jesus' fulfilment, as stated in v. 18, by spelling out its implications to the disciples in terms of their behaviour in the present age, in the prospect of his *parousia*. By doing this, with v. 18, this verse guards against a possible antinomian interpretation of v. 17. It would therefore be possible to suppose that this verse was intended to function as a warning against a certain antinomian tendency of disciples within (or even outside) Matthew's community. Lastly, one further point needs to be noted in v. 19—that obeying or setting aside the law (i.e. 'the *messianic* νόμος'), though it is an extremely important matter for the disciples, does not constitute the criterion of entering the kingdom of heaven; to this criterion Matthew will turn in v. 20.

iv. *Mt. 5.20—The greater righteousness.* As a number of scholars suggest, v. 20 plays a double function as a bridge (or a pivot)—on the one hand, concluding the previous verses (vv. 17-19), and, on the other hand, introducing the following antitheses (vv. 21-48).[76]

---

75. *Law*, p. 99.

76. Meier, *Law*, pp. 108, 116; Luz, *Matthew 1–7*, p. 270. Some suggest that v. 20 exclusively introduces the antitheses and is not related to the previous section, but they seem to overlook the inferential force of γάρ too readily; cf. G. Strecker, *Der Weg der Gerechtigkeit: Untersuchungen zur Theologie des Matthäus* (FRLANT, 82; Göttingen: Vandenhoeck & Ruprecht, 1962), pp. 151-52; Sand, *Gesetz*, p. 203; B. Przybylski, *Righteousness in Matthew and his World of Thought* (SNTSMS, 41; Cambridge: Cambridge University Press, 1980), pp. 80, 85; *et al.* The proposal by Broer, *Freiheit*, p. 73, may be also worth considering: vv. 18-20 develop the first part of v. 17 (I have come not to abolish the law), and vv. 21-48 develop the second part (I have come to fulfil the law).

ἡ βασιλεία τῶν οὐρανῶν here once again may be understood 'in the final, ultra-historical sense', that is, as the consummated kingdom at the end of history.[77] 'The greater righteousness' which the disciples are to possess is presented as the criterion of entering the consummated kingdom of heaven; without this righteousness nobody can enter the kingdom. This righteousness is thus a more serious matter than just obeying or setting aside the law which only affects status within the kingdom as stated in v. 19.

The usage of the verb περισσεύειν in the New Testament and in non-biblical Greek shows that it carries a qualitative sense as well as a quantitative sense.[78] The addition of πλεῖον heightens the contrast between the righteousness of the disciples and that of οἱ γραμματεῖς καὶ Φαρισαῖοι.

Though scribes and Pharisees are not synonymous in Matthew, and they literally refer to two different groups within the first century historical Jewish world (but with some overlap, especially after 70 CE),[79] the phrase οἱ γραμματεῖς καὶ Φαρισαῖοι seems to blur the distinction and to function as a hendiadys. For Matthew, the scribes and Pharisees are transparent figures representing the Jewish opponents, whose religion may be characterized as legalism and hypocrisy, and 'who lead the attack against Jesus and who in return bear the brunt of Jesus' rebuke'.[80] Matthew thus turns his attention from the antinomian tendency within (v. 19) to the Jewish legalistic opponents outside who rejected Jesus and his disciples partly because of their adherence to the law (cf. 12.1-14; 15.1-20).

The crux of this verse is clearly the phrase ὑμῶν ἡ δικαιοσύνη. The interpretation of this phrase, however, is not an easy task. Since the disciples' righteousness is compared with that of the scribes and Pharisees, one of the crucial questions is whether the comparison is quantitative or qualitative. In the light of its relationship with the antitheses (vv. 21-48),

77.   Meier, *Law*, p. 114; cf. Guelich, *Sermon*, pp. 160-61; Davies and Allison, *Matthew*, I, p. 501.

78.   McConnell, 'Law', pp. 37-38; cf. Luz, *Matthew 1–7*, p. 270.

79.   The attempt to regard the scribes and Pharisees as identical by E. Rivkin, *A Hidden Revolution* (Nashville: Abingdon, 1978), is properly refuted by D.E. Orton, *The Understanding Scribe: Matthew and the Apocalyptic Ideal* (JSNTSup, 25; Sheffield: JSOT Press, 1989), p. 187 n. 71. For Matthew's understanding of the scribes, see Orton, *Scribe*, pp. 20-38, 137-76.

80.   Meier, *Law*, p. 111. For further discussion of the Pharisees in Matthew's Gospel, see below, Excursus 2.

it seems clear that the disciples' righteousness requires quantitative advance on that of the scribes and Pharisees. It seems, however, also quite clear, as most scholars argue, that the disciples' righteousness has a qualitative distinction from that of the scribes and Pharisees.[81] As Meier convincingly argues, the disciples' righteousness here means the moral activity which is based on and enabled by their fundamental relationship to a personal God through Jesus Messiah who has inaugurated the kingdom of God, that is, God's reign, in his fulfilling the will of God revealed in the law and the prophets (vv. 17-18).[82] The righteousness of the scribes and Pharisees, however, lacked this fundamental relationship.[83]

Since 'the new eschatological relationship' is, for Matthew, the starting point and the foundation of the righteousness necessary for entrance into the kingdom, the righteousness of the scribes and Pharisees which lacked this new relationship falls short of the criterion for entering the kingdom.[84] It is, of course, now clear that Matthew is waging battle on a double front, against antinomianism and legalism. According to Matthew's presentation in vv. 19 and 20, however, Jesus' warning in v. 20 against the legalism represented by the scribes and Pharisees (i.e. exclusion from the kingdom) is much more severe than that in v. 19 against antinomianism among the disciples (i.e. the lowest status in the kingdom). A good disciple, however, is to give full attention to both of these complementary warnings in vv. 19 and 20, and to guard not only against legalism but also against antinomianism. He needs to be equipped primarily with the new relationship with God through Jesus Messiah

81. For a detailed discussion of this issue, see Przybylski, *Righteousness*, pp. 83-87; see also Banks, *Jesus*, p. 225; Betz, *Essays*, p. 53; *et al.* We have already seen that the comparative verb περισσεύειν can carry a qualitative sense as well as a quantitative sense.

82. Meier, *Law*, pp. 109-10. His argument is based on his comprehensive investigation of all the examples of Matthew's use of δικαιοσύνη; see his *Law*, pp. 73-79.

83. This by no means suggests that the historical parties of scribes and Pharisees in the first century generally showed such understanding of righteousness. For further discussions of this issue, see below, Excursus 2.

84. In fact, their one-sided understanding of righteousness blinded them from seeing Jesus as the messiah they had long waited for, and from doing the will of God in the light of the messiah's coming (cf. 12.1-14; 23.25-26); cf. Guelich, *Sermon*, p. 160; M. Maher, 'Take my Yoke upon You (Matt. XI. 29)', *NTS* 22 (1975), pp. 102-103.

who has fulfilled the will of God revealed in the whole Scripture (vv. 17, 18), but without lacking the conduct in keeping with God's will (v. 19), which is the necessary consequence of God's reign which has been inaugurated in Jesus' coming as messiah.

Most of the conclusions reached so far may appear to be to a certain degree tentative and therefore provisional; we now turn to the antitheses (vv. 21-48) which are directly related to not only v. 20 but also vv. 17-20 as a whole, to see whether these conclusions can be sustained.

b. *Matthew 5.21-48—Six Antitheses*

The intimate relationship between Mt. 5.21-48 (the so-called 'six antitheses') and Mt. 5.17-20 is undeniable. Matthew may have positioned the antitheses straight after the key passage (vv. 17-20) either in order to provide concrete examples of how the principles, presented in the key passage work out practically, or in order to make the key passage the requisite introduction to the antitheses. In either case it seems beyond question that the conclusions reached in the previous section are to be applied to and examined in the light of these antitheses in order to establish their reliability.

The origin of the six antitheses in their present structural format is so widely debated without scholarly consensus that certainty on it may be neither obtainable nor necessary.[85] Once again, therefore, I will focus my attention primarily on the pericope as it stands and treat it in its entirety as reflecting Matthew's viewpoint. It seems, nevertheless, quite possible to suggest that the introductory formula and the antithetical form and/or content of at least some of the antitheses go back to Jesus himself.[86]

The introductory formula, which all six share with some variations,

---

85.   There are three major views: (i) R. Bultmann, *The History of the Synoptic Tradition* (trans. J. Marsh; Oxford: Blackwell, 2nd edn, 1968), pp. 134-36, and others assign the first, second, and fourth antitheses to pre-Matthean tradition and the third, fifth, and sixth to Matthew's redaction—see also Klostermann, *Matthäus-evangelium*, p. 42; Guelich, *Sermon*, pp. 179, 265-71; Luz, *Matthew 1-7*, p. 276; Davies and Allison, *Matthew*, I, p. 505; (ii) Jeremias, *Theology*, pp. 251-53, and others assign all six antitheses to pre-Matthean tradition—see also Wrege, *Berg-predigt*, pp. 56-57; Sand, *Gesetz*, p. 48; (iii) M.J. Suggs, *Wisdom, Christology, and Law in Matthew's Gospel* (Cambridge, MA: Harvard University Press, 1970), pp. 109-15, and others attribute the structural formulation of all six antitheses to Matthew himself—see also I. Broer, 'Die Antithesen und der Evangelist Matthäus', *BZ* 19 (1975), pp. 56-63.

86.   Cf. Luz, *Matthew 1-7*, pp. 274-79.

finds its full form in the first and fourth antitheses: Ἠκούσατε ὅτι ἐρρέθη τοῖς ἀρχαίοις...ἐγὼ δὲ λέγω ὑμῖν (vv. 21-22, 33-34). ἠκούσατε could be taken either in a rabbinic technical sense as meaning 'you have understood the law in a literal but misleading way'[87] or in a non-technical sense as referring to the reading of the Scriptures in the synagogue.[88] If we recognize, however, the strong probability that 'the Scripture was usually read in interpreted ('targumized') form' in the synagogue,[89] in either case ἠκούσατε could involve interpretive elements not originally intended by the written Torah. The real gravity of the first part of the formula, however, seems to be placed on the second verb ἐρρέθη, which, rather than ἠκούσατε, is the proper counterpart of λέγω of the second part. It is highly probable that ἐρρέθη, as a divine passive, refers back to God's words spoken at Sinai. In that case τοῖς ἀρχαίοις could only refer to the Sinai generation. The first part of the formula as a whole then may mean 'you have heard (*in the synagogue with scribal interpretation*) / understood (*in a literal but misleading way*) that God said to the Sinai generation that...' If we give due weight to the direct relationship between v. 20 and the six antitheses, it seems probable that the traditional scribal/Pharisaic interpretation, which explained the written Torah but frequently distorted the will of God revealed in it, may be a substantial, though subsidiary, element in the first part of the formula (cf. τῶν γραμματέων καὶ Φαρισαίων in v. 20). Considering the main issue in vv. 17-20 as a whole (i.e. Jesus as the fulfiller of *the law*), however, the primary focus of the formula must be on what God said at Sinai as recorded in the written Torah.

In itself the expression of the second part of the formula (ἐγὼ δὲ λέγω ὑμῖν) has parallels in rabbinic literature.[90] Considering the authoritative character of the instructions which it introduces, however, its use in the present co-text is unique.[91] First of all this latter expression

---

87. See especially Daube, *Rabbinic Judaism*, pp. 55-62; see also Branscomb, *Jesus*, p. 240; Davies, *Setting*, pp. 101-102; Wrege, *Bergpredigt*, p. 58; *et al.*

88. Banks, *Jesus*, pp. 201-203; Luz, *Matthew 1–7*, p. 278; *et al.*

89. Moo, 'Jesus', p. 18; cf. Dalman, *Jesus-Jeshua*, p. 70.

90. See especially E. Lohse, 'Ich aber sage euch', in *idem, Der Ruf Jesu und die Antwort der Gemeinde: Festschrift für Joachim Jeremias* (BZNW, 26; Göttingen: Vandenhoeck & Ruprecht, 1970), pp. 193-96; see also Daube, *Rabbinic Judaism*, pp. 56-62.

91. I will discuss the authoritative character of Jesus' instructions later; see Banks, *Jesus*, pp. 202-203; Guelich, *Sermon*, pp. 184-85; cf. Lohse, 'Ich aber sage

contrasts Jesus' instructions (ἐγὼ δὲ λέγω), as I have just suggested, not only with the scribal interpretation and/or understanding of the written Torah (ἠκούσατε) but also and primarily with the written Torah itself given to Moses at Sinai (ἐρρέθη). Secondly, the expression contrasts Jesus' disciples (ὑμῖν) with the Israelites at Sinai (τοῖς ἀρχαίοις). But what is the nature of these contrasts? This question can be properly answered by considering the individual antitheses.

i. *First, second and sixth antitheses.*[92] *The first antithesis (Mt. 5.21-26)*—The thesis in v. 21 contains two statements. The first (οὐ φονεύσεις) is an Old Testament quotation (Exod. 20.13; Deut. 5.18). The second (ὃς δ' ἂν φονεύσῃ, ἔνοχος ἔσται τῇ κρίσει), though not itself directly from the Old Testament, may be best understood as a summary of the Old Testament passages prescribing the penalty for murder (Exod. 21.12; Lev. 24.17; Num. 35.16-31).

Numerous parallels to the demands in Jesus' tripartite antithesis in v. 22 have been cited from the Old Testament and Jewish literature in order to demonstrate that Jesus' demands were nothing new to his contemporary Jews.[93] It seems quite clear, however, that his demands go far beyond that of the supposed Jewish parallels and 'No real parallel therefore occurs'.[94] Furthermore Jesus' conjunction of the anger and the hatred with the sixth commandment makes his demands more distinctive.[95]

The second antithesis (Mt. 5.27-30)—The thesis in v. 27 is a straightforward Old Testament citation (Exod. 20.14; Deut. 5.18), and, unlike

euch', pp. 194-200. France, *Matthew*, p. 118, points out that 'The emphatic and repeated use of *I* is striking'.

92.   For a selected bibliography on these antitheses, see Meier, *Law*, pp. 136-38 nn. 27, 29 and 31; and, for more recent literature, Luz, *Matthew 1-7*, pp. 279-80, 290-91, 337-38. These three antitheses are grouped together because they are, in my view, less problematic in relation to the issue of abrogating the Old Testament law than the other three; as we shall see, whereas in these three the law is affirmed, in the other three Jesus' teaching sets the law aside. Similar groupings are found in Stonehouse, *Witness*, pp. 188, 198-208; Meier, *Law*, pp. 135-61.

93.   Cf. Branscomb, *Jesus*, p. 240; G. Friedlander, *The Jewish Sources of the Sermon on the Mount* (New York: KTAV, 1969), pp. 40-53; Strack and Billerbeck, *Kommentar*, I, p. 276-82; more recently, Luz, *Matthew 1-7*, pp. 282-84; Davies and Allison, *Matthew*, I, p. 521.

94.   Banks, *Jesus*, pp. 187-89, quotation from p. 189.

95.   Cf. Moo, 'Jesus', pp. 18-19; Davies and Allison, *Matthew*, I, p. 521.

the first, with no further addition. More numerous and more impressive parallels to Jesus' statement in the antithesis in v. 28 have been cited from the Old Testament (e.g. Exod. 20.17) and rabbinic writings;[96] once again, however, they do not really parallel the severity and seriousness of Jesus' antithetical statement which is further demonstrated in the following verses (vv. 29-30).[97]

The sixth antithesis (Mt. 5.43-48)—In the thesis (v. 43) the quotation from Lev. 19.18 (ἀγαπήσεις τὸν πλησίον σου) is followed by an additional element (καὶ μισήσεις τὸν ἐχθρόν σου) which is not a quotation from the Old Testament and can hardly be described as a summary of Old Testament teaching. The latter element rather reflects a false but popular inference drawn from, for example, such passages as Deut. 7.2, 5; 23.3-6; 25.19; 30.7 (cf. Ps. 139.21-22), which is well attested in the Qumran Community Rule (1QS 1.3-4, 9-11; 9.21-22).[98]

Despite all the numerous parallels to Jesus' demands in the antithesis (v. 44) which can be drawn from Judaism and Greek philosophy (especially Stoicism),[99] a number of scholars note their distinctively universal and imperative character and conclude that they have no genuine parallel in Jewish and Hellenistic literature.[100]

96.   See especially Strack and Billerbeck, *Kommentar*, I, pp. 298-301; Moore, *Judaism*, II, pp. 167-72, among others.

97.   Banks, *Jesus*, p. 191; France, *Matthew*, p. 121; *pace* Luz, *Matthew 1–7*, pp. 295-96. At any rate most of the impressive parallels come from the rabbis after Jesus.

98.   Daube, *Rabbinic Judaism*, p. 56; Davies, *Setting*, p. 245; *pace* Banks, *Jesus*, pp. 199-200—his argument is largely based on the arbitrary assumption that Matthew should do the same thing (i.e. summarizing the Old Testament position) in v. 21b, v. 33b and here.

99.   A list of literature, which covers not only Jewish and Hellenistic parallels but also those in Indian literature, in Buddhism and in Taoism, is found in Luz, *Matthew 1–7*, p. 340 n. 18. For Jewish parallels, see also Strack and Billerbeck, *Kommentar*, I, pp. 369-70.

100.   See especially Bultmann, *History*, p. 105—he claims that Jesus' saying here contains 'something characteristic, new, reaching out beyond popular wisdom and piety and yet...in no sense scribal or rabbinic nor Jewish apocalyptic'; see also N. Perrin, *Rediscovering the Teaching of Jesus* (London: SCM Press, 1967), pp. 148ff.; Banks, *Jesus*, pp. 200-201; Luz, *Matthew 1-7*, pp. 340-42; Davies and Allison, *Matthew*, I, p. 552; *et al.*

Conclusions—What, then, is Jesus' teaching in these three (1st, 2nd, and 6th) antitheses doing to the law (1, 2, 6) and/or the scribal understanding of it (6)? On the one hand, as most scholars agree, his teaching in them neither merely affirms the Old Testament commandments nor abrogates them but rather surpasses or transcends them by internalizing (1, 2), intensifying (1, 2, 6), radicalizing (1, 2, 6) or extending (6 and perhaps 1, 2) them without weakening their literal force.[101] These are some of the concrete illustrations of his fulfilment of the law, that is, fulfilling the ultimate will of God, to which the law pointed forward, by drawing out the radical but original intention behind it. These radical demands can only be given to his disciples who are now, through their relationship with Jesus Messiah, living in the kingdom of heaven, in which any broken relationships are out of the question and 'anything less than the restored relationship' therefore 'leaves one culpable before God' (cf. v. 48: ἔσεσθε οὖν ὑμεῖς τέλειοι ὡς ὁ πατὴρ ὑμῶν ὁ οὐράνιος τέλειός ἐστιν).[102] This shows how the 'greater' righteousness of the disciples is different from that of the scribes and Pharisees. On the other hand, Jesus' teaching may also aim to rebuke the current scribal legalistic and casuistic interpretation as reflected in the sixth thesis. Furthermore Jesus may well be echoing the current Jewish casuistry in all these three antitheses but only in an ironic way,[103] in order to show the 'greater' righteousness more graphically.

ii. *Third, fourth and fifth antitheses.*[104] *The third antithesis (Mt. 5.31-32)*—The thesis in v. 31 is a free paraphrase of Deut. 24.1, where divorce is simply assumed (though not commanded) when a man finds עֶרְוַת דָּבָר ('something indecent') in his wife—it is clear that its meaning here cannot be 'adultery' because the penalty for adultery in Old

101. See, among many others, McConnell, 'Law', p. 54; Jeremias, *Theology*, pp. 251-52; Meier, *Law*, pp. 136-39; for further references, see Mohrlang, *Matthew*, p. 144 n. 121. For a different view as regards the sixth antithesis, however, see Sand, *Gesetz*, p. 53.

102. Guelich, *Sermon*, p. 241; see also p. 194. Cf. L. Goppelt, 'Das Problem der Bergpredigt', in *idem*, *Christologie und Ethik* (Göttingen: Vandenhoeck & Ruprecht, 1968), p. 40; Luz, *Matthew 1–7*, pp. 285-86, 296-97; Hagner, *Matthew 1–13*, pp. 116, 118, 120.

103. Cf. Moo, 'Jesus', p. 18; France, *Matthew*, p. 119; Luz, *Matthew 1–7*, p. 285.

104. For a selected bibliography on these antitheses, see Meier, *Law*, pp. 140-41 n. 38, p. 151 n. 62, and p. 157 n. 76; and, for more recent literature, Luz, *Matthew 1–7*, pp. 298-99, 310-11, 322-23.

Testament times was death (cf. Deut. 22.22).[105] In fact, the main issue in Deut. 24.1-4 is not divorce but reunion of a divorced couple after the termination of the woman's remarriage; here the remarriage of a divorced woman is taken for granted.

In the time of Jesus the permissible grounds for divorce were much debated: the school of Shammai interpreted ערות דבר in Deut. 24.1 to refer only to sexual sins, whereas the school of Hillel understood it as referring to any cause of complaint.[106] It is generally agreed that the latter represented the dominant Jewish view. Though the syntactical use of ἀπολῦσαι in Mt. 19.7 is not clear, it seems possible to suspect that Deut. 24.1 was understood by Jesus' contemporaries not as permitting but rather as commanding (ἐνετείλατο) the divorce; Jesus, however, disagrees with such a view by using the verb ἐπέτρεψεν ('[Moses] permitted'—Mt. 19.8).

The word πορνεία in the antithesis (v. 32) may refer rather to 'adultery' than to 'incest'.[107] In either case, however, Jesus' antithesis makes the exception stricter than that of Deut. 24.1, not to speak of that of the school of Hillel.[108] The latter part of Jesus' antithesis is also stricter than

---

105. Cf. Craigie, *Deuteronomy*, p. 305, esp. n. 3—he suggests, 'In this context, the words may indicate some physical deficiency in the woman...A physical deficiency such as the inability to bear children may be implied'.

106. *m. Git.* 9.10; cf. Strack and Billerbeck, *Kommentar*, I, pp. 313-15.

107. For fuller discussions of the meaning of πορνεία, see Carson, 'Matthew', pp. 414-18; Davies and Allison, *Matthew*, I, pp. 529-31. The former option is supported by most of the recent commentators, for example, Allen, *Matthew*, p. 52; Schweizer, *Matthew*, pp. 123-26; R.H. Gundry, *Matthew: A Commentary on his Literary and Theological Art* (Grand Rapids: Eerdmans, 2nd edn, 1994 [1982]), p. 91; Carson, 'Matthew', pp. 417-18; France, *Matthew*, pp. 123-24; J. Gnilka, *Das Matthäusevangelium*, I (2 vols.; Freiburg: Herder, 1986, 1988), pp. 167-69; Luz, *Matthew 1–7*, pp. 304-306; Davies and Allison, *Matthew*, I, pp. 530-31; D.J. Harrington, *The Gospel of Matthew* (Sacra Pagina, 1; Collegeville, MN: The Liturgical Press, 1991), pp. 87-88; Hagner, *Matthew 1–13*, pp. 124-25; *et al.*. The latter option is supported by a significant number of scholars (esp. Roman Catholic scholars), for example, H. Baltensweiler, 'Die Ehebruchsklauseln bei Matthäus. Zu Matth. 5,32; 19,9', *TZ* 15 (1959), pp. 340-56; J.A. Fitzmyer, 'The Matthean Divorce Texts and Some New Palestinian Evidence', *Theological Studies* 37 (1976), pp. 208-11; Meier, *Law*, pp. 147-50; Guelich, *Sermon*, pp. 204-209; B. Witherington, 'Matt. 5.32 and 19.9—Exception or Exceptional Situation?', *NTS* 31 (1985), pp. 571-75; *et al.*

108. To this extent, Jesus' view as represented in v. 32 is by and large similar to that of the school of Shammai in its understanding of ערות דבר in Deut. 24.1.

the Old Testament divorce regulation because it defines the remarriage of the divorced wife, which is taken for granted in Deut. 24.1-2, as adultery. At this stage, Mt. 19.4-9 throws further light on the character of the relation between the thesis and the antithesis here. According to Mt. 19.8, Jesus is, in fact, setting aside the Old Testament divorce regulation in relation to his disciples; he rather instructs them to go back to the first principle of marriage as revealed in Gen. 2.24. Jesus' appeal to the first principle, however, does not necessarily involve repudiating the divorce regulation as such; it is rather insisting, as France suggests, that each principle/regulation 'is given its proper function, the one as a statement of the ideal will of God, the other as a (regrettable but necessary) provision for' the people who had hardened hearts and failed to maintain the ideal.[109] Jesus' fulfilment has enabled the disciples to attain the ideal will of God; Jesus, therefore, commands them to go back to the first principle, because the provision for the old age is no longer meaningful for them.[110] Lastly, the exception in the Matthean antithesis is not a real exception, because adultery, by its nature, has already broken the marital relationship and a 'divorce' in such a case is only a recognition of an already broken marriage.[111] For Jesus, according to Matthew's presentation, divorce proper (i.e. the deliberate ending of a marriage which is still intact) which was partly allowed in the Old Testament, is absolutely prohibited (cf. Mk 10.11-12; Lk. 16.18).

The fourth antithesis (Mt. 5.33-37)[112]—The two statements of the thesis in v. 33 are not exact quotations from the Old Testament but crystallized summaries of the Old Testament teaching on the subject (v. 33a—Lev. 19.12; cf. Exod. 20.7; v. 33b—Num. 30.2; Deut. 23.21-23; cf. Ps. 50.14). In the Old Testament oaths or vows were not only taken for granted but sometimes imposed (e.g. Exod. 22.7-10; Num. 5.19-22; cf. Deut. 6.13); in such a context false/unfulfilled oaths or vows were prohibited, and this

    109. *Matthew*, p. 281.
    110. Hagner, *Matthew 1–13*, p. 125; cf. E.P. Sanders, *Jesus and Judaism* (London: SCM Press, 1985), p. 260; Luz, *Matthew 1–7*, pp. 301-302.
    111. France, *Matthew*, p. 281; Luz, *Matthew 1–7*, p. 306; *et al.*
    112. For the question of the authenticity of the prohibition of swearing, see A. Ito, 'The Question of the Authenticity of the Ban on Swearing (Matthew 5.33-37)', *JSNT* 43 (1991), pp. 5-13—this article is a critical reply to G. Dautzenberg, 'Ist das Schwurverbot Mt 5,33-37; Jak 5,12 ein Beispiel für die Torakritik Jesu?', *BZ* 25 (1981), pp. 47-66, who denies the authenticity of Jesus' prohibition, which is usually accepted; cf. Luz, *Matthew 1–7*, p. 313, esp. n. 16.

prohibition may well be understood as pointing forward to the ultimate truthfulness.

It is generally admitted that Jesus' absolute rejection of oaths in vv. 34-37 is not paralleled by the Old Testament and the current Jewish literature.[113] The Old Testament law as well as the contemporary Jewish teaching is surpassed by Jesus' proclamation. This surpassing, however, once again does not necessarily involve contradicting or abrogating the oath-taking regulations in the Torah.[114] The oath-taking regulations, which presupposed the unreliability of one's word, were required only for the people of the old age because of their untruthfulness. For the disciples who are living in the kingdom of heaven, however, those regulations are no longer necessary and consequently they are to be set aside, because the requirement for disciples is rather absolute truthfulness, a greater righteousness. The real issue of this antithesis is then not the oath-taking itself; it is rather focused on the truthfulness of the disciples which is expected by Jesus, who has fulfilled the ultimate goal of the Old Testament regulations of truthful swearing—that is, the unconditional truth.[115]

The fifth antithesis (Mt. 5.38-42)—The thesis, ὀφθαλμὸν ἀντὶ ὀφθαλμοῦ καὶ ὀδόντα ἀντὶ ὀδόντος, in v. 38 is a citation from Exod. 21.24; Lev. 24.20; Deut. 19.21. In these passages, the *lex talionis* was intended to set strict limits on revenge rather than to sanction it. By Jesus' day physical penalties were replaced by monetary recompense.

Jesus' command of 'no resistance' in the antithesis is strikingly contrasted to the Old Testament principle of *lex talionis* and to the current application of it. What is then the character of the contrast, and in what sense does Jesus' antithesis fulfil the law? First of all the antithesis intensifies and radicalizes the Old Testament restrictions on the degree of vengeance: his command first of all involves renouncing their right to revenge; however, it goes one step further and, in fact, demands nothing less than no resistance.[116] What is the ground for such a demand? Once again it is because his demand is addressed to a different context; his

---

113. See especially Banks, *Jesus*, pp. 195-96; cf. Davies and Allison, *Matthew*, I, pp. 534-35.

114. *Pace* Meier, *Law*, p. 156; Luz, *Matthew 1–7*, p. 317.

115. Cf. Jeremias, *Theology*, p. 220; Davies and Allison, *Matthew*, I, p. 536; Hagner, *Matthew 1–13*, pp. 126-29.

116. Hare, *Matthew*, p. 55; cf. Meier, *Law*, p. 158.

command of 'no resistance' is given to those who now live in the kingdom of heaven and therefore are called to be subject only to the will of God, which the *lex talionis* alone falls short of attaining, that is, limitless forgiveness (vv. 39b-42) and love of enemy (the sixth antithesis), 'the lifestyle governed by the free grace of God'.[117] We may then conclude that Jesus' 'no resistance' antithesis does not so much abolish or contradict the Old Testament *lex talionis* as fulfil it, by transcending, going beyond, and even bypassing it[118] in order to reveal the ultimate will of God behind it.

Conclusion—According to the investigation above, all these three (3rd, 4th, and 5th) antitheses do not involve contradiction to and/or abrogation of the Old Testament law as frequently assumed.[119] They rather reveal and turn the disciples' attention to the original will of God behind the law as represented in the three theses. This, however, necessarily results in transcending, going beyond, setting aside or bypassing certain literal regulations of the law, because they were provisions for the people of the old age who had hardened hearts and failed to maintain the ideal. Jesus' fulfilment of the law, however, has enabled the disciples to attain the ideal will of God, and consequently those provisions for the old age are no longer suitable, meaningful or necessary for them. The requirement for them now is nothing less than the perpetual unity in marriage relationship, absolute truthfulness, no resistance under any circumstances, that is, a lifestyle governed by the heavenly Father who is τέλειος (v. 48); this is nothing else but the greater righteousness which is required for every disciple who wishes to enter the kingdom of heaven (v. 20).

My interpretation of the six antitheses so far now seems to suggest the following conclusions: (1) The suggested meaning of πληρῶσαι in section 2a is in harmony with the overall picture of fulfilment which the six antitheses illustrate; one may add a final comment here that the illustrations clearly suggest that the meaning of πληρῶσαι includes an element of totality and fullness which only Jesus can accomplish.[120]

---

117. Hagner, *Matthew 1–13*, p. 132.

118. Banks, *Jesus*, p. 199; France, *Matthew*, p. 126; cf. Luz, *Matthew 1–7*, p. 330.

119. For a brief list of scholars who assume this in various ways, see Mohrlang, *Matthew*, p. 144 n. 121.

120. Luz, *Matthew 1–7*, p. 265.

(2) The tension between 'already' and 'not yet' in Jesus' fulfilment is well demonstrated by the two facts (i) that all six antitheses have already fulfilled the six theses by surpassing, transcending, going beyond them, or setting them aside or by revealing the ultimate will of God in/behind them, and (ii) that the disciples are still required to keep the law as Jesus reinterpreted it in the six antitheses probably until Jesus' second coming. (3) It is now clear that τῶν ἐντολῶν τούτων in v. 19 is, as I suggested above, nothing else than the new messianic νόμος which is already fulfilled by Jesus; Jesus' six antitheses over against the six theses are all illustrations of this fulfilled new messianic Torah which the disciples are required to keep. (4) Jesus' six antitheses show what is the greater righteousness over against that of the scribes and Pharisees who were still bound only to the old Torah as a literal code of behaviour; the six antitheses show that the greater righteousness involves not only extending the scope of the law but also proceeding towards the higher and deeper level of godly life.

c. *Other Passages*

In addition to the key text (5.17-20) and the six antitheses (5.21-48), there are still some substantial passages in Matthew's Gospel which are related to Matthew's understanding of the law in relation to Jesus. In this section I will survey those passages without detailed exegetical discussions with the aim of examining whether the conclusions reached in sections 2a and 2b are in harmony with those other law-related passages in the Gospel and therefore reliable.

i. *Jesus, tradition, and law (Mt. 15.1-20; 23.1-36; cf. 16.12; 19.17).* In Mt. 15.1-20 Jesus, in responding to the criticism of the Pharisees and scribes, criticizes ἡ παράδοσις τῶν πρεσβυτέρων (= the Pharisaic oral law)[121] primarily because people are invited to transgress ἡ ἐντολὴ τοῦ θεοῦ for the sake of the παράδοσις. The crucial issue here is a question of authority. The Pharisaic way of using a legal provision like '*Korban*'[122] makes it directly conflict with the will of God as revealed in the fifth commandment and in effect override the authority of the ἐντολή. Such a παράδοσις deserves no respect and has no authority for Jesus and his

---

121. See Hill, *Matthew*, pp. 250-51; France, *Matthew*, p. 241; Davies and Allison, *Matthew*, II, p. 520; *et al.* See also Gnilka, *Matthäusevangelium*, II, p. 21— 'die Überlieferung der Alten, die die Pharisäer als Zaun für die Thora errichtet hatten'.

122. Cf. Mk 7.11; the tractate *Nedarim* in the Mishnah.

disciples (vv. 3-6). The Pharisees who teach such a παράδοσις are characterized by Jesus as a plant which has not been planted by God and therefore will be rooted up (v. 13) and as blind guides who will fall into a pit with those whom they guide (v. 14). In vv. 11 and 18-20, as in 5.21-48, Jesus' concern is again focused on what lies behind the outward act; for him, 'what counts above all is the heart'.[123] The question of what implications this passage have for the Old Testament food laws is not simple. A number of scholars rightly argue that in this passage Matthew, perhaps deliberately, is not tackling the question directly;[124] nevertheless there is no compelling reason to deny that 'the principle for the abandonment of the food-laws is [already] there' (cf. v. 11).[125] Is this not then contradictory to 5.17 (οὐκ ἦλθον καταλῦσαι ἀλλὰ πληρῶσαι)? This seeming contradiction may be, however, best explained by suggesting that Jesus, for Matthew, does not attack or conflict with the Old Testament by explicitly abandoning the food law; rather as Banks properly points out after an extensive discussion, Jesus' principle behind v. 11 'expresses an entirely new understanding of what does and does not constitute defilement'.[126] In that case, Jesus' radical teaching of defilement, for Matthew, is another concrete example of what Jesus' fulfilment of the Old Testament involves; God's will behind the food law, which prophesied and pointed forward to Jesus' fulfilment until John (cf. 11.13), is now revealed in *Jesus' new standard of defilement*— 'not foods which go into the mouth but evil things (cf. vv. 18-19) which come out of the heart defile a man'. This is, then, another case of the fulfilment in terms of internalization.

In Mt. 23.1-36 Matthew presents another impressive critique of the scribes and Pharisees. Here, as in 15.1-20, Jesus criticizes their teaching and practice mainly because their excessive interest in more minute legal prescriptions leads them to neglect more fundamental demands of God

123. Davies and Allison, *Matthew*, II, p. 531.

124. Note the omission of the comment in Mk 7.19b—καθαρίζων πάντα τὰ βρώματα; note also the addition of Mt. 15.20b which goes back to the discussion of the hand-washing issue. See Green, *Matthew*, pp. 143-44; Banks, *Jesus*, pp. 140-46; Mohrlang, *Matthew*, p. 11; France, *Matthew*, pp. 244-45; Davies and Allison, *Matthew*, II, pp. 526-31, 534-35; Harrington, *Matthew*, p. 233; *et al.* Cf. Barth, 'Law', p. 90.

125. France, *Matthew*, p. 245; cf. Banks, *Jesus*, p. 139: 'there is every indication that Matthew understood his alteration in v. 11b in the widest possible fashion'. *Pace* Barth, 'Law', p. 90; Davies and Allison, *Matthew*, II, pp. 526-31.

126. *Jesus*, p. 141.

in the law. For example, their scrupulous concern for tithing even in respect of the smallest herbs has blinded them to τὰ βαρύτερα τοῦ νόμου—that is, ἡ κρίσις, τὸ ἔλεος, and ἡ πίστις (v. 23; cf. Mic. 6.8). Not surprisingly, therefore, they are once again characterized as blind guides (cf. vv. 16-17, 19, 26).[127] The issue here is a question of priority as the phrase τὰ βαρύτερα τοῦ νόμου in v. 23 implies; such inward virtues as justice, mercy, and faithfulness are much more important than those casuistic regulations regarding tithing and oath-taking (cf. vv. 16-22).[128]

ii. *Greater righteousness (Mt. 7.12; 9.13; 12.7; 19.16-21; 22.40; etc.).* According to Mt. 19.16-21, 'to be a disciple' (ἀκολούθει μοι) requires 'to be perfect' (τέλειος εἶναι[129]). As we have seen, the requirement for entering the kingdom of heaven, that is, the greater righteousness in 5.20, is nothing less than the perfection as stated in 5.48; and the same perfection is required here for the rich young man who wishes to have/enter eternal life (= to be a disciple).[130] The perfection required here by Jesus is, as in 5.48 (cf. 5.43-47), closely related with the right understanding of the love commandment in Lev. 19.18 (cf. v. 19b: ἀγαπήσεις τὸν πλησίον σου ὡς σεαυτόν)—that is, πώλησόν σου τὰ ὑπάρχοντα καὶ δὸς [τοῖς] πτωχοῖς (v. 21). This close relationship between perfection and the radical understanding of the love commandment does not seem to be accidental. As many scholars note, Matthew

127. There are some other characterizations in ch. 23—e.g. hypocrites (vv. 13, 15, 27, etc.); fools (v. 17); serpents and brood of vipers (v. 33); etc. Such a negative assessment of the Pharisaic teaching can be also found in 16.12.

128. Moo, 'Jesus', p. 11. The question whether vv. 3 and 23 endorse the validity of the rabbinic teaching or not is not directly related to my topic and I do not discuss it here; for a detailed discussion of it, see Banks, *Jesus*, pp. 175-80—he concludes that 'For neither evangelist...nor for Christ, was a recognition of the validity of the scribal teaching either intended or implied'; similarly, France, *Matthew*, pp. 324, 328; *contra* Barth, 'Law', pp. 86, 88-89.

129. Matthew alone characteristically (cf. 5.48) includes this clause; cf. Mk 10.21; Lk. 18.22.

130. Mt. 19.16-26 does not afford a real foundation for the two-level (i.e. 'the ordinary Christians' who simply have eternal life [cf. vv. 17-19] and 'the members of religious orders' [cf. vv. 20-21]) ethic which many Catholics hold; see Barth, 'Law', pp. 95-100; France, *Matthew*, p. 286; Gnilka, *Matthäusevangelium*, II, p. 165; cf. Davies, *Setting*, pp. 209-14; Strecker, *Gerechtigkeit*, p. 142 n. 1. Harrington (a Catholic commentator), *Matthew*, p. 281, does not explicitly affirm the two-level ethic, though suggests the possibility of it only indirectly.

tends to attach a special significance to the love commandment,[131] and such a tendency is further demonstrated by 7.12 and 22.40.

The so-called 'Golden Rule' of Mt. 7.12 states that loving kindness for one's neighbour is ὁ νόμος καὶ οἱ προφῆται (cf. 5.17; 22.40). From this statement alone, however, it is difficult to determine the nature of the relationship between the commandment of love for one's neighbour and the Old Testament. We may at best suggest that love for neighbour represents the Old Testament in a certain way.[132] We may expect a more concrete picture of the relationship from the following discussion of 22.34-40.

In Mt. 22.34-36 one of the Pharisees tests Jesus by raising a question about the greatest commandment (ἐντολὴ μεγάλη)[133] in the law. In response to this question, in 22.37-40 Jesus cites two love commandments from the Old Testament—love for God (Deut. 6.5) and love for neighbour (Lev. 19.18). According to vv. 37-39, it is quite apparent that for Jesus a certain logical connection between the 'first' and 'second' love commandments is presupposed. But the use of the 'first' and 'second' does not mean that one is on a different level of authority from the other (cf. v. 39, ὁμοία); rather for him they stand together 'on a level of their own', because 'each depends on the other for its true force'.[134] Thus these two commandments are inseparable.[135] The final

131. Barth, 'Law', pp. 75-85; Banks, *Jesus*, pp. 164-71; *et al.*

132. Luz, *Matthew 1–7*, pp. 428-31, interprets 7.12 in the light of 'fulfilment' as stated in 5.17, and says (pp. 429-30), 'this fulfillment is bundled up in the practice of the Golden Rule' (similarly, E. Schweizer, 'Matthäus 5, 17-20. Anmerkungen zum Gesetzesversändnis des Matthäus', in *idem, Neotestamentica* [Zürich: Zwingli Verlag, 1963], p. 402). His view, however, is only possible on the basis of his presupposition that 7.12 constitutes a bracket with 5.17 (p. 425; 'inclusio' in Davies and Allison's term—see their *Matthew*, I, p. 685) and serves as the conclusion of the whole content between the bracket, a view which, as pointed out by Banks, *Jesus*, pp. 227-28, is not without problems.

133. Cf. Mk 12.28: ἐντολὴ πρώτη. In the light of Mt. 22.38, however, we may assume that for Matthew the two terms (i.e. μεγάλη and πρώτη) have a similar meaning; see Banks, *Jesus*, p. 165.

134. France, *Matthew*, p. 320; cf. Mohrlang, *Matthew*, p. 95; Hare, *Matthew*, pp. 259-60.

135. Moo, 'Jesus', pp. 6, 33 n. 27. Such an implication can be also discerned in Lk. 10.25-28, which is frequently considered as originated from a separate incident from that in Mt. 22.34-40 (and Mk 12.28-34); cf. Manson, *Sayings*, pp. 259-61; E.E. Ellis, *The Gospel of Luke* (NCB; London: Marshall, Morgan & Scott, 2nd edn, 1974), p. 159; Banks, *Jesus*, p. 164. For a different view, however, which sees the

part of his reply (v. 40), however, raises a controversial question, a question about the relation between the two great commandments and all the law and the prophets (ὅλος ὁ νόμος...καὶ οἱ προφῆται). The crucial key to this question is the meaning of the word κρεμάννυμι. Various views have been suggested without scholarly consensus,[136] and one cannot expect a definite conclusion. After an extensive discussion, however, D.J. Moo convincingly concludes, 'For Jesus, it is not a question of the "priority of love over law" but of the priority of love *within* the law'.[137] The two commandments are the greatest but they do not displace all the rest. The rest depend on them, but the validity and applicability of the rest cannot be decided by appeal to these love commandments.[138]

From the discussions so far in this subsection, one may draw some conclusions: (1) It is the teaching and practice of the scribes and Pharisees rather than the law itself which is criticized. (2) Though the validity of the law is frequently taken for granted (cf. also 19.17), the literal application of every law is no longer expected (15.11—the food law is, at least implicitly, abandoned). (3) As an aspect of the fulfilment, Jesus' concern is directed to the heart and the inward fundamental virtues. (4) A certain priority of importance among the commandments of God is presumed or, at least, implied. (5) To the love commandment a special significance is attached. (6) Though the two love commandments are greatest, they do not displace the rest of the Old Testament law; they are by no means a sole commandment.[139] (7) We may, therefore, conclude that the love commandment is the centre of the greater righteousness (= perfection), but it is by no means all that it entails.

The observations and discussions in section 2c as a whole, then, suggest that my conclusions in the first part of this chapter are in harmony with the other law-related passages in the whole Gospel. It would appear that no passage in the Gospel either explicitly or implicitly contradicts these

two pericopes as based on one event with different channels of tradition, see Bultmann, *History*, pp. 23, 51.

136. For various views suggested so far, see G. Bertram, 'κρεμάννυμι', *TDNT*, III, pp. 919-21; Moo, 'Jesus', pp. 6-7, 34-35 nn. 30-35.

137. 'Jesus', p. 11.

138. Banks, *Jesus*, p. 169; Moo, 'Jesus', p. 11; Harrington, *Matthew*, p. 316; *et al.* In that case, this passage cannot be a support for the so-called 'situationalism' advocated by P. Lehmann and J. Fletcher.

139. Such a verdict may be applicable to 9.13 and 12.7 (cf. 18.12-35) where Hos. 6.6 is cited. I will come back to these passages in Chapter 4.

conclusions. Rather, this discussion, on the one hand, further confirm the previous conclusions (e.g. the concept of fulfilment in terms of radical-izing, internalizing, transcending, etc.; the perfection which characterizes the greater righteousness), and, on the other, adds some more aspects of Matthew's understanding of the law in the light of Jesus (e.g. the priority among the commandments; the prominent status of the love command-ment in Jesus' teaching). These conclusions will be presupposed in what follows.

Excursus 2
'Pharisees' in Matthew's Gospel

The aim of this excursus is to clarify the use of the term 'Pharisees' in the following chapters by drawing the picture of the Pharisees as shown in Matthew's Gospel. Its aim is thus purely descriptive. It is beyond my scope here to reconstruct the historical identity of the Pharisees in the first century CE (especially in the time of Jesus) as Sanders and many others have attempted but still without firm consensus,[140] or to evaluate the historical reliability of Matthew's picture of the Pharisees.[141]

1. *The Uses of 'Pharisees' and Other Related Terms in the Synoptic Gospels* (according to Luz, *Matthew 1–7*, pp. 52-70)[142]

Terms	Matthew	Mark	Luke
Φαρισαῖος	30	12	27
γραμματεῖς/Φαρισαῖοι	11	3	5
Φαρισαῖοι καὶ Σαδδουκαῖοι	5	0	0
ἀρχιερεῖς/Φαρισαῖοι	2	0	0
γραμματεύς	23	21	14
Σαδδουκαῖοι	7	1	1
ἀρχιερεύς	25	22	15
πρεσβύτερος	12	7	5
ἀρχιερεῖς/πρεσβύτεροι	8	1	1

---

140. Jeremias, *Jerusalem*, pp. 246-67; Schürer, *History*, II, pp. 381-403; A.J. Saldarini, *Pharisees, Scribes and Sadducees in Palestinian Society* (Edinburgh: T. & T. Clark, 1988); J. Neusner, *Jews and Christians: The Myth of a Common Tradition* (London: SCM Press, 1991), and many other books; Sanders, *Law*; idem, *Practice*, pp. 380-490; Wright, *People*, pp. 181-203; *et al.*

141. Cf. Mohrlang, *Matthew*, p. 20. However, some brief comments on both issues may be made when they are invited in the course of discussions.

142. Another convenient list of the uses of the terms can be found in D.E. Garland, *The Intention of Matthew 23* (NovTSup, 52; Leiden: Brill, 1979), pp. 218-21, though his summary statement at the end is not free from problems.

The following are my observations from the figures in the above table. (i) In Matthew Pharisees are more frequently mentioned than the other groups listed, and this phenomenon is remarkable when compared with Mark—in Mark scribes (21) and chief priests (22) appear nearly twice as frequently as Pharisees (12); according to Garland's list, on five occasions Matthew has Pharisees where Mark has scribes, whereas Matthew retains all Mark's references to Pharisees. In Luke the figure for Pharisees (27) is similar to that of Matthew (30), though the other groups (35) are less prominent than in Matthew (67) and Mark (51). (ii) Matthew combines Pharisees with other groups more often (18) than Mark (3) and Luke (5)—the most frequent combination is that with scribes (11) and it seems Matthew's characteristic use;[143] his combination of Pharisees with Sadducees (5) is unique and most striking;[144] his combination of Pharisees with the chief priests (2) is also unique and the latter case (27.62) is especially noteworthy because it is the only case where Pharisees appear in the passion narrative through all the synoptics.

A general tendency can be observed in all the three synoptics that scribes and Pharisees[145] are mentioned more frequently in the earlier part whereas the chief priests and elders become predominant figures in the later part (i.e. the passion narrative).

2. Areas of Conflict between Jesus and Pharisees in Matthew's Gospel

In Matthew Pharisees come into conflict with Jesus over his association with sinners (9.9-13; cf. Mk 2.13-17; Lk. 5.27-32), and over the failure of his disciples to observe the traditional regulations of fasting (9.14-15; cf. Mk 2.18-20; Lk. 5.33-35), sabbath (12.1-8, 9-14; cf. Mk 2.23-28; 3.1-6; Lk. 6.1-5, 6-11) and purity (15.1-20; cf. Mk 7.1-23; Lk. 11.37-41). A certain conflict is also implied in the dispute regarding the propriety of divorce (19.3-9; cf. Mk 10.2-12). Furthermore a significant portion of Jesus' teaching is set explicitly or implicitly in contrast to the Pharisaic teachings and practices of the law (e.g. 5.17-20, 21-48; 6.1-8, 16-18; 11.28-30 versus 23.4; etc.),[146] and such teaching as well as his direct criticisms against the Pharisees (especially ch. 23) may also have roused their hostility (cf. 15.12).

---

143. Seven cases out of eleven are found in ch. 23 alone. Mark has only three cases. Luke has five cases of the combination but interestingly without any overlap with those in Matthew.

144. For discussions of this controversial phenomenon, see on the one side S. van Tilborg, *Jewish Leaders in Matthew* (Leiden: Brill, 1972), p. 35; Meier, *Law*, pp. 18-19; *et al.*; on the other side, D.A. Carson, 'The Jewish Leaders in Matthew's Gospel: a Reappraisal', *JETS* 25 (1982), pp. 167-69; Stanton, 'Origin', p. 1919; Saldarini, *Pharisees*, pp. 166-67; France, *Evangelist*, pp. 106-107; *et al.*

145. Because of the limited scope of this excursus, I will not attempt to discuss the relation between the scribes and Pharisees and the implication of the combination of the two groups (and also of other combinations). For a brief account of these issues, see Garland, *Intention*, pp. 41-43; Saldarini, *Pharisees*, pp. 163-66; for the lists of literature covering the issues, see Garland, *Intention*, pp. 42-43 nn. 26, 28 and 29.

146. For further cases of contrasts, see Davies, *Setting*, pp. 291-92; Mohrlang, *Matthew*, pp. 20-21.

3. *Characterization of 'Pharisees' in Matthew's Gospel*

As an antithesis to the followers of Jesus, Pharisees are consistently portrayed as Jesus' opponents throughout the Gospel even when they are not specifically mentioned in Mark or Luke.[147] In Matthew they are always critical of Jesus' behaviour (e.g. 9.11; 12.24), and in their questions to Jesus they are hostile in their attitude[148] and malicious in their intent.[149] Moreover, they do not hesitate even to take counsel against him in order to kill him (12.14), and they take part in the request for a guard at Jesus' tomb after his burial (27.62).[150] It is true that in Matthew the Pharisees are neither the only opponents of Jesus nor are they always made the focal point of opposition.[151] But it is nonetheless undeniable that in Matthew the Pharisees receive a greater prominence in their opposition to Jesus.[152]

4. *Jesus' Verdict on 'Pharisees' in Matthew's Gospel*

Jesus' verdict on the Pharisees in Matthew is, as expected from the above observation, thoroughly negative. Jesus bitterly denounces their hypocrisy and ostentatiousness (15.1-12; 23.25-27, 28 and seven woes against them as 'hypocrites' in ch. 23; cf. 6.1-8, 16-18; 7.1-5), distorted casuistry (e.g. 23.23), self-righteousness (e.g. 9.13), self-glorification (e.g. 23.5-7), and legalism without genuine compassion and concern for others (9.10-13; 12.7; 23.4, 13, 23).[153] It is not surprising, then, that Jesus calls them 'evil and adulterous' (12.39; 16.4),[154] and 'brood of vipers' (12.34;

---

147. The followings are the passages with synoptic parallels where only Matthew refers to the Pharisees:

    12.24 (cf. 9.34)—Mk 3.22 (scribes); Lk. 11.14-15 (crowds)

    21.45—Mk 12.12 (scribes *et al.*); Lk. 20.19 (scribes *et al.*)

    22.34—Mk 12.28 (scribes); Lk. 10.25 (a lawyer)

    22.41—Mk 12.35 (scribes); Lk. 20.41 (scribes; cf v.46)

    23.2—Mk 12.36 (scribes); Lk. 20.46 (scribes)

    23.13—no Markan parallel; Lk. 11.52 (lawyers)

    23.29—no Markan parallel; Lk. 11.47-48 (lawyers)

    (cf. 3.7 no Markan parallel; Lk. 3.7 [crowds])

See H.F. Weiss, 'φαρισαῖος', *TDNT*, IX, pp. 37-38; cf. Hummel, *Auseinandersetzung*, pp. 12-14. There are also some other references to Pharisees which have no synoptic parallels: 5.20; 22.15; 23.15, 26; 27.62; cf. G.D. Kilpatrick, *The Origins of the Gospel according to St Matthew* (Oxford: Clarendon Press, 1946), p. 106.

148. Especially compare 22.34 with Mk 12.28; cf. Lk. 10.25.

149. Matthew's consistency in describing the Pharisees as hostile adversaries of Jesus and/or his disciples is further highlighted when it is compared with Luke's Gospel in which, though conflicts between the two parties remain, some of the Pharisees are at times favourable to Jesus when they eat with him (Lk. 7.36; 11.37; 14.1) or warn him of Herod's plots (Lk. 13.31).

150. No parallels in Mark and Luke. This is, in fact, the sole reference to the Pharisees after Jesus' arrest in all the synoptics.

151. Note the role of the chief priests and elders in the passion narrative. See Garland, *Intention*, p. 45; *pace* Weiss, 'φαρισαῖος', p. 39.

152. Garland, *Intention*, p. 45; France, *Evangelist*, p. 220; *et al.*

153. Mohrlang, *Matthew*, p. 20.

154. Such a verdict is not found in Mark (cf. Mk 8.11-12), and in Luke the verdict is directed to the crowds (cf. Lk. 11.29).

23.33; cf. 3.7). Furthermore, Jesus categorizes them as false leaders who, as 'blind guides' (15.14; 23.16, 17, 19, 24, 26), not only themselves reject God's agents and their message of the kingdom (23.34) but also become a hindrance to those who sincerely want to enter it (23.13). If 23.33-39 is, as D.E. Garland and others suggest, to be understood in direct relation to the previous part of the chapter,[155] Matthew seems to attribute Jerusalem's doom to the sins of the 'scribes and Pharisees' as false leaders of the people. At any rate, such righteousness of the Pharisees, as we have seen in section 2a, clearly falls short of the criterion for entering the kingdom (5.20).

5. *Conclusions*

Though the anti-Pharisaic attitude, as D.E. Garland points out, is not unique to Matthew,[156] his consistency in portraying the Pharisees as hostile opponents of Jesus is remarkable especially when it is compared with Luke's way of presenting the Pharisees.[157] Jesus' verdict on them in Matthew makes the picture of the Pharisees more striking. It may not be strange, therefore, that such a striking picture makes many scholars uncomfortable and leads them to seek some relieving solutions. Some scholars explain the problem in terms of Matthew's context, and often conclude that Matthew is simply reading his own context back into the situation of Jesus' ministry.[158] An extreme and regrettable corollary of such an explanation is to regard Matthew's portrayal of the Pharisees as purely prejudiced and to attribute little or no historical value to his Pharisaic materials.[159] Other scholars like Garland argue that, for Matthew, all the categories of opponents like Pharisees, Sadducees, scribes, high priests and elders constitute 'a homogeneous group' who are all 'stereotyped as false' most often 'under the rubric of Pharisees', and Pharisees (or more exactly scribes and Pharisees) is therefore used as a general term for 'the genus, false leaders of Israel'.[160] It is true that both these approaches are insightful

---

155. Garland, *Intention*, pp. 26-32, 170-209. See also E. Schweizer, 'Matthäus 21-25', in *Gemeinde*, pp. 116-25; *idem, Matthew*, pp. 401-403; he outlines thus: 22.15-46—the trial; 23.1-32—the verdict; 23.33-36—the sentence; 23.37–24.2—the execution (*Matthew*, p. 402).

156. *Intention*, p. 221.

157. For a brief account of Luke's more complex picture of the Pharisees, see S. Westerholm, 'Pharisees', *DJG*, p. 614.

158. Cf. Davies, *Setting*, pp. 290-92; D.R.A. Hare, *The Theme of Jewish Persecution of Christians in the Gospel according to St Matthew* (SNTSMS, 6; Cambridge: Cambridge University Press, 1967), pp. 80-96, 126-29; *et al.*

159. For a brief account and criticism of such a view, see France, *Evangelist*, pp. 221-22; to his list of literature on p. 221 n. 45 we may add Sanders's two recent books, *Law and Practice*, and J.D.G. Dunn, 'Pharisees, Sinners, and Jesus', in *idem, Jesus, Paul and the Law: Studies in Mark and Galatians* (London: SPCK, 1990), pp. 61-88, in which a response to Sanders's earlier view in his *Jesus* is found.

160. Garland, *Intention*, pp. 44-46; cf. Weiss, 'φαρισαῖος', pp. 38-39; J.D. Kingsbury, *Matthew—Proclamation Commentary* (Philadelphia: Fortress Press, 1977), p. 8; Sand, *Gesetz*, pp. 81-82. The term 'leaders', while regularly used by scholars, may not be entirely appropriate here, since Pharisees as such did not necessarily have a position of official 'leadership' during the first century CE in Palestine.

and viable to some extent. Yet Matthew does not seem to be either totally uncon-
scious of such distinctions or carelessly to dismiss the historical aspects of
Pharisaism in Jesus' time, especially when we pay enough attention to, for example,
Matthew's editorial note in 22.34 which clearly indicates that he did distinguish
between Sadducees and Pharisees, and also to their disappearance from the scene in
the passion narrative which is perfectly in keeping with the power structure of the
time as Sanders and others suggest.[161] We may then rather suggest, following
France's conclusion, that

> Matthew has focused on the Pharisees not so much because this is a convenient
> term of abuse for any religious opponent (this would rather reflect modern usage),
> but because he sees the essence of Jesus' conflict with the official religion of his
> time as falling in those areas of theology and ethics which were (and continued to
> be in his day) the special concern of the Pharisees (and particularly of those of
> them who were scribes).[162]

Finally, Matthew's anti-Pharisaism by no means provides any ground for anti-
Judaism or anti-Semitism, though it has tragically served in that way through the
centuries. It seems fairly arguable that the Gospel is still open to Jews who may yet
respond to the gospel (cf. 28.19).[163] The only reason that the Pharisees (and other
leaders) are so severely criticized by Jesus in Matthew is the fact that they as
religious guides not only failed to respond to the teaching and work of Christ and his
kingdom but also misguided other Jews and became a hindrance to them. May we
then conclude that in Matthew Jesus criticizes or rejects not Israel as a whole but only
its unresponsive and therefore unworthy religious specialists, especially Pharisees?
The referent of 'Pharisees' in the following chapters, then, is these unresponsive
Pharisees as characterized in Matthew.

---

161. See especially Sanders, *Practice*, pp. 380-490; cf. Weiss, 'φαρισαῖος', p. 37.

162. France, *Evangelist*, p. 222. Cf. Mohrlang, *Matthew*, pp. 20-21: 'it is clearly Pharisaic
interpretation and practice of the law that Matthew is here concerned to combat, and from
which he wishes to protect the Christian community' (p. 20); Stanton, 'Judaism', pp. 156-57:
'The harsh words directed against the scribes and Pharisees are not to be explained as a setting
up of *straw men* as an example of the reverse of Christian discipleship' (p. 157—italics mine).

163. J.P. Meier, 'Nations or Gentiles in Matthew 28.19?', *CBQ* 39 (1977), pp. 94-102;
France, *Evangelist*, pp. 235-37; Stanton, 'Judaism', pp. 157-61; T. De Kruijf, 'Go Therefore and
Make Disciples of All Nations', *Bijdragen* 54 (1993), pp. 19-29. For a different view, see
D.R.A. Hare and D.J. Harrington, '"Make Disciples of all the Gentiles" (Mt. 28.19)', *CBQ* 37
(1975), pp. 359-69.

Chapter 4

JESUS AND THE SABBATH IN MATTHEW'S GOSPEL:
TEXTS, CO-TEXTS AND CONTEXTS (I)

In Matthew the term σάββατον appears eleven times (12.1, 2, 5 [twice], 8, 10, 11, 12; 24.20; 28.1 [twice]).[1] Most of these references (8 out of 11) are found in two consecutive passages (12.1-8, 9-14), both of which have parallels in Mark (Mk 2.23-28; 3.1-6) and Luke (Lk. 6.1-5, 6-11); it will naturally be on these two passages that our investigation is focused. The sabbath reference in 24.20 is unique to Matthew (cf. Mk 13.18), and needs to be discussed substantially.[2] Though the term σάββατον appears twice in 28.1, the reference is, in fact, to an event which happened on Sunday and not on the sabbath; therefore they will not be the immediate object of our investigation in this chapter. There is, however, a further passage worthy of note, 27.62-66, which has no synoptic parallel, and in which, though the term σάββατον is not used, the Pharisees' request and activity *on the sabbath*[3] is presented.

In this chapter and the following I will thus concentrate my investigation on the three sabbath passages (Mt. 12.1-8, 9-14; 24.20) which explicitly mention the sabbath issue, though the significance and implication of 27.62-66 will also be considered whenever it is deemed appropriate.

1.   In 28.1 the term is once used not to mean the sabbath but the week in the phrase μίαν σαββάτων ('the first day of the week'). Four of these references (12.5 [twice]; 12.11; 24.20) are unique to Matthew, while all the rest have parallels in Mark and Luke. In Mark and Luke the term appears 13 (1.21; 2.23, 24, 27 [twice], 28; 3.2, 4; 6.2; 15.42; 16.1, 2, 9) and 20 times (4.16, 31; 6.1, 2, 5, 6, 7, 9; 13.10, 14 [twice], 15, 16; 14.1, 3, 5; 18.12; 23.54, 56; 24.1) respectively; cf. Turner, 'Sabbath', pp. 100, 139 nn. 3 and 4—he miscounts one appearance in Lk. 6.5 as two and makes the total appearances in Luke 21 rather than 20. See Chapter 6 Chart 1 (pp. 298-99).

2.   This verse will be discussed separately in Chapter 5.

3.   In 27.62 we find an odd expression τῇ δὲ ἐπαύριον, ἥτις ἐστιν μετὰ τὴν παρασκευήν ('on the next day, that is, after the day of Preparation') which must refer to the sabbath.

Their synoptic parallels (Mk 2.23-3.6; Lk. 6.1-11; cf. Mk 13.18) will, of course, also be kept in view throughout the investigation.

This chapter will demonstrate why the preliminary studies in Chapters 1-3 needed to be undertaken at some length. The observations and conclusions in Chapter 1 will provide a solid ground for the discussion as we are in a position to discuss the primary intention and ultimate goal of the sabbath and its fulfilment. The investigation in Chapter 2 will supply a balanced, though still limited, picture of the views of and practices on the sabbath in the time of Jesus and Matthew, and enable me to reconstruct a probable context for the text under discussion. The necessity for Chapter 3 can hardly be exaggerated: Jesus' attitude to the sabbath is only one aspect of his attitude to the Old Testament (especially to the law), and no study of Jesus' attitude to the sabbath in Matthew can be reliable until it has been set in the context of Matthew's more general presentation of Jesus' view of the law in Matthew.[4]

1. Co-texts of the Sabbath Controversy Pericopes (12.1-8, 9-14)

For the proper understanding of the two sabbath controversy pericopes, seeing the pericopes in the light of their co-texts seems indispensable.

a. Interrelation between the Two Pericopes

It is quite clear that Mt. 12.1-8 and 12.9-14 are two separate pericopes.[5] These two pericopes, however, are linked together in all the synoptic Gospels, and this may strongly suggest that all synoptists wanted to see them as interrelated, probably because both deal with the same issue, that of Jesus' attitude to the sabbath and the objection to it by his opponents. In Matthew's presentation their relation is still clearer: (1) his redaction in v. 9 (μεταβὰς ἐκεῖθεν)[6] makes Mark's implication that both events occurred on the same sabbath (cf. Mk 3.1) more apparent; (2) while in Luke the opponents in each pericope are different groups (6.1-5, 'some of the Pharisees'; 6.6-11, 'the scribes and the Pharisees), in Matthew (and also in Mark) the same opponents are in view for both pericopes; (3) in that case, the decision to destroy Jesus in the final verse (v. 14) not only concludes the second pericope but may also serve as the

---

4.   Cf. Carson, 'Sabbath', p. 58; Turner, 'Sabbath', p. 108.
5.   Note they report different incidents.
6.   Cf. Mk 3.1, in which the clause is lacking; cf. also Lk. 6.6, which reads Ἐγένετο δὲ ἐν ἑτέρῳ σαββάτῳ! See Lohse, 'σάββατον', p. 24, esp. n. 194.

overall conclusion to both pericopes. In my co-text study it will be then more appropriate to deal with them as a unit, and regard the pericopes immediately before 12.1-8 and after 12.9-14 as the immediate co-text of the unit.

b. *Broader Co-text: 11.2–12.50*

Before we go into the study of the immediate co-text, it seems proper to consider the broader co-text first, since it may enable us not only to see the text and its relation to the immediate co-text in the light of the flow of its broader narrative block (chs. 11–12—see below) but also eventually to see the place and function of the text (12.1-14) and of its co-text in the light of the plot of the whole Gospel.

Many scholars rightly note that chs. 11–12 constitute a narrative block which is not only 'framed' between two discourses (chs. 10, 13), but also has certain recurrent theme(s).[7] These are some of the suggested themes: on the one hand, the unbelief, opposition, and rejection of Israel,[8] and, on the other, the invitation of Jesus.[9] The motif of unbelief and rejection appears throughout the two chapters: for example, 'this generation' who do not respond to Jesus and John (11.16-19); woes against the three Galilean cities which failed to repent in the face of Jesus' mighty works (11.20-24); two sabbath controversies in which the Pharisees oppose Jesus' attitude to the sabbath (12.1-8, 9-14); the Beelzebul controversy in which once again the Pharisees attribute Jesus' healing power to Beelzebul (12.22-37); the request for a sign by some of the scribes and Pharisees and Jesus' condemnation of 'this generation' (12.38-45). Though the negative response to Jesus by various groups/ cities of Israel (cf. even John's response in 11.2-3) is thus a predominant theme, it is also noteworthy that Jesus' positive attitude to various other groups, especially his invitation and the result of the positive response to

---

7.   For example, classically Bacon, *Studies*, pp. 205-15, 288-93, and his followers; C.H. Lohr, 'Oral Techniques in the Gospel of Matthew', *CBQ* 23 (1961), p. 427; Kingsbury, *Structure*, p. 20; A. Sand, *Das Evangelium nach Matthäus* (RNT; Regensburg: Verlag Friedrich Pustet, 1986), pp. 235-36; Howell, *Story*, pp. 138-41; *et al.* Cf. C. Deutsch, *Hidden Wisdom and the Easy Yoke* (JSNTSup, 18; Sheffield: JSOT Press, 1987), pp. 21-22—though she argues that her text (11.25-30) must be understood in the light of 11.2–13.58 rather than that of 11.2–12.50, she still considers 11.2–12.50 as a sub-section which constitutes a narrative unit.

8.   Kingsbury, *Structure*, p. 20; Deutsch, *Yoke*, p. 22; Howell, *Story*, pp. 138-39; Davies and Allison, *Matthew*, II, p. 234; *et al.*

9.   Howell, *Story*, p. 140; Davies and Allison, *Matthew*, II, p. 234.

it, constitutes another key theme; in 11.25-30 Jesus shows his positive attitude to the babes and offers his invitation to all who are heavy laden; in 12.18-21 Jesus is portrayed as the hope for the Gentiles; in 12.46-50 family membership is offered to anybody (the disciples in particular are in view here—cf. v. 49) who does the will of his Father in heaven.[10]

Along with these themes a crucial issue running through the two chapters is that of Christology. In 11.2-6 it is indicated that he is the Christ who is to come;[11] in 11.10-14 and 12.25-29 it is implied that Jesus himself is the one who has already brought the kingdom of heaven; in 11.19 (cf. vv. 25-27) Jesus seems to identify himself with wisdom; in 11.25-30 Jesus reveals himself as the one who reveals the Father and his will and who invites people to himself; in 12.5-6, 41-42 Jesus proclaims that he is greater than the temple, Jonah and Solomon (cf. also vv. 3-4); in 12.8 he pronounces that he is Lord of the sabbath; in 12.15-21 he is described as the chosen servant upon whom God puts his Spirit—this pericope is impressively linked with the following pericope (vv. 22-37), in which the Pharisees attribute Jesus' work of the Spirit to Beelzebul.

In addition to these thematic tendencies, W.D. Davies and D.C. Allison attempt to show that the structure of chs. 11–12 also demonstrates their unity as a narrative block.[12] They divide chs. 11–12 into three triads, and present the following pattern:

		1	2	3
Unbelief/rejection	1	11.2-19	12.1-8	12.22-37
Unbelief/rejection	2	11.20-24	12.9-14	12.38-45
Invitation/acceptance	3	11.25-30	12.15-21	12.46-50[13]

10.   Cf. 11.5-6, in which the good news is preached to the poor and various disabled people are restored.

11.   Cf. also 11.7-15, in which Jesus reveals the identity of John the Baptist and his relation to the kingdom of heaven.

12.   *Matthew*, II, pp. 233-34; cf. B.C. Lategan, 'Structural Interrelations in Matthew 11-12', *Neotestamentica* 11 (1977), pp. 115-29.

13.   *Matthew*, II, p. 234. For the division of ch. 11 into three units, see further F.W. Beare, *The Gospel according to St Matthew: A Commentary* (Oxford: Basil Blackwell, 1981), p. 255; France, *Matthew*, pp. 192-201; *et al.*; cf. Hare, *Matthew*, p. 120. For the division of ch. 12 into six units, see further Meier, *Matthew*, pp. 128-40; Gnilka, *Matthäusevangelium*, I, pp. 442-72; *et al.* For a different picture of the structural relationship between the two chapters, see U. Luz, *Das Evangelium nach Matthäus (8–17)* (EKKNT, 1/2; Zürich and Brauschweig: Benziger Verlag, 1990), p. 225.

As Davies and Allison confess, Matthew might not have intended such a neatly symmetrical structure.[14] For example, at least two-thirds of 11.2-19 does not necessarily represent the unbelief/rejection of Israel, since 11.2-15 is rather concerned with the identity of Jesus (vv. 2-6) and that of John the Baptist (vv. 7-15). Having said this, however, when we consider Matthew's frequent use of the triad throughout the Gospel,[15] their pattern may well represent Matthew's literary intent, at least in terms of the overall flow of the narrative in the two chapters. In that case, the pattern above, along with the thematic tendencies as observed, may help us to a certain extent to see the role and place of these pericopes (primarily, 12.1-8, 9-14; and also 11.25-30; 12.15-21) in the flow.

c. *Immediate Co-text: 11.25–12.21*
According to Davies and Allison's pattern of the structure of chs. 11–12 above, 11.25-30 and 12.15-21, both of which are interestingly invitation/acceptance pericopes, constitute the immediate co-text of these texts, that is, the two unbelief/rejection (or controversy) pericopes (12.1-8, 9-14). The function of 11.25-30 and 12.15-21 as the immediate co-text of our text (12.1-14), however, is demonstrated not simply by their position immediately next to the text, but more significantly by their themes which are intimately linked with that of the text.

i. *Mt. 11.25-30*. The phrase ἐν ἐκείνῳ τῷ καιρῷ of 12.1 is characteristically Matthean,[16] and ties our text to its preceding pericope (11.25-30) thematically (or theologically),[17] if not chronologically.[18]

---

14.   *Matthew*, I, p. 69.
15.   Cf. Allen, *Matthew*, p. lxv; Luz, *Matthew 1–7*, p. 38; Davies and Allison, *Matthew*, I, pp. 86-87. For the frequent use of it in Jewish literature, see, for example, *m. Ab.* ch. 1; cf. G. Delling, 'τρεῖς κτλ.', *TDNT*, VIII, pp. 216ff.
16.   This phrase is lacking in both Mk 2.23 and Lk. 6.1. Mark and Luke instead have καὶ ἐγένετο and ἐγένετο δὲ respectively. The same phrase also occurs in Mt. 11.25 and 14.1, and they are, in fact, the only three occurrences in the New Testament in that form; cf. Sand, *Matthäus*, p. 254; Deutsch, *Yoke*, p. 25.
17.   Schweizer, *Matthew*, p. 277; Luz, *Matthäus (8–17)*, pp. 198, 229; D.J. Harrington, 'Sabbath Tensions: Matthew 12:1-14 and other New Testament Texts', in Eskenazi *et al.* (eds.), *Sabbath*, p. 47; *et al.*
18.   Davies and Allison, *Matthew*, II, p. 305; cf. L. Morris, *The Gospel according to Matthew* (Leicester: IVP, 1992), p. 291, esp. n. 64. Carson, 'Four Gospels', p. 75, however, is not so sceptical about the chronological significance of the phrase: 'As if such a juxtaposition were not enough, Matthew then carefully points out that

Thematic correspondence between 11.25-30 and our text is apparent. The following are the more impressive examples of this correspondence: (i) Σόφοι καὶ σύνετοι of v. 25 may most naturally (though, of course, not exclusively)[19] refer to the immediately following opponents of Jesus, the Pharisees of 12.2, 14, 24, 38 (and probably also the scribes of 12.38)—this suggestion is further supported by the fact that they are wise and well instructed in terms of Torah, and that they usually appear as the opponents of Jesus in Matthew's Gospel.[20] (ii) The sonship and the authority to reveal all things given to the Son by the Father, which are affirmed in the clause Πάντα μοι παρεδόθη ὑπὸ τοῦ πατρός μου of v. 27, become the source of the authority of his interpretation of Torah over against the Jewish tradition in 12.1-14 and of his declaration of the lordship of the sabbath in 12.8.[21] (iii) In the light of 23.4, we may assume that οἱ κοπιῶντες καὶ πεφορτισμένοι of v. 28 refers to those who are under the burden of the Pharisaic interpretation of Torah;[22] a more specific referent of the burden in the immediate co-text then may well be the Pharisaic interpretation of the sabbath law.[23] (iv) Jesus' ζυγός of v. 29, which is described as 'easy' (χρηστός) in v. 30,[24] may most likely refer to Jesus' teaching including his interpretation of Torah over against that of the Pharisees,[25] and the sabbath controversies which immediately follow (12.1-14) may illustrate the contrast between the two kinds of burden/yoke.[26] (v) Jesus' gentleness, as characterized in v. 29, is

the Sabbath conflicts occurred "at that time" (ἐν ἐκείνῳ τῷ καιρῷ)—presumably at or near the time when Jesus had spoken of His rest'.

19.   The referent of the phrase may also include this generation of 11.16 and the three cities of 11.20-24, and perhaps even all the unresponsive Israelites throughout the Gospel; see Deutsch, *Yoke*, p. 31.

20.   Davies and Allison, *Matthew*, II, p. 275; Hagner, *Matthew 1–13*, p. 318; *et al.*; cf. Deutsch, *Yoke*, pp. 30-31.

21.   Deutsch, *Yoke*, p. 34.

22.   Suggs, *Wisdom*, p. 106; Deutsch, *Yoke*, p. 41; *et al. Contra* G.N. Stanton, 'Matthew 11.28-30: Comfortable Words?', in *idem*, *People*, pp. 372-75.

23.   Suggs, *Wisdom*, p. 107; Deutsch, *Yoke*, p. 41.

24.   Cf. also τὸ φορτίον μου of v. 30, which is described as ἐλαφρόν.

25.   Strecker, *Gerechtigkeit*, p. 173; Deutsch, *Yoke*, pp. 42-43; *et al.* The following clause, καὶ μάθετε ἀπ' ἐμοῦ, may also support this suggestion. See our further discussion below, section 2b.

26.   Cf. Deutsch, *Yoke*, p. 43; *idem*, 'Wisdom in Matthew: Transformation of a Symbol', *NovT* 32 (1990), p. 38; Hare, *Matthew*, pp. 128-30.

once again well illustrated and highlighted in the two sabbath controversies (12.1-14), especially in contrast to the contentiousness of the Pharisees, and further affirmed in the following citation of the Servant Song of Isa. 42.1-4 (12.15-21). (vi) Ἀνάπαυσις of v. 29, which is promised to all who come to Jesus (cf. v. 28) and take his yoke (cf. v. 29), may refer to the experience of the eschatological sabbath which has been anticipated through Israel's history but is now fulfilled by Jesus;[27] in that case it effectively anticipates the following sabbath controversies.

We may then conclude with some confidence that, for Matthew, understanding our text in the light of its immediately preceding pericope (11.25-30) is imperative. This conclusion is further affirmed when we add a comparative observation of the co-text of the sabbath controversies in Mark and Luke. In both Gospels the sabbath controversies are preceded by Jesus' saying about new wineskins (Mk 2.21-22; Lk. 5.36-39; cf. Mt. 9.16-17). This saying signifies that by Jesus' presence there are now new forms as well as new content;[28] this saying, then, introduces the two sabbath controversies perfectly well,[29] since in both controversies the sabbath is supposed to have a new form in the presence of 'Lord of the sabbath'. In that case, and if Matthew knew this order from his material which seems highly plausible, Matthew may have had a strong reason for separating these two well-related pericopes in order to place the latter in a new setting; and we may suppose that such a careful writer as Matthew may have done so because he saw it as more appropriate.[30]

The immediately preceding pericope (11.25-30) of our text, and especially the latter part (vv. 28-30) of it, thus demonstrates a significant link with our text, and it seems imperative to understand our text in the light of its relation to its preceding pericope. It is therefore appropriate

27. Bacchiocchi, *New Testament*, pp. 263-70; Davies and Allison, *Matthew*, II, pp. 288-89; *et al.*

28. Carson, 'Sabbath', p. 74.

29. Cf. J. Nolland, *Luke 1–9.20* (WBC, 35a; Dallas: Word Books, 1989), p. 253. This does not deny, however, that this saying is more closely attached to the previous fasting–wedding pericope (Mk 2.18-20; Lk. 5.33-35). For the question of unity between the two pericopes, see F. Hahn, 'Die Bildworte vom neuen Flicken und vom jungen Wein', *EvT* 31 (1971), p. 362; R.H. Gundry, *Mark: A Commentary on his Apology for the Cross* (Grand Rapids: Eerdmans, 1993), pp. 138-39; Nolland, *Luke 1–9.20*, p. 243; cf. *Gos. Thom.* 47.

30. Cf. A. Lindemann, 'Der Sabbat ist um des Menschen willen geworden...', *WD* 15 (1979), pp. 95-96.

for us to include 11.25-30, especially vv. 28-30,[31] as a part of the object of our exegetical study.

ii. *Mt. 12.15-21.* Whereas the Markan version of the sabbath controversies is followed by and very loosely associated to a pericope which offers 'a fairly general statement of Jesus' activity and its effect'[32] (3.7-12), Matthew adds to our text a well-designed pericope which offers a brief summary report of Jesus' ministry (12.15-16) and a long quotation from Isa. 42.1-4 with an introductory formula (12.17-21).[33] Matthew's heavily abbreviated report of Jesus' ministry (12.15-16) in comparison with that of the Markan version (3.7-12), in effect, functions as an introduction of the formula quotation[34] into the broader co-text, rather than as an independent statement which solely governs the quotation. Though the quotation formula of v. 17 (ἵνα πληρωθῇ τὸ ῥηθὲν...λέγοντος) is grammatically attached to vv. 15-16, that link is not to be pressed too much. If Matthew intended to relate the quotation solely to vv. 15-16,[35] only a single verse (v. 19) out of four (vv. 18-21) would be enough.[36] How could Matthew then include the unnecessary three verses here, if, as B. Gerhardsson properly observes, he is 'strictly economical in the length of his quotations'?[37] We may, therefore, rather suppose that Matthew intended his longest quotation to be understood in the light of a more extended co-text (immediately, 11.25–12.14; but more broadly,

31.   Most scholars note three subunits of 11.25-30: (i) vv. 25-26; (ii) v. 27; (iii) vv. 28-30—e.g. Bultmann, *History*, pp. 159-60; Davies and Allison, *Matthew*, II, pp. 271-72; *et al.* In my exegetical studies my concern will be focused on the last part of the pericope (vv. 28-30).

32.   Gundry, *Mark*, p. 159; Gundry points out that the statement does not summarize the preceding pericopes, 'since the element of controversy in most of 2.1–3.6 is missing'.

33.   This quotation is unique to Matthew; and it is the longest one in Matthew.

34.   Cf. France, *Evangelist*, pp. 181-82.

35.   Cf. Strecker, *Gerechtigkeit*, pp. 69-70; Stendahl, *School*, pp. 110-15; Barth, 'Law', pp. 125-26.

36.   Luz, *Matthäus (8–17)*, p. 246; cf. O.L. Cope, *Matthew: A Scribe Trained for the Kingdom of Heaven* (CBQMS, 5; Washington, DC: The Catholic Biblical Association of America, 1976), p. 34; J.H. Neyrey, 'The Thematic Use of Isaiah 42.1-4 in Matthew 12', *Bib* 63 (1982), p. 458. For detailed discussions of the theme of v. 19 and its relation to the preceding two verses, and of other themes of the quotation, see below, section 5.

37.   *The Mighty Acts of Jesus according to Matthew* (Lund: Gleerup, 1979), p. 26.

chs. 11–12,[38] and perhaps even beyond the two chapters).[39]

We need then to ask whether 11.25–12.14 along with 12.15-16 provides any identifiable basis for the quotation of Isa. 42.1-4; and my answer to the question is affirmative, as the following thematic correspondences and/or contrasts[40] demonstrate[41]: (i) If we suppose that Matthew understood Isa. 42.1-4, and especially the clause ὁ ἀγαπητός μου εἰς ὃν εὐδόκησεν ἡ ψυχή μου (cf. 3.17; 17.5), in messianic terms, Matthew may well have intended to strengthen Jesus' two crucial Christological statements of vv. 6 and 8 (τοῦ ἱεροῦ μεῖζόν ἐστιν ὧδε; κύριος γάρ ἐστιν τοῦ σαββάτου ὁ υἱὸς τοῦ ἀνθρώπου) by including v. 18 in the quotation. (ii) Moreover, the picture of Jesus as the bearer of the Spirit as mentioned in v. 18 (θήσω τὸ πνεῦμά μου ἐπ' αὐτόν) is already present, though implicit, in his healing activity in 12.9-14; Matthew here seems to contrast such an implicit picture of Jesus with the implicit spiritual state of 'their [the Pharisees'] synagogue' (v. 10)[42] which not only lacks the Spirit but fails to recognize Jesus as the bearer of the Spirit,[43] as shown in their antagonistic attitude to Jesus and his

---

38. Especially 12.22-50 where the themes of the quotation are further developed and/or illustrated; cf. Cope, *Scribe*, pp. 32-52, esp. pp. 37-46—he rather suggests 12.1-50 as a co-text of the quotation (pp. 46-52). Cf. also Neyrey, 'Use', p. 459.

39. Cf. Luz, *Matthäus (8–17)*, pp. 246-50; Davies and Allison, *Matthew*, II, pp. 323-24.

40. If we suppose that a certain consistent thematic flow is running through chs. 11–12, and that the character of the Pharisees, who are Jesus' opponents throughout ch. 12, is contrasted with that of Jesus, the factors of contrast as well as correspondence are to be noted carefully. The lack of controversy and the absence of the Pharisees in 12.15-21 (cf. also 11.25-30; 12.46-50) does not mean that the pericope is independent from its surrounding controversy materials; we may rather suggest that the pericope belongs to a positive part of the whole well-organized structure (see Davies and Allison's three triads pattern above, section 1b), and is to be understood, therefore, in the light of its surrounding controversy (and also other two positive) materials. In that case contrast is an important element in the thematic flow of this section.

41. *Pace* Cope, *Scribe*, pp. 34-35.

42. For the significance of the repeated use of 'their synagogue', see J.C. Anderson, *Matthew's Narrative Web: Over, and Over, and Over Again* (JSNTSup, 91; Sheffield: JSOT Press, 1994), pp. 57-59. Cf. Banks, *Jesus*, p. 123.

43. Harrington, *Matthew*, p. 181. If Matthew's community was still in tension with the synagogue(s), as I supposed above, this narrative may have been understood by Matthew's reader as a powerful criticism against the current rabbinic Judaism and its synagogue by implication; see Neyrey, 'Use', p. 459.

work (cf. vv. 10, 14); this implicit picture of conflict becomes explicit in 12.22-32 where the Pharisees attribute Jesus' work by the Holy Spirit to Beelzebul. (iii) Whereas God loves and is well pleased with his chosen servant Jesus (ὁ ἀγαπητός μου εἰς ὃν εὐδόκησεν ἡ ψυχή μου), the Pharisees are not pleased with Jesus and his disciples (vv. 2, 10), but rather condemn them (v. 7) and finally take counsel against him to kill him (v. 14). (iv) The referent of κάλαμος συντετριμμένος and λίνον τυφόμενον in the co-text is not easy to define, and perhaps needs to be discerned rather in the Gospel as a whole;[44] G. Barth, however, convincingly holds that these phrases may refer to οἱ κοπιῶντες καὶ πεφορτισμένοι of 11.28 and various groups of the poor people of 11.5, rather than the [ὄχλοι] πολλοί of 12.15 who are supposed to be ill.[45] (v) Jesus' humility and gentleness as characterized in vv. 19-20 may be most naturally understood in the light of Jesus' own statement in 11.28-30 (especially v. 29—πραΰς εἰμι καὶ ταπεινὸς τῇ καρδίᾳ); his gentleness, in particular, is further illustrated in 12.1-14.[46]

It may thus be confidently suggested that Matthew put his longest quotation in the present co-text because he thought it appropriate to understand it in the light not just of 12.15-16 but rather of its more extended preceding pericopes. Indeed it may also be suggested that the sabbath controversy materials, especially in their positive implications, may be better understood by seeing them as a deliberate preparation for the subsequent quotation. In that case it seems appropriate to include the quotation as part of the object of my exegetical investigation.

d. *The Place of 12.1-14 and its Co-text in the Plot of Matthew*
It becomes quite clear from the co-text investigation that our text (12.1-14) is not a section independent of its co-text but fits into its immediate co-text and also into its broader co-text perfectly well. The question now is what the place and function of our text and its co-text is in the plot of the whole Gospel.

According to my preliminary considerations in Chapter 3, 11.2–12.50 belongs to the second phase (4.17–16.20) of the Gospel story, and comprises the third narrative block of the Gospel enclosed by two discourses

---

44. E.g. 9.36; see Barth, 'Law', p. 128; cf. Davies and Allison, *Matthew*, II, p. 326; Luz, *Matthäus (8–17)*, p. 250.

45. Barth, 'Law', p. 128; cf. France, *Matthew*, p. 206.

46. See my exegetical studies below. Cf. Luz, *Matthäus (8–17)*, p. 250; Howell, *Story*, p. 238.

(9.35–11.1, on the commissioning and encouragement; 13.1-53, parables of the kingdom)[47]. To identify the referent of τὰ ἔργα τοῦ Χριστοῦ of 11.2 which appears in the first verse of the narrative block seems crucial in clarifying the relationship between these two chapters and the previous ones. The fact that Jesus relates it to 'hearing' and 'seeing' in 11.4 and 'healing' and 'preaching' in 11.5 shows that the phrase refers back not only to the miracles of chs. 8–9 but also to Jesus' teaching of chs. 5-7, both of which are interpreted as messianic by Matthew (cf. τοῦ Χριστοῦ). We may even include ch. 10 in the referent of the phrase, because 'the disciples' words and deeds are in effect a re-enactment or continuation of their master's words and deeds'.[48] The phrase, thus, comprehensively summarizes the content of 4.17–11.1,[49] in which Matthew presents primarily the ministry of Jesus in words and deeds (see especially 4.23; 9.35) which has fulfilled the Old Testament (5.17) and inaugurated the kingdom of heaven (4.17; cf. 5.3, 10), and also the role of disciples in the kingdom (4.18-22; 8.18-22; 9.9-17; 9.35–10.4). These words and deeds of Jesus naturally expect responses from various people, and it is these responses, mostly negative, which, along with Jesus' still open invitation, form the themes of chs. 11–12. Such various responses are explained in Jesus' parables of ch. 13, and further exemplified in chs. 14–16 'until the true response is found in Peter's confession in 16.13-20', which completes the second phase of the Gospel story.[50]

My preliminary considerations in Chapter 3 also show that Matthew's story of the life and ministry of Jesus is divided into three phases according to the time line in the story: (i) the birth of Jesus and John's preparation (1.1–4.16); (ii) the ministry of Jesus and Israel's response (4.17–16.20); (iii) Jesus' suffering, death, and resurrection (16.21–28.20). His story begins with the birth of Jesus, which has fulfilled the predictions of the Old Testament (cf. especially the formula quotations in

47. As regards the relationship between the narrative and the discourses under the threefold division (i.e. 1.1–4.16; 4.17–16.20; 16.21–28.20) in Matthew, see Bauer, *Structure*, pp. 129-32.

48. Davies and Allison, *Matthew*, II, p. 240; cf. H.J. Held, 'Matthew as Interpreter of the Miracle Stories', in Bornkamm, *et al.*, *Tradition*, pp. 250-52; Gerhardsson, *Acts*, pp. 31-32.

49. Held, 'Miracle', pp. 250-52; cf. Kingsbury, *Story*, pp. 72, 76, 161; cf. also France, *Matthew*, p. 191; Davies and Allison, *Matthew*, II, p. 240.

50. France, *Matthew*, p. 191; cf. Kingsbury, *Structure*, pp. 19-20; Bauer, *Structure*, pp. 93-95.

chs. 1–2), and the preparation of John the Baptist who has fulfilled the prophecy about Elijah (3.1-12; cf. 11.2-19). In this first phase, Matthew presents Jesus as the Davidic messiah, the Son of God (cf. 3.16-17).[51] In the second phase (4.17–16.20), Matthew tells of Jesus' ministry to Israel which has fulfilled the law and the prophets and inaugurated the kingdom of heaven, and of Israel's various responses to him. Whereas variousJewish groups of people, especially the Pharisees, repudiate, reject, and conspire to kill him (cf. especially 12.1-14), and the crowds falsely regard him merely as a prophet of one kind or another (cf. 16.13-14), the disciples follow him, are taught by him, and finally confess him to be the Christ, Son of God (16.20; cf. 11.27; 14.33). In the third phase (16.21–28.20), Matthew completes his story of Jesus by presenting his movement towards Jerusalem and his suffering, death, and resurrection, which have fulfilled the will of God as revealed in the Old Testament, and have brought the kingdom of heaven even to Gentiles as well as to Jews.

The place and function of chs. 11–12 (and 11.25–12.21 in particular) in the plot of the Gospel story as I have described it just above may thus be understood as follows: (1) 11.2–12.50 serves as a turning point in the second phase of the story, that is, it starts to present various responses to Jesus' messianic words and deeds; and our text (12.1-14), in particular, presents two outstanding negative responses to Jesus' messianic teaching about and deeds on the sabbath, by the Pharisees, the most prominent opponents of Jesus in the Gospel story. (2) Moreover, 12.1-14 provides the first clear indication that at the end of the Gospel story Jesus' messianic words and deeds will lead his opponents to kill him (12.14; cf. 27.7).[52] (3) 11.2–12.50, though not so markedly as the preceding chapters (i.e. 4.17–11.1), still continues to present Jesus as the fulfilling messiah through his words and deeds, as 11.25-30 and 12.15-21 show; even 12.1-14, which is characterized by the Pharisees' negative responses, may be taken as presenting Jesus as the messiah who fulfils the sabbath (cf. 12.8) which, being a part of the Old Testament law, has awaited this fulfilment; this notion is further supported not only by the content of 11.28-30 which may refer to the eschatological sabbath which is now fulfilled by Jesus but also by the fact that our text (12.1-14) is program

---

51. Kingsbury, *Story*, pp. 43-58.

52. For the significance of the repeated use of συμβούλιον λαμβάνειν (take counsel) in Matthew's Gospel, see Anderson, *Web*, pp. 113-16, esp. p. 114.

matically placed between those two eschatological and Christological pericopes (11.25-30; 12.15-21).[53]

If Matthew's plot is focused on Jesus as the messiah who fulfilled the whole scriptural revelation in the Old Testament and inaugurated the kingdom of heaven, and on the responses to himself and his words and deeds, our text with its surrounding immediate co-text plays a significant role in the plot (i) by showing an important aspect of the messianic fulfilment, that is, the fulfilment of the sabbath which played a central part in Judaism at the time of Jesus as well as in Matthew's day, and (ii) by presenting a fatally negative response by the Pharisees to such an important aspect of the messianic fulfilment as the eschatological significance of the sabbath shown by Jesus—that response is fatal because it results, for the first time in the flow of the Gospel story, in the decision to kill Jesus.

2. God's Revelation and Jesus' Yoke (11.25-30)

The two sabbath controversy pericopes (Mt. 12.1-8, 9-14) have parallels in both Mark (2.23-28; 3.1-6) and Luke (6.1-5, 6-11). These pericopes, however, are preceded by the pericope concerning Jesus' invitation and promise of rest (11.25-30) only in Matthew, and, as we have observed above, the link between these two pericopes and the preceding one is intimate. In order therefore to understand the two sabbath controversy pericopes in the light of their relation to the preceding pericope, I shall commence my exegetical investigation with 11.25-30.[54]

The importance attached to Mt. 11.25-30 (as a whole or in part) is well demonstrated by the scholarly attention given to it since D.F. Strauss's publication of the first significant modern study of the pericope in 1863,[55] and A.M. Hunter's statement that Mt. 11.25-30 provides 'perhaps the most important verses in the Synoptic Gospels'[56] may not

---

53. The fact that both 11.28-30 and 12.17-21 are unique to Matthew may show how Matthew programmatically constructed the co-text of the two sabbath pericopes.

54. A partial parallel to this pericope is found in Lk. 10.21-22.

55. 'Jesu Weheruf über Jerusalem und die σοφία τοῦ θεοῦ. Matth. 23, 34-39, Luk. 11,49-51. 13,34-35. Ein Beitrag zur johanneischen Frage', *ZNW* 6 (1863), pp. 84ff; I owe this information to H.D. Betz, 'The Logion of the Easy Yoke and of Rest', *JBL* 86 (1967), p. 11.

56. 'Crux Criticorum—Matt. XI. 25-30—A Re-appraisal', *NTS* 8 (1962), p. 241.

be a gross exaggeration.[57] In spite of such a keen interest among scholars, the meaning of the pericope is far from agreed, perhaps because 'the deception lies in the character of the passage itself', as H.D. Betz suggests, which 'is open to meaning...like a vessel which itself has no content, but which stands ready to be filled'.[58] In fact, while the pericope raises a series of vital and interesting questions regarding its nature and origin as well as the respective referent of various words/ phrases (e.g. ταῦτα, σοφῶν καὶ συνετῶν, νηπίοις of v. 25, πάντα of v. 27, πάντες οἱ κοπιῶντες καὶ πεφορτισμένοι of v. 28, ζυγός of vv. 29 and 30, etc.), present scholarship has not reached a firm agreement on any of them. I shall first briefly survey the history of investigation regarding the nature and origin of the pericope, and present my own positions on them. On the ground of those positions I will then attempt to clarify the referent of each problematic and/or significant word/phrase of the pericope (especially of vv. 28-30). Only then will we be able to see the significance of the pericope in relation to the following controversy material.

Following the appearance of E. Norden's *Agnostos Theos* in 1913,[59] the original unity of the whole pericope was supported by numerous scholars;[60] according to them the entire pericope Mt. 11.25-30 was already present in Q. But after R. Bultmann's challenge to the unity of 11.25-30,[61] most scholars have tended to agree that only 11.25-27 was present in Q,[62] though they do not agree where 11.28-30 came from.[63]

57.   On the prominent use of this pericope (esp. v. 28) in various liturgies, see Stanton, 'Matthew 11. 28-30', pp. 364-66.

58.   'Logion', p. 10.

59.   E. Norden, *Agnostos Theos* (Leipzig and Berlin: Teubner, 1913), pp. 277-308.

60.   E.g. M. Rist, 'Is Matt. 11.25-30 a Primitive Baptismal Hymn?', *Journal of Religion* 15 (1935), pp. 63-64; E. Meyer, *Ursprung und Anfänge des Christentums*, I (3 vols.; Stuttgart and Berlin: J.G. Cotta, 1924), pp. 286-89; M. Dibelius, *From Tradition to Gospel* (trans. B.L. Woolf; London: Ivor Nicholson & Watson, 1934), p. 279, esp. n. 2; *et al.*; most recently, Davies and Allison, *Matthew*, II, pp. 237-38—they suggest Q^mt as the source of the unified whole pericope; cf. Hagner, *Matthew 1–13*, p. 316.

61.   *History*, pp. 159-60.

62.   Cf. Strecker, *Gerechtigkeit*, p. 172; Betz, 'Logion', pp. 19-20; Suggs, *Wisdom*, pp. 79-82; Schweizer, *Matthew*, p. 268; Sand, *Matthäus*, p. 251; Gnilka, *Matthäusevangelium*, I, p. 433; *el al.* For the grounds of such argument, see especially Deutsch, *Yoke*, pp. 48-49; Suggs, *Wisdom*, pp. 79-81, among many others.

63.   For example, *a lost Jewish wisdom writing*—Bultmann, *History*, pp.

Considering the fact that vv. 28-30 are absent in the Lukan parallel (11.21-22), and that vv. 28-30 are found in the *Gospel of Thomas* (saying 90) independent of vv. 25-27, it seems best simply to describe vv. 25-27 as Q material[64] and vv. 28-30 as M *Sondergut*.[65]

The question of the authenticity of the pericope is more complex and there is no scholarly consensus about it.[66] We may, therefore, leave the issue unsettled; in fact, for my purpose the question is not crucial, since Matthew clearly presents the whole pericope as Jesus' words and links it with the following sabbath controversy material.

As regards the background(s) of the pericope there are three main suggestions: (1) Since Strauss's pioneering essay the majority of scholars have traced its background in Sir. 51 and some other Second Temple

159-60; *M Sondergut*—Schniewind, *Matthäus*, p. 149; Gnilka, *Matthäusevangelium*, I, p. 433 ('Sonderüberlieferung des Mt'); Deutsch, *Yoke*, p. 49; cf. Strecker, *Gerechtigkeit*, p. 172 ('einer Sonderüberlieferung'); *Matthew's redaction*—Bacon, *Studies*, p. 290; cf. H. Frankemölle, *Yahwe-Bund und Kirche Christi: Studien zur Form und Traditionsgeschichte des 'Evangeliums' nach Matthäus* (NTAbh, NS 10; Münster: Aschendorff, 2nd edn, 1984), p. 290 n. 74; Sand, *Matthäus*, p. 251; etc.

64. As I affirmed above, my work is not based specifically on the two-source hypothesis, and I do not, therefore, assume the document customarily called 'Q' which, as generally supposed, Matthew and Luke had in common along with Mark, according to the two-source hypothesis. For a selected bibliography on Q, see Davies and Allison, *Matthew*, I, p. 115 n. 68. By the alternative phrase '*Q material*' I refer rather to what may have been several sources used in common by Matthew and Luke but not by Mark, some in written, but some in oral form; cf. Wrege, *Bergpredigt, passim*; Jeremias, *Theology*, pp. 38-39; Ellis, *Luke*, pp. 21-29; cf. also Davies and Allison, *Matthew*, I, pp. 115-21, esp. p. 121.

65. By '*M Sondergut*' I refer not to a particular document but, as an inclusive term, rather to multiple sources in either oral or written form, which are used by Matthew but not by Mark and Luke; cf. Meier, *Law*, p. 2; Deutsch, *Yoke*, pp. 14, 49; Davies and Allison, *Matthew*, I, pp. 121-25, esp. p. 125, among many others. M *Sondergut* is to be distinguished from Matthew's redaction, though the distinction is not always possible.

66. For the complexity of the question and various views presented, see Deutsch, *Yoke*, pp. 50-52. She argues that 'there is no solid evidence for authenticity in any of the three' logia (i.e. vv. 25-26, v. 27, and vv. 28-30), and this may be true; cf. Norden, *Agnostos*, pp. 303-304; Barth, 'Law', p. 103 n. 1; *et al.* But the opposite argument that there is no solid evidence against authenticity may be also true—cf. O. Cullmann, *The Christology of the New Testament* (trans. S.C. Guthrie and C.A.M. Hall; London: SCM Press, 2nd edn, 1963), pp. 288-90; Hunter, 'Criticorum', pp. 241-49; for a further list of scholars arguing for authenticity, see U. Wilckens, 'σοφία κτλ.', *TDNT*, VII, p. 516 n. 356.

period wisdom writings (e.g. Sir. 6.23-31; ch. 24; Bar. 3.9–4.4; Wis. *passim*; *1 Enoch* 42; 4 Ezra 5.9-12; etc.).[67] (2) Not a few scholars suggest that the background is to be traced primarily in the Old Testament (e.g. Exod. 33.12-14; Lev. 26.13; Deut. 12.9; 28.47-48; 30.11; 34.10; Jer. 2.20; 5.5; 6.16; 30.8; Lam. 5.5; Mic. 2.10; Ezek. 34.15, 27; Zeph. 3.9-13; cf. Job. ch. 28; Prov. chs. 1–9).[68] (3) Stanton suggests that this pericope (especially vv. 28-30) is to be understood not in the light of these backgrounds (especially Sir. 51) but in the light of several other passages within the Gospel itself.[69] In my judgment, the three views above are not necessarily in conflict with each other; rather they are complementary if we are to understand the pericope properly. In the following investigation, I will therefore refer to the Old Testament as well as to Sir. 51 and other Second Temple period Jewish literature as the backgrounds of the pericope, but with a clear view that there are differences as well as similarities between the background material and the pericope. The most important and promising way of interpretation, however, would be, as Stanton suggests, to see the pericope in the light of other passages of the Gospel itself, including both its immediate and broader co-text.

a. *11.25-27—Thanksgiving for Revelation*

The first question raised from vv. 25-27 is what ταῦτα (v. 25) are which are revealed not to the wise and understanding but to the babes. In its present co-text it may most probably refer to the ἔργα of Jesus (11.2, 19),[70] that is, Jesus' words and deeds which disclose the presence of the

---

67.   Norden, *Agnostos*, pp. 277-308; Bultmann, *History*, pp. 159-60; Betz, 'Logion', pp. 19-20; Suggs, *Wisdom*, pp. 83-108; Deutsch, *Yoke*, pp. 55-143; *et al.* Some who follow this line suggest that the pericope (as a whole or in part) should be understood in the light of Hellenistic mysticism; cf. Dibelius, *Tradition*, pp. 279-86; Bultmann, *History*, pp. 159-60. Others who also follow this line find its background in Qumran and rabbinic writings as well; see Suggs, *Wisdom*, *passim*; Deutsch, *Yoke*, *passim*; *idem*, 'Wisdom', p. 29; cf. W.D. Davies, '"Knowledge" in the Dead Sea Scrolls and Matthew 11.25-30', in *idem*, *Origins*, pp. 119-44.

68.   Among others, M'Neile, *Matthew*, p. 166; W. Manson, *Jesus the Messiah* (London: Hodder & Stoughton, 1943), pp. 71-72; more recently, D.C. Allison, 'Two Notes on a Key Text: Matthew 11.25-30', *JTS* 39 (1988), pp. 477-85; B. Charette, 'To Proclaim Liberty to the Captives', *NTS* 38 (1992), pp. 290-97.

69.   'Matthew 11.28-30', pp. 366-77.

70.   Note in the Lukan co-text the referent of ταῦτα is less apparent than in the Matthean co-text; cf. Lk. 10.21-22; see I.H. Marshall, *The Gospel of Luke: A*

kingdom.[71] The content of ταῦτα is thus eschatological. It is noteworthy that the same motif of a concealing and a revealing of the eschatological truth reappears in 13.11, where 'the secrets of the kingdom of heaven' must be the same as the content of ταῦτα here.[72]

The next question is what are the referents of σοφῶν καὶ συνετῶν and νηπίοις of v. 25. 'The wise and understanding' in the present Matthean co-text most likely represent the opponents of Jesus in the Gospel, and may refer to the Pharisees and scribes in particular,[73] who are, on the one hand, well instructed in terms of Torah (cf. 23.2), and who are, on the other hand, the most outstanding opponents of Jesus throughout the Gospel as well as the immediately following opponents in ch. 12. The idea of the wise and understanding who paradoxically do not really understand the true wisdom of God is already present in Isa. 29.14: ἀπολῶ τὴν σοφίαν τῶν σοφῶν καὶ τὴν σύνεσιν τῶν συνετῶν κρύψω (LXX), and v. 25 may well be an echo of this idea.[74] 'The babes' (νήπιοι),[75] conversely, represent those who are chosen by Jesus the Son (cf. v. 27, ᾧ ἐὰν βούληται ὁ υἱὸς ἀποκαλύψαι) not because they have the full knowledge of the (oral) Torah but because they are unlearned, weak and simple and perhaps therefore humble and receptive.[76] It is

---

Commentary on the Greek Text (NIGTC; Exeter: Paternoster, 1978), p. 434.

71.   Deutsch, *Yoke*, p. 104; cf. Hill, *Matthew*, p. 205: 'the "mighty works" of the previous paragraph, the events of eschatological significance witnessing to the appearance of the Kingdom'; France, *Matthew*, p. 198: 'the significance of Jesus' mission'.

72.   Davies and Allison, *Matthew*, II, p. 277; Hagner, *Matthew 1–13*, p. 319.

73.   Hill, *Matthew*, p. 205; Bacchiocchi, *New Testament*, p. 259; cf. Deutsch, *Yoke*, p. 111: 'the religious leadership and the crowds who do not truly understand'; Luz, *Matthäus (8–17)*, pp. 206, 229: 'die ganze religiöse Aristokratie' (p. 206).

74.   Cf. 1 Cor. 1.19, where Paul quotes Isa. 29.14. For a positive picture of the wise and understanding, however, see esp. *2 Apoc. Bar.* 46.5; cf. Prov. 16.21; Dan. 2.21; 1QH 1.35.

75.   Davies and Allison, *Matthew*, II, p. 275, note that in the LXX the term νήπιος is sometimes used technically, referring to the righteous (cf. Ps. 18.7 [EVV 19.7]; 114.6 [EVV 116.6]; 118.130 [EVV 119.130]), and assert that this technical use is assumed here. For a further discussion of the use of the term in the LXX, see G. Bertram, 'νήπιος', *TDNT*, IV, pp. 914-17. In Philo the term is used differently and refers simply to those in the elementary stage in the pursuit for wisdom; see *Sobr.* 9; *Congr.* 9-11; *Leg. Gai.* 27; cf. Deutsch, *Yoke*, pp. 87-89.

76.   Cf. Suggs, *Wisdom*, pp. 86-87; France, *Matthew*, p. 198; Davies and Allison, *Matthew*, II, p. 275; Hagner, *Matthew 1–13*, pp. 318-19. Luz, *Matthäus (8–17)*, p. 206, identifies them with the 'Am ha aräz'.

such people who have the privilege of being the recipients of 'these things' and through the true knowledge of 'these things' become Jesus' disciples. We may then identify the νήπιοι of v. 25 with Jesus' disciples or the entire Christian community (perhaps, Matthew has his community in view here).

Finally, what is the referent of πάντα of v. 27? The immediate co-text (especially the latter part of v. 27) suggests that πάντα refers primarily to Jesus' sonship[77] which expresses his intimate relationship with God; the mutual knowledge which is shared exclusively between the Father and the Son as described in v. 27 is, in fact, an essential part of this intimate relationship. Since the Son's knowledge of the Father is based on this exclusive Father–Son relationship, sharing his knowledge with anyone else is a matter of revelation;[78] and the authority to reveal the knowledge belongs to Jesus as a part of his sonship. The revelation of his knowledge of the Father, however, is not open to everybody but only given to his elect (= his disciples; cf. v. 25). What then is the content of Jesus' knowledge of the Father which is revealed to his elect? Considering its relation to vv. 25-26, Jesus' revelation of the Father may well be the same as the whole eschatological revelation of God in Jesus[79] which includes the knowledge of 'these things' of v. 25 by implication. Jesus' sonship, knowledge of the Father and authority to reveal it are thus correlative. In short, πάντα of v. 27 refers to Jesus' sonship which accompanies the knowledge of the Father and the authority to reveal that knowledge; and the knowledge revealed to the elect comprises the whole revelation of God in Jesus' eschatological deeds and words.

b. *11.28-30—Jesus, Yoke and Rest*

The first two questions we may raise from 11.28-30 concern the identity of πάντες οἱ κοπιῶντες καὶ πεφορτισμένοι and the nature of the burden they carry. First of all, those who are invited are not yet the disciples of Jesus;[80] rather they are those who are now invited to

77. Deutsch, *Yoke*, p. 33.
78. France, *Matthew*, pp. 199-200.
79. Davies and Allison, *Matthew*, II, pp. 279-80; cf. Bacchiocchi, *New Testament*, p. 260; Deutsch, *Yoke*, pp. 106-107.
80. Most modern scholars favour this view; see esp. Deutsch, *Yoke*, p. 41; Hagner, *Matthew 1–13*, p. 323; cf. Davies and Allison, *Matthew*, II, p. 288. *Pace*, Stanton, 'Matthew 11.28-30', p. 374—there seems to be no necessity in his argument that the audience of vv. 25-27 must be the same as that of vv. 28-30, even if we admit that Matthew linked the two logia.

become his disciples. They are not to be equated, therefore, with the 'babes' of v. 25 or with the elect of v. 27 both of which clearly refer to Jesus' disciples. What are then the toil and the burden they suffer from? Three options seem possible: (1) the burden of sin;[81] (2) 'the costly nature of discipleship';[82] (3) the burden of legalistic interpretation of the Torah by the Pharisees and scribes.[83] With the vast majority of modern scholars, I favour the last option, because: (i) the anti-Pharisaic polemic is evidenced not only in the immediately following pericopes (12.1-8, 9-14) but also throughout the Gospel; (ii) the unusual word φορτίζω does not occur elsewhere in Matthew; but the related substantive φορτίον appears in 23.4,[84] where it refers to the burden of legalistic interpretation by the Pharisees and scribes, and it seems most natural to understand our phrase in the light of this;[85] (iii) this option provides the most sensible interpretation of the ζυγός and ἀνάπαυσις of this logion in the light of their backgrounds as well as the immediate co-text.[86]

The key to the interpretation of the present logion seems to lie in the phrase ὁ ζυγός μου (vv. 29, 30). The ζυγός (Heb. עֹל) is sometimes used in the Old Testament as a symbol of foreign oppression (e.g. Lev. 26.13; Isa. 9.4; 58.6; Jer. chs. 27–28; 30.8; Ezek. 34.27), but it is also used in a positive sense of the service of God (e.g. Jer. 2.20; Lam. 3.27) or of instruction by the law of God (Jer. 5.5). In the Second Temple Jewish literature the word is commonly used for instruction and/or control (or rule)[87] of the Torah (2 *Apoc. Bar.* 41.3; *m. Ab.* 3.5; *m. Ber.* 2.2;

---

81. Most of the early Church Fathers—e.g. Chrysostom, *Hom. on Mt.* 38.3; Eusebius, *Dem. ev.* 88d—I owe this information to Davies and Allison, *Matthew*, II, p. 288.

82. Stanton, 'Matthew 11.28-30', p. 374.

83. Most scholars favour this option—Allen, *Matthew*, p. 124; Barth, 'Law', p. 148 n. 2; Betz, 'Logion', pp. 22-23; Deutsch, *Yoke*, p. 41; Luz, *Matthäus (8–17)*, p. 219; *et al.* Charette, 'Captives', pp. 294-95, suggests rather the burden of captivity than that of legalistic interpretation, though he includes the latter in the category of the former.

84. In Matthew it appears only once again in 11.30, which is closely related to the present verse.

85. The fact that the Lukan parallel (11.46) of Mt. 23.4 is the only other place in the New Testament where the verb φορτίζω is used makes our suggestion more probable.

86. See the discussion below in this subsection.

87. Not a few scholars equate the idea of submission or obedience with the 'yoke' (e.g. Davies and Allison, *Matthew*, II, p. 289). But they disregard that the obedience/disobedience is the result of taking/rejecting (or breaking) the yoke, not the

cf. 1QH 6.19; Acts 15.10; Gal. 5.1), the commandments (*m. Ber.* 2.2; cf.
2 En. 34.1-2), Wisdom (Sir. 6.30; 51.26), the messiah (*Pss. Sol.* 7.9;
17.30), or heaven (= God; *b. Ber.* 10b).[88] In the New Testament the
'yoke' refers to the law itself (Acts 15.10; Gal. 5.1; cf. *2 En.* 34.1-2).
The picture of the use of the word 'yoke' is thus complicated and it is
not easy to simplify it. For our purpose, however, one may make the
following observations: (1) the term 'yoke' can mean either 'control/
rule' or 'instruction/teaching'; (2) the object of 'yoke' can be either a
personal character (e.g. God, Wisdom, the messiah, foreign king) or the
law/commandments; (3) for Christians the yoke could refer to the law in
the negative sense. Another significant point which is noteworthy is that
no Jewish teacher or prophet (even Moses) ever told his disciples or
Israel, 'Take *my* yoke upon you'. In Sir. 51.26, the closest parallel to our
logion, Ben Sira says 'Put your neck under *her* [= of Wisdom] yoke';
this is striking because in v. 23 he issues his own invitation, 'Draw near
to *me*, you who are uneducated...', as Jesus does in v. 28 ('Come to
me').

What, then, does Jesus' invitation ἄρατε τὸν ζυγόν μου ἐφ' ὑμᾶς
mean? First of all, Jesus who issues this invitation cannot be simply
identified with Wisdom (either as the personified one or as the Torah) or
a teacher (like Ben Sira or the rabbis);[89] Matthew rather identifies him
with the Son to whom God has delivered all things (cf. v. 27) and who is
going to reveal his own teaching about the sabbath over against that of
the Pharisees (12.1-14). Secondly, it appears clear that Jesus' yoke primarily refers to his 'teaching' including his interpretation of the Torah
over against that of the Pharisees.[90] Having said this, however, Jesus'

yoke itself. I therefore rather suggest the idea of 'control' or 'rule' alongside the idea
of 'instruction' or 'teaching' for the 'yoke', which fits well in most examples
presented below; a similar notion is taken by Maher, 'Yoke', p. 99.

88.   Cf. Strack and Billerbeck, *Kommentar*, I, pp. 608-10; Deutsch, *Yoke*,
pp. 113-39 (*passim*).

89.   Though the similarities between Sir. 51.23-30 and Mt. 11.28-30 are
striking, the differences between the two are obvious. For example, as I have
mentioned just above, whereas Ben Sira commands the reader to take '*her* yoke',
Jesus offers '*my* yoke'; likewise, whereas Wisdom herself does not issue her invitation, Jesus himself issues his own invitation. France's verdict is, then, right: 'The
wording is familiar, but the sense is new' (*Evangelist*, p. 304).

90.   Among others, see Deutsch, *Yoke*, p. 42; Hagner, *Matthew 1–13*, p. 324.
See also above, in this subsection, my interpretation of πάντες οἱ κοπιῶντες καὶ
πεφορτισμένοι.

yoke is not to be restricted to his teaching alone; it may well also refer to the personal relationship with him (i.e. being 'ruled'/'controlled' by him, or his discipleship).[91] This is well demonstrated by the fact that Jesus' invitations, δεῦτε πρός με, μάθετε ἀπ' ἐμοῦ, and promise, κἀγὼ ἀναπαύσω ὑμᾶς, as well as his description of his own character, πραΰς εἰμι καὶ ταπεινὸς τῇ καρδίᾳ, are all focused on Jesus himself rather than his teaching. Especially μάθετε ἀπ' ἐμοῦ suggests that 'we are dealing here with an invitation to discipleship'.[92] In fact, these two suggestions are not necessarily in conflict with each other. Those who come to Jesus and become the disciples of Jesus (i.e. take his yoke) are to learn from Jesus, who gives a new teaching which not only includes the new interpretation of the Torah over against that of the Pharisees (cf. 12.1-14; 23.4; cf. also 5.17-20, 21-48) but also reveals the whole eschatological truth of the kingdom of heaven (cf. vv. 25-27; 13.11).

If we admit this interpretation of ὁ ζυγός μου, the seemingly paradoxical clause, ὁ γὰρ ζυγός μου χρηστὸς καὶ τὸ φορτίον μου ἐλαφρόν ἐστιν, of v. 30 is not difficult to explain. According to 5.20, Jesus' demand in his teaching is by no means lighter than that of the Pharisees; rather the disciples are required to have the *greater* righteousness (cf. also 5.18-19)! The clue is in v. 29 as I have interpreted it. Jesus' invitation is not simply to his new teaching but to the relationship with himself, who is πραΰς...καὶ ταπεινὸς τῇ καρδίᾳ (v. 29; cf. 12.7, 18-21). Being based on this relationship (= discipleship) which is characterized by the mercy and lowliness of Jesus, who is the fulfiller of the ultimate will of God as revealed in the Scriptures (cf. 5.17) and the inaugurator of God's reign upon his people (cf. 12.28), his teaching is, in spite of its more radical character (cf. 5.21-48), paradoxically not heavy like that of the Pharisees[93] but easy and light. Matthew will illustrate this characteristic of Jesus' yoke in the immediately following two sabbath controversies, especially in contrast to that of the Pharisees (12.1-8, 9-14).

Finally, in v. 29 Jesus promises 'rest' for those who come to him (v. 28—here 'rest' is already promised) and take his yoke. How can those who take his yoke secure the rest? The reason is that (note γάρ in

91. Cf. Betz, 'Logion', p. 23; Maher, 'Yoke', p. 103; Bacchiocchi, *New Testament*, p. 270; Deutsch, *Yoke*, p. 135; Stanton, 'Matthew 11.28-30', p. 375; *et al.*
92. Deutsch, *Yoke*, pp. 43, 135 (quotation from p. 43).
93. It is noteworthy that in 23.4 the Pharisees' 'burdens' (φαρτία; note the same word is used in 11.30), which refer to the Pharisaic interpretation of the Torah, are described 'heavy' (βαρέα).

v. 30) his yoke is easy and his burden is light. The lightness of Jesus' yoke and his promise of rest are thus correlative. The clause εὑρήσετε ἀνάπαυσιν ταῖς ψυχαῖς ὑμῶν may be an echo of the MT of Jer. 6.16,[94] where the rest is offered by God to those who follow the good way. Jesus now issues that promise in his own name to those who come to him, take his yoke and learn from him; thus the 'rest' promised by God is now fulfilled by Jesus. In the Old Testament the concept of 'rest' frequently accompanies the notion of the national redemption and salvation of the people from their enemies (Deut. 12.9; 25.19; Ps. 95.11; Isa. 14.3), which God will provide. Though the notion of redemption described in those passages is mostly political in character, Hebrews ch. 4 links such a notion (especially that of Ps. 95) with God's rest of Gen. 2.2 and understands it in terms of eschatological redemption.[95] Such an eschatological understanding of the concept of 'rest' is not peculiar to the writer of Hebrews; a number of the Second Temple Jewish writings also associate the messianic age with the notion of rest (*2 Esdr.* 8.52; *4 Ezra* 7.36, 38; 8.52; *T. Dan* 5.11-12; *LAE* 51.1-2; *2 Apoc. Bar.* 72.2; 73.1), and in some of these passages as well as in Hebrews ch. 4 the sabbath appears in relation to the concept of the rest.[96] All these witness that the eschatological understanding of the concept of rest, especially in relation to the notion of the sabbath, was well established by the first century CE. In that case Matthew's reference to the ἀνάπαυσις promised by Jesus may well refer to the fulfilment of this expected eschatological messianic rest. Such an interpretation fits not only the eschatological character of the present pericope as I have interpreted it but also the immediately following pericopes which, as we shall see, deal with the sabbath issue in terms of Jesus' fulfilment of it. Moreover this interpretation also fits well the overall plot of the Gospel which is focused on Jesus the messiah who has fulfilled the whole revelation of the Old Testament and inaugurated the eschatological kingdom of heaven (which is to provide the eternal rest for his people).[97]

In short, the pericope (11.25-30) as a whole effectively prepares the

---

94. ומצאו מרגוע לנפשם. LXX has ἁγνισμόν instead of ἀνάπαυσιν.

95. Cf. von Rad, *Hexateuch*, pp. 94-102, esp. pp. 99-101.

96. In *2 En.* 33.1-2 the messianic age is conceived as the great sabbath; cf. *T. Levi* 18; *LAE* 51.1-2. It is also noteworthy that in Isa. 66.23 the universal sabbath gathering and worship is presented as the concluding promise of the new creation; see above, Chapter 1.

97. Cf. Bacchiocchi, *New Testament*, pp. 266-67.

way for the following sabbath controversy pericopes (12.1-8, 9-14), and Matthew's intention of linking the Q material (vv. 25-27) with M *Sondergut* (vv. 28-30) and placing them immediately before the two sabbath pericopes becomes clear. Verse 25 provides, first of all, the fundamental reason for the Pharisees' lack of the true understanding of the sabbath; it is simply because the Father has hidden it from them. Alongside this vv. 25 and 27 contrast Jesus—to whom 'everything' (= primarily the sonship) has been delivered and who, therefore, now has the authority to reveal it to his elect—with the Pharisees, from whom these things are hidden. Furthermore in vv. 28-30 Jesus' yoke and burden which are easy and light are contrasted with those of the Pharisees which are heavy (as implied in v. 28; cf. 23.4). Jesus' gentle and lowly character (cf. 12.18-21) seems also to anticipate the contrast with the Pharisees' unmerciful and judgmental character (cf. 12.1, 2, 7, 10, 14). Jesus' Christological proclamations in 12.6, 8 are well preluded by his statement of the Father–Son relationship in v. 27. The discussion of the fulfilment of the sabbath by Jesus is anticipated by the introduction of the notion of rest in a Christological and eschatological setting. With these implications in mind we now turn to the first sabbath pericope.

3. *Plucking Grain on the Sabbath (12.1-8)*

The literary relation of Mt. 12.1-8 to its two synoptic parallels (Mk 2.23-28; Lk. 6.1-5) is not simple. The complexity of the matter derives largely from two problems:[98] (i) minor agreements between Mt. 12.1-8 and Lk. 6.1-5 over against Mk 2.23-28,[99] especially the omission of Mk 2.27;

---

98.   Here I will not go into the complicated discussion of the tradition-history of Mk 2.23-28, because it is not immediately relevant for my investigation. The issue, however, is well discussed by F. Neirynck, 'Jesus and the Sabbath. Some Observations on Mk II,27', in J. Dupont (ed.), *Jésus aux origines de la christologie* (BETL, 40; Leuven: Leuven University Press, 1975), pp. 227-70; see also, F.W. Beare, 'The Sabbath was Made for Man', *JBL* 79 (1960), pp. 130-36; Lohse, 'σάββατον', pp. 21-22; A.J. Hultgren, 'The Formation of the Sabbath Pericope in Mark 2:23-28', *JBL* 91 (1972), pp. 38-43.

99.   E.g. omission of ὁδὸν ποιεῖν (Mk 2.23); insertion of ἐσθίειν/ἤσθιον (v. 1/Lk. 6.1); εἶπαν (v. 2/Lk. 6.2); εἶπεν (v. 3/Lk. 6.3); omission of χρείαν ἔσχεν (v. 3/Lk. 6.3); omission of ἐπὶ Ἀβιαθὰρ ἀρχιερέως (Mk 2.26); insertion of μόνοις/μόνους (v. 4/Lk. 6.4); omission of Mk 2.27; order of v. 8/Lk. 6.5; etc.; for further examples, see H. Aichinger, 'Quellenkritische Untersuchung der Perikope

(ii) the addition of Mt. 12.5-7. The first problem causes embarrassment especially for advocates of the two-source hypothesis, and invites them to present various solutions. For example, H. Aichinger appeals to the hypothesis of a Deutero-Mark.[100] H. Hübner suggests that Matthew and Luke have used a Q version of Mk 2.23-28 as well as the Markan version itself.[101] Lohmeyer again suggests that Matthew uses here 'eine parallele Tradition', the origin of which is, however, not yet known.[102] The second problem makes the situation more complicated. Davies and Allison suggest that vv. 5-7 are Matthew's redaction.[103] Bultmann and others, however, attribute vv. 5-6 to Matthew's source(s), though they think v. 7 is Matthew's redaction.[104] Furthermore T.W. Manson and others argue for the pre-Matthean origin of vv. 5-7 as a whole.[105]

Such a variety of suggestions without any scholarly consensus regarding the source(s) of the pericope may be a pointer to the fact that no simple hypothesis can explain the complicated problems completely.[106]

vom Ährenraufen am Sabbat. Mk 2,23-28 par Mt 12,1-8 par Lk 6,1-5', in A. Fuchs (ed.), *Jesus in Der Verkündigung der Kirche* (SNTU, a1; Freistadt: Plöchl, 1976), p. 141.

100. 'Ährenraufen', pp. 141-53, esp. pp. 148-49; cf. Luz, *Matthäus (8–17)*, p. 229—he uses the phrase, 'spätere Mk-Rezension' for the same idea.

101. *Gesetz*, pp. 113-28, esp. pp. 117-21. He conjectures a five-stage tradition-history of Mk 2.23-28 and suggests that the Q version has been influenced by the third stage Markan version (i.e. >Mk< 2,23-24, 25-26, 28[C]), which lacks v. 27. For the difficulties of such a Mark-Q overlap theory, however, see Sanders and Davies, *Synoptic Gospels*, pp. 74-83.

102. *Matthäus*, p. 183. Gnilka, *Matthäusevangelium*, I, p. 443, however, thinks this suggestion unlikely.

103. *Matthew*, II, pp. 312-13, esp. n. 36; cf. Hill, 'Hosea VI. 6', pp. 114-15; Gnilka, *Matthäusevangelium*, I, p. 443. Cf. also Luz, *Matthäus (8–17)*, p. 229—he considers the present form of vv. 5-7, which he thinks is a unified thought-unit, as Matthew's product, regardless its source(s); Hummel, *Auseinandersetzung*, p. 44, esp. n. 57.

104. Bultmann, *History*, p. 16; see Barth, 'Law', p. 82; J. Schmid, *Das Evangelium nach Matthäus* (RNT; Regensburg: Verlag Friedrich Pustet, 5th edn, 1965), p. 206; Schweizer, 'Matthäus 12,1-8: Der Sabbat—Gebot und Geschenk', in J. Kilunen *et al.* (eds.), *Glaube und Gerechtigkeit* (Helsinki: Finnischen Exegetischen Gesellschaft, 1983), pp. 170-72; cf. Luz, *Matthäus (8–17)*, p. 229; Gnilka, *Matthäusevangelium*, I, p. 443.

105. Manson, *Sayings*, p. 187; see Allen, *Matthew*, pp. lviii, 127-28 (Matthean Logia); Banks, *Jesus*, p. 118.

106. Luz, *Matthäus (8–17)*, p. 229, also concludes similarly—'Eine wirklich befriedigende Erklärung gibt es nicht'.

The difficulties for the two-source hypothesis caused by the above problems suggest perhaps that the literary relations among the three synoptic pericopes are much more complex and indirect than generally supposed, and may have involved various sources, the origins and developments of which are unfortunately not known to us. Can we, however, be more precise about the relations? If we do not stick to the two-source hypothesis, it may be possible to put forward a more reasonable solution. For example, the minor agreements can be explained simply by supposing 'common tradition';[107] one version of this tradition was used by Mark, and certain different versions of it[108] rather than Mark itself were used by Matthew and Luke respectively.[109]

107. By '*common tradition*' I refer not to a particular document but, as an inclusive term, rather to stories and sayings of Jesus known to all the synoptists which may have been existed in variety of forms either oral or written. In fact, the 'common tradition' may represent something not unlike the 'Proto-Mark' or 'Deutero-Mark' as proposed by a number of two-source advocates (see Sanders and Davies, *Synoptic Gospels*, pp. 93-102). I do not, however, envisage the tradition at this stage as yet having distinctively Markan character nor do I regard it as necessarily existing in the form of a proto-gospel. I, therefore, prefer a more general term, 'common tradition' to Proto- or Deutero-Mark.

108. For example, as regards the presence of the saying of Mk 2.27 in 'common tradition' we have some options all of which are more or less plausible: (i) the saying was not present in any versions of 'common tradition'—then we have to explain why and from where Mark inserted this saying; (ii) the saying was present in one version of 'common tradition' which was available for Mark but not in other versions of 'common tradition' which were available for Matthew and Luke—then we need to explain why the latter versions came to exist without it; (iii) the saying was present in all versions of 'common tradition'—then we must ask why Matthew and Luke together omitted it from their Gospels. It is generally assumed (though mostly based on the Markan priority) that both Matthew and Luke deliberately omitted the saying of Mk 2.27 because of its radical implications or some other reasons (i.e. option [iii])—cf. Lohse, 'σάββατον', p. 22 n. 175; Beare, 'Sabbath', p. 134; V. Taylor, *The Gospel according to St Mark: The Greek Text with Introduction, Notes, and Indexes* (London: Macmillan, 2nd edn, 1966), p. 218; E. Schweizer, *The Good News according to Mark* (trans. D.H. Madvig; London: SPCK, 1970), p. 71; Neirynck, 'Sabbath', pp. 230-31; Davies and Allison, *Matthew*, II, p. 315. The first option, however, is also plausible if we suppose that Mark inserted it into his Gospel from his special material because of its close thematic relationship with the main body—cf. J. Roloff, *Das Kerygma und der irdische Jesus: Historische Motive in den Jesus-Erzählungen der Evangelien* (Göttingen: Vandenhoeck & Ruprecht, 1970), pp. 58-59. I will take up this issue in the following exegetical discussions.

109. Cf. W.F. Albright and C.S. Mann, *Matthew: a New Translation with*

The inclusion of vv. 5-7 can be explained by supposing that Matthew took it from M *Sondergut* and adapted it into his 'common tradition'. There are good reasons for not supposing the unit (vv. 5-7) as Matthew's redaction: (i) if v. 6 is a simply adjusted reproduction of Q material in vv. 41 (something greater than Jonah, a prophet) and 42 (something greater than Solomon, a king) by Matthew himself, we may rather expect, for example, 'something greater than Aaron' (that is, a high priest; cf. Heb. 4.14–5.10) which is a good counterpart of Jonah a prophet and Solomon a king in vv. 41-42, than 'something greater than the temple' which is not a good counterpart to the persons of vv. 41-42; (ii) if Matthew was written after 70 CE, the issue of temple service is much more relevant to the situation of the pre-70 CE church or even more to that of Jesus himself than to that of Matthew; (iii) if, as many scholars suppose (though mistakenly in my view), Matthew is conservative in matters of Old Testament law, we can hardly imagine that he invented such a radical saying as v. 6 and inserted a rather uncomfortable word like v. 7 in the present co-text; (iv) if the sabbath was one of the central issues of the conflict between Jesus and the Pharisees,[110] such a saying as vv. 5-7 may well have existed in M *Sondergut*, independently or in a different sabbath controversy co-text which is not preserved in Matthew.

Since Bultmann's challenge to the historicity of this sabbath conflict story, the question of the historicity of the story has been much debated; in recent years a most notable challenge to its historicity has been put forward by Sanders. His challenge, however, heavily depends on questionable assumptions.[111] Recently many scholars have tended to favour

---

Introduction and Commentary (AB, 26; New York: Doubleday, 1971), p. 150: 'The Greek verbal agreements of Matthew and Luke against Mark in vss. 1-8, especially in vss. 1-4, are good illustrations of the dependence of these two evangelists on traditions other than Mark'.

110. *Pace* Sanders, *Law*, pp. 19-23. The point will be more fully developed below in my exegetical discussions; cf. Mt. 12.9-14 par.; Lk. 13.10-17; 14.1-6; Jn 5.1-18; 9.1-41.

111. For example, too low a view of the influence of the Pharisees in first-century Palestine, and too negative a view of the historical value of the synoptic reports in general. In his 'Jesus and the Constraint of the Law', *JSNT* 17 (1983), p. 20, he simply says, 'the scene is imaginary, having been created to give a setting for the Son of man saying of Mark 2.28. Pharisees did not actually spend their sabbaths patrolling cornfields' (cf. Schweizer, *Mark*, p. 70; Hultgren, 'Formation', pp. 41-42). The reason for this statement is provided in his *Law*, pp. 19-23. One of his crucial

the historicity of the story,[112] and R. Pesch provides five forceful arguments to support the historicity of the story over against more sceptical views.[113] The first three of these are especially relevant also to our study of the Matthean pericope: (i) Markan tradition (2.23-28 par.; 3.1-6 par.), Lukan *Sondergut* (13.10-17; 14.1-6), and John's Gospel (5.1-18; 9.1-41) all witness that Jesus' sabbath practice caused conflict with certain Jewish authorities; moreover, the situation described in Mk 2.23-26 cannot be considered as a typical practice of the early Christians; (ii) Jesus and his disciples were poor itinerant preachers, as other traditions witness (e.g. Mk 10.28; Mt. 8.20; Lk. 8.3) and as the present story assumes (Mk 2.23; cf. Mt. 12.1)—Sanders's doubt about the historicity on the grounds that they would have been able to return to their base for the meal is then refutable; (iii) that Jesus was made legally responsible for his disciples (Mk 2.24) is historically plausible (cf. Mk 2.18; 7.5)[114]— Bultmann's view against the historicity thus loses its ground.[115] As Davies and Allison point out, the story as it stands in Mark does not, in fact, provide any really helpful defence of early Christian practice on the sabbath or of observance of the first day of the week, because 'Jesus' reasoning does not open itself up to easy generalisations'. If the early

arguments, for example, is that if the disciples were less than 2000 cubits (*c.* 1000 yards, i.e. the sabbath limit) from a town/village, they could return to their previous base for the meal! This assumption, however, is well refuted by Casey, 'Historicity', pp. 1-5, by appealing to the system of *Peah*. For a classic argument against the historicity of the story, see Bultmann, *History*, p. 16. For further counter-arguments against Sanders and Bultmann, see the immediate discussion below and the following exegetical investigations.

112. Rordorf, *Sunday*, pp. 59-61, 72-75; E. Haenchen, *Der Weg Jesu: Eine Erklärung des Markus-Evangeliums und der kanonischen Parallelen* (Berlin: Töpelmann, 1966), p. 122, esp. n. 4; Roloff, *Kerygma*, pp. 55-58; Banks, *Jesus*, pp. 113-23; J. Gnilka, *Das Evangelium nach Markus*, I (2 vols.; Zürich: Benziger Verlag, 1980), p. 122; M.J. Borg, *Conflict, Holiness and Politics in the Teachings of Jesus* (New York and Toronto: Edwin Mellen Press, 1984), p. 152; R. Pesch, *Das Markusevangelium*, I (2 vols.; Freiburg: Herder, 4th edn, 1984), p. 183; Casey, 'Historicity', *passim*; Davies and Allison, *Matthew*, II, pp. 304-305; Gundry, *Mark*, pp. 148-49; *et al.*

113. *Markusevangelium*, I, p. 183; the same arguments are reproduced in Davies and Allison, *Matthew*, II, pp. 304-305.

114. See D. Daube, 'The Responsibilities of Master and Disciples in the Gospels', *NTS* 19 (1972), pp. 1-15. *Contra* Bultmann, *History*, p. 16.

115. A similar criticism against Bultmann's argument is already found in Roloff, *Kerygma*, pp. 55-56.

church had sought to justify their sabbath practice, would they not 'have created a story whose implications are a little more patent?'[116] There seems then to be good reason to accept the originality and historicity of the story.[117]

a. *12.1—The Situation*

Matthew's description of the situation of the first sabbath conflict story is notably different in some points from its synoptic parallels.

The phrase ἐν ἐκείνῳ τῷ καιρῷ is characteristically Matthean, and has the effect of tying the present pericope to its preceding pericope (11.25-30) which is concerned with Jesus' invitation to take up his easy yoke and his promise of messianic rest.

The verb ἐπείνασαν seems to be a stylistic addition which may serve, on the one hand, to clarify the actual situation which is simply presupposed in the Markan and Lukan accounts, and, on the other, to anticipate ἐπείνασεν of v. 3 and thereby to enhance the parallelism between the situation of Jesus' disciples and the situation of David and his companions. The significance of this addition, therefore, is not to be exaggerated.[118]

---

116. Davies and Allison, *Matthew*, II, p. 305. For further arguments for the historicity and authenticity of the story especially in relation to the way of using the Old Testament by Jesus, see Gundry, *Mark*, pp. 148-49.

117. The historicity of the story, however, by no means guarantees the authenticity of the pericope as a whole or of individual sayings. The question of authenticity will be taken up in the following exegetical discussions.

118. Cf. Hummel, *Auseinandersetzung*, p. 41; Banks, *Jesus*, p. 113, esp. n. 3 (pp. 113-14); France, *Matthew*, p. 202; Davies and Allison, *Matthew*, II, p. 306, esp. n. 10. *Pace* Kilpatrick, *Origin*, p. 116; G. Bornkamm, 'End-expectation and Church in Matthew', in *idem*, *Tradition*, p. 31 n. 2; Barth, 'Law', pp. 81-82—Barth claims that the insertion of ἐπείνασαν indicates that Matthew's community still kept the sabbath, though not so strictly as the Rabbinate; such a claim is based on his suggestion that this insertion supplies a reasonable ground for the disciples' action and thus guards 'against the conclusion [by his community] that *everything* is permissible on the Sabbath'; his suggestion, however, is not convincing, because: (i) in the flow of the argument in the whole story the insertion, in fact, does not play such a significant theological role at all, as we shall see below; (ii) as we have seen in Chapter 3, Matthew's concern about the law is primarily focused on Jesus' fulfilment of it rather than on the degrees of strictness, and, even when he is concerned about the strictness, Jesus' demands are much stricter than those of the Rabbinate anyway (cf. esp. 5.20, 21-48); (iii) it is hard to provide a theological motivation for the addition of καὶ ἐσθίειν, which is the natural counterpart of ἐπείνασαν as ἔφαγον of v. 4 is the

The phrase καὶ ἐσθίειν (Luke also adds καὶ ἤσθιον) is another stylistic addition which also serves double functions: clarification of the actual situation presupposed in Mark and anticipation of ἔφαγον of v. 4. Its addition, in fact, is expected by the addition of ἐπείνασαν.

The lack of the Markan ὁδὸν ποιεῖν is much less significant than the other changes in this verse. Perhaps it was not present in the 'common tradition' and was added by Mark for clarification of the situation.[119]

12.1 as a whole presents the situation of the story—the people involved in the event (Jesus' disciples [and Jesus]), what happened (plucking heads of grain and eating them), when (sabbath), where (grainfields), and why (hunger [and they were with Jesus]) it happened. It is evident that the following controversy was developed because the event happened on the sabbath. The location of the event is described simply as τὰ σπόριμα,[120] and it is not clear how far it was from a town/village. As far as the event is concerned the disciples are the main characters. It is note-worthy, however, that Matthew put the name ὁ Ἰησοῦς, instead of the Markan/Lukan pronoun αὐτόν, at the forefront of the story and made it the subject of the opening sentence: '(At that time) *Jesus* went on *the sabbath*...' This change becomes especially significant when we read it in relation to the closing saying of the story: 'For *the Son of man* is lord of *the sabbath*'. Matthew may well have changed the structure of the opening sentence in order to make a kind of *inclusio*.[121] Matthew, thus, made it clear from the outset that the central figure of the story is not the disciples but Jesus himself. A final brief comment on the hunger

natural counterpart of ἐπείνασεν of v. 3 (see the following discussion).

119. Note Matthew and Luke both lack the phrase; for the problem of minor agreements and my solution for it, see above. For various interpretations of this phrase in its Markan co-text, see Neirynck, 'Sabbath', pp. 254-59. J.D.M. Derrett, 'Judaica in St. Mark', in *idem, Studies in the New Testament*, I (Leiden: Brill, 1977), pp. 85ff., and some others (e.g. M. Hooker, *The Gospel according to St Mark* [London: A. & C. Black, 1991], p. 102) suggest that the problem in the disciples' behaviour was not the plucking as such, but the creation of a road. The improbability of such a suggestion, however, is well demonstrated by Gundry, *Mark*, p. 140; cf. also E.P. Gould, *A Critical and Exegetical Commentary on the Gospel according to St Mark* (ICC; Edinburgh: T. & T. Clark, 1896), p. 48; Neirynck, 'Sabbath', pp. 257-58.

120. In the New Testament it occurs only here and in the parallels (Mk 2.23; Lk. 6.1).

121. For the examples of *inclusio* in Matthew's Gospel, see Davies and Allison, *Matthew*, I, pp. 92-93.

motive may be necessary at this stage; though the disciples' hunger is the surface reason for their behaviour, as the story is developing, it will become clear that the fundamental ground which makes the disciples guiltless (cf. v. 7) even according to the Pharisaic standard is not their hunger but the presence of Jesus, Lord of the sabbath, with them.

b. *12.2—The Pharisees' Accusation*

Now the Pharisees, the most outstanding opponents of Jesus (and his disciples) in Matthew's Gospel, come into the scene as the accusers of Jesus. It is not strange that they accuse Jesus (not the disciples!) of his disciples' behaviour, since the master was responsible for his disciples.[122]

The historicity of the accusation is questioned by a number of scholars. E. Schweizer, for example, asks: 'Where do these Pharisees come from, since one is permitted to go only about half a mile on the Sabbath?... Why do they reproach the disciples for picking the heads of wheat but not for walking on the Sabbath, which was a more serious transgression?'[123] A.J. Hultgren also asserts, 'the appearance of the Pharisees to criticize the disciples for plucking grain on the sabbath seems to be contrived'.[124] Sanders again says, 'the scene is imaginary...Pharisees did not actually spend their sabbaths patrolling cornfields'.[125] The objections are twofold though interrelated. First, they doubt the presence of the Pharisees in the grainfields on the sabbath. Second, they think it improbable that the Pharisees patrolled grainfields every sabbath to keep people from breaking the sabbath. As regards the first objection, we need to consider the Erub practice[126] among the first-century Pharisees. If the Erub was designed to be placed at the sabbath limit (= 2000 cubits, *c.* 915 metres)[127] from the boundaries of one's own village/town, on the way to the next village/town, it first of all presupposes that it was quite common during that time that the distance between villages/towns was

122. See Daube, 'Responsibility', pp. 1-15, esp. pp. 4-8.
123. *Mark*, p. 70.
124. 'Formation', p. 41.
125. 'Constraint', p. 20.
126. 'Erub' is a practice of depositing food on the eve of the sabbath at the sabbath limit whereby the length of permitted sabbath journey could be doubled. For a fuller definition of the term, see Danby, *Mishnah*, p. 793, app. I.8. For my discussions of Erub regulations, see above, Chapter 2.
127. There seems to be no disagreement about the sabbath limit of 2000 cubits among the Pharisees, though CD 10.21 suggests 1000 cubits rather than 2000. See above, Chapter 2.

less than two kilometres,[128] and it also presupposes the situation that the Pharisees from time to time travelled from their own village to the next, for example, to visit a house of mourning or feasting (cf. *m. 'Erub.* 8.1).[129] If the villages/towns were farming ones, it seems most natural to suppose that they travelled along the road beside grainfields.[130] There was thus every probability that the Pharisees were present in the grainfields where the disciples plucked the heads of grain.[131] It is not necessary then to assume that the Pharisees spent their sabbaths patrolling grainfields. It seems highly probable to suppose a situation that some Pharisees on their journey to the next village came across Jesus' disciples who were just then plucking the heads of grain. M. Casey, however, suggests a more positive involvement of the Pharisees. Since 'the Pharisees were quite free to go and see whether Jesus was teaching in accordance with the Law', there is a strong probability that some Pharisees would follow Jesus and his disciples and watch them so that they might accuse him (cf. Mk 3.2; Mt. 12.10).[132] The second objection, thus, is an unnecessary deduction.

Having watched the disciples plucking the heads of grain on the sabbath, the Pharisees raised an objection against their behaviour. Why should they have objected to such behaviour? It is clear that plucking the heads of grain from the edge of the fields was not unlawful in itself, because such a practice was permitted in the Old Testament (Lev. 19.9; 23.22; Deut. 23.25; cf. *m. Peah passim*; *t. Peah passim*; 4Q159;

---

128. In that case, Sanders's further question is why the disciples did not return to their previous base. However, as Pesch, *Markusevangelium*, I, p. 183, and Casey, 'Historicity', pp. 1-4, properly suggest, if the disciples were poor and if they did not have any food prepared in their previous base, there must have been no other option for them but to eat from the grain in the fields (cf. the custom of *Peah*). We may also doubt the possibility that the disciples had their 'base' in the nearby village/town; cf. Sigal, *Halakah*, p. 129, esp. n. 59.

129. Otherwise they would not have needed to develop complicated regulations regarding Erub at such a length.

130. Cf. *b. Šab.* 127a, where the possibility of rabbis' presence in a field on the sabbath is taken for granted.

131. Schweizer, *Mark*, p. 70, and Sanders, *Law*, p. 20, raise the pointless question why the Pharisees did not reproach the disciples for exceeding the sabbath limit. If the disciples, on the one hand, were beyond the sabbath limit, how could the Pharisees be present there? If the disciples, on the other hand, were within the sabbath limit, there is no reason why the Pharisees should raise the question of travelling. According to our considerations above, I am convinced that the latter was the case.

132. Casey, 'Historicity', pp. 4-5.

Josephus, *Ant.* 4.231-39). In Exod. 34.21, however, harvest on the sabbath is forbidden, and *m. Šab.* 7.2 confirms the prohibition more explicitly (cf. *Jub.* 50.12). The question then is what kinds of activities constitute reaping. The Pharisees' accusation of v. 2 implies that they regarded plucking the heads of grain in the fields as an act of reaping.[133] They said, ἰδοὺ οἱ μαθηταί σου ποιοῦσιν ὃ οὐκ ἔξεστιν ποιεῖν ἐν σαββάτῳ. It is noteworthy that Matthew turns a question into an accusation by eliminating the interrogative τί which is present in the both Markan and Lukan texts. This may heighten the Pharisees' antagonistic attitude to Jesus. Their accusation, however, is valid only if their halakhic interpretation of Exod. 34.21 is accepted without dispute. But, as Sanders properly suggests, the Pharisees' view of the sabbath was shared neither by ordinary Jews nor by other parties (e.g. Sadducees,[134] Essenes[135]),[136] and Jesus himself may well not have accepted their view.[137] The crucial focus of Jesus' argument, however, is not, in fact, to demonstrate that he/his disciples did not violate the sabbath. His argument will be rather

133. The Tannaitic literature contains no real parallel to the practice of the disciples as described in v. 1; see above, Chapter 2; cf. Sigal, *Halakah*, p. 129. However, a later text, *y. Šab.* 7.2 (9c), states that plucking of grain is reaping, and therefore is forbidden on the sabbath; cf. also Philo, *Vit. Mos.* 2.22; cf. *Spec. Leg.* 2.66-70. Another later text, *b. Šab.* 128a, however, allows plucking with fingers on the sabbath as long as no tool is used; this regulation may be perhaps a reflection of the movement towards leniency in the later rabbinic tradition.

134. They, for example, did not accept the Pharisees' Erub practice.

135. They did not agree with them, for example, about the sabbath limit.

136. Sanders, *Law*, pp. 22-23; cf. Sigal, *Halakah*, p. 125. This does not deny, however, that the Pharisees were more influential than any other groups, perhaps except the priesthood, in the pre-70 period, nor that they kept on seeking to increase their influence among the Jews (cf. Sanders, *Practice*, pp. 380-412, esp. p. 412), as the present accusation betrays. As we observed in Chapter 2, however, it is further noteworthy that even among the Pharisees, a number of specific regulations regarding the sabbath were not agreed, not only between the leading factions (i.e. the Shammaites and Hillelites) but also between individual rabbis.

137. It is true that Jesus' arguments of vv. 3-4 and 5-6 are about doing what is formally unlawful and yet being guiltless. But this does not necessarily suggest that Jesus accepts the Pharisees presupposition that the disciples behaved unlawfully. In my view, Jesus' hidden argument is that the disciples, in fact, did not break the Old Testament law at all, but, even if they did, they are still guiltless because, as we shall see below, he is greater than David and the temple as well as being 'Lord of the sabbath'. It seems, thus, clear at least that no positive indication of breach of the sabbath by the disciples is given in Jesus' responses.

established on the level of fulfilment of the Old Testament than on the level of simply keeping it without blemish,[138] whereas the Pharisees are accusing him on the ground of their halakhah, which represents only one of many interpretations of the law, and one which neither every Jew[139] nor Jesus would have accepted as authoritative.

c. *12.3-4—Jesus' First Response: David and the Shewbread*

Jesus' first response to the Pharisees' objection is a question which directs their attention to Scripture, specifically to David's breach of the law in 1 Sam. 21.1-6. Several scholars question the authenticity of this response on various grounds, of which the following are most important: (i) Jesus' response does not sufficiently justify the conduct of the disciples;[140] (ii) Jesus' response does not contain 'reference to the fact that he has brought about a completely new state of affairs'.[141] I shall, however, demonstrate that, in fact, precisely the opposite of both arguments is true,[142] in which case, the saying has rather good claims to authenticity.[143]

In the Matthean text a couple of serious discrepancies between Jesus' first response and the episode in 1 Sam. 21.1-6, which are present in the Markan text (2.25-26), are missing.[144] One may feel, however, that there

138. *Pace*, Sigal, *Halakah*, pp. 125-28—he suggests that Jesus simply provides here another sabbath halakhah based upon his interpretation and application of the traditional rabbinic hermeneutics and principles.

139. For example, Sadducees did not, like the Pharisees, regard the oral law (halakhah) as authoritative; see Josephus, *Ant.* 13.297; cf. Sanders, *Practice*, pp. 332-36.

140. E.g. Rordorf, *Sunday*, pp. 59-61.

141. Schweizer, *Mark*, pp. 70-71, quotation from p. 71. For a more detailed discussion of the authenticity of the saying from a sceptical viewpoint, see Neirynck, 'Sabbath', pp. 236-37, 261-70; see also Hultgren, 'Formation', pp. 38-43; Hübner, *Gesetz*, pp. 120-21.

142. See Banks, *Jesus*, pp. 115-18, esp. p. 116.

143. Cf. my considerations above (section 3) of the implausibility of the suggestion that the first sabbath conflict story is a community product, which partially demonstrate the authenticity of the present saying; see Borg, *Conflict*, p. 152; Pesch, *Markusevangelium*, I, p. 183; Davies and Allison, *Matthew*, II, pp. 304-305, 311; cf. also Roloff, *Kerygma*, p. 58; R.A. Guelich, *Mark 1–8:26* (WBC, 34a; Dallas: Word Books, 1989), p. 121.

144. These are the absence of ἐπὶ Ἀβιαθὰρ ἀρχιερέως (Mk 2.26), which conflicts with the text of 1 Samuel (Ahimelech instead of Abiathar), and the suppression of the clause, καὶ ἔδωκεν καὶ τοῖς σὺν αὐτῷ οὖσιν (Mk 2.26; cf. Lk. 6.4), which

remains one further significant discrepancy—David had companions with him according to Jesus' response, whereas in the 1 Samuel episode David visited Ahimelech alone. The problem, however, is not as definite as it first appears. The episode itself in 1 Samuel, in fact, neither denies nor confirms the presence of his companions, and it is not surprising that some Old Testament commentators suspect their presence.[145] More importantly, however, since the story is focused on David,[146] Jesus' words may well have reflected David's own reference to his companions (cf. 1 Sam. 21.2-5), regardless of the factuality of their presence in the scene. One may see still another discrepancy in Jesus' account that David and his companions were hungry. It seems quite clear, however, that in the episode in 1 Samuel David's hunger is presupposed;[147] in that case, Jesus' account simply makes explicit what is implicit in the narrative. Here we may need to note that in Matthew the words on both sides of ἐπείνασεν which are present in the Markan text (i.e. χρείαν ἔσχεν καί...αὐτός) are missing. If the Markan text reflects the 'common tradition' more faithfully, Matthew's change may once again indicate his concern to enhance the parallelism between the situation of Jesus' disciples and that of David and his companions.[148]

The phrase οἱ ἄρτοι τῆς προθέσεως ('the shewbread') corresponds to the Hebrew לחם הפנים ('the bread of the Presence') in the LXX along with other renderings.[149] It describes the twelve loaves which were placed every sabbath in two rows on the table before the Holy of Holies

is devoid of any warrant in 1 Samuel. For the significance of these changes, see Daube, 'Responsibility', p. 7.

145. E.g. R.P. Gordon, *1 & 2 Samuel* (Exeter: Paternoster, 1986), p. 170; G. Robinson, *Let Us Be Like the Nations: A Commentary on the Books of 1 and 2 Samuel* (ITC; Grand Rapids: Eerdmans, 1993), p. 115; cf. R.W. Klein, *1 Samuel* (WBC, 10; Waco, TX: Word Books, 1983), p. 213. For a different view, however, see H.W. Hertzberg, *I & II Samuel* (trans. J.S. Bowden; OTL; London: SCM Press, 1964), p. 180.

146. It is noteworthy that in Jesus' reconstruction of the story the role of the priest has completely disappeared from sight 'in favor of a total emphasis on the initiative and responsibility of David' (Nolland, *Luke 1–9:20*, p. 257); cf. Roloff, *Kerygma*, p. 56.

147. Cf. Klein, *1 Samuel*, p. 213.

148. J.M. Hicks, 'The Sabbath Controversy in Matthew: An Exegesis of Matthew 12.1-14', *RevQ* 27 (1984), pp. 81-82, 84. For a different view, however, see Aichinger, 'Ährenraufen', p. 126.

149. E.g. ἄρτοι τοῦ προσώπου, ἄρτοι τῆς προσφορᾶς, ἄρτοι ἐνώπιοι.

and later eaten by the priests.[150] Jesus makes it clear that it is unlawful for David and his companions to eat those loaves, and Matthew emphasizes the unlawfulness by adding μόνοις at the end of v. 4.

S.S. Cohn takes Jesus' first response as an attempt to justify the disciples' behaviour by using a precedent from David. He is convinced that Jesus uses here a rabbinic way of argument, that is, *Gezera Shava* (analogy).[151] As D.M. Cohn-Sherbok and others point out, however, the analogy between the disciples' conduct and the David story is poor: (i) whereas the issue in David's case was eating the shewbread, the issue in the disciples' case was working on the sabbath;[152] (ii) whereas David and his companions, according to Jewish tradition,[153] were in danger of their lives, Jesus and his disciples were not;[154] (iii) whereas David himself was involved in eating the shewbread, Jesus was not personally involved in plucking grain.[155] If Jesus had indeed tried to justify the disciples' behaviour according to the rabbinic analogy of *Gezera Shava*, Jesus' first response must have been a very poor answer to the Pharisees' accusation; it was poor simply because it was not valid from their

---

150. Cf. Exod. 25.23-30; Lev. 24.5-9; Num. 4.1-8; 1 Chron. 9.32; 23.29; cf. also Philo, *Spec. Leg.* 1.168-76; Josephus, *Ant.* 3.142-43, 255-56.

151. 'The Place of Jesus in the Religious Life of his Day', *JBL* 48 (1929), p. 97; cf. D.E. Nineham, *The Gospel of St Mark* (Pelican Gospel Commentaries; London: A. & C. Black, rev. edn, 1968), pp. 105-106; Sigal, *Halakah*, pp. 131-32; S. Kuthirakkattel, *The Beginning of Jesus' Ministry according to Mark's Gospel (1,14-3,6); a Redaction Critical Study* (Rome: Editrice Pontificio Istituto Biblico, 1990), p. 223.

152. Some suggest, following Jewish tradition (cf. *b. Men.* 95b; *Yalkut* on 1 Sam. 21.5—these rabbinic evidences, however, are unlikely to be early), that David's action took place on the sabbath, and therefore that the two incidents are related to the sabbath law (see Casey, 'Historicity', pp. 9-13; cf. Sigal, *Halakah*, p. 131). As Guelich, *Mark*, p. 122, properly points out, however, the issue in Jesus' first response is not the sabbath at all but the shewbread; see also M. Hooker, *The Son of Man in Mark* (London: SPCK, 1967), p. 97, esp. n. 3; Banks, *Jesus*, p. 115, esp. n. 2; Borg, *Conflict*, pp. 153, 337 n. 40. Perhaps his response is indirectly related to the sabbath only through the fact that the shewbread was replaced every sabbath.

153. Cf. *b. Men.* 95b-96a; see Strack and Billerbeck, *Kommentar*, I, pp. 618-19.

154. Borg, *Conflict*, pp. 153-54, unsatisfactorily argues that Jesus' disciples were on a mission of some urgency, as David had been. In the scene of the pericope such a missiological urgency is neither clear nor implied.

155. D.M. Cohn-Sherbok, 'An Analysis of Jesus' Arguments concerning the Plucking of Grain on the Sabbath', *JSNT* 2 (1979), pp. 31-36. Cf. Daube, *Rabbinic Judaism*, pp. 67-71.

hermeneutical point of view. It is probably true that Jesus was familiar with rabbinic hermeneutics. Yet it must be more true that Jesus neither depended on nor subjected himself to it. He was rather, according to Cohn-Sherbok, 'teaching on his own authority...far removed from the technical casuistry of the Scribes, Sadducees and Pharisees'.[156] This may partly help to explain why, at the end of the two sabbath controversies, the Pharisees, instead of being persuaded, took counsel against him with hostility.

So what precisely is Jesus arguing for by appealing to 1 Sam. 21.1-6? If Jesus' argument is not based on the rabbinic principle of analogy, *Gezera Shava*, what kind of parallel/comparison is Jesus thinking of? It is first of all very clear from the above observation that Jesus is not arguing that, since such a righteous man as David once broke the law, the disciples also could break the law now.[157] Such an argument is not likely, not only because of the poor analogy as illustrated above, but because Jesus, in fact, nowhere in the pericope positively accepts that his disciples actually broke the sabbath law. From this last point one may hold that Jesus was attacking the rabbinic halakhah, not the Torah, or more positively that 'Jesus was upholding the Torah against its false interpreters'.[158] Such an argument is much more attractive than the previous one, because it takes the problem of the poor analogy seriously. Yet there is another crucial problem in the fact that Jesus does not indicate anywhere in the pericope that the literal regulations of the sabbath in the Old Testament are still applicable to his disciples. On the contrary, his second (vv. 5-6), third (v. 7), and fourth (v. 8) responses strongly indicate that the sabbath law is no longer literally applicable to his disciples, as we shall see below. Furthermore, we have already seen that at

---

156. 'Plucking', p. 34; see also, Davies and Allison, *Matthew*, II, p. 308: 'Jesus was not an adept in rabbinic debate. He may well have learned much from the Scripture scholars of his day, but he apparently did not expend his energies trying to master their methods. Rather...he shows very little interest in halachic minutiae but a very strong interest in the central ethos of the mother-tradition, which may be summarized in formulas such as "the great and first commandment" (Matt 22.38), "the weightiest matters of the law" (Matt 23.23) or in some other way' (the last sentence is a quotation from B. Gerhardsson, *The Gospel Tradition* [Lund: Gleerup, 1986], p. 26); cf. Bacchiocchi, *Sabbath*, p. 50.

157. *Pace* Hultgren, 'Formation', p. 41; Sigal, *Halakah*, p. 132.

158. Davies and Allison, *Matthew*, II, p. 312. Cf. C.E.B. Cranfield, *The Gospel according to St Mark* (Cambridge Greek Testament Commentary; Cambridge: Cambridge University Press, 1977 [1959]), p. 115; Carson, 'Sabbath', p. 61.

least in Matthew's Gospel the literal application of every law is no longer expected by Jesus.

One may find a real parallel between the disciples' behaviour and the David story in the element of 'hunger'. On these grounds, some may hold that Jesus is arguing here that in exceptional cases a lesser good (ceremonial law) should be subordinated to a higher good (human need).[159] Others may also similarly hold that one divine demand may overrule the other, therefore the love commandment which is the first and greatest commandment of all (cf. Mt. 23.34-40) may overrule the sabbath commandment as well as the ceremonial legislation.[160] These suggestions appear to have some truth at least in Matthew's Gospel for the following reasons: (i) The element of 'hunger' indeed provides a real parallel especially in Matthew's Gospel, because, as we have seen above, Matthew highlights the parallelism by adding ἐπείνασαν in v. 1 and by dropping in v. 3 the words which surround ἐπείνασεν in the Markan text (2.25). (ii) In Matthew a certain priority of importance among the commandments of God is presumed or, at least, implied (cf. vv. 5, 7 of the present pericope). (iii) Furthermore, to the love commandment a special significance is attached. Nevertheless, I am inclined to conclude that the above suggestions are only partially true and therefore cannot be sustained as they stand, mainly for the following reasons: (i) Though the parallel between the disciples' behaviour and the David story is high-lighted, the real focus of Matthew's concern in the whole pericope is more on Jesus himself than on the disciples, as vv. 6, 8 further indicate; we may, therefore, rather suggest that the parallelism of hunger between the disciples and David/his companions is a surface analogy which, though real, plays only the role of introducing a more fundamental comparison, the comparison between Jesus and David. (ii) The hunger element alone is not sufficient to make the two incidents significantly parallel;[161] hunger without threat to life is too vague a ground for breaking the law, and could easily lead into anarchy.[162] (iii) As I pointed out above, Jesus, in fact, nowhere in the pericope positively accepts that his disciples actually broke the sabbath law. (iv) The focus of vv. 5-7, as we shall see, is not

159. Allen, *Matthew*, p. 127; Schlatter, *Matthäus*, pp. 394-95; Hagner, *Matthew 1-13*, p. 329.

160. Cf. Hummel, *Auseinandersetzung*, pp. 42-43; Davies and Allison, *Matthew*, II, pp. 311-12.

161. France, *Matthew*, p. 202.

162. Cf. Guelich, *Mark*, p. 123.

on the Old Testament precedent or on the priority among the laws, as it first appears, but rather on the authority of Jesus even over the temple (vv. 5-6) and on the character of Jesus over against that of the Pharisees (v. 7). (v) More importantly, as we have seen in Chapter 3, in Matthew the love commandment does not displace the rest of the Old Testament; it is by no means a sole commandment, though it is the centre of the greater righteousness.[163]

It is not surprising, then, that many scholars detect the Christological claim as the fundamental reason for Jesus' appeal to 1 Sam. 21.1-6.[164] They suggest that the underlying question here is, as in vv. 5-6, 8, the authority of Jesus. If David, the great king (= type), had the authority to reinterpret the law, Jesus, the greater king/messiah (= antitype), must have that authority to a higher degree. As France points out, 'Without the idea of the superiority of Jesus to David...the argument is a *non sequitur*, and that superiority...is best established by a typological relationship'.[165] Behind Jesus' appeal to the David story, an implicit David-typology is thus present, and this typology is requisite for a proper understanding of Jesus' argument. This implicit typological argument by itself might be not powerful enough to claim his messianic authority. In Matthew, however, this implicit claim is followed by an explicit claim in Jesus' following response, the temple-typology: 'something greater than the temple is here' (v. 6). In the flow of Jesus' argument in the Matthean pericope, Jesus' first response thus prepares the way to the explicit temple-typology in his second response by saying implicitly that 'something greater than David is here'. This implicit typology is especially significant in Matthew's Gospel, because Matthew has a clear concern to present Jesus as the Davidic messiah (cf. 1.1-17; 12.23; 21.9, 15).[166] This messianic interpretation of the David story, in fact, is in line with the flow of Matthew's argument in its immediate and wider co-texts. The Christological and eschatological character of 11.25-30, especially Jesus' Father–

---

163. Furthermore, neither in the disciple's behaviour nor in the David story is the love commandment actively involved.

164. Roloff, *Kerygma*, pp. 56-58; R.T. France, *Jesus and the Old Testament: His Application of Old Testament Passages to Himself and his Mission* (London: Tyndale Press, 1971), pp. 46-47; Gnilka, *Markus*, I, p. 122; Pesch, *Markusevangelium*, I, p. 182; *et al.*

165. France, *Jesus*, p. 47. Cf. L. Goppelt, *Theology of the New Testament*, I (2 vols.; Grand Rapids: Eerdmans, 1981), p. 94; Roloff, *Kerygma*, pp. 56-58; Gnilka, *Markus*, I, p. 122; Guelich, *Mark*, p. 123.

166. Note all these 'son of David' references are unique to Matthew.

Son relationship with God (11.27) and the eschatological fulfilment of the sabbath by Jesus (11.28-30), and the messianic character of the quotation in 12.18-21 point to the Christological and eschatological interpretation of the present pericope. In that case, it is most natural that Jesus' first response in the pericope should also have that implication. Furthermore, the double typology in 12.41-42 may also point to the messianic interpretation of the David story; if Matthew places Jesus alongside some of the greatest 'authorities' of the Old Testament (the temple, the king Solomon, the prophet Jonah), he may well place him alongside another great figure, the king David.[167] This messianic significance of the first and the subsequent two responses of Jesus will become the basis of the culminating messianic proclamation of v. 8, κύριος γάρ ἐστιν τοῦ σαββάτου ὁ υἱὸς τοῦ ἀνθρώπου.

d. *12.5-6—Jesus' Second Response: the Temple and Jesus*

Matthew alone includes Jesus' second response (vv. 5-6) to the Pharisees' accusation in the present pericope.[168] The sayings of the response, as I have suggested in section 3, may well have come from M *Sondergut*, which probably had preserved Jesus' own sayings whose original setting had been another similar sabbath controversy between Jesus and the Pharisees which is now lost.[169]

Davies and Allison and some others suggest that Matthew's inclusion of these sayings in the present co-text was 'motivated by the belief that the argument in 12:3-4 is of itself insufficient'.[170] The David story, according to them, has no direct relevance to the question of the sabbath and more importantly it belongs to the province of haggada[171] which

167. France, *Evangelist*, p. 170.

168. Mark, instead of these sayings and the following saying (Mt. 12.7), has another saying, τὸ σάββατον διὰ τὸν ἄνθρωπον ἐγένετο καὶ οὐχ ὁ ἄνθρωπος διὰ τὸ σάββατον; Luke does not have any of those sayings.

169. Allen, *Matthew*, p. 128: 'It seems probable…that the editor here…adds to a particular incident sayings spoken on other similar occasions'; Manson, *Sayings*, p. 187; Schmid, *Matthäus*, p. 206; Schweizer, *Matthew*, p. 278; cf. also Bultmann, *History*, p. 16; Aichinger, 'Ährenraufen', pp. 128-30. *Pace* Beare, 'Sabbath', pp. 134-35; Davies and Allison, *Matthew*, II, pp. 312-13, esp. n. 38.

170. Davies and Allison, *Matthew*, II, p. 313; similarly, D. Hill, 'On the Use and Meaning of Hosea VI. 6 in Matthew's Gospel', *NTS* 24 (1978), pp. 114-15; cf. also Hummel, *Auseinandersetzung*, pp. 41-42; Neirynck, 'Sabbath', p. 230.

171. For rabbinic Judaism, the David story is haggadic, because it is not a part of Torah but of historical data; cf. Daube, *Rabbinic Judaism*, pp. 68-69.

cannot form a final authority in a legal dispute; the case of the priests in
the temple, by contrast, is not only directly related to the question of the
sabbath, but also forms a final authority in the present dispute because
of its halakhic nature.[172] I doubt, however, that Matthew believed that
Jesus' argument in vv. 3-4 was insufficient because of its haggadic
character or its lack of sabbath relevance. On the one hand, Jesus neither
depended on nor subjected himself to rabbinic hermeneutics, and, on
the other, the focus of Jesus' argument in vv. 3-4 is not on the parallel
between the two incidents but rather on the authority of Jesus himself.[173] In my judgment, Matthew's purpose in including the sayings of
vv. 5-6 was rather to strengthen the force of Jesus' Christological claim
in vv. 3-4, which is implicit as we have seen above, by adding another
Christological claim of Jesus in vv. 5-6, which is this time explicit as we
shall see shortly.

Jesus' second response seems to appeal to one of the well-known
rabbinic exceptions. According to the Tannaitic literature, as we have
seen in Chapter 2, the first-century rabbis allowed violations of the sabbath for at least six occasions,[174] and temple service was one of them.
Jesus may well have been familiar with those exceptions. We do not
need, however, to suppose that Jesus is here dealing with a rabbinic
halakhic casuistry, since Jesus clearly indicates that he is appealing to the
Old Testament itself (cf. ἢ οὐκ ἀνέγνωτε ἐν τῷ νόμῳ ὅτι... of v. 5)
rather than to the rabbinic halakhah. In Num. 28.9-10 God commands
the offering of sabbath sacrifices; in order to carry out this command the
priests are inevitably expected to be involved in work which is forbidden

---

172. For rabbinic Judaism, the case would be halakhic if it makes Jesus'
argument rest upon a definite precept promulgated in Torah (cf. Lev. 24.8-9; Num.
28.9-10); see Daube, *Rabbinic Judaism*, pp. 67-71; Davies and Allison, *Matthew*, II,
p. 313.

173. Cf. Banks, *Jesus*, pp. 116-17; his argument is noteworthy: 'No more than
the previous illustration, however, does this yield a suitable precedent for the disciples' conduct, since their activity and that of the priests are scarcely parallel. Nor is it
intended to add a more technically astute halakhic proof though, from a formal point
of view, the example would have carried more weight with rabbinic hearers'.

174. The six occasions are: (1) circumcision (*m. Šab.* 19.1, 4; *t. Šab.* 15.10; cf.
Jn 7.22-23); (2) the Passover (*m. Pes.* 6.1-2); (3) saving Scriptures and food from
fire (*m. Šab.* 16.1, 3); (4) self-defensive war (*Mek. Šab.* 1 (L. 3.200-201); cf.
Josephus, *Ant.* 12.276-77; 13.12-14); (5) saving life (*t. Šab.* 15.16); (6) the temple
service (*t. Šab.* 15.16; *Mek. Šab.* 1 [L. 3.198]). For fuller discussions and references,
see above, Chapter 2.

on the sabbath. It is thus taken for granted that the priests in the temple violate (βεβηλοῦσιν) the sabbath in order to offer the sabbath sacrifices but remain guiltless (ἀναίτιοι).[175] E. Levine, however, alternatively suggests that Jesus' second response appeals 'to the widely contested and rigorously defended Pharisaic practice of reaping the first sheaves (i.e. *'omer*) offering'.[176] The reason for his alternative suggestion is that the example of the priests in the temple is not analogous to the disciples' behaviour;[177] and it is true that the practice of reaping *'omer* on the sabbath offers a tighter analogy to the disciples' behaviour in the fields. Nevertheless, as we shall see shortly, if the focus of Jesus' argument is not so much on the precedent of the disciples' behaviour as on Jesus' authority, Levine's alternative may not be necessary. In addition, the phrase ἐν τῷ νόμῳ in Jesus' introductory formula once again points to the written Torah rather than to the rabbinic oral tradition. Furthermore, the phrase ἐν τῷ ἱερῷ clearly shows that the priests violate the sabbath not in the field as Levine suggests but in the temple. Levine's suggestion thus is not very convincing.

What is Jesus then arguing for by appealing to the case of the priests in the temple? As we have noted above, there seems to be first of all a more apparent surface parallel between the disciples' behaviour and the priests' practice in the temple, that is, both are related to the issue of working on the sabbath. We may therefore suggest that Jesus' argument to some extent relies on the precedent of the priests' breach of the sabbath. On the basis of this fact and Jesus' statement of v. 6, a number of scholars suggest that Jesus uses here a rabbinic way of argument, *qal wahomer* ('the light and the weighty').[178] The flow of argument then may be something like this: (i) Scripture ordains that the observance of the sabbath must yield to the temple ministry, and naturally the priests who serve in it (or its ministry) are allowed to breach the sabbath;[179]

175. Cf. also Lev. 24.5-9, where the change of shewbread on the sabbath is commanded.

176. 'The Sabbath Controversy according to Matthew', *NTS* 22 (1975/76), p. 481. This was, in fact, a matter on which Pharisees deliberately defended their practice against Sadducean opposition. Cf. *m. Men.* 10.3, 9.

177. Levine, 'Sabbath', p. 481; cf. also Albright and Mann, *Matthew*, p. 149.

178. Daube, *Rabbinic Judaism*, pp. 67-71; Sigal, *Halakah*, p. 132; Davies and Allison, *Matthew*, II, p. 313; *et al.*

179. Cf. *t. Šab.* 15.16, where R. Akiba says, 'Now in what regard did the Torah impose a more strict rule, in the case of the Temple service or in the case of the

(ii) Jesus is greater than the temple; (iii) therefore, the observance of the sabbath must yield to Jesus' ministry, and the disciples who serve him (or his ministry) are even more justified in breaching the sabbath. As Cohn-Sherbok once again rightly points out, however, Jesus' argument does not strictly reflect the rabbinic hermeneutical rule, *qal wahomer*. First of all, the parallel between the disciples and the priests is not precise enough to meet the rabbinic standard of the rule. Unlike the priests who were engaged in the direct ministry of the temple and therefore entitled to violate the sabbath, the disciples were neither engaged in any religious practice nor in direct service to Jesus by plucking the grain, but they were simply concerned to satisfy their own hunger, and therefore they could not be entitled to violate the sabbath.[180] Furthermore, unlike the rabbinic *qal wahomer* only one premise (premise [i]) of Jesus' argument has its basis in the Torah, and premise (ii) does not have any support from the Torah at all.[181] Jesus' argument thus is not valid at all according to the rabbinic *qal wahomer*. We may then rather suggest once again as in the case of the David story that Jesus, though he may have been familiar with the rabbinic *qal wahomer*, in his second response neither depended on nor subjected himself to it, but was rather teaching on his own authority. His second response is thus, like his first one, proclamatory rather than explanatory and therefore becomes provocative rather than persuasive. This may once again explain why in v. 14 the Pharisees, instead of being persuaded, took counsel to destroy him.

The focus of Jesus' argument then is not on the precedent for the disciples' behaviour as it first appears in v. 5. The real focus in the flow of argument is rather found in v. 6, where Jesus proclaims his own authority even without the support of any particular passage from the Torah. The parallel of the priests in the temple in v. 5 is not a true precedent, but plays only a preparatory role for the Christological proclamation of v. 6, which now introduces the explicit typology. Several scholars note that μεῖζον in v. 6 is not masculine but neuter, and suggest that the

---

Sabbath? It was more strict in the case of the Temple service than in the case of the Sabbath.'

180. Cf. Cohn-Sherbok, 'Plucking', p. 39. Bacchiocchi, *Sabbath*, pp. 53-54, rightly points out the redemptive nature of the priests' sabbath work, but wrongly regards the disciples' behaviour (i.e. plucking the grain) as a parallel redemptive ministry.

181. Cf. Cohn-Sherbok, 'Plucking', p. 38.

referent of μεῖζον therefore is 'the kingdom of God',[182] 'the love commandment',[183] 'the mercy of God' (cf. v. 7),[184] 'the phenomenon of the ministry of Jesus',[185] or 'the community around Jesus',[186] rather than Jesus himself. The neuter form, μεῖζον, however, is not necessarily to be counted as an impersonal 'thing', for in the similar sayings in 12.41-42 the neuter form (πλεῖον) is used where it is *persons* (Jonah and Solomon) in the Old Testament who are undoubtedly set in contrast with Jesus himself. Most probably then by μεῖζον Jesus refers to himself here as well.[187]

What then is the force of this explicit temple-typology in the flow of the argument? First of all, this temple-typology makes explicit what the previous implicit David-typology (vv. 3-4) suggested;[188] and in this way the Christological claim to a messianic authority as the focus of the argument of the whole pericope becomes more apparent and powerful. As the presence of God has been specially experienced by Israelites (especially by the priests) in the temple, now the presence of God is more fully experienced by the disciples who are with Jesus, for Jesus is greater than the temple. The role and authority of the temple as the focus of God's presence thus is transferred to and fulfilled by Jesus. This notion of transference to and fulfilment by Jesus of God's presence seems especially significant for Matthew, as is shown not only explicitly by this temple-typology, but also implicitly by the fact that the whole Gospel falls within the *inclusio* Ἐμμανουήλ ('God with us', 1.23)/ἐγὼ μεθ' ὑμῶν εἰμι πάσας τὰς ἡμέρας ('I am with you always...', 28.20), as well as by Jesus' saying, οὗ γάρ εἰσιν δύο ἢ τρεῖς συνηγμένοι εἰς τὸ ἐμὸν ὄνομα, ἐκεῖ εἰμι ἐν μέσῳ αὐτῶν (18.20).[189] In the present co-

---

182. Manson, *Sayings*, p. 187; Schweizer, *Matthew*, p. 278.

183. Sigal, *Halakah*, p. 132.

184. Luz, *Matthäus (8–17)*, p. 231.

185. Hagner, *Matthew 1–13*, p. 330.

186. Harrington, *Matthew*, p. 172; cf. Hill, *Matthew*, p. 211.

187. Barth, 'Law', p. 82; Banks, *Jesus*, p. 117; Gundry, *Matthew*, p. 223: 'The neuter gender of μειζον stresses the quality of superior greatness rather than Jesus' personal identity'; France, *Matthew*, p. 203; Sand, *Matthäus*, p. 255; Davies and Allison, *Matthew*, II, p. 314.

188. Beare, 'Sabbath', pp. 134-35; France, *Jesus*, p. 47.

189. For the significance of this saying in relation to Jesus' replacement of the temple, see B. Gärtner, *The Temple and the Community in Qumran and the New Testament: A Comparative Study in the Temple Symbolism of the Qumran Texts and*

text the significance of the notion is clear. If the temple has more authority than the sabbath because of its role as the focus of God's presence, Jesus who is the replacement and fulfilment of the role of the temple has even more authority than the sabbath. This notion of Jesus' authority over the temple and therefore also over the sabbath prepares the way to the culminating pronouncement of Jesus' messianic claim in v. 8 that κύριος γάρ ἐστιν τοῦ σαββάτου ὁ υἱὸς τοῦ ἀνθρώπου.

As we briefly noted above, this temple-typology is, in fact, part of the threefold (or even fourfold) typology of ch. 12. Through this threefold (or fourfold) typology Matthew effectively proclaims that Jesus is the messiah who is greater than the temple, the great king Solomon (and probably David), and the prophet Jonah, that is, the three central features of the Old Testament, since he is the fulfilment of the Old Testament (cf. 5.17). Thus far 12.5-6 (and also 3-4) is not simply an illustration of a precedent for the disciples' behaviour, but a Christological claim that Jesus' authority is greater than that of the temple (and of David) and therefore prevails over the sabbath (and ultimately the law).

Finally, there is, in fact, a real parallel between the practice of the priests and the disciples' behaviour, that is, both the priests and the disciples are 'guiltless' (cf. ἀναίτιοι of v. 5 for the priests, and ἀναιτίους of v. 7 for the disciples).[190] Why are the priests guiltless in spite of their breach of the sabbath? The presupposed reason is because they are *in the temple*, which has authority over the sabbath because of its role as the focus of God's presence. The natural subsequent question is how about the disciples. Jesus' implied answer is that they are still more guiltless, because they are *with Jesus* (cf. 1.23; 18.20; 28.20), who has authority over the temple (v. 6) and therefore over the sabbath (v. 5) because of his fulfilment and replacement of the role of the temple.[191] Even this real parallel then also witnesses that the focus of Jesus' appeal to the practice of the priests in the temple is not so much on its role as

---

the New Testament (SNTSMS, 1; Cambridge: Cambridge University Press, 1965), p. 114.

190. As we have seen above, however, it is not necessary to suppose that Jesus here assumes that his disciples broke the sabbath law.

191. One should point out that Carson, 'Sabbath', p. 67 (and some others, in fact) makes a mistake when he compares Jesus' authority with that of the priests rather than the temple itself. The Matthean text does not have the notion of Jesus as the high priest as he supposes! That notion is well developed in the epistle to the Hebrews, but not clearly in the present Matthean text. A similar mistake can be seen in Bacchiocchi, *Sabbath*, p. 53.

the precedent for the disciples' behaviour as on the priests' relation to the temple in comparison with the disciples' relation to Jesus, the messiah, who is the fulfilment/replacement of the temple and the fulfilment/Lord of the sabbath (cf. v. 8).

e. *12.7—Jesus' Third Response: Mercy not Sacrifice*

Jesus' third response (v. 7) to the Pharisees' accusation again appears in Matthew alone. His response now appeals to Hos. 6.6 which, in fact, is already found in 9.13, where the quotation serves to respond to the Pharisees' criticism of Jesus' association with tax collectors and sinners.[192] The saying of v. 7 as a whole is linked with vv. 5-6 in the present form through the reference to τοὺς ἀναιτίους (cf. ἀναίτιοι of v. 5),[193] and, it seems not at all improbable, as Banks suggests, that the whole block (vv. 5-7) was 'derived from earlier tradition, and...that it had its original basis in an encounter between Jesus and the Pharisees' which might have been distinct from but similar to the present incident.[194] In that case v. 7, along with vv. 5-6, most probably came from M *Sondergut*.

The crucial question to be raised for a proper understanding of the verse is what the precise force of the quotation is. Commonly an antithesis between moral law and ritual law is seen in the quotation.[195] It is not likely, however, that ἔλεος here refers to the moral law; furthermore, the disciples' behaviour in plucking the heads of grain 'could scarcely be justified in terms of obedience to the moral law'.[196]

Some suggest that the quotation serves to defend Jesus' tolerance of the disciples' behaviour.[197] Others suggest that the quotation serves to show the priority of the 'love commandment' over the sabbath law and

---

192. For a discussion of the exact force of the quotation in 9.13, see Banks, *Jesus*, pp. 108-13; according to him, 'The quotation...is not primarily intended as an evaluation of the Law, or as a definition of the character of God, but as a christological affirmation' (p. 110). Some other scholars also see the Christological purpose of the quotation: e.g. Held, 'Miracle', pp. 257-59; Lohmeyer, *Matthäus*, p. 174; *et al.*

193. Hummel, *Auseinandersetzung*, pp. 43-44; Banks, *Jesus*, p. 118. *Pace* Davies and Allison, *Matthew*, II, p. 315.

194. *Jesus*, p. 118; cf. also M'Neile, *Matthew*, pp. 119, 169: 'It was probably a genuine utterance spoken on another occasion'; Beare, 'Sabbath', p. 135; *pace* Bultmann, *History*, p. 16; Hill, 'Hosea vi. 6', pp. 107-109.

195. E.g. Strecker, *Gerechtigkeit*, pp. 32-33.

196. Banks, *Jesus*, p. 117; cf. also Gundry, *Matthew*, p. 224.

197. Hagner, *Matthew 1–13*, p. 330.

thus requests the Pharisees to have mercy on the disciples.[198] At first sight both suggestions seem to fit the flow of the surface argument quite well. These suggestions, however, presume Jesus' agreement that his disciples committed sin by breaking the sabbath law, which, according to our investigation so far, does not fit either Jesus' or Matthew's argument in the present pericope (cf. especially τοὺς ἀναιτίους of v. 7). Moreover, either suggestion involves a response by Jesus which sounds too passive especially immediately after his authoritative Christological pronouncement in v. 6. Having said this, however, Jesus' third response does, on the one hand, justify his approval (not merely tolerance) of the disciples' behaviour, not in such a passive way but by demonstrating the fact that his disciples did nothing wrong according to God's will as revealed in the Old Testament; on the other hand, Jesus criticizes the Pharisees' condemning attitude, not because they did not show mercy to the disciples[199] but because they did not understand the original will of God (i.e. mercy not sacrifice) and as a result condemned the disciples who were guiltless.[200]

Another more probable suggestion is that mercy, which is superior to sacrifice, is not a principle which serves to justify Jesus' tolerance or to criticize the Pharisees' unmerciful attitude, but rather a principle according to which the disciples behaved. According to this suggestion, the disciples in the field on the sabbath had two options to follow: one was to follow the principle of mercy which allowed them to alleviate their real, though not life-threatening, hunger even though it made them breach the sabbath rest; the other was to follow the sabbath law in the Pharisaic way according to which they could not breach the sabbath rest unless they were in a life-threatening situation. Since the disciples knew the priority of the principle of mercy over the sabbath law, they behaved as such, and they were therefore guiltless, though the Pharisees who did not understand the priority of mercy condemned them.[201] This

---

198. Cf. Hare, *Matthew*, p. 132.

199. In fact, they were not in a position to show mercy to the disciples, according to the flow of Jesus' argument in the pericope.

200. Note εἰ δὲ ἐγνώκειτε τί ἐστιν·...οὐκ ἂν κατεδικάσατε τοὺς ἀναιτίους of v. 7.

201. See especially Saldarini, *Community*, pp. 130-31; cf. also Bacchiocchi, *Sabbath*, pp. 52-53; Hicks, 'Sabbath', pp. 84, 88; J.D.G. Dunn, 'Mark 2.1-3.6: A Bridge between Jesus and Paul on the Question of the Law', in *idem*, *Law*, p. 22. It is interesting to note that the rabbis had already acknowledged the importance of mercy as Simon the Just (3rd cent. BCE) had said, 'By three things is the world

suggestion is more convincing than any of the above suggestions, not only because it does not presuppose the disciples' sin, but also because it explains why the disciples are guiltless in spite of their breach of the sabbath, and also because it provides a good reason for Matthew's redactional insertion of ἐπείνασαν in v. 1. Nevertheless, this suggestion is not completely satisfactory either, since, on the one hand, it still presupposes that the disciples did actually break the sabbath (though not that they sinned), even though nowhere in the present pericope does Jesus positively accept that they did so; and on the other, 'real' hunger is too vague a ground for breaking the sabbath and to accept it as such could easily lead into anarchy.

These last three suggestions, though each of them may have some truth in it, are not satisfactory as they stand. Is there, then, any other more satisfactory explanation of the force of the quotation? A satisfactory explanation should, on the one hand, embrace all the elements of truth in the suggestions above, and give links between them. On the other hand, it should respect the fact that Jesus seems to argue that the disciples did not break the sabbath, and consequently should lead to a more positive interpretation of Jesus' third response. Such an explanation can once again be found in a Christological understanding of the quotation. The saying, ἔλεος θέλω καὶ οὐ θυσίαν, here first of all shows the character of God who is to be understood primarily as the merciful one rather than the demanding one,[202] and who is, therefore, looking for loving-kindness rather than blind sacrifice from his people.[203]

---

sustained: by the Law, by the [temple-]service, and by deeds of loving-kindness' (*m. Ab.* 1.2); a teaching attributed to Johanan ben Zakkai that the practice of loving-kindness replaces the temple sacrifices after the destruction of the temple is also noteworthy (*ARN*, version A, ch. 4).

202. Barth, 'Law', p. 83.

203. A brief investigation of the meaning with which ἔλεος is employed by Matthew, especially in the light of the use of חסד in the Old Testament (and in Hosea in particular) and the use of ἔλεος in Mt. 23.23, is found in Hill, 'Hosea vi. 6', pp. 109-10, 118-19—according to him the meaning of ἔλεος in Matthew is 'the compassionate attitude and merciful action which give concrete expression to one's faithful adherence to and love for God', or 'loyal love to God [i.e. God-ward meaning] which manifests itself in acts of mercy and loving-kindness [i.e. human-ward meaning]' (p. 110); he thus gives the covenantal overtone to the term which, therefore, has God-ward meaning as well as human-ward meaning; cf. Bacchiocchi, *Sabbath*, p. 54. See also Davies and Allison, *Matthew*, II, p. 105: 'Perhaps, then, we should consider the possibility that ἔλεος still carries for Matthew the connotations

It is now Jesus who assumes that character as the fulfiller of God's will as revealed in Hos. 6.6,[204] and his merciful character is well demonstrated in the two sabbath controversies and much more so in the immediate co-texts (i.e. 11.28-30 and 12.18-21). It is significant here to note that this saying immediately follows the temple-typology which declares that Jesus himself is greater than the temple; Jesus, the merciful one, now declares that mercy is more important than temple-sacrifice. The quotation thus develops the Christological claim of the temple-typology further, and provides the ground for the disciples' guiltlessness (τοὺς ἀναιτίους) in spite of the Pharisees' accusation. They were guiltless not because they had not violated the rabbinic regulations of the sabbath or, perhaps, even the sabbath law itself in its 'old' (or 'unfulfilled') sense,[205] but because they acted under the authority of Jesus, the merciful one, who had fulfilled the sabbath and become 'Lord of the sabbath' (cf. v. 8). In other words, the disciples, under the authority of Jesus, rightly understood the fulfilled meaning and ultimate aim of the sabbath and behaved according to that right understanding, and therefore they were guiltless. Jesus' merciful attitude to his disciples is thus fully justified, and on the contrary the Pharisees' condemning attitude is clearly criticized. Here the contrast between Jesus' merciful character and the Pharisees' antagonistic and unmerciful character reaches its culmination.[206]

We may need to ask at this stage whether there is any relation between God's merciful character and the sabbath. God's mercifulness, in fact, seems not irrelevant to the original intention of the sabbath

of *hesed* and that he understands Hos 6.6 as did the prophet: cultic observance without inner faith and heart-felt covenant loyalty is vain'; cf. France, *Matthew*, p. 168. For a discussion of the covenantal connotation of חסד in Hos. 6.6, see Wolff, *Hosea*, p. 120; cf. also Stuart, *Hosea–Jonah*, p. 110.

204. Cf. 5.17—Jesus is the fulfiller not only of the law but also of the prophets; see above, Chapter 3.

205. See my discussion of the contrast between the new νόμος (or the messianic νόμος as fulfilled) and the old νόμος (or the νόμος as it was) in Chapter 3.

206. It may have been in deliberately ironical contrast with this account of the legalistic condemning attitude of the Pharisees that Matthew later included the story about the Pharisees (27.62-66) who along with the chief priests asked Pilate for the stone of the sepulchre to be sealed on the sabbath and thus did what was surely not allowed according to their own regulation. Cf. H. Weiss, 'The Sabbath in the Synoptic Gospels', *JSNT* 38 (1990), p. 16—he contrasts the Pharisees' 'flagrant violation of the Sabbath' with 'the Christian women who were rather anxious to anoint Jesus' body wait until after the Sabbath to go about their business' (28.1).

institution. First of all, we saw in Chapter 1 that the sabbath institution is a reflection of the blessing of the seventh day which has its ultimate purpose in the eternal rest for the people of God as is implied in his rest after his creation which has no end (cf. Gen. 2.2-3; Exod. 20.8-11) and as is also exemplified in his redemptive deliverance of Israel from Egypt (cf. Deut. 5.12-15). The sabbath thus is not a burden in its origin but an expression of God's grace and mercy.[207] It is also noteworthy that in Isa. 1.13 YHWH hates the institutionalized sabbath assemblies (along with other cultic activities) because they are vain; the reason why they are vain is because of Israel's unmerciful behaviour (cf. Isa. 1.15-17); the Old Testament thus already shows that legalistic observance of the sabbath without the merciful attitude towards the oppressed, the orphan and the widows cannot achieve God's original will for the sabbath. We may then suggest that the sabbath institution from its origin has an intimate relation with God's mercifulness, especially with his merciful plan of redemption for his people, and that, when Israel was keen to keep the sabbath without understanding that this was God's original intention for the sabbath, God was not pleased with them. Such an idea is not foreign to Matthew. First of all 11.28-30 clearly shows the link between *Jesus' merciful character* which assumes God's merciful character reflected in the sabbath institution and *eschatological rest* which fulfils the ultimate goal of the sabbath. Moreover, this link is preceded by Jesus' mention in 11.25 of the lack of understanding of 'the wise and understanding' which may refer to the Pharisees in particular, who as a result lay burdens upon others instead of giving them rest.

If my suggestion is right, v. 7 can be understood in the light of the stream of thought which was already present throughout the Old Testament and is now more concretely expressed in 11.25-30. The sabbath was originally instituted as an expression of God's mercy for his people rather than as a burden; but, since the Pharisees, like Israel in Isaiah's period, do not understand this original intention (cf. εἰ δὲ ἐγνώκειτε τί ἐστιν), they condemn the innocent disciples (τοὺς ἀναιτίους) on the basis of their own mechanical burdensome regulations. In that case the saying of Jesus in v. 7 achieves, as France suggests, 'the same effect as the pronouncement', τὸ σάββατον διὰ τὸν ἄνθρωπον ἐγένετο καὶ οὐχ ὁ ἄνθρωπος διὰ τὸ σάββατον (Mk 2.27), which Matthew

---

207. That is why in Isa. 58.13 YHWH expects Israel to call the sabbath 'a delight' (ענג) rather than a burden. A similar notion is detected in *Jubilees* (cf. 2.21-33; 50.9-10, 12); cf. Hooker, *Son of Man*, pp. 95-96.

replaces.[208] It seems then quite wrong to suppose this replacement to be an expression of Matthew's conservatism,[209] or to regard it as an indication of the continued observance of the sabbath among Matthew's community.[210] By quoting Hos. 6.6 in v. 7, Jesus shows what God's original intention for the sabbath was—that is, the sabbath was instituted for the benefit of the people and was presented not as a burden but as an expression of mercy; that intention is now fulfilled by Jesus himself, the merciful one, under whose authority the disciples are guiltless because they rightly understood and behaved according to the true meaning and intention of the sabbath.

f. *12.8—Jesus' Fourth Response: Lord of the Sabbath*
Matthew, like Mark and Luke, records as the climax of his narrative the saying, κύριος γάρ ἐστιν τοῦ σαββάτου ὁ υἱὸς τοῦ ἀνθρώπου. The

---

208. *Matthew*, p. 204; cf. also Banks, *Jesus*, p. 120; Carson, 'Sabbath', p. 68. A strikingly similar saying is found in *Mek. Šab.* 1 on Exod. 31.14 which is attributed to R. Simon b. Meahsiah (*c.* 180), but may represent earlier tradition: 'The Sabbath is given to you but you are not surrendered to the Sabbath'; see above, Chapter 2. On this ground Davies and Allison, *Matthew*, II, p. 315, suggest that 'maybe Matthew was aware that the sentiment [of Mk 2.27] was used by his opponents' and therefore replaced it. For a comprehensive investigation of Mk 2.27, see Neirynck, 'Sabbath', pp. 227-70. For an explanation of Luke's omission of Mk 2.27, see, for example, Turner, 'Sabbath', p. 103—after evaluating some possible explanations, he concludes that 'Luke has dropped Mark 2:27 in order to heighten the christological comparison between David and Jesus and to eliminate what may have been, to him, a relatively obscure step in logic of Jesus' teaching' (p. 104). Similarly, Banks, *Jesus*, p. 120; S.G. Wilson, *Luke and the Law* (SNTSMS, 50; Cambridge: Cambridge University Press, 1983), pp. 31-35, esp. pp. 34-35.

209. E.g. Kilpatrick, *Origins*, p. 116; Schweizer, *Matthew*, p. 277; Weiss, 'Sabbath', p. 21; Hagner, *Matthew 1–13*, p. 327. Casey, 'Historicity', p. 19, properly, though indirectly, points out a pitfall of such a view: 'The view that 2.27 is more radical than this [= 2.28] results from removing it from its [Jewish] context and interpreting it against a background of Gentile Christianity, which does not obey the Law and which needs a higher Christology than that of Jesus or the apostles to enable it to hold together'.

210. E.g. Saldarini, *Community*, p. 131; cf. Kilpatrick, *Origins*, p. 116; Davies and Allison, *Matthew*, II, p. 315; E.K.C. Wong, 'The Matthean Understanding of the Sabbath: A Response to G.N. Stanton', *JSNT* 44 (1991), pp. 6-7, 14-15. In fact, it is quite questionable whether the proclamation of Mk 2.27 was present in 'common tradition' used by Matthew, especially considering the fact that it is also wanting in Luke; see above, section 3; cf. Barth, 'Law', p. 91 n. 1. For a different view, however, see Beare, 'Sabbath', p. 134.

question of the authenticity of this saying has been much debated without any scholarly consensus,[211] especially in relation to the term ὁ υἱὸς τοῦ ἀνθρώπου and its link with the term ὁ ἄνθρωπος of Mk 2.27. Whatever tradition-history the saying has, however, the following two interrelated points are very evident: (i) Matthew most probably did not create the saying but rather took it from his version of 'common tradition'; (ii) Matthew regards the saying as Jesus' own and presents it as his concluding response.

Jesus' final response is linked by γάρ to the preceding verse(s): on the one hand, it provides the ground for the claim in v. 7 (i.e. the disciples' guiltlessness); on the other, it relates to the whole of vv. 1-7 as 'both the goal and ground of the various Christological assertions that have preceded it'.[212]

The term ὁ υἱὸς τοῦ ἀνθρώπου poses some of the most perplexing problems in the Gospels, and numerous treatments of its origin and meaning have been presented in detail without any solid scholarly consensus. It is clearly beyond the scope of the present study even to survey those treatments.[213] A more directly relevant question for this study is to

---

211. The following accept the authenticity of the saying—Hooker, *Son of Man*, p. 98; Schweizer, *Mark*, p. 71; Roloff, *Kerygma*, pp. 58-62; Banks, *Jesus*, pp. 122-23; Carson, 'Sabbath', pp. 63-64; S. Kim, *The 'Son of Man' as the Son of God* (WUNT, 30; Tübingen: Mohr, 1983), pp. 36-37, 93-94; Casey, 'Historicity', pp. 13-22; Gundry, *Mark*, pp. 144, 148-49; *et al.*; cf. E. Schweizer, 'Der Menschensohn (Zur eschatologischen Erwartung Jesu)', *ZNW* 50 (1959), pp. 185-205; *idem*, 'The Son of Man Again', *NTS* 9 (1962/63), pp. 256-61; I.H. Marshall, *The Origins of New Testament Christology* (Leicester: IVP, 2nd edn, 1990), pp. 63-82. The following are sceptical of its authenticity—(i) *a product of the early community*—Beare, 'Sabbath', pp. 131-35; E. Käsemann, *Essays on New Testament Themes* (trans. W.J. Montague; SBT, 41; London: SCM Press, 1964), p. 102; H.E. Tödt, *The Son of Man in the Synoptic Tradition* (trans. D.M. Barton; London: SCM Press, 1965), pp. 130-32; A.J.B. Higgins, *Jesus and the Son of Man* (London: Lutterworth, 1964), p. 30; Taylor, *Mark*, p. 220; Hultgren, 'Formation', p. 41; *et al.*; (ii) *Mark's addition*—Lane, *Mark*, pp. 118-20; B. Lindars, *Jesus Son of Man: The Doctrinal Significance of the Old Testament Quotations* (London: SPCK, 1983), pp. 103-106; Davies and Allison, *Matthew*, II, p. 316; cf. Cranfield, *Mark*, p. 118. For a useful overview of the divergent scholarly opinions, which frequently contradict each other outright, with regard to the authenticity of the Son of man sayings, see C.C. Caragounis, *The Son of Man: Vision and Interpretation* (Tübingen: Mohr, 1986), pp. 145-67.

212. Banks, *Jesus*, p. 120.

213. For a selected bibliography on these issues, see J. Nolland, *Luke 9:21–*

be found in the discussion of the Aramaic background and the referent of the term in Mk 2.28, especially in relation to ὁ ἄνθρωπος in Mk 2.27. Three views are outstanding and noteworthy. First, it is commonly held that the phrase here did not originally carry a 'titular' sense, but represents the basic generic sense of the Aramaic phrase בר נשא meaning 'human being', so that it may be taken as synonymous with ὁ ἄνθρωπος in Mk 2.27.[214] According to this view Mk 2.28 is no more than a logical continuation of or even a mere repetition of what the preceding sentence is saying—that is, if the sabbath was made for 'man' (v. 27), it follows that 'man' is 'Lord of the sabbath' (v. 28). As many scholars point out, however, it is extremely unlikely that Jesus would have declared humankind in general to be 'lord' of the sabbath which the Old Testament repeatedly describes as distinctively YHWH's.[215] Secondly, T.W. Manson, reversing his original view, argues that 'man' in Mk 2.27 is a misunderstanding for 'the Son of man', and we should read Mk 2.27-28 thus: 'The sabbath was made for the Son of man and not the Son of man for the sabbath; and so the Son of man is lord of the sabbath'. For Manson, 'the Son of man' has a collective nuance (cf. 'the saints of the Most High' of Dan. 7.18; cf. also Dan. 7.13-14) referring to Jesus in particular but also to the disciples.[216] His suggestion, however, suffers from grave

---

18:34 (WBC, 35b; Dallas: Word Books, 1993), pp. 468-69. A useful overview, though rather brief, of the issues involved in the term is found in I.H. Marshall, 'Son of Man', *DJG*, pp. 775-81. For more recent full scale discussions of the term, see, among others, Kim, *Son of Man*; Lindars, *Jesus*; Caragounis, *Son of Man*; D.R.A. Hare, *The Son of Man Tradition* (Minneapolis, MN: Fortress Press, 1990).

214. E.g. J. Wellhausen, *Das Evangelium Marci* (Berlin: Georg Reimer, 2nd edn, 1909), p. 20; F.J.F. Jackson and K. Lake, *The Beginnings of Christianity*, I (5 vols.; London: MacMillan, 1920–33), pp. 378-79; T.W. Manson, *The Teaching of Jesus: Studies of its Form and Content* (Cambridge: Cambridge University Press, 1955), p. 214; R. Bultmann, *Theology of the New Testament*, I (2 vols.; trans. K. Grobel; London: SCM Press, 1952, 1955), p. 30; Rordorf, *Sunday*, p. 64; Sigal, *Halakah*, pp. 132, 234 n. 74; J.D. Crossan, *The Historical Jesus: The Life of a Mediterranean Jewish Peasant* (Edinburgh: T. & T. Clark, 1991), p. 257; *et al.*

215. A.E.J. Rawlinson, *The Gospel according to St Mark with Introduction Commentary and Additional Notes* (Westminster Commentaries; London: Methuen, 1925), p. 34; Hooker, *Son of Man*, p. 94; Taylor, *Mark*, pp. 219-20; Guelich, *Mark*, p. 125; *et al.*

216. 'Mark ii. 27-28', in *Coniectanea neotestamentica*, XI (Lund: Gleerup, 1947), pp. 138-46; cf also *idem*, 'The Son of Man in Daniel, Enoch, and the Gospels' (1949), in *Studies in the Gospels and Epistles* (Manchester: Manchester University Press, 1962), p. 143. Though Beare, 'Sabbath', p. 131, agrees with Manson's first

criticisms especially against the idea that the Son of man has corporate significance in the New Testament.[217] Lastly, M. Hooker suggests that these two verses were originally two separate sayings, that the referent of 'man' in v. 27 is 'Israel' (cf. *Jub.* ch. 2), the people of God, and that Jesus himself is at least implicitly identified with the 'Son of man' of v. 28 whose authority goes beyond any merely human authority and is at least equal to that of the Mosaic law.[218] This last suggestion is most convincing, not only because, by supposing the independent origins of the two sayings, it eliminates unnecessary conjecture of mistranslation and it explains the lack of Mk 2.27 both in Matthew and Luke more easily,[219] but also because it gives a convincing explanation of how these two verses fit in with the flow of argument of the whole pericope (Mk 2.23-28).[220]

At this stage we may need to inquire into the use of the term in Matthew.[221] J.D. Kingsbury argues that in Matthew 'the Son of man', unlike the other Christological titles, functions not as a 'confessional title' to set forth the identity of Jesus, but as a 'public title', by means of which Jesus and he alone refers to himself 'in view of the "public" (or "world") in order to point to himself as "the man", or "the human being" (earthly, suffering, vindicated), and to assert his divine authority in the face of opposition'.[222] His observations seem generally correct, though not all the Matthean uses of the term fit neatly into the scheme he proposes.[223] A crucial weakness of his proposal, however, is found in

idea (cf. *Teaching*, p. 214), he interprets the Son of man as 'an individual designation for Jesus himself, a designation which in the Synoptic tradition is a surrogate for "Messiah"'.

217. Hooker, *Son of Man*, pp. 95-102; A.J.B. Higgins, 'Son of Man—*Forschung* since "The Teaching of Jesus"', in A.J.B. Higgins (ed.), *New Testament Essays* (Manchester: Manchester University Press, 1959), pp. 126-27; *et al.*

218. *Son of Man*, pp. 94-102; cf. Tödt, *Son of Man*, pp. 130-31.

219. We may suppose that the saying of Mk 2.27 existed only in the Markan version of 'common tradition' or that Mark inserted it from his special material.

220. See esp. Hooker, *Son of Man*, pp. 96-98.

221. In contrast to the voluminous discussion of the term in general, comparatively little attention has been paid to Matthew's use of the term. Cf. France, *Evangelist*, p. 288, esp. n. 27; in his note a brief bibliography on the subject is found.

222. 'The Figure of Jesus in Matthew's Story: a Literary-Critical Probe', *JSNT* 21 (1984), pp. 27-32; quotation from p. 27.

223. See France, *Evangelist*, p. 289; cf. D. Hill, 'Son and Servant: an Essay on Matthean Christology', *JSNT* 6 (1980), pp. 2-3. As France, *Evangelist*, pp. 289-90, rightly points out, however, 'these features are', in fact, 'not particularly distinctive of

his failure to admit the possibility of Dan. 7.13-14 as the background of the term.[224] This possibility, in fact, seems especially strong in the case of Matthew, since

> the majority of Matthew's distinctive uses fall in the group which focus on the future vindication and glory of the Son of Man…And in many of these passages the echoes of Daniel 7:13-14 are unmistakable not only in the title itself but also in references to clouds, heaven, coming, glory, kingdom, judgement and the like.[225]

In that case, it seems highly probable that Matthew employs this term, and expects his readers to understand it, neither as a colourless empty public title nor as a mere self-designation of Jesus as many suppose,[226] but as a Christological title which has its background in Dan. 7.13-14 and functions as a pointer to Jesus' authoritative eschatological mission as the fulfiller of God's ultimate will.[227]

From the observations above, one may suggest with some confidence that ὁ υἱὸς τοῦ ἀνθρώπου in Mt. 12.8 is employed by Matthew (whatever its original use by Jesus himself) neither as a generic term signifying humanity nor as a collective term for Israel/disciples nor just as a self-designation of Jesus but rather as a Christological title, which points to the authority of Jesus who fulfils his eschatological mission and is, therefore, greater than David and the temple, and which is thus perfectly suitable for Jesus' pronouncement of his own Lordship of the sabbath especially in the face of the Pharisees' opposition.

The meaning of the whole verse and its function in the flow of Jesus'

Matthew; they could equally be discerned in the usage of the other gospels'.

224. D. Hill, 'The Figure of Jesus in Matthew's Story: a Response to Professor Kingsbury's Literary-critical Probe', *JSNT* 21 (1984), p. 50; cf. France, *Evangelist*, p. 290. For fuller accounts of this background, see esp. Kim, *Son of Man*, pp. 15-37; Caragounis, *Son of Man*, pp. 61-119, 168-243.

225. France, *Evangelist*, p. 291; cf. G. Vermes, *Jesus the Jew* (London: SCM Press, 2nd edn, 1983), pp. 178-79.

226. E.g. G. Vermes, 'The Use of בר נשׁא/בר נשׁ in Jewish Aramaic', in M. Black, *An Aramaic Approach to the Gospels and Acts* (Oxford: Clarendon Press, 3rd edn, 1967), pp. 310-28. For a brief criticism of it, see Jeremias, *Theology*, p. 261 n. 1.

227. For the connection between 'the kingdom of God' and 'the Son of man' in Matthew, see France, *Evangelist*, p. 291; cf. M. Pamment, 'The Son of Man in the First Gospel', *NTS* 29 (1983), p. 122. For a comprehensive investigation of the connection (but in the teaching of Jesus as a whole), see Caragounis, *Son of Man*, pp. 232-43; cf. also Kim, *Son of Man*, pp. 74-81.

argument in the Matthean pericope are now very obvious. His final response (v. 8) is no longer indirect but declares outright his own Lordship of the sabbath (κύριος...τοῦ σαββάτου). In the Old Testament, as we have observed in Chapter 1, God's Lordship (or ownership) of the sabbath is repeatedly presupposed or expressed (cf. such expressions as 'to/for YHWH' in, for example, Exod. 16.23, 25; 20.10; 31.15; 35.2; Lev. 23.3; Deut. 5.14; and such phrases as 'my/your sabbath' in, for example, Exod. 31.13; Lev. 19.3, 30; 26.2; Neh. 9.14; Isa. 56.4; 58.13. Ezek. 20.12ff.; 22.8, 26; 23.38; 44.24), and this Lordship frequently provides the ground for the covenantal orientation of the sabbath. This Lordship of the sabbath which was exclusively claimed by God alone in the Old Testament is now claimed by Jesus, the Son of man. This claim is then unparalleled, since it is tantamount to a claim to be God or at least to have an authority equal to God. The Christological note could hardly be raised higher than this.[228]

This is, of course, not an abrupt claim. From the very beginning of his Gospel (cf. the genealogy of 1.1-17; the formula quotations of chs. 1–2) and throughout the following chapters (cf. Jesus' baptism in 3.13-17; the sermon on the mount in chs. 5–7; the healing miracles of chs. 8–9), Matthew has consistently presented Jesus as the promised one, the messiah, who fulfils the Old Testament and brings the kingdom of heaven to his disciples. More immediately in 11.25-30 and in the present pericope, Matthew builds up the ground for the claim more concretely by showing that Jesus the messiah, who fulfils the eschatological rest and brings it to his disciples, is greater than David the king and than the temple; now what will follow is expected to be a greater claim than those, and it is the claim to Lordship over the sabbath.

Jesus the Son of man, who brings the age of salvation and delivers his disciples from their burden, now fulfils God's ultimate will for the sabbath by providing the eternal rest which was looked forward to through the sabbath institution. Hence he has the absolutely legitimate right to claim Lordship over the sabbath. It is then not so much Jesus' stance towards the sabbath that really matters; it is rather how the sabbath law stands with regard to him, as the one who brings it to fulfilment and on whom all attention must now be focused.[229] Now the matter of real importance is no longer merely keeping the literal regulations of the

228. Note the emphasis in the Greek construction is on the predicate κύριος; cf. Hicks, 'Sabbath', p. 88; Davies and Allison, *Matthew*, II, p. 316.
229. This is an adapted quotation from Banks, *Jesus*, p. 226.

sabbath law, but accepting Jesus as the messiah and receiving the eschatological rest (= redemption)[230] present in him.

The disciples, being with the messiah who is Lord of the sabbath, are not bound to keep the Old Testament sabbath law as such. They are no longer obliged to keep it as the people in the Old Testament period did, because they are now participating in the eschatological rest, the ultimate goal of the sabbath which is now fulfilled and provided by Jesus. Jesus now transcends the sabbath law by fulfilling its original and fundamental purpose. It is, of course, still not very clear how this transcendence should affect the way the disciples keep the sabbath;[231] but the transcendence does provide the crucial Christological key with which the early church could later determine the issue—for some at least, that would involve setting aside the sabbath. Jesus' fulfilment of the sabbath, like other laws, has thus the elements of both 'continuity' in the sense that Jesus' redemption fulfils the sabbath ultimately and 'discontinuity' in the sense that the sabbath is transcended by Jesus' fulfilment of it. This is then another good example which shows what Jesus' saying of 5.17[232] signifies.[233] Jesus, the Son of man, has come not to abolish the sabbath as some (e.g. the Pharisees in his time; the antinomians in Matthew's community) may have suspected or thought, but to fulfil it. Now it becomes more than ever clear why the disciples are guiltless; it is exactly because their behaviour in the grainfield on the sabbath is by no means

230. For the background of the link of these two concepts, see Hooker, *Son of Man*, pp. 99-102; cf. E.C. Hoskyns, 'Jesus, the Messiah', in G.K.A. Bell and A. Deissmann (eds.), *Mysterium Christi* (London: Longmans, Green, 1930), pp. 74-78; Carson, 'Sabbath', p. 66; Kim, *Son of Man*, pp. 93-94; cf. also the investigations above. Cf. Heb. 4.1-11.

231. On this fact the comment by Lincoln, 'Perspective', p. 364, is noteworthy: 'This is only to be expected because of the veiled nature of His [= Jesus'] earthly ministry. Only after the consummation of this ministry in His death and Resurrection would the significance of both His person and work become clear... The veiled nature of Jesus' ministry accounts for the slight ambiguity in regard to His relation to the Sabbath and for the fact that for a time in the early church there were those who continued Sabbath observance while the full implications of the entry of the new age accomplished by Christ were being worked out.' In that case the women's observance of the sabbath as indicated in 28.1 (cf. Lk. 23.56) is not an unexpected one.

232. Μὴ νομίσητε ὅτι ἦλθον καταλῦσαι τὸν νόμον ἢ τοὺς προφήτας· οὐκ ἦλθον καταλῦσαι ἀλλὰ πληρῶσαι.

233. A certain link between the present pericope and 5.17 is also recognized by Gnilka, *Matthäusevangelium*, I, p. 446; cf. also Luz, *Matthäus (8–17)*, p. 233; Saldarini, *Community*, p. 131.

the consequence of Jesus' abolition of the sabbath but the result of their acknowledgment of and participation in his fulfilment of it.

This pericope began with an opening sentence describing *Jesus'* going through the grainfield on *the sabbath*.[234] It now comes to an end with a closing statement pronouncing who Jesus, *the Son of man*, is in relation to *the sabbath*. As I suggested above, Matthew may well have thought of the effect of an *inclusio* here in order to highlight the centrality of Jesus' role in the pericope in relation to the sabbath. The question which was raised by Jesus' journey on the sabbath finds its ultimate answer in this final response which proclaims Jesus' Lordship of the sabbath. Each of the preceding three responses, of course, was a proper, though to some degree indirect, answer in its own right. It is noteworthy that all these answers are grounded upon the Old Testament (one upon the Former Prophets [= historical writings]; one upon the Torah; one upon the Prophets) and that they adopt various ways of argument (one by means of implicit typology; one by means of explicit typology; one by means of quotation). By piling up all these answers, therefore, the effect of Jesus' argument has already become extremely powerful. For Matthew, however, all these answers, in some sense, function as a preparation for the final response, the climax of the story, which pronounces the ultimate authority of Jesus over the sabbath and thus provides the ultimate answer to the original question. Jesus' authority which has already been the focus of the previous answers now finds its culminating expression in the final answer. This culminating pronouncement, however, functions not only as the answer to the original question, but also adds another important dimension by injecting a high Christological note in the flow of the Gospel story as a whole.[235] It seems then natural that this climactic pronouncement extends its effect even to the next sabbath controversy pericope.

4. *Healing the Man with a Withered Hand on the Sabbath (12.9-14)*

The literary relation of Mt. 12.9-14 to its two synoptic parallels (Mk 3.1-6; Lk. 6.6-11; cf. Lk. 14.5; 13.15) is slightly different in character from that of the previous pericope. Many scholars who adopt the two-source

234. It is noteworthy that the disciples are not mentioned in this sentence, and also that only Matthew includes the name ὁ Ἰησοῦς.

235. Cf. Banks, *Jesus*, pp. 120-21.

hypothesis readily identify Mark and Q as the two main sources of the Matthean pericope (i.e. vv. 9-10, 12b-14 from Mark; v. 11 from Q; v. 12a probably from Matthew himself).[236] It may be possible to explain most of the differences between Mt. 12.9-10, 12b-14 and Mk 3.1-6 simply as Matthew's redactional changes. It seems, however, much easier to explain those differences by supposing 'common tradition' as suggested in section 3.[237] Mt. 12.11 and Lk. 14.5 may well have been based on Q material (rather than Q),[238] though it is equally plausible that each of them come from M *Sondergut* and L *Sondergut* respectively.[239] A number of scholars suggest that v. 12a is a Matthean redaction.[240] Their suggestion is, however, by no means conclusive; we may well suppose that it comes either from M *Sondergut* or from Q material.[241]

The historicity of the sabbath healing story is generally admitted by most scholars.[242] The authenticity of Jesus' sayings in the present pericope perhaps apart from πόσῳ οὖν διαφέρει ἄνθρωπος προβάτου of

236. E.g. C.M. Tuckett, *Reading the New Testament: Methods of Interpretation* (London: SPCK, 1987), pp. 90-93; Davies and Allison, *Matthew*, II, p. 316; Weiss, 'Sabbath', p. 19; *et al.*

237. Cf. addition of ἰδού in v. 10 (cf. Lk. 14.2); omission of ἦν ἐκεῖ of Mk 3.1 (cf. Lk. 6.6); substitution of ξηράν in v. 10 for ἐξηραμμένην of Mk 3.1 (cf. ξηρά of Lk. 6.6); omission of αὐτόν of Mk 3.2 (minor agreement?); omission of μετ' ὀργῆς, συλλυπούμενος ἐπὶ τῇ πωρώσει τῆς καρδίας αὐτῶν of Mk 3.5 (minor agreement!)—these may be some examples which are less explicable by means of the two-source hypothesis than by supposing 'common tradition'. Cf. also the alteration of Mk 3.6 in Lk. 6.11.

238. It is less likely that these two verses are based on a written document (e.g. 'Q'), considering the significant differences in form and content between them; cf. Turner, 'Sabbath', p. 107: 'Matthew and Luke used different recensions of that material'.

239. Cf. Allen, *Matthew*, p. 129; Davies and Allison, *Matthew*, II, p. 319; Nolland, *Luke 9:21–18:34*, p. 746. It seems most probable that Lk. 13.15 comes from L *Sondergut*; it is too distinctive to be considered a real parallel to Mt. 12.11 sharing a common source (i.e. 'Q material'). See below, Chapter 6, section 3.

240. Hummel, *Auseinandersetzung*, p. 44; H. Hendrickx, *The Miracle Stories* (London: Geoffrey Chapman, 1987), p. 162; Luz, *Matthäus (8–17)*, p. 238; Davies and Allison, *Matthew*, II, pp. 316, 321.

241. Cf. Tuckett, *Reading*, pp. 91, 133. In that case, Luke omitted the saying in his redaction in 14.5.

242. E. Lohse, 'Jesu Worte über den Sabbat', in W. Eltester (ed.), *Judentum Urchristentum Kirche* (Berlin: Töpelmann, 1960), pp. 83-84; Schweizer, *Matthew*, pp. 279-80; Tuckett, *Reading*, pp. 113-14; Davies and Allison, *Matthew*, II, pp. 316-17; *et al.* Pace Bultmann, *History*, p. 12.

v. 12a is mostly assumed and/or well attested by many scholars;[243] and even the saying of v. 12a is probably authentic,[244] especially if it came from M *Sondergut*.

Most scholars agree that the narrative of the present pericope is that of a 'pronouncement-story' rather than a miracle story.[245] The healing of v. 13 is not the focus of attention; the primary concern of the whole pericope is clearly the question of the sabbath. U. Luz points out a possible chiastic scheme ABCDC´B´A´, according to which vv. 11-12a forms the centre.[246] The climax of the narrative, however, is reached in v. 12b which picks up the elements from vv. 11-12a and by doing so provides the answer to the question raised by the Pharisees in v. 10b.[247]

a. *12.9-10—The Setting and the Pharisees' Challenge*
Matthew's description of the setting and of the Pharisees' role in the story are significantly different from the synoptic parallels (Mk 3.1-2; Lk. 6.6-7).

The phrase μεταβὰς ἐκεῖθεν is characteristically Matthean, and makes the tie between the previous and present stories more apparent. According to Matthew Jesus and his disciples continued their journey from the grainfield where the controversy had happened and entered into a town perhaps to attend the synagogue service on the same sabbath.[248] In that case, it seems highly probable that the Pharisees who had

243. Lohse, 'Worte', pp. 84, 86-89; Schweizer, *Matthew*, pp. 279-80; Tuckett, *Reading*, pp. 113-14; Davies and Allison, *Matthew*, II, pp. 316-17; *et al.* Even Bultmann, *History*, p. 147, himself admits the probable authenticity of Mk 3.4 (= Mt. 12.12b).

244. Cf. Allen, *Matthew*, p. 129; Lohse, 'Worte', pp. 84, 88-89; Rordorf, *Sunday*, pp. 58 (esp. n. 2), 74; Banks, *Jesus*, pp. 127, 130.

245. V. Taylor, *The Formation of the Gospel Tradition* (London: MacMillan, 1935), pp. 63-64; cf. Dibelius, *Tradition*, p. 43 (paradigm); Bultmann, *History*, p. 12 (apophthegm); G. Theissen, *The Miracle Stories of the Early Christian Tradition* (trans. F. McDonagh; Edinburgh: T. & T. Clark, 1983), pp. 106-12 (justificatory rule miracle); *et al.*

246. *Matthäus (8–17)*, p. 237.

247. Hagner, *Matthew 1–13*, p. 333.

248. It is quite clear that Jesus often visits the synagogue on the sabbath (Mk 1.21; 3.1 par.; 6.2 par.; cf. also Mt. 9.35; Mk 1.39 par.; Jn 18.20). The significance of this fact, however, must not be exaggerated. Rordorf, *Sunday*, pp. 67-68, comments on the fact thus: 'This behaviour [= Jesus' visit to the synagogue on the sabbath] does not necessarily mean that Jesus was a zealous observer of the Jewish law or that he was very strict about the sabbath commandment. It stands to reason that

been involved in the earlier controversy were also present in the synagogue of the same town.[249]

In this context Matthew's addition of the personal pronoun αὐτῶν to
τὴν συναγωγήν is highly significant. In Matthew the synagogue is 'a
place of confrontation' (cf. 10.17; 23.34).[250] By adding αὐτῶν to it (i.e.
'*their* synagogue') Matthew highlights 'the gulf which was developing
between Jesus and the Jewish establishment'[251] especially that of the
Pharisees (cf. v. 14, and also v. 2). The synagogue of the Pharisees is no
longer neutral to Jesus and his disciples;[252] it was already charged with
an antagonistic atmosphere, and now it becomes more so after the confrontation in the grainfield.

Matthew makes the antagonism of the Pharisees to Jesus more apparent by converting the Pharisees' unspoken thought (cf. Mk 3.2; Lk. 6.7)
into an explicit question. They are thus more positively involved in this
test-case. Their question is by no means out of genuine interest in Jesus'
halakhic stance with regard to the sabbath, but simply betrays their
antagonistic zeal to search for further evidence to accuse him (ἵνα

Jesus used the opportunity to deliver his message in the synagogues where people
were assembled on the sabbath'; cf. Marshall, *Luke*, p. 181; Turner, 'Sabbath', pp.
101-102; Nolland, *Luke 1–9:20*, p. 195; *pace* Bacchiocchi, *Rest*, pp. 145-46. For
further discussion, see below, Chapter 6.

249. Mark seems to assume this as well (cf. καί), though Luke presents the
situation rather differently—Ἐγένετο δὲ ἐν ἑτέρῳ σαββάτῳ; cf. also οἱ γραμματεῖς
καὶ οἱ Φαρισαῖοι of Lk. 6.7 which seem to be assumed as a different group of
people from those Pharisees of the previous story. Hagner, *Matthew 1–13*, p. 333,
rather suggests, perhaps because of the conflict between the Matthean and Lukan
versions of the situation, that the phrase is a 'general transitional phrase that provides
little actual information other than the narrative function of getting Jesus to the
synagogue where the interchange and healing take place'. It seems, however, evident
that Matthew at least intended to link the two stories more intimately regardless of
the actual historical sequence.

250. Davies and Allison, *Matthew*, II, p. 317; cf. also *idem*, *Matthew*, I, pp.
413-14.

251. France, *Matthew*, p. 204.

252. This may well be a reflection of the situation of Matthew's community in
relation to its neighbouring synagogues—that is, Matthew's community was no
longer a part of the synagogue of the Pharisaic Jews, though, as I suggested in
Chapter 3, the relation between the two was still a live issue; cf. France, *Evangelist*,
pp. 107-108. For further discussions of this issue, see Kilpatrick, *Origin*, pp. 109-
11; Hummel, *Auseinandersetzung*, pp. 28-71; Hare, *Persecution*, pp. 135, 141-45,
167-71; Cope, *Scribe*, pp. 51-52, esp. n. 92; Saldarini, *Community*, pp. 66-67.

κατηγορήσωσιν αὐτοῦ) if not yet to destroy him (cf. v. 14). In this converted question, Matthew's text has two significant differences from that of Mark: (i) the presence of the verb ἔξεστιν; (ii) the lack of the pronoun αὐτόν. Firstly, the presence of ἔξεστιν in the question on the one hand 'strengthens the link between 12.1-8 and 12.9-14 (cf. 12.2, 4)',[253] and on the other 'moves the question of the Law more explicitly into the foreground'.[254] Furthermore, it creates the verbal and structural correspondence between the question and the answer (v. 12). Secondly, the absence of Mark's αὐτόν in the question makes the issue purely halakhic. In Matthew the question is no longer about healing the particular man at the scene but about healing in general. The Pharisees' concern is not reserved for the man in need at all, but is solely focused on accusing Jesus by means of their halakhic question. Their lack of concern for the man as such on the one hand provides the very ground of Jesus' argument in his response to their challenge in vv. 11-12, and on the other hand well prepares us for the Pharisees' plot to destroy Jesus in v. 14.

The crucial question now is whether the act of healing was prohibited on the sabbath. There is no first-hand material which explicitly witnesses the view of the contemporary Jews of Jesus' day.[255] Even in the list of 39 categories of prohibited work on the sabbath in *m. Šab.* 7.2 healing is not mentioned (cf. also *m. Beṣ.* 5.2).[256] The prohibition of healing, however, is assumed rather than argued in the various rabbinic writings (e.g. *m. Šab.* 14.3; 22.6; cf. *t. Šab.* 16.22)[257], and the only exception to it is when life is in immediate danger. In *m. Yom.* 8.6 R. Mattithiah b. Heresh (*c.* 130) provides an interesting case regulation with a general principle: 'If a man has a pain in his throat they may drop medicine into his mouth on the Sabbath, since there is doubt whether life is in danger, and whenever there is doubt whether life is in danger this overrides the Sabbath'

253. Davies and Allison, *Matthew*, II, p. 317.

254. Banks, *Jesus*, pp. 123-24; cf. also Barth, 'Law', p. 79.

255. Cf. the overall discussions of the sabbath material to the first century CE in Chapter 2.

256. R.T. France, in his not yet published commentary on Mark's Gospel, points out that healing 'is not, after all, part of normal work for most people'. I am most grateful to Dr France for allowing me to read his commentary in typescript.

257. According to *m. Šab.* 22.6, healing on the sabbath is practically possible, but only if the healing is not purposively intended and the actions involved are allowed on the sabbath. In *t. Šab.* 16.22, the house of Shammai forbids one even to pray for a sick person, though the house of Hillel permits it.

(cf. *Mek. Kaspa* 4 [L. 180-81]).[258] Though the dates of these materials are uncertain or significantly later than Jesus' time, the Pharisees' question in Matthew and their attitude in Mark and Luke clearly suggest that the Pharisees at the scene already recognized and adopted such a rabbinic opinion that the act of healing must not be allowed on the sabbath unless life is in immediate danger. It seems then quite clear that healing the man with a withered hand (ἄνθρωπος χεῖρα ἔχων ξηράν) on the sabbath was not lawful according to the Pharisaic halakhic stance, because a withered hand could hardly be classified as an immediate danger to life.

Jesus is thus put into a seemingly perfect test-case by the Pharisees. As far as the Pharisees' halakhic stance is concerned, there can be only one answer to their question, and that must be 'No'. Nevertheless the clause ἵνα κατηγορήσωσιν αὐτοῦ, in fact, implies that the Pharisees already anticipated what Jesus' answer would be; otherwise their question seems to lose its point. And as they may have expected, Jesus' answer will not be 'No'. Once he is challenged, there would have been no other choice but to confront them with the authority of the Lord of the sabbath. Before we go on to discuss Jesus' response, however, we should recall also an additional but most significant fact that, according to the investigation above in Chapter 1, the Torah itself (and the Old Testament as a whole) nowhere states or even implies that healing must not be allowed on the sabbath.

b. *12.11-12—Jesus' Response*

Matthew alone includes Jesus' saying of vv. 11-12a in the present pericope, though the saying has a close but partial parallel in Lk. 14.5.[259] Davies and Allison suggest that Matthew's inclusion of this saying in the present co-text was intended to sharpen 'Jesus' halakhic logic' and to make him 'a first-rate debater'.[260] It is, however, doubtful whether Jesus' argument in the Matthean pericope is really halakhic. As we will

---

258. The principle that saving life overrides the sabbath is well established throughout Judaism from the fairly early period, as we have seen in Chapter 2; cf. 1 Macc. 2.39-41; 9.43-49; CD 11.16-17; 4Q251 2.6-7; *t. Šab.* 15.16; *Mek. Šab.* 1 (L. 3.197-201); etc. For further references to sabbath healing in the rabbinic literature, see Strack and Billerbeck, *Kommentar*, I, pp. 623-29.

259. Cf. also Lk. 13.15, which is, however, too distinctive to be considered a real parallel to Mt. 12.11.

260. *Matthew*, II, p. 319. Immediately after this comment, however, they add: 'Nonetheless…the First Gospel's legal debates remain relatively unsophisticated'.

see later, though he is using the Pharisees' halakhic tradition, his argument by no means appeals to their halakhic tradition but rather points to the inconsistency of their halakhic system. His argument then is far from halakhic; on the contrary it is anti-halakhic.

In the present pericope the function of the sayings of vv. 11-12 is to respond to the Pharisees' challenge in v. 10 (ὁ δὲ εἶπεν αὐτοῖς); therefore the immediate audience of these sayings (especially that of the counter-question of v. 11; cf. τίς ἔσται ἐξ ὑμῶν ἄνθρωπος) is clearly the Pharisees.

It is not clear whether (ὃς ἕξει) πρόβατον ἕν is simply a Semitism for 'a sheep'[261] or whether it is an emphatic expression meaning '(who has) only one sheep' which might be then an anticipation of the story of one lost sheep in 18.12-14.[262] Preferring the latter option, Luz asserts, 'Matthew, like the Nathan story of 2 Sam. 12.3, surely has in mind the single sheep of a poor man'.[263] If Luz's assertion is right, the imperative necessity of rescuing the sheep seems to be increased, though not on the legal level but on the humanitarian level. In Lk. 14.5 we have υἱός[264] ἢ βοῦς instead of Matthew's πρόβατον.[265] Not a few scholars regard this combination to be original.[266] If the saying of v. 11 came from M *Sondergut*, however, it is not necessary to suppose that the phrase πρόβατον ἕν is secondary.

In the time of Jesus different opinions may presumably have existed side by side as to whether one should rescue an animal from a pit (βόθυνος)[267] on the sabbath. According to CD 11.13-14, it is clearly

261. Zahn, *Matthäus*, p. 347 n. 4; Beare, *Matthew*, p. 272; F. Neirynck, 'Luke 14:1-6: Lukan Composition and Q Saying', in C. Bussmann and W. Radl (eds.), *Der Treue Gottes trauen* (Feiburg: Herder, 1991), pp. 252-53.

262. Cf. Gundry, *Matthew*, p. 226; Hagner, *Matthew 1–13*, p. 333.

263. *Matthäus (8–17)*, p. 239 (translation mine); cf. Fenton, *Matthew*, p. 192; Sigal, *Halakah*, p. 138.

264. א K L Ψ f[1,13] 33 etc. have ὄνος instead.

265. For the effect of paronomasia in the Lukan version when rendered into Aramaic (i.e. ברא [son], בעירא [ox], and בירא [well]), see Lohse, 'Worte', p. 87; Marshall, *Luke*, p. 580; *et al.* For another but rather unconvincing explanation, see M. Black, 'The Aramaic Spoken by Christ and Luke 14⁵', *JTS* 1 (1950), pp. 60-62.

266. Gundry, *Matthew*, p. 226; Tuckett, *Reading*, p. 92; Nolland, *Luke 9.21–18:34*, p. 746; *et al.*

267. Lk. 14.5 has φρέαρ instead. Would 'well' cause more immediate danger than 'pit'? In that case the Matthean version may be more lenient than the Lukan version.

forbidden to lift a (newborn) beast out on the sabbath, if it falls into a cistern or pit. In 4Q251 2.5-6 a similar prohibition is found: 'A man should not lift out cattle which has fallen in[to] the water on the Sabbath day'.[268] These are, in fact, the only places outside the Gospels where this issue is discussed in the extant literature before or around the time of Jesus. In a rabbinic tradition recorded in the Talmud (*b. Šab.* 128b),[269] however, the issue is discussed once again. According to it, the rabbis had different opinions about the issue:

> Rab Judah said in Rab's name: If an animal falls into a dyke, one brings pillows and bedding and places [them] under it, and if it ascends it ascends. An objection is raised: If an animal falls into a dyke, provisions are made for it where it lies so that it should not perish. Thus, only provisions, but not pillows and bedding?

It is clear, however, that neither the milder view (i.e. the former which allows throwing articles into the pit to enable the animal to climb out) nor the stricter view (i.e. the latter which allows only feeding the animal to keep it alive until the next day) allows one to pull the animal out of the pit.[270] We find, thus, a significant discrepancy between Jesus' assumption and the extant rulings before or around and even after the time of Jesus. This fact leads many scholars to suggest that Jesus is here not appealing to any accepted legal ruling but to the actual/common practice of his hearers or simply to their common sense/conscience.[271] In this connection, it is interesting to note the editor's comment in *b. Šab.* 128b: '[The avoidance of] suffering of dumb animals is a Biblical [law],[272] so the Biblical law comes and supersedes the [interdict] of the Rabbis'. If such a priority of relieving an animal from suffering over the

268. In CD 11.16-17, however, it is permitted to pull a human being out of water or a pit 'with the aid of a ladder or rope or (some such) utensil'; cf. also 4Q251 2.6-7: '[...But if it is a human being who has fallen into the water on the day of] the Sabbath, he will throw him his garment to lift him out with it'. See above, Chapter 2.

269. Rab Judah, one of the speakers in the passage, is not too long after the New Testament period.

270. *Pace* Barth, 'Law', p. 79, n. 3, where he argues, 'Here Matthew appeals to the milder!'; a similarly mistaken view is also found in Hummel, *Auseinandersetzung*, p. 45. For further rabbinic materials which are to some extent related to the issue, see Strack and Billerbeck, *Kommentar*, I, pp. 629-30.

271. Manson, *Sayings*, pp. 188-89; Borg, *Conflict*, p. 150; Hare, *Matthew*, p. 133; *et al.*

272. The editor may have had in mind such verses as Prov. 12.10; Deut. 22.14; Exod. 23.5.

rabbinic sabbath rulings had already been commonly recognized in Jesus' time, Jesus may well have appealed to such a common practice. This suggestion thus seems to solve the problem raised by the lack of contemporary supportive sources, and also it sounds in line with my previous suggestion that Jesus' argument is not halakhic. Nevertheless, when we are reminded of the fact that the immediate audience of Jesus' saying of v. 11 is the Pharisees (cf. especially αὐτοῖς and ἐξ ὑμῶν), it is not easy to explain how Jesus' appeal to such a common practice could provide any real force to his argument against those who were seeking to accuse him on the basis of their halakhic casuistry. His argument could be really meaningful only if the Pharisees agree at least with Jesus' primary assumption in accordance with their casuistic rulings. We must then suppose that the Pharisees, or at least those in front of Jesus, either indeed had such a ruling as Jesus assumes in his question or at least regarded such a practice as not a violation of their own halakhah. In such a situation where there is insufficient evidence on either side (especially in relation to the Pharisees in Galilee),[273] we seem to have good reason to take the Gospel evidence(s) (cf. also Lk. 14.5) itself as the evidence for the actual situation in the time of Jesus.[274] Considering the observation in Chapter 2 that there were differing Pharisaic halakhic opinions about the sabbath from an early stage, it seems highly likely that the Pharisees, especially those in the Galilean district,[275] in the time of Jesus were different in their view(s) of the present issue not only from the Qumran community but also from the rabbis represented in *b. Šab.* 128b, and they instead allowed one to pull the animal out of the pit on the sabbath.[276] If my suggestion is right, Jesus' question provides a proper starting point for his subsequent argument in v. 12.

To this rhetorical question Jesus adds an emphatic statement: πόσῳ

---

273. Cf. Hübner, *Gesetz*, p. 140. For the lack of sources regarding the 'Galilean Pharisees' in general during the first century CE, see, for example, Saldarini, *Pharisees*, pp. 291-97.

274. The possibility of this argument has already been suggested by Tuckett, *Reading*, pp. 65-66, though he has at the same time recognized the danger of circularity.

275. As regards the presence of the Pharisees in Galilee and their influence upon the Galilean Jews, see, among others, S. Freyne, *Galilee from Alexander the Great to Hadrian: A Study of Second Temple Judaism* (Wilmington, DE: Glazier/Notre Dame University Press, 1980), esp. ch. 8; *idem*, *Galilee, Jesus and the Gospels* (Dublin: Gill & Macmillan, 1988); Saldarini, *Pharisees*, pp. 291-97.

276. Cf. Saldarini, *Community*, p. 132.

οὖν διαφέρει ἄνθρωπος προβάτου. This *a fortiori* argument may indeed be an appeal to their common sense (cf. 6.26; 10.31).[277] Jesus' argument then is clear, though partly implicit: if you are ready to relieve an animal from its suffering on the sabbath, it should surely be proper to relieve a man from his suffering even on the sabbath (regardless of whether his life is in immediate danger or not; but your halakhic rulings unduly forbid this proper behaviour). As I have suggested above, even if Jesus uses one of the Pharisees' halakhic rulings, his argument is far from rabbinic or halakhic;[278] it is rather anti-halakhic in pointing out the inconsistency and inhumanity of their halakhic system.

Jesus, therefore, concludes his argument by presenting a general principle, which is based not on the Pharisaic halakhah[279] but on his own authority as 'Lord of the sabbath' (v. 8):[280] ὥστε ἔξεστιν τοῖς σάββασιν καλῶς ποιεῖν. It is interesting to compare the original question by the Pharisees in v. 10 (εἰ ἔξεστιν τοῖς σάββασιν θεραπεῦσαι;) with this statement. The structure of Jesus' answer, on the one hand, exactly corresponds to that of the Pharisees' question (ἔξεστιν τοῖς σάββασιν + infinitive). This may show Matthew's intention to relate the question and

277. In 6.26 and 10.31, however, Jesus' argument has some theological weight, because his argument there is based, though implicitly, on the fact that God is the Father of the disciples; cf. Luz, *Matthew 1–7*, p. 405.

278. Cf. Banks, *Jesus*, p. 127. Once again, Jesus' argument is by no means that of *qal wahomer* for reasons similar to those given above in relation to 12.5-6; *pace* Sigal, *Halakah*, pp. 136-41; Hicks, 'Sabbath', pp. 89-90; Harrington, *Matthew*, p. 173; Saldarini, *Community*, p. 132. Unlike the rabbinic *qal wahomer*, none of the premises of Jesus' argument has its basis in the Torah; cf. Cohn-Sherbok, 'Plucking', pp. 36-39. Jesus' argument is thus proclamatory again rather than explanatory and therefore provocative rather than persuasive. This may once again explain why the Pharisees in v. 14 took counsel against him instead of being persuaded by him.

279. There is no such general principle as the one presented by Jesus in v. 12b in the extant rabbinic writings. On the contrary, there are specific rulings which contradict the principle—for example, in *t. Šab.* 16.22 the house of Shammai forbids one to distribute charity to the poor on the sabbath in the house of assembly, or even to pray for a sick person, though the house of Hillel permits them. The author of *The Epistle to Diognetus* implies that the Jews of his time forbade one to perform a good deed on the sabbath; see *Diogn.* 4.3: 'And what can it be but impious falsely to accuse God of forbidding that a good deed should be done on the Sabbath day?' (...ἐν τῇ τῶν σαββάτων ἡμέρᾳ καλόν τι ποιεῖν...); see below, Chapter 7, section 4.

280. Cf. Hagner, *Matthew 1–13*, p. 334: 'It is because of who he is...that his interpretation of the meaning of the commandments is authoritative (cf. v 8)'.

the answer more intimately. The focus of the answer, on the other hand, is different from that of the question; whereas the Pharisees' question is more specific (θεραπεῦσαι) and therefore casuistic in its character, Jesus' answer is more general (καλῶς ποιεῖν) and therefore non-casuistic. This may show Matthew's intention to emphasize the contrast between Jesus' concern and that of the Pharisees.[281] The Pharisees are enslaved by their halakhic concern and that concern on the one hand leads them to be eager to accuse Jesus by means of their halakhic question and on the other blinds them to the need of the man with a withered hand; while Jesus is rather concerned with restoring the original will of God for the sabbath and revealing the meaning of the fulfilment of the sabbath in himself, Lord of the sabbath (v. 8), and this concern naturally leads him to see the need of the man with a withered hand and leads him to proclaim a more general principle as regards the sabbath especially in a situation when it is fulfilled.

Jesus' answer in Matthew is then neither defensive nor conditioned by the Pharisees' question, but it is rather proclamatory. His answer (ἔξεστιν τοῖς σάββασιν καλῶς ποιεῖν) is based, as I pointed out above, not on the Pharisaic halakhah but on his own authority as 'Lord of the sabbath' (v. 8). If we judge this answer according to the Pharisees' halakhic standard, it must be a poor answer.[282] His answer, however, is by no means an addition to the Pharisaic halakhah. And yet his answer is certainly not a simple repetition or representation of the Old Testament sabbath law either, since in the Old Testament such a positive commandment is nowhere given. The statement of his answer becomes possible just because Jesus, who brings the age of salvation, brings the fulfilment of the sabbath which has been anticipated and awaited by the Old Testament, and becomes 'Lord of the sabbath' (cf. 4.3, 6). It seems

281. Note in the Markan and Lukan versions the question is more specific—ἀγαθὸν ποιῆσαι/ἀγαθοποιῆσαι ἢ κακοποιῆσαι, ψυχὴν σῶσαι ἢ ἀποκτεῖναι/ἀπολέσαι;' Matthew may have omitted ἢ κακοποιῆσαι, ψυχὴν σῶσαι ἢ ἀποκεῖναι/ἀπολέσαι in order to make Jesus' answer more general and by doing that to contrast it with the question of the Pharisees more impressively. The omission may also have the effect of increasing the structural correspondence between the question and the answer.

282. *Pace* Tuckett, *Reading*, p. 132—Matthew's Jesus is far from arguing 'in a typically rabbinic manner' as he suggests; on the contrary Jesus' argument in Matthew, as in Mark, is based on his own authority rather than on rabbinic hermeneutics. Cf. Banks, *Jesus*, p. 127.

then quite clear that his answer assumes the messianic authority,[283] and it, therefore, needs to be understood Christologically.[284] Jesus' underlying argument seems clear: I am not abolishing the sabbath but fulfilling it and showing the meaning of the fulfilment of it in this statement! His statement, which is rather provocative than persuasive, may naturally anticipate such an antagonistic response from the Pharisees as is shown in v. 14.

On the basis of the observations above, we may now investigate more closely the meaning of Jesus' final statement, ὥστε ἔξεστιν τοῖς σάββασιν καλῶς ποιεῖν. First, ὥστε indicates that Jesus' statement is the conclusion drawn from the preceding two sayings (12.11-12a).[285] As we have seen just above, however, Jesus' conclusion is not in accordance with the rabbinic way of argument; it is rather a free pronouncement on his own authority: if you are ready to relieve an animal from its suffering on the sabbath, it should certainly be right to relieve a human being from his or her suffering even on the sabbath (regardless of whether his or her life is in immediate danger or not, though your halakhic rulings would forbid you to do so); *therefore*, generally speaking, it is perfectly right to do good (to a human being)[286] on the sabbath. What then does 'to do good' (καλῶς ποιεῖν) mean? Does it mean simply 'to love one's neighbour', as some scholars suggest?[287] Certainly it may include the love commandment. Nevertheless, it hardly seems a right understanding to limit the scope of καλῶς ποιεῖν just to the love commandment. More probably he may be referring to the principle of mercy in Hos. 6.6 which he directly quoted in v. 7 in his previous

283. Cf. Rordorf, *Sunday*, pp. 69-71; Roloff, *Kerygma*, p. 66; Banks, *Jesus*, pp. 125-28, esp. p. 127.

284. Otherwise, his answer (doing good) to the Pharisees' question (healing) would make little sense, especially from the Pharisaic viewpoint, as we have pointed out just above. 'Doing good' is by no means the point of the Pharisees' question; cf. Saldarini, *Community*, p. 133: 'No Jew would hold the opposite, that it is not permitted to do good on the Sabbath. The quarrel, then, is over exactly which types of good are permitted on the Sabbath when work is involved'; cf. also Carson, 'Sabbath', pp. 69-70: 'the Pharisees would surely argue that keeping the Sabbath is good, and breaking it is evil'.

285. Note in Mk 3.4 and Lk. 6.9 this statement takes the form of a rhetorical question.

286. Davies and Allison, *Matthew*, II, p. 321, include this qualifying phrase in their paraphrase.

287. E.g. Barth, 'Law', p. 79; Luz, *Matthäus (8–17)*, pp. 239-40.

conflict.[288] This suggestion is attractive, since it fits in well with the Pharisees' unmerciful attitude in v. 10. 'To do good (to a human being)' then may refer to any act which is beneficial to a human being in need. In that case Jesus' statement becomes so radical that we may expect that no one except the 'Lord of the sabbath' (or God himself) could pro-nounce it. Together with the principle quoted in v. 7 (ἔλεος θέλω καὶ οὐ θυσίαν) this statement (ἔξεστιν τοῖς σάββασιν καλῶς ποιεῖν) reveals the true meaning and intention of the sabbath which is now fulfilled by Jesus himself, the merciful one, who, therefore, has the au-thority not only to pronounce the meaning and intention but also to act in accordance with it. 'To do good (especially to a human being)' is perfectly permissible on the sabbath, because it is in line with God's original will for the sabbath; since the sabbath was instituted as an expression of God's mercy for human beings, it is right to do merciful acts (= to do good) for them on the sabbath. 'To do good' is not an act of breaking (still less abolishing) the sabbath; nor is it just an act of keep-ing the sabbath, either. More properly speaking, it is a necessary require-ment as the result of the fulfilment of the sabbath. In short, Jesus does not abolish the sabbath but fulfils it and acts according to the principle which is revealed through his fulfilment (cf. v. 13).

c. *12.13—Jesus' Healing*

Straight after the pronouncement of the principle, Jesus now changes his addressee and speaks to the man in need. The lack of the two phrases of Mk 3.5a (καὶ περιβλεψάμενος αὐτοὺς μετ᾽ ὀργῆς, συλλυπούμενος ἐπὶ τῇ πωρώσει τῆς καρδίας αὐτῶν), especially of the latter one, is surprising considering Matthew's interest in highlighting the Pharisees' unmerciful attitude, if they were present in 'common tradition'. Some scholars, in fact, suspect that these phrases are Mark's own redactional notes, though not simply for this reason, but more because the phrases witness a number of Markan stylistic features.[289] Even if they were part

288. See France, *Matthew*, p. 205; Saldarini, *Community*, p. 133; cf. Hicks, 'Sabbath', p. 89.

289. Kuthirakkattel, *Beginning*, p. 228, points out four features: (i) two or more participles before or after the main verb is Markan style (cf. E.J. Pryke, *Redactional Style in the Marcan Gospel: A Study of Syntax and Vocabulary as Guides to Redaction in Mark* [SNTSMS, 33; Cambridge: Cambridge University Press, 1978], pp. 119-26); (ii) μετά with genitive is a Markan preference; (iii) six out of seven uses of περιβλέπεσθαι are in Mark; (iv) πώρωσις/πωρόω (cf. 6.52; 8.17) has no parallel in the other synoptics. See also Gnilka, *Markus*, I, p. 126; Guelich, *Mark*, p. 137.

of 'common tradition', however, Matthew may well have omitted them on purpose—probably in order to emphasize the intimate link between Jesus's pronouncement of the principle (v. 12b) and his subsequent deed of healing (v. 13), and at the same time to highlight the climactic effect of the pronouncement (v. 12b).

In any case, in the present form of the narrative in Matthew Jesus' healing appears as an immediate application of the principle which he has just pronounced. Having pronounced the principle, and by doing so having justified his healing activity in advance, Jesus now heals the man's withered hand without any hesitation. He says to the man: ἔκτεινόν σου τὴν χεῖρα. Then the man obeys what he says and the healing miracle happens: καὶ ἐξέτεινεν καὶ ἀπεκατεστάθη ὑγιὴς ὡς ἡ ἄλλη.[290] It is interesting, however, to note that Jesus' healing, as a matter of fact, does not involve any breach of the Old Testament sabbath law[291] or perhaps even the rabbinic rulings. Jesus neither himself stretches forth his own hand, nor touches or holds the man; he simply speaks which would surely be allowed on the sabbath even according to the strictest rabbinic stance. Nevertheless, the Pharisees' reaction in the next verse (v. 14) seems to indicate that they think differently. Probably they are distracted by the result of Jesus' command (i.e. healing itself in v. 13b) if not by the command itself (v. 13a), since they seem to share the later rabbinic assumption that purposively intended healing is not allowed on the sabbath.[292] Having said this, however, healing simply by speech may by no means have been a clear area even among the Pharisees, and that may be why they 'went out' of the synagogue rather than stay in it and further argue against Jesus (cf. v. 14). Davies and Allison's suggestion that 'his act of healing is far less provocative than his words in vv. 11-12', then, seems to be a fair judgment.[293]

---

290. J.D.M. Derrett, 'Christ and the Power of Choice (Mark 3,1-6)', *Bib* 65 (1984), pp. 184-86, attempts to demonstrate the close link between this miracle and the incident of Moses' stretching out his arm over the sea in Exod. 14 (cf. YHWH's command in v. 16 and Moses' obedience in v. 21) which saved Israel from Egypt. He also attempts (pp. 179-82) to expound Jesus' saying ἔκτεινόν σου τὴν χεῖρα in the light of the various biblical and Jewish uses of the image of 'stretching out the hand/arm'. Both attempts, however, seem to read too much into the text.

291. As I have already mentioned, the Old Testament, in fact, nowhere states or even implies that healing must not be allowed on the sabbath.

292. In that case, Jesus' healing may have disturbed the Pharisees not because of the action involved in the healing but because of his purposive intention.

293. *Matthew*, II, p. 321.

Even though I said in above that Jesus' healing of v. 13 is not the focus of attention, this healing miracle itself nevertheless seems to have some significance in the present narrative. First, this miracle brings additional support to Jesus' authoritative statement in v. 12b (and perhaps also to his authority as 'Lord of the sabbath'); instant restoration of the withered hand may exhibit the effectiveness of Jesus' word, and this effectiveness seems to be still more highlighted by the phrase, ὑγιὴς ὡς ἡ ἄλλη, which is unique to Matthew. Secondly, the result of the miracle (i.e. the restoration of the withered hand—ἀπεκατεστάθη[294]) may indicate the fulfilment of the sabbath in terms of the rescue from bodily disability (= bodily burden); Matthew's unique phrase, ὑγιὴς ὡς ἡ ἄλλη, seems to emphasize the completeness of the healing, that is, the complete rescue from the bodily burden.[295] Thirdly, and more fundamentally, this miracle itself, like the previous healing miracles of chs. 8–9, may be a further witness to Jesus as the promised one, the messiah, who fulfils the Old Testament and brings God's reign upon his people. Lastly, the obedience of the man, which makes God's reign operative upon his body, stands in contrast with the unresponsive attitude of the Pharisees upon whom therefore God's reign cannot be operative;[296] since the Pharisees missed the real significance of the miracle as the sign of the inbreaking of the kingdom, they could not respond to the miracle properly, but, on the contrary, sought to kill Jesus. Jesus then has ample reasons to heal the man on the sabbath in terms of his own ministry, though his act has been motivated by the Pharisees' testing question.

d. *12.14—The Pharisees' Reaction*

Now the Pharisees (οἱ Φαρισαῖοι), who appear consistently as Jesus' opponents throughout our two pericopes, at last ἐξελθόντες... συμβούλιον ἔλαβον κατ' αὐτοῦ ὅπως αὐτὸν ἀπολέσωσιν. The lack of the Markan phrase μετὰ τῶν Ἡρῳδιανῶν (3.6) in this verse highlights the Pharisees' role as opponents of Jesus.[297] Jesus, as we have seen

294. Some scholars seek the background of this incident from the Jeroboam story in 1 Kgs 13.1-10; see Derrett, 'Christ', p. 182; Gnilka, *Matthäusevangelium*, I, pp. 448-49. Taylor, *Mark*, p. 223, however, is sceptical about this.

295. Hagner, *Matthew 1–13*, p. 334.

296. Probably the crowd's response and Jesus' healing them all in v. 15 may also be contrasted with the Pharisees' unresponsive attitude; see Derrett, 'Christ', p. 170.

297. Note Matthew does mention Ἡρῳδιανοι in 22.16 (= Mk 12.13); note that in 22.15 a saying similar to the present verse appears. Cf. Banks, *Jesus*, p. 127;

above, did not violate the Old Testament sabbath law and perhaps not even the Pharisaic sabbath regulations. The verb ἐξελθόντες may indicate the Pharisees' failure to forge an accusation with respect to the sabbath law at least on the theological level.[298] They could not stay in the synagogue any longer[299] because of this failure and perhaps also because of Jesus' overwhelming authority in the synagogue after the healing. There was no other option for them but to go out of the synagogue. Even if they were aware of their failure, they still could not give up their original intention. On the contrary, they came to a firm conclusion that they had to remove Jesus himself (ὅπως αὐτὸν ἀπολέσωσιν) not merely refute his teaching (cf. v. 10: κατηγορήσωσιν αὐτοῦ). They were probably disturbed by Jesus' saying in v. 12b (and also by his sayings in vv. 6-8) and even further by the result of the miracle (i.e. the healing itself in v. 13b) if not by Jesus' behaviour involved in the healing (i.e. the saying in v. 13a). They were probably also threatened by Jesus' overwhelming authority. The lack of genuineness in their question is thus demonstrated. The real tragedy for the Pharisees, then, as Hagner points out, was not simply their failure to understand and accept Jesus' argument but more fundamentally their failure to receive Jesus himself as the messiah who brings the kingdom and becomes 'Lord of the sabbath'.[300]

The phrase συμβούλιον ἔλαβον is characteristically Matthean.[301] The expression is a Latinism (*consilium capere*) meaning 'to take counsel', which in Matthew is exclusively used to describe Jesus' adversaries[302]

Davies and Allison, *Matthew*, II, p. 322; Hagner, *Matthew 1–13*, p. 332. For the identity of the Herodians, see an extensive overview of opinion in H. Hoehner, *Herod Antipas* (SNTSMS, 17; Cambridge: Cambridge University Press, 1972), pp. 331-42. Though there is no consensus of opinion, a majority of scholars take them to have been the political supporters of Herod Antipas; see Cranfield, *Mark*, p. 122; W. Grundmann, *Das Evangelium nach Markus* (THNT, 2; Berlin: Evangelische Verlaganstalt, 7th edn, 1977), p. 97; Kuthirakkattel, *Beginning*, p. 238.

298. Cf. Gundry, *Mark*, p. 152—he sees such an indication from the Pharisees' coalition with the Herodians in the Markan text.

299. Cf. εὐθύς in the Markan text.

300. See *Matthew 1–13*, p. 334.

301. Matthew: 5 (12.14; 22.15; 27.1, 7; 28.12); Mark: 0 (cf. 3.6; 15.1); Luke: 0. Mark instead has συμβούλιον ἐδίδουν which is most unusual. The only occurrence of the noun συμβούλιον in the New Testament apart from the above seven occurrences is found in Acts 25.12.

302. The Pharisees—12.14; 22.15; the groups within the Sanhedrin—27.1, 7; 28.12.

when they proceed in consultation against him or form plans.[303] In the present verse, the phrase does not necessarily imply an official decision. The Pharisees may have simply consulted each other against Jesus, and/or formed a plan (without any official binding force) how to destroy Jesus.[304] This interpretation suits the power structure of the time. As I have suggested just above, in a situation where their authority in the synagogue and among the people was threatened by Jesus' authority, the Pharisees may have intuitively realized that Jesus must be removed if their influence and authority was to remain intact.[305] Furthermore, if they thought that Jesus had indeed broken the sabbath by healing the man, they may have had good reason to decide to kill Jesus, at least on the grounds of their own rulings (cf. *m. Sanh.* 7.1, 4, and 8; cf. also Exod. 31.14). Since the Pharisees, however, did not have such an authority to kill somebody simply on the grounds that he or she did not follow their halakhic rulings (even though they may have wished to do so),[306] they needed to find other measures to kill Jesus, and they attempted to do so. If the Pharisees' plan, however, did not have any official binding force at that time, and if Jesus did not, in fact, break the sabbath law (even though he might have broken some of the unsettled Pharisaic halakhic rulings), it is not so strange that in the final trial of Jesus no charge was made against him in relation to sabbath breaking.

The Pharisees' ultimate reaction to Jesus' pronouncement of the principle (v. 12b) and his healing miracle (v. 13) thus betrays the irreconcilable difference between Jesus' radical approach to the sabbath in terms of its fulfilment and the Pharisees' traditional approach in terms of their casuistic halakhah. Ironically, whereas Jesus delivers the man from his bodily burden and gives him wholeness of life as a gift of the age of salvation, the Pharisees use this merciful action as an occasion to conspire to destroy his life. By bringing the wholeness of life which the kingdom offers, Jesus puts his own life at stake.[307] Again ironically, the so-called guardians of the sabbath arrange to remove the Lord of the

303. Cf. G. Schneider, 'συμβούλιον, ου, τό', *EDNT*, III, p. 286.

304. Similarly, in 22.15; note that in both places the Pharisees are the subjects and the construction ὅπως + subjunctive follows; compare them with other occurrences in 27.1, 7; 28.12, where the subjects are the groups of the Sanhedrin and there is no ὅπως construction.

305. Hagner, *Matthew 1–13*, p. 334; cf. Sigal, *Halakah*, p. 142.

306. See esp. Sanders, *Practice*, pp. 380–490; see also above Excursus 2.

307. Guelich, *Mark*, p. 139.

sabbath,[308] just because he teaches God's ultimate aim and intention for the sabbath (vv. 6-8, 11-12) and behaves according to the principle (v. 13) which is now revealed through his fulfilment of it (cf. v. 8).

As we have observed, this pericope does not stand alone. It is linked with the previous pericope by the opening phrase μεταβὰς ἐκεῖθεν. The two incidents, according to Matthew, happened on the same sabbath, and Jesus' opponents are most probably the same Pharisees as those in the previous incident. If these two pericopes are so closely tied, the Pharisees' reaction in v. 14 may well be the reaction not only to Jesus' argument and healing in vv. 11-13 but also to Jesus' argument and pronouncement in vv. 3-8. Nevertheless the present pericope has a self-sustaining structure. The question raised by the Pharisees in the beginning (v. 10) is answered by Jesus (vv. 11-12) with its climax in his pronouncement of the principle for the sabbath (v. 12b). The Pharisees' original intention to accuse Jesus (v. 10) is carried out in v. 14, though probably in a rather different way than they initially anticipated. Whereas Jesus enters into their synagogue (v. 9), the Pharisees go out of the synagogue. The fact that after the healing miracle no comment is made of the positive response to it by either Pharisees or the crowds may further prove our suggestion that the climax of the pericope is reached in Jesus' pronouncement in v. 12b and the focus is not the miracle itself but Jesus' teaching of the principle for the sabbath in the age of the messiah who is the Lord of the sabbath.

From the investigation so far one may draw out some outstanding features of this pericope. First, the Pharisees' opposition and unmerciful character is most apparent in the pericope (and more than in other synoptic pericopes): (i) the Pharisees' unspoken thought in Mark and Luke is converted into an explicit question (v. 10); (ii) the lack of αὐτόν in their question (v. 10) makes the question purely halakhic; their obsession with halakhic casuistry has made it impossible for them to pay any attention to the man in need; they have lost nearly every sense of mercy in spite of Jesus' teaching in v. 7 in the previous incident;[309] (iii) the underlying intention of their question is not a genuine enquiry into Jesus' halakhic stance but an antagonistic search for evidence to accuse him (v. 10—κατηγορήσωσιν αὐτοῦ); (iv) after Jesus' argument and

---

308. Gundry, *Mark*, p. 152.

309. Note, however, that in the Markan text the man in need is in view, though there also the Pharisees' concern is not focused on the man's welfare at all.

miracle they are taking counsel against him rather than being persuaded.

Secondly, the legal issue which dominates the pericope is ultimately focused on Jesus' authority over the Pharisaic halakhah and even over the law itself, so that the legal issue gives way to the Christology: (i) the presence of ἔξεστιν in the Pharisees' question not only highlights the tie between 12.1-8 (cf. vv. 2, 4) and 12.9-14, but also brings the question of the law into the foreground especially in relation to Jesus' stance to it; in that case, the term, though used on the opponents' lips, seems to indicate implicitly that the present pericope is to be understood Christologically like the previous one in terms of Jesus' relation to the law (particularly the sabbath law) as the fulfiller of it; (ii) though in Matthew Jesus uses the Pharisaic halakhah (v. 11), it does not mean that Jesus is bound to it but his concluding statement clearly shows that he is arguing not on the level of the halakhah but beyond it; (iii) Jesus' answer in v. 12b (ἔξεστιν τοῖς σάββασιν καλῶς ποιεῖν), though its structure is akin to that of the Pharisees' halakhic question, is based on his own authority as 'Lord of the sabbath' (v. 8). It is thus clear that the legal flavour of the pericope only serves to demonstrate Jesus' Christological stance and authority as the Lord of the sabbath who is fulfilling it. This fulfilment is not just in terms of revealing (or reinterpreting) the true meaning of the sabbath law, but also in terms of restoring God's original will for the sabbath (i.e. bringing mercy [not burden] upon his people through his teaching and healing) and more fundamentally and more comprehensively in terms of filling up or completing the ultimate goal of the sabbath (i.e. bringing the eschatological rest upon God's people through Jesus' redemptive work). The sabbath law in the Old Testament pointed forward to all of these, and they are now all fulfilled in Jesus' person (as the messiah, the merciful one, and the Lord of the sabbath), teachings (cf. 11.25–12.21 as a whole, and particularly, 11.28-30; 12.3-8, 11-12) and actions (12.13; cf. 12.15).

Thirdly, though the healing miracle is not the focus of the pericope, it still witnesses to Jesus as the messiah who brings wholeness of life upon those who are under a bodily burden, and thus presents Jesus as the merciful as well as powerful one who exercises his messianic authority and power to relieve people from Satanic bondage (i.e. the withered hand here).

Lastly, the Pharisees' plan to kill Jesus also has Christological significance in the flow of Matthew's Gospel. Though the rejection of the messiah has already been an important theme in the Gospel (e.g.

Herod's attempt to kill Jesus in 2.1-18), the Pharisees' attempt to kill Jesus in the face of his authoritative teaching and miracle as the messiah seems to anticipate that it is the messiah's fate to be killed by his opponents just because of his messiahship, a fate which will be first explicitly explained in 16.21 and will be finally accomplished in chs. 26–27 (cf. also 22.15; 27.1).[310] In spite of such antagonistic opposition, Jesus carries on his messianic task (vv. 15-16) as a merciful one who 'will not break a bruised reed or quench a smouldering wick' (v. 20).

5. Jesus the Servant (12.15-21)

We have already observed in section 1 that the link between this pericope and the two preceding sabbath controversy pericopes (12.1-8, 9-14) is intimate. It seems then imperative to include this pericope in the exegetical study and examine it in the light of the conclusions which are drawn from the exegetical investigations of the preceding pericopes (12.1-8, 9-14, and also 11.25-30).[311]

a. 12.15-16—Jesus' Withdrawal and Further Healings

The structure of vv. 15-17 is similar to that of 8.16-17, where we also have a summary of Jesus' healing ministry (cf. πάντας...ἐθεράπευσεν) followed by a fulfilment formula quotation from Isaiah. Though most of the vocabulary of these verses is found in Mk 3.7-12, the brevity of Matthew's report of Jesus' ministry in these two verses is striking as compared with that of the Markan version (3.7-12).[312] In Matthew these verses function as an introduction of the formula quotation into the broader co-text, rather than as a self-sufficient narrative like that in Mark (3.7-12). The intimate connection between these verses and the previous

310. Cf. Luz, *Matthäus (8–17)*, p. 240; Hare, *Matthew*, p. 133.

311. I will not attempt to present a comprehensive study of this pericope. My investigation will cover only the limited number of exegetical issues raised from this pericope which are more relevant for the purpose of this study. Moreover, my investigation will concentrate on the link between the present pericope and the preceding pericopes rather than the following ones, though the latter will be in view whenever it is deemed appropriate; this, of course, by no means implies that the latter are less important than the former for a proper understanding of the present pericope.

312. Cf. also Lk. 6.17-19—this Lukan pericope, however, can hardly be considered as a real parallel to the present two verses in Matthew; note the Lukan pericope is immediately followed by the Sermon on the Plain (6.20-49), and therefore has a more natural parallel in Mt. 4.24-25 (+ chs. 5–7, i.e. the Sermon on the Mount).

pericope(s) (particularly v. 14) is made more evident by the introduction of the two words, γνούς[313] and ἐκεῖθεν, in v. 15, which are both peculiar to Matthew.[314]

Jesus' merciful and gentle character is further highlighted by his withdrawal (ὁ δὲ Ἰησοῦς...ἀνεχώρησεν ἐκεῖθεν) in the face of the Pharisees' unjustifiable project to destroy him (v. 14), without mounting 'an active resistance against them' or passing immediate judgment upon them (cf. v. 19),[315] though he ultimately brings justice to victory (v. 20).[316] His mercifulness and gentleness is thus so impressively contrasted with the Pharisees' aggressive opposition that no serious reader would miss the contrast.

In v. 15b we have another interesting contrast—whereas the Pharisees left Jesus, many crowds followed him (ἠκολούθησαν αὐτῷ [ὄχλοι] πολλοί). As commonly in Matthew, among the crowds were the sick, and Jesus ἐθεράπευσεν αὐτοὺς πάντας.[317] Jesus' healing ministry here, like the previous healing miracles of chs. 8–9 and of 12.13, may be once again a further witness to Jesus as the promised one, the servant messiah, who fulfils the Old Testament, and particularly the messianic Servant Song of Isa. 42.1-4 (cf. vv 18-21). Matthew's typical use of πάντας[318] here emphasizes the comprehensiveness of Jesus' ministry (cf. 11.28).

Jesus' command ἐπετίμησεν αὐτοῖς ἵνα μὴ φανερὸν αὐτὸν ποιήσωσιν may correspond to the Isaiah quotation (especially v. 19 = Isa. 42.2).

313. The construction, γνοὺς δὲ ὁ Ἰησοῦς/ὁ δὲ Ἰησοῦς γνούς, may be characteristically Matthean. Whereas Matthew uses this construction four times (12.15; 16.8; 22.18; 26.10), it is not found in either Mark or Luke; see Luz, *Matthew 1–7*, p. 56; Davies and Allison, *Matthew*, II, p. 322. This construction may well highlight Jesus' supernatural knowledge (cf. Davies and Allison, *Matthew*, II, p. 322), though here its major function seems to be as a bridge between v. 15 and v. 14.

314. γνούς has no counterpart in Mark (nor Luke). For ἐκεῖθεν Mark has πρὸς τὴν θάλασσαν which has no clear relation with the preceding pericope.

315. Harrington, *Matthew*, pp. 179-81. Cf. Stendahl, *School*, pp. 111-12.

316. Jesus' withdrawal then must not be understood as a passive escape from the threat of killing. Such behaviour would be strange immediately after the authoritative Christological pronouncements (cf. vv. 6-8, 12) and healing (v. 13). Furthermore, the Pharisees' plan to destroy Jesus, in fact, could not be an immediate threat to Jesus' life, as we have seen above. Cf. France, *Matthew*, p. 205.

317. A very close parallel to v. 15bc is found in 19.2 but without πάντας. Cf. also 8.16.

318. Cf. (4.23); 8.16; (9.35); πᾶς is never used with θεραπεύω in Mark and Luke. Mark here and elsewhere (1.34; 6.13) has πολύς instead; cf. also Lk. 7.21—ἐθεράπευσεν πολλούς.

The servant's demeanour in Isa. 42.2 corresponds closely to Jesus' character, 'particularly in regard to the messianic secret and the non-triumphalist character of Jesus'.[319] Jesus' demand for silence is thus seen as the 'fulfilment of the role of the Servant'.[320]

b. *12.17-21—Jesus the Servant*

The fulfilment formula and the Isaiah quotation of vv. 17-21 are peculiar to Matthew. Matthew's ten quotations followed by his special formula (ἵνα) πληρωθῇ τὸ ῥηθὲν (ὑπὸ κυρίου) διὰ (...) τοῦ προφήτου λέγοντος[321] (1.22-23; 2.15; 2.17-18; 2.23; 4.14-16; 8.17; 12.17-21; 13.35; 21.4-5; 27.9-10)[322] are, in fact, all without synoptic parallels. The formula itself is unique to Matthew,[323] and we may well suspect that Matthew himself designed it (or at least used it) 'to prepare the reader for a solemn declaration of how God's previously announced purpose has reached its due conclusion in Jesus'.[324] By quoting then the Servant Song (Isa. 42.1-4) in vv. 18-21 introduced by this fulfilment formula (v. 17), Matthew affirms the truth that in Jesus Isaiah's prophecy concerning the servant has reached its fulfilment.[325]

319. Hagner, *Matthew 1–13*, p. 337; cf. France, *Matthew*, p. 206 and his remark on the messianic secrecy in Matthew on p. 153: 'This motif of secrecy…is better understood as reflecting a real danger that Jesus could achieve unwanted popularity merely as a wonder-worker, or worse still as a nationalistic liberator, and so foster a serious misunderstanding of the true nature of his mission'. Strecker, *Gerechtigkeit*, p. 69, also points out the contact between v. 16 and v. 19. *Pace* Neyrey, 'Use', pp. 460-70.

320. France, *Matthew*, p. 206.

321. The formula varies slightly, but the basic structure is much the same.

322. Though its formula is different, 2.5-6 is also generally regarded as part of this group for other reasons; see France, *Evangelist*, p. 171; cf. Stendahl, *School*, pp. 97, 99-101.

323. For the detailed examination of the formula and its background, see G.M. Soares-Prabhu, *The Formula Quotations in the Infancy Narrative of Matthew* (AnBib, 63; Rome: Biblical Institute Press, 1976), pp. 46-63.

324. France, *Evangelist*, p. 172.

325. Kingsbury, *Structure*, p. 95. Matthew apparently understood the Song as a prophecy of the messiah. Cope, *Scribe*, p. 36, points out that 'The Targum translation of the opening verse (משיחא עבדי) "my servant, the Messiah…" attests to the use of the passage as a Messianic text in Judaism'. Cf. J. Jeremias, 'Παῖς Θεοῦ', *TDNT*, V, p. 681.

The text of Matthew's quotation differs from all known Greek versions, and it does not closely follow the Masoretic Text either.[326] Matthew probably translated the Hebrew text independently or with some influence from sources available to him (e.g. the Targums, the LXX)[327] but with a clear view to his own purpose in quoting the Song, that is, to demonstrate how Jesus' ministry fulfilled the servant's mission. K. Stendahl, therefore, asserts that 'the form of the text in Matthew is an *interpretation* of the prophecy in the light of what happened to Jesus'.[328]

Matthew, like the LXX, has παῖς rather than δοῦλος in v. 18a.[329] The fact that παῖς can mean either 'servant' or 'son' makes Matthew's choice of the term highly significant. If the words spoken by the heavenly voice at the baptism (3.17) and transfiguration (17.5) are, as many suppose, considered as a quotation from (or at least allusion to) Isa. 42.1,[330] the word παῖς effectively provides a link between this quotation and the other two quotations where υἱός is used, but without losing the basic meaning of 'servant'.[331] Matthew's ὁ ἀγαπητός μου for בחירי ('my elect') is once again explained by Matthew's concern for bringing this quotation into conformity with the other two quotations at baptism and transfiguration where both run ὁ υἱός μου ὁ ἀγαπητός. The first half of v. 18 then is nearly the same as the other two quotations: ἰδοὺ ὁ παῖς μου ὃν ᾑρέτισα, ὁ ἀγαπητός μου εἰς ὃν εὐδόκησεν ἡ ψυχή μου / οὗτός ἐστιν ὁ υἱός μου ὁ ἀγαπητός, ἐν ᾧ εὐδόκησα. By assimilating

326. Some thorough studies of the text are found in Stendahl, *School*, pp. 107-15; R.H. Gundry, *The Use of the Old Testament in St Matthew's Gospel with Specific Reference to the Messianic Hope* (NovTSup, 18; Leiden: Brill, 1967), pp. 110-16; J. Grindel, 'Matthew 12,18-21', *CBQ* 29 (1967), pp. 110-15; Cope, *Scribe*, pp. 32-52; Neyrey, 'Use', pp. 457-73.

327. Grindel, 'Matthew 12,18-21', p. 110; Gnilka, *Matthäusevangelium*, I, pp. 451-53; Davies and Allison, *Matthew*, II, p. 323. For a different view, however, see Strecker, *Gerechtigkeit*, pp. 67-70; B. Lindars, *New Testament Apologetic: The Doctrinal Significance of the Old Testament Quotations* (London: SCM Press, 1961), pp. 144-52.

328. *School*, p. 112; italics mine. Cf. also Cope, *Scribe*, p. 49: 'freely shaped to suit his own purposes in applying the servant text to Jesus'.

329. The Masoretic Text has עבדי. Note Aquila and Symmachus both have δοῦλος here instead, though Theodotion has παῖς like the LXX and Matthew.

330. See Stendahl, *School*, pp. 109-10; Gundry, *Use*, pp. 29-32; Grindel, 'Matthew 12,18-21', p. 110; *et al.*

331. Cf. Schweizer, *Matthew*, p. 282; Cope, 'Scribe', p. 45; *et al.*

this quotation to the two key Christological quotations, Matthew pitches the Christological note of this quotation as high as that of the other two. Furthermore, the next line which mentions the bestowal of the Spirit (θήσω τὸ πνεῦμά μου ἐπ' αὐτόν) reinforces the link between this quotation and that at the baptism (cf. 3.16). By linking these two quotations in this way Matthew seems to claim effectively, though implicitly, that the messiah's mission inaugurated at the baptism is now being fulfilled.[332]

It is highly important in ch. 12 to quote this Servant Song which authorizes Jesus as the servant messiah, God's Son and servant, whom God has chosen, with whom God is pleased, and upon whom God has put his Spirit. By repeating this key messianic quotation after Jesus' extraordinary claims in relation to the sabbath (vv. 3-8, 11-13; cf. also 11.28-30), Matthew solidly affirms that Jesus' authority is ordained by God and therefore that his claims are genuine, in spite of the Pharisees' hostile response (v. 14). The Pharisees fail to recognize Jesus as God's chosen servant simply because they lack the Spirit which God has put upon Jesus—a fact which will be more explicitly demonstrated by their attribution of Jesus' work by the Spirit to Beelzebul (v. 24). 'God's verdict about Jesus, then, serves as an important apologetic response to the hostility of the Pharisees.'[333] In this setting the statement εἰς ὃν εὐδόκησεν ἡ ψυχή μου is particularly significant, because the contrast between God's attitude to Jesus and that of the Pharisees is inescapable. Whereas the Pharisees are deeply displeased with Jesus and unjustly take counsel how to kill him (v. 14), God is well pleased with Jesus and commissions him to proclaim justice to the nations (v. 18d: κρίσιν τοῖς ἔθνεσιν ἀπαγγελεῖ) and to bring justice to victory (v. 20c: ἐκβάλῃ εἰς νῖκος τὴν κρίσιν).[334] 'Bringing justice to victory', as France points out, is more than 'mere legal vindication'.[335] It is rather, as Barth puts it, 'a matter of the complete establishing of' and carrying out of 'the will of God' which is the goal of Jesus' ministry.[336] Verses 18d and 20c then

332. Cf. France, *Matthew*, p. 206.

333. Neyrey, 'Use', p. 460; cf. Hummel, *Auseinandersetzung*, pp. 125-27.

334. The formation of v. 20c is not simple. Perhaps it may be 'a conflation' of Isa. 42.3c and 4b (Davies and Allison, *Matthew*, II, p. 326). Many suspect that Matthew's εἰς νῖκος comes from Hab. 1.4 (לנצח); see Stendahl, *School*, p. 113; Grindel, 'Matthew 12,18-21', p. 114; Gundry, *Use*, pp. 114-15; *et al.*

335. *Matthew*, p. 207.

336. 'Law', p. 141. It is not easy to decide whether 'justice' or 'judgment' is the proper rendering for κρίσις here. Gundry, *Matthew*, p. 229, may be right in asserting that 'Matthew's emphasis on discipling Gentiles requires that κρίσιν be taken

may well witness that Jesus' proclamation of his Lordship of the sabbath (v. 8) and of other truths regarding it (vv. 3-7, 11-12) together with his healing(s) on the sabbath (v. 13; cf. also v. 15) are part and parcel of the fulfilment of the will of God, particularly his will for the sabbath.

A remaining question in relation to v. 18d is whether the ἔθνη here (cf. also v. 21) embraces Jews as well as Gentiles or exclusively refers to Gentiles. Inasmuch as many crowds are following Jesus (v. 15) and some of them are confessing Jesus as 'Son of David' (v. 23) and since the disciples themselves are also Jews, it seems improbable to argue that ἔθνη here refers only to Gentiles. Nevertheless, the repeated appearance of ἔθνη in the present quotation[337] provides a definite scriptural ground for rejecting unrepentant Jews and particularly the Pharisees (cf. 11.20-24, 25-27; 12.30-37, 39-42) and offering their privilege also to Gentiles[338] because of the Jews' failure to respond to Jesus' message and his messianic miracles (cf. 12.2, 10, 14, 24; cf. also 11.16-27; 12.25-50).[339] The two sabbath controversies (12.1-14) then, along with Jesus' verdict on this generation and his woes to unrepentant cities (11.1-24), seem to provide a concrete occasion for Matthew to introduce this pivotal quotation which declares Jesus' attitude to Jews (particularly the Pharisees) and Gentiles. This attitude will be revealed more expressly as the Gospel continues (cf. 12.30-50; 15.1-12, 21-28; 21.28-22.11; ch. 23; 24.14; 26.13; 28.18-19; etc.).

As I indicated above, v. 19 may be best understood in relation to vv. 15-16. Even though Jesus is involved in the controversies with the Pharisees (vv. 1-14), his intention is not to court popularity but to make a necessary Christological proclamation which fulfils the role of the messianic servant (cf. vv. 18d, 20c).[340] His withdrawal, however, in the

positively as "justice"...instead of negatively as "judgment"'; see also W. Grundmann, *Das Evangelium nach Matthäus* (THNT, 1; Berlin: Evangelische Verlagsanstalt, 1968), p. 326; Schweizer, *Matthew*, p. 282; Hagner, *Matthew 1–13*, p. 338. For a different view, however, see Luz, *Matthäus (8–17)*, pp. 247-49.

337. Note Isa. 42.3c-4a (or 4ab) is omitted in Matthew's quotation for some reason. Matthew could also have omitted ἔθνη if it did not fit into his purpose.

338. There have already been in Matthew indications for offering the privilege to Gentiles; cf. four presumably non-Israelite women in Jesus' genealogy (1.3-6); wise men from the East (2.1-12); Jesus' flight into Egypt (2.13-15); Jesus' response to a Gentile centurion (8.5-13); etc.

339. Cf. Neyrey, 'Use', p. 466: 'the mention of ἔθνη is controversial in tone and so belongs to the polemic against the Jews in ch. 12'.

340. *Pace*, therefore, Neyrey, 'Use', pp. 468-69.

face of the Pharisees' unjustifiable pursuit of him to destroy him (v. 15) may be another aspect of fulfilling his role as the messianic servant who does not wrangle or cry aloud and whose voice no one will hear in the street (v. 19: οὐκ ἐρίσει οὐδὲ κραυγάσει οὐδὲ ἀκούσει τις ἐν ταῖς πλατείαις τὴν φωνὴν αὐτοῦ; cf. also 11.29: πραΰς εἰμι).[341] This character of the servant's ministry is further demonstrated by Jesus' command not to make him known in v. 16 (cf. 11.29: ταπεινὸς τῇ καρδίᾳ). In spite of his deep concern about this 'messianic secrecy', however, he does not withhold his authority and power to care for the needy who are under unbearable burdens, as revealed in his invitation in 11.28-30 and his teaching and healing ministry in vv. 1-15. This merciful ministry is, in fact, still another aspect of fulfilling the role of the messiah who does not break a bruised reed or quench a smouldering wick (v. 20: κάλαμον συντετριμμένον οὐ κατεάξει καὶ λίνον τυφόμενον οὐ σβέσει).[342] The messiah's merciful character which is thus fulfilled in Jesus (cf. 11.27, 28-30; 12.3-8 [especially v. 7], 11-13, 15) is once again in sharp contrast with the Pharisees' unmerciful character as revealed in vv. 2, 7, 10, 14 (cf. also 11.28).

In short, the introductory pericope (vv. 15-16) and the formula quotation (vv. 17-21) as a whole effectively confirm the Christological nature of the two preceding sabbath controversy pericopes by revealing their fulfilling aspects even more clearly. Matthew appears to handle his material very carefully in order to achieve such an effect.

First, the striking brevity of Matthew's report of Jesus' ministry in vv. 15-16 compared with that of the Markan version (3.7-12) effectively enables this report to function as a bridge between the preceding pericopes and the following quotation. In spite of its brevity, however, this report, in effect, has another efficient function, that is, balancing the character of the messiah in relation to the messianic secrecy (ἐπετίμησεν

---

341. Cf. Stendahl, *School*, pp. 111-12; Barth, 'Law', p. 127; France, *Evangelist*, p. 301. Matthew's ἐν ταῖς πλατείαις for בחוץ (Targum, בברא) is once again unique to Matthew. The natural translation may be ἔξω as in the LXX. As Stendahl, *School*, p. 113, suggests, however, Matthew may well split up 'the adverbial expression into its component parts and obtains something more concrete which fitted into the context where the reluctant attitude of Jesus to publicity is stressed'. Stendahl continues to suggest that 'This preference for the concrete is further shown by the active construction "nobody will hear his voice" for the MT's "he will not let his voice be heard" and the LXX's "his voice will not be heard"'.

342. Cf. Barth, 'Law', p. 128.

αὐτοῖς ἵνα μὴ φανερὸν αὐτὸν ποιήσωσιν; cf. v. 19) which the previous pericopes do not reveal.

Secondly, Matthew's characteristic quotation formula followed by one of the Servant Songs of Isaiah emphatically affirms the fact that in Jesus the Old Testament prophecy concerning the servant has reached its fulfilment.

Thirdly, Matthew's quotation of Isa. 42.1-4 introduced by the fulfilment formula endorses the fact that Jesus' proclamations regarding the sabbath and his healing on the sabbath are essential aspects of the fulfilment of the servant's mission as revealed in the Servant Song, and Matthew's unique rendering of the Song increases the effectiveness of the quotation in showing how Jesus' ministry fulfilled the mission of the servant messiah. His choice or replacement of words in v. 18 (e.g. παῖς, ἀγαπητός) brings this quotation into conformity with the other two quotations at the baptism and transfiguration. By thus assimilating this quotation to the two key Christological quotations, Matthew pitches the Christological note of this quotation as high as that of the other two. With this highly Christological quotation, Matthew effectively affirms the fact that Jesus' proclamations and healing(s) on the sabbath in the previous pericopes are authorized by God himself. Jesus' ministry on that sabbath is nothing else but part and parcel of the fulfilment of God's will for the sabbath (cf. vv. 18d, 20c).

Additionally, the contrast between Jesus' merciful (vv. 7, 20; cf. 11.29) and gentle (vv. 15, 19-20; cf. 11.29) character with God-given authority (v. 18; cf. vv. 6, 8, 12-13; 11.25-30) and the Pharisees' unmerciful (vv. 7, 10; cf. 11.28) and aggressive (v. 14) character but without God-given authority is outstanding throughout the pericopes that I have investigated so far. The reason why they fail to recognize Jesus as the messiah is simply because they lack the Spirit which God has put upon Jesus (v. 18), as their attribution of Jesus' work by the Holy Spirit to Beelzebul witnesses (v. 24; cf. 11.25-27). Since Jesus' messianic work is rejected by unresponsive Jews (cf. 11.20-24, 25-27) and particularly by the Pharisees (cf. vv. 1-14), Jesus' invitation is now open even to Gentiles who are ready to recognize his messianic work as the fulfilment of God's will (vv. 18d, 21; cf. 11.28). Thus vv. 18d and 21 show another aspect of the fulfilment of the Servant Song, and the two sabbath controversy incidents provide a concrete occasion for Matthew to include such critical verses in his quotation.

6. Conclusion: Significance and Implication of the Two Sabbath Controversy Pericopes

I am now in a position to draw together the exegetical investigations in the previous sections and summarize the various conclusions reached so far, with some further consideration of the significance and implications of those conclusions.

a. *Co-texts*

The co-text study shows that (1) the two sabbath pericopes (Mt. 12.1-8, 9-14) are interrelated very closely; (2) chs. 11–12 constitute a narrative block with certain recurrent themes (i.e. the unbelief, opposition, and rejection of Israel, on the one hand, and the invitation of Jesus, on the other) and with a crucial issue running through them (i.e. Christology); (3) 11.25-30 (especially vv. 28-30) is intimately linked to the two sabbath pericopes, and it is imperative to understand it in the light of its relation to the preceding pericope; (4) 12.15-16 functions as an introduction of the formula quotation into the broader co-text, and 12.17-21, therefore, is to be understood in the light not just of 12.15-16 but rather of the more extended pericopes which precede it (and, of course, also of the pericopes which follow); (5) chs. 11–12 (and 11.25–12.21 in particular) play a significant role in the plot of Matthew by showing important aspects of the messianic fulfilment (especially, the fulfilment of the sabbath) and also by presenting a fatally negative response by the Pharisees to Jesus' messianic ministry, which results in the decision to kill Jesus.

b. *The Flow of Argument*

The preceding pericope (11.25-30) as a whole prepares the way for the following sabbath controversy pericopes very effectively. Verse 25 explains, in anticipation, the fundamental reason for the Pharisees' lack of true understanding of the sabbath; it is because the Father has hidden it from them. Alongside this vv. 25 and 27 contrast Jesus, to whom πάντα have been delivered and who now has the authority to reveal it to those whom he chooses, with the Pharisees, from whom ταῦτα are hidden. Furthermore in vv. 28-30 Jesus' yoke and burden which are easy and light are contrasted with those of the Pharisees which are heavy. Jesus' gentle and lowly character seems also anticipate the contrast with the Pharisees' unmerciful and judgmental character (cf. 12.2, 7, 10, 14). Jesus' Christological proclamations in 12.6, 8 follow appropriately from his statement of the Father–Son relationship in v. 27. The discussion of the fulfilment of the sabbath by Jesus is anticipated by the introduction of the notion of rest (v. 29—ἀνάπαυσις) in a Christological and eschatological setting.

The issue in the first sabbath controversy pericope (12.1-8) seems at first sight to be the question of the interpretation of the sabbath law. But as we move through the pericope, we can see that what is asserted is not simply that Jesus' interpretation of the law is better than that of the Pharisees, but that someone dramatically significant is present who is greater than David and the temple and that he is none other than the Lord of the sabbath. By piling up Jesus' first three responses to the Pharisees' accusation, which are all grounded in different ways upon the Old Testament, Matthew has already produced an extremely powerful argument. For Matthew, however, all these answers, in some sense, function as a preparation for the final response, the climax of the story, which pronounces the ultimate authority of Jesus over the sabbath. Jesus' authority which has already been the focus of the previous responses now finds its culminating expression in the final response. This culminating pronouncement, however, functions not only as the response to the Pharisees' accusation (v. 2) but also adds another important dimension by injecting a high Christological note into the flow of the Gospel story as a whole. This climactic pronouncement then also extends its effect naturally into the next sabbath controversy pericope.

The second controversy pericope (12.9-14) does not stand alone but is closely linked with the first one. According to Matthew the two incidents happened on the same sabbath, and Jesus' opponents are most probably the same Pharisees as those in the previous incident. If these two pericopes are so closely tied, the Pharisees' reaction in v. 14 may be seen as the reaction not only to Jesus' argument and healing in vv. 11-13 but also to Jesus argument in vv. 3-8. Nevertheless the present pericope has a coherent structure of its own. The question raised by the Pharisees in the beginning (v. 10) is answered by Jesus (vv. 11-12) culminating in his pronouncement of the principle for the sabbath (v. 12b). The Pharisees' original intention to accuse Jesus (v. 10) is carried on in v. 14. Whereas Jesus enters into their synagogue (v. 9), the Pharisees go out of the synagogue (v. 14). These are some outstanding features of this pericope: (1) the Pharisees' opposition and unmerciful character is most apparent; (2) the legal issue which dominates the pericope is ultimately focused on Jesus' authority over the Pharisaic halakhah and even over the law itself, so that the legal issue gives way to the Christology; (3) though the healing miracle is not the focus of the pericope, it still witnesses to Jesus as the messiah who brings wholeness of life upon those who are under a bodily burden; (4) the Pharisees' plan to kill Jesus has Christological significance in the flow of the whole Gospel—the Pharisees' attempt to kill Jesus in the face of his messianic ministry seems to anticipate the fact that it is the messiah's fate to be killed by his opponents simply because of his messiahship (cf. 16.21; chs. 26–27).

The formula quotation with its introductory pericope (12.15-21) effectively confirms the Christological nature of the two preceding sabbath controversy pericopes by revealing their fulfilling aspects even more clearly: (1) the striking brevity of Matthew's report of Jesus' ministry in vv. 15-16 (cf. Mk 3.7-12) effectively enables this report to function as a bridge between the preceding pericopes and the following quotation; (2) the quotation formula followed by one of the Servant Songs affirms the fact that in Jesus the Old Testament prophecy concerning the servant has reached its fulfilment; (3) Matthew's quotation of Isa. 42.1-4 introduced by the fulfilment formula endorses the claim that Jesus' proclamations regarding the sabbath and his healing on the sabbath are essential aspects of the fulfilment of the servant's mission as revealed in the Song, and Matthew's unique rendering of the Song increases the effectiveness of the quotation in showing how Jesus' ministry fulfilled the servant's mission. Additionally, vv. 18d and 21 show another aspect of the fulfilment of the Servant Song, in that the failure of the Pharisees to respond to Jesus' messianic ministry corresponds to the opening of Jesus' invitation even to Gentiles who are ready to recognize his messianic work as the fulfilment of God's will.

c. *The Theological Significance of Jesus' Fulfilment of the Sabbath*
We may now consider the theological significance of the conclusions in this chapter in the light of the investigations in the previous chapters. First of all, Jesus is shown in 11.25–12.21 as the fulfiller of God's original intention and ultimate goal for the sabbath. This intention and this goal were revealed well in the Old Testament as we observed in Chapter 1. My study there shows that the sabbath institution is a reflection of the blessing of the seventh day which has its ultimate purpose in the eternal rest for the people of God; this rest is implied in God's rest after his creation which has no end (cf. Gen. 2.2-3; Exod. 20.8-11) and is also exemplified in his redemptive deliverance of Israel from Egypt

(cf. Deut. 5.12-15; cf. also Heb. 4.1-11). The sabbath law thus was not originally given as a burden but as an expression of God's covenantal blessing. The fundamental importance of the recognition of the covenantal relationship in keeping the sabbath is effectively indicated by the creation and Exodus motive clauses in the sabbath commandments (Exod. 20.11; Deut. 5.15; cf. Exod. 31.17). But the original intention and goal were frequently forgotten or seriously distorted in Israel (in the Old Testament period as well as in the time of Jesus) as we observed in Chapters 1 and 2. In some Old Testament passages we can already note legalistic observance of the sabbath without recognition or appreciation of the covenantal character of the institution; such observance is rejected by YHWH (Isa. 1.13; Hos. 2.11; Amos 8.5). By the time of Jesus' ministry the recognition of and emphasis on the covenantal significance of the sabbath seems to have been strikingly weakened as the Qumran Scrolls, Philo and rabbinic literature witness. Instead, through the centuries up to 100 CE, the rather general rules in the Old Testament regarding works prohibited on the sabbath had been developed in the direction of an increasingly more specific and meticulous casuistry. Though some of the sabbath regulations had moved towards leniency in the course of this period, the growing number of more specific and meticulous regulations must inevitably have made the sabbath law more inconvenient and burdensome and directed the concern of the people away from *why* they should keep it to *how* they should keep it. The sabbath which was originally instituted as an expression of God's covenantal blessing now became a burdensome institution (cf. 11.28). In such a situation Jesus came to recover the original intention and fulfil the ultimate goal for the sabbath. He invites people to take his yoke (= his new teaching and the relationship with him) which gives them the eschatological rest, that is, redemption. His teaching on the original intention for the sabbath (12.7), his proclamation of his Lordship over the sabbath (12.8), his pronouncement of the general principle of the sabbath (12.12) and his healing on the sabbath (12.13) all emphatically witness that he is the recoverer and fulfiller of God's original and ultimate will for the sabbath.

Secondly, the fulfilment theology of the two sabbath pericopes and also of their surrounding pericopes is perfectly in line with that of 5.17-20 and other law-related passages that were investigated in Chapter 3. As I pointed out in section 3, Jesus' fulfilment of the sabbath as revealed in 11.25–12.21 is another good example which shows what Jesus' saying of 5.17 signifies. Jesus, the Son of man, has come not to abolish the sabbath as some (e.g. the Pharisees in his time; the antinomians in Matthew's community) may have suspected or thought, but to fulfil it. Jesus' fulfilment of the sabbath, like other laws, has the elements of both 'continuity' in the sense that Jesus' redemption fulfils the sabbath ultimately and 'discontinuity' in the sense that the sabbath is no longer the same after Jesus' fulfilment of it but is rather transcended by the fulfilment. Since the disciples are now participating in the eschatological rest (= redemption), the ultimate goal for the sabbath, which is now fulfilled and provided by Jesus, they are no longer obliged to keep the Old Testament sabbath law in the same way as the people in the Old Testament period did. This is indeed strongly implied in 12.5-6. If the priests are not obliged to keep the sabbath as far as they are in the temple, the disciples are still less obliged to keep the sabbath because they are with Jesus who is greater than the temple (cf. also 12.7, 12b). Such an implication can be even further stretched in Matthew. If the temple, which is greater than the sabbath (12.6), ceases to function in its role as type after Jesus' fulfilment of it (ch. 24; cf. also 27.51), the sabbath can even more easily cease to function in its role as sign/type after Jesus' fulfilment of it (cf. 12.8; 11.28-29). It is, of course, still not spelled out explicitly how Jesus' transcendence of the sabbath should affect the way the disciples keep the sabbath. But the transcendence does provide the crucial key with which the early church (especially the Apostolic Fathers) could later determine the issue, as we will see in Chapter 7.

Thirdly, since Jesus' fulfilment of the sabbath as revealed in 11.25–12.21 has an eschatological character, it naturally involves the eschatological tension—that is, the sabbath is *already* fulfilled by Jesus' ministry but it is *still* looking forward to its consummation when Jesus' redemption is completed at the close of the age (cf. 28.20).[343] Jesus is already the Lord of the sabbath (12.8); he is already providing the eschatological rest/redemption (11.28-30; 12.13); and he also expounds the true meaning of the sabbath as fulfilled already (11.28-30; 12.3-7, 11-12). Nevertheless, the eschatological rest Jesus provides has also a futuristic element (cf. 11.29: εὑρήσετε ἀνάπαυσιν); Jesus' Lordship over the sabbath is not yet recognized by many Jews as well as by most Gentiles; and more importantly Jesus' proclamation of justice to the Gentiles is not yet completed (12.18, 20-21; cf. also 28.19-20).

In short, the question of the sabbath in Matthew, like the question of

---

343. See the discussion of the 'already' but 'not yet' dimension in Jesus' fulfilment of the law in Chapter 3. Cf. Heb. 4.11.

the law in general, is a question of fulfilment, eschatology, and high Christology—that is, a question of salvation-history.[344]

d. *The Practical Implication of Jesus' Fulfilment of the Sabbath*
What implication then would this theological significance have for the contemporaries of Jesus and more importantly for Matthew's community? First, for the contemporaries of Jesus, not only his proclamation of his Lordship over the sabbath (12.8) but his teaching on the true meaning of the sabbath (12.3-7, 11-12) and his healing ministry on the sabbath (12.13) must have appeared so radical that they must surely have suspected that something unprecedented was happening and someone extraordinary was present. Having said this, however, they may not have grasped the full meaning and impact of Jesus' fulfilment of the sabbath, because they lived in a period when much of Jesus' redemptive work was not yet accomplished—for example, his trial, death, resurrection and second coming. Would this explain why the women visited the tomb, where Jesus was buried, on the first day of the week (28.1), probably in order to keep the sabbath according to the commandment (cf. Lk. 23.56)? Such an attitude is, of course, not necessarily an inappropriate one, yet it may possibly betray that they were still bound to the sabbath law without proper understanding of the full implication that Jesus had fulfilled the sabbath and become the Lord of the sabbath. If this was their attitude, we may suppose that, even if they could grasp the theological meaning of Jesus' fulfilment of the sabbath, it may have taken time for them to draw from the theological meaning its implication for their practice in relation to the sabbath.

Secondly, Matthew's community may certainly have had some different level of understanding from that of Jesus' contemporaries. Through their struggle against unbelieving Jews, Jesus' relation to the Old Testament law (including the sabbath law) and also their relation to it must have been a live issue. In the course of the conflict, some may have compromised themselves and adopted the legalistic tendency and others may have reacted too extremely and chosen to be antinomian. In such a situation Matthew has presented a foundational principle in 5.17-20, which pronounces Jesus' fulfilment of the Old Testament (vv. 17-18) and explains its implication for his disciples' relation to the law, especially against the two dangers, that is, legalism (v. 20) and antinomianism (v. 19). He has also presented some concrete examples of applying the

344. Cf. Meier, *Law*, pp. 88-89.

principle for particular commandments (e.g. 5.21-48). In 11.25–12.21, Matthew now aims to apply the principle for the sabbath commandment, one of the crucial issues of his time. What implication does Jesus' fulfilment of the sabbath have for his community? As I have concluded above, Matthew presents Jesus' fulfilment of the sabbath, as of other laws, as having the elements of both 'continuity' and 'discontinuity'. What is the implication of this double continuity–discontinuity character for his community?

In Matthew there is, of course, no indication of whether the sabbath was still observed or not among the groups[345] of the Matthean community.[346] Perhaps some groups may still have kept the sabbath while others did not. If there were some groups who still observed the sabbath legalistically, Matthew's message for them must have been clear and strong: Turn your attention to the significance of Jesus' fulfilment of the sabbath, because the day as it stands does not have the same significance as it had before it was fulfilled (cf. 12.3-8, 12; 5.17). For other groups who may have disregarded or even hated the observance of the sabbath, however, Matthew may at most have reminded them that the sabbath commandment itself is not such a bad thing as they supposed, provided that their focus is on Jesus who has fulfilled it (cf. 5.19). If this was the case, Matthew's understanding of the fulfilment of the sabbath is once again in line with 5.17-20 where Jesus' warning against legalism (5.20) is much graver than that against antinomianism (5.19). For Matthew, the sabbath is perpetual only until its fulfilment, like the temple (cf. ch. 24; cf. also 12.6[347]) and accordingly the priesthood and offerings.[348] After the fulfilment of the sabbath, the function of the sabbath as the sign/type is no longer required, because Jesus' redemption, the antitype of the sabbath, makes the type unnecessary. Matthew may then have good reason

345. I have proposed, following Stanton, that the community was composed of a number of local house groups in and around a city; these groups probably showed some distinctive tendencies of their own as well as the commonalty.

346. 24.20 is by no means a positive indicator for the community's sabbath observance, as we will see in Chapter 5.

347. If the temple is perpetual only until fulfilment, the sabbath, which according to Matthew is less important than the temple, could well be more so regarded.

348. Cf. Lincoln, 'Perspective', pp. 352-53—he properly points out that all those institutions and also the Noahic, Abrahamic, and Davidic covenants which are all described as perpetual just as the sabbath (cf. Exod. 27.21; 28.43; 29.28; 30.21; 40.15; Lev. 6.18, 22; 7.34, 36; 24.8; Num. 18.19; Gen. 9.16; 17.7, 13; 2 Sam. 7.13, 16; 23.5) are perpetual only until their fulfilment.

to encourage his community to give up sabbath observance and instead to focus on Jesus who is the Lord of the sabbath and on his redemption which is the ultimate goal of the sabbath. Such encouragement may have been necessary especially in the face of the danger of legalism within the community as well as the threat of casuistic Pharisaism outside it, both of which endangered the true meaning and significance of Jesus' fulfilment of the sabbath.

While this conclusion may seem to have gone well beyond what is clearly implied in Mt. 11.25–12.21, we will see later (in Chapter 7) that the Apostolic Fathers did in fact interpret Matthew's understanding of the sabbath in its relation to Jesus in just this way, if not indeed more radically, as we may see in their opposing of the Lord's day to the sabbath.

Chapter 5

JESUS AND THE SABBATH IN MATTHEW'S GOSPEL: TEXTS, CO-TEXTS AND CONTEXTS (II)

The last text (24.20) we are to investigate is very short, but it is necessary to investigate various questions raised in the text carefully in order to interpret it properly. Before I investigate those questions, it would be helpful to summarize the various ways of interpreting the verse offered so far. Since Stanton already provides an excellent survey of six different ways,[1] I will simply adopt his summary, but with the addition of his own view and of E.K.-C. Wong's criticism of his view.[2] I will also add Banks's view which Stanton leaves out.

1. *Various Views on Matthew 24.20*

1) E. Klostermann[3] and others maintain that Mt. 24.20 witnesses that Matthew's community kept the sabbath strictly.[4] Klostermann rejects the view of B. Weiss[5] and A. Loisy[6] that Matthew preserved the original form of the tradition here whereas Mark abbreviated it. He rather claims

---

1. '"Pray that your Flight may not be in Winter or on a Sabbath": Matthew 24.20', in *idem, People*, pp. 193-98. This article was originally published in *JSNT* 37 (1989), pp. 17-30.

2. 'The Matthean Understanding of the Sabbath: A Response to G.N. Stanton', *JSNT* 44 (1991), pp. 3-18.

3. *Matthäusevangelium*, p. 194.

4. Cf. Allen, *Matthew*, p. 256; C.G. Montefiore, *The Synoptic Gospels*, II (2 vols.; London: Macmillan, 2nd edn, 1927), p. 312; Hummel, *Auseinandersetzung*, p. 41; D. Patte, *The Gospel according to Matthew: A Structural Commentary on Matthew's Faith* (Philadelphia: Fortress Press, 1987), p. 35; *et al.*

5. *Das Matthäus-Evangelium* (Göttingen: Vandenhoeck & Ruprecht, 9th edn, 1898), pp. 402-403, 410, 413.

6. *Les Evangiles Synoptiques*, II (Ceffonds: Prés Montier-en-der, 1908), pp. 422-23.

that Mt. 24.20 is one of the Judaizing passages in Matthew: 'Christians keep the Sabbath strictly, just as they also still sacrifice (5.23) and pay the Temple tax (17.27)'.[7] As we shall see, however, it is difficult to defend this view, particularly in the light of 12.1-14.

2) A. Schlatter, who claims that Matthew was the first Gospel to be written, believes that Mt. 24.20 reflects the fears of Palestinian followers of Jesus who announced 'complete separation from the temple' and departed 'from Jewish piety' and who did not keep the sabbath. For them, 'Flight on the sabbath was especially dangerous, because every fugitive would be recognized at once'.[8] E. Hirsch similarly claims that this verse implies dangers from the hate-charged Jewish authorities: 'a Christian congregation fleeing on the sabbath would have been as recognizable in Palestine as a spotted dog'.[9] This view is perceptive, yet it is not free of problems, to which we shall return later.

3) G. Strecker, who insists that 'the Jewish elements of the Gospel are the result of the community-tradition and need not be characteristic of the redactor', claims that the extra phrase μηδὲ σαββάτῳ in Mt. 24.20 may reflect the original form of the Jewish apocalyptic tradition.[10] Rordorf similarly suggests that 'the addition μηδὲ σαββάτῳ in Mt. 24.20 (or even the whole verse?) derives from a late Jewish...milieu', that is, 'from late Jewish apocalyptic or from nationalist and zealot circles'.[11] It seems, however, arbitrary to set aside those redactional changes as community tradition simply because they do not conform to the interpreter's particular understanding of Matthew's distinctive viewpoint. It is hardly convincing to suppose that such a careful writer as Matthew carelessly added the material which did not fit into his viewpoint.

4) G. Barth, who rightly points out that Mt. 24.20 by no means implies that 'on the whole Sabbath question he [Matthew] adopted a stricter view than that known by the rest of Judaism', claims that Matthew adds the phrase μηδὲ σαββάτῳ in Mt. 24.20 so that his community may not give offence against current Judaism.[12] In other words, as Stanton puts it, 'Matthew's community was prepared to keep the Sabbath more

---

7. Quoting Stanton's English translation in his 'Pray', p. 193.
8. Schlatter, *Matthäus*, p. 706 (translation mine).
9. *Die Frühgeschichte des Evangeliums*, II (Tübingen: Mohr, 1941), p. 313 (translation from Barth, 'Law', p. 92).
10. *Gerechtigkeit*, p. 18, esp. n. 3 (translation mine); see Stanton, 'Pray', p. 194.
11. *Sunday*, pp. 68, 120.
12. 'Law', p. 92.

strictly than was necessary according to his own convictions for the sake of good relationships with the Jewish authorities'.[13] Barth's claim, however, contradicts his own prior conclusion that 'an escape on the Sabbath not only occurred frequently in the Jewish wars, but it was no longer regarded as scandalous'.[14] If, as Barth properly concludes, by the time of Matthew flight on the sabbath was generally accepted even by Jews whenever they were seriously threatened by enemies, there is no reason why Matthew's community would give offence to their contemporary Jews by fleeing on the sabbath. Stanton's verdict is, therefore, quite right: 'So the Matthean addition can hardly reflect a desire to maintain reasonable relationships with Jewish leaders'.[15]

5) E. Lohse claims that 'Mt. 24:20 offers an example of the keeping of the Sabbath' by Jewish Christian congregations which still remained within Judaism.[16] Since he notes, however, that flight on the sabbath was generally regarded as legitimate by contemporary Judaism when there was danger to life, he needs to provide further explanation of the additional phrase μηδὲ σαββάτῳ in Mt. 24.20. So he suggests: 'if desecration of the Sabbath was required in face of the terrors of the last time, this could only mean an escalation of the catastrophe'.[17] Though his suggestion is attractive at first sight, Lohse unfortunately can offer no evidence from contemporary Jewish literature to confirm that such a view was current in Matthew's time. Furthermore, as Stanton points out and as we will see shortly, the co-text in ch. 24 does not support the view that the flight which Matthew describes will be caused by the terrors of the end-time.[18]

6) R. Walker proposes that the additional phrase μηδὲ σαββάτῳ in Mt. 24.20 'is already an anachronism for Matthew (like today's "Gentile church") and therefore is irrelevant in the text as it stands'.[19] If we

---

13. 'Pray', p. 196.

14. 'Law', pp. 91-92; cf. Strack and Billerbeck, *Kommentar*, I, pp. 952-53. See also above, the discussion of 'war on the sabbath' in Chapter 2.

15. 'Pray', p. 196.

16. 'σάββατον', p. 29.

17. 'σάββατον', pp. 29-30. Cf. also Harrington, *Matthew*, pp. 337, 339, 341— according to him the addition indicates that for Matthew 'Sabbath observance remained important, and he feared the *crisis of conscience* that might develop for pious Jews forced to travel on the Sabbath' (p. 341—italics mine).

18. Stanton, 'Pray', pp. 196-97.

19. *Die Heilsgeschichte im ersten Evangelium* (FRLANT, 91; Göttingen: Vandenhoeck & Ruprecht, 1967), p. 86 (translation mine); similarly, J. Lambrecht,

assume that Matthew merely preserved the original form of the tradition here, such a statement may be possible, though the explanation of the phrase still remains open. If we assume, however, that Matthew added the phrase in order to point out to his readers that earlier disciples of Jesus did once keep the sabbath very strictly, such an explanation sounds unlikely. If the sabbath is no longer a live issue in his community and in its surroundings, there seems to be no clear reason for Matthew to insert the phrase here. Furthermore, as Stanton points out, if Matthew is adding an anachronistic historicizing phrase, then he is sharply differentiating earlier disciples of Jesus (who kept the sabbath strictly) from Christians in his own day (who presumably have abandoned it). But in Matthew's Gospel 'the evangelist uses the disciples as models for Christians in his own day'.[20]

7) Stanton, who presupposes a non-Palestinian setting for Matthew and believes that Matthew's community is *extra muros* yet still defining itself over against Judaism,[21] first of all suggests that with the additional phrase ἡ φυγὴ ὑμῶν, 'disciples, who include readers or listeners in the evangelist's day, are addressed directly', and concludes that the persecution causing the flight came from Jewish religious leaders.[22] He also concludes that 'in the light of Matt 12.1-14 it is impossible to accept that it kept the Sabbath strictly and was therefore reluctant to flee on a Sabbath'.[23] On the ground of these preliminary suggestions and conclusions, he explains the additional phrase μηδὲ σαββάτῳ thus: 'since they [disciples] do not keep the Sabbath strictly, they would not hesitate to escape on the Sabbath; however, they know that in so doing they would antagonize still further some of their persecutors',[24] and, therefore, 'it was to be avoided if at all possible'.[25] Hence Matthew added the phrase. Stanton's suggestion is thoroughly investigated and carefully argued, though not without some weaknesses, as Wong partly points out, and we will come back to some of his detailed arguments.

'The Parousia Discourse: Composition and Content in Mt. XXIV-XXV', in M. Dider (ed.), *L'Evangile selon Matthieu: Rédaction et théologie* (Gembloux: Duculot, 1972), p. 322. See Stanton, 'Pray', p. 197.

20. Stanton, 'Pray', p. 197; cf. also U. Luz, 'The Disciples in the Gospel according to Matthew', in Stanton (ed.), *Interpretation*, pp. 98-128.

21. See his 'Pray', pp. 198-203, 206; see also *idem*, 'Origin', pp. 1914-21.

22. 'Pray', p. 203.

23. 'Pray', p. 205.

24. 'Pray', p. 203.

25. 'Pray', p. 206.

8) After criticizing Stanton's view,[26] Wong suggests that Matthew's admonition to 'pray that your flight may not be...on a Sabbath' implies that 'at least some of the members of the Matthaean community (probably some of the conservative Jewish Christians who still behave according to their tradition) would hesitate to flee on a Sabbath, even though their lives were thus in increased danger'. He further suggests that by adding the phrase μηδὲ σαββάτῳ 'Matthew wants to keep the community intact by taking care of the "weak" ones (who might hesitate to flee even at the critical time)...and prays...that they will not be led into temptation' (cf. Mt. 6.13).[27] Though Wong's suggestion is interesting, it is still open to the same difficulty as Klostermann's view.

9) Banks suggests that 'the hindrances posed by the sabbath arise not so much from Jewish-Christian principles as from the sabbatarian scruples of the Jews, e.g. shutting of gates of the cities, difficulty in procuring provisions, etc.'[28] R.H. Gundry, who thinks that the flight on the sabbath is taken for granted in Mt. 24.20, similarly suggests that Matthew 'has in mind hindrances to flight because of rabbinic restrictions, suspension of services to travellers, and especially inability to purchase supplies'.[29] Meier also points out that the co-text of the phrase[30] 'speaks of external circumstances which will make flight difficult, not impossible'.[31] This line of explanation is the most probable, and I will come back to it shortly.

2. *'And Not on the Sabbath'—My Proposal*

Some of the explanations presented above (e.g. options 2, 4, 7-9) have some truth in them, though most of them have problems and weaknesses as I have briefly pointed out above. Could there be any fully satisfactory explanation of the additional phrase(s) in 24.20? I will

26. Wong's criticism in part I is disappointing, yet that in parts II and III provides fair observations and valuable suggestions, though still not without crucial weaknesses.

27. 'Sabbath', p. 15.

28. *Jesus*, p. 102. Not a few scholars, in fact, follow his explanation—Meier, *Matthew*, p. 284; Gundry, *Matthew*, p. 483; C.L. Blomberg, *Matthew* (NAC; Nashville: Broadman, 1992), p. 358.

29. *Matthew*, p. 483.

30. E.g. 'being pregnant, having to care for new-born infants, trying to flee amid the chilling rains and flooded roads of a Palestinian winter' (vv. 19-20).

31. *Matthew*, p. 284.

attempt to present one; in order to do this I first of all need to raise and investigate some issues which, in my view, are crucial in explaining the phrase μηδὲ σαββάτῳ more properly.

a. *The Source*

Many scholars assume that the phrase μηδὲ σαββάτῳ in Mt. 24.20 came from Matthew himself,[32] mainly on the grounds of Matthew's preference for μηδέ[33] and perhaps also of Matthew's tendency to form pairs with conjunctions.[34] But such an assumption is not conclusive at all, and, as a matter of fact, there are not a few scholars who seek the source of the phrase from earlier tradition[35] or logia,[36] and some recognize the possibility of or presuppose the authenticity of the phrase.[37] If the question of the source and the authenticity of the phrase is not settled definitely, it may be necessary to explain the phrase at least on the two different levels—that is, on the level of Jesus and on the level of Matthew.

b. *The Co-text and Context*

The broader co-text (i.e. ch. 24), whatever the understandings of vv. 4-14, and 29-44 are, shows that vv. 15-21 point to the events of the Jewish War of 66–70 CE (cf. particularly vv. 3, 15), but in the form of future prediction not in the form of description of past events. It is, in fact, extremely difficult to fit the extant accounts of the actual events[38] into the details of the prediction in vv. 15-21. Christian flight to Pella in

32. E.g. Banks, *Jesus*, pp. 102-103; Barth, 'Law', p. 91; Stanton, 'Pray', p. 192; Wong, 'Sabbath', p. 14; *et al.*

33. It occurs eleven times in Matthew as opposed to six in Mark and eight in Luke. Do these statistics, however, really show Matthew's preference for the word? Note this word does not appear either in the list of Matthew's favourite words and phrases in J.C. Hawkins, *Horae Synopticae* (Oxford: Clarendon Press, 1909), pp. 3-10, nor that in Davies and Allison, *Matthew*, I, pp. 77-79, nor that in Luz, *Matthew 1–7*, pp. 54-70, though that in Gundry, *Matthew*, pp. 641-52, includes it.

34. Cf. Banks, *Jesus*, p. 103 n. 1.

35. Strecker, *Gerechtigkeit*, p. 18; Braun, *Spätjüdischhäretischer*, p. 69 n. 4; Schweizer, *Matthew*, p. 452; *et al.*

36. Allen, *Matthew*, p. lv n. 1, and p. 256.

37. M'Neile, *Matthew*, p. 349; Carson, 'Matthew', p. 501; Morris, *Matthew*, p. 605; *et al.*

38. Mainly, Josephus, *War* 2.271–7.455; *Life* 17-413; Tacitus, *Histories* 5.1-13; Cassius Dio, *Historia Romana* 66.4-7; *et al.* See Schürer, *History*, I, pp. 484-85.

Transjordan before the war in response to 'a divine oracle'[39] can hardly be an incident which Jesus predicts here. Not only is Pella not in the mountains (cf. v. 16), but also nothing had yet happened to the 'holy place' (cf. v. 15). B. Reicke together with many others even doubts that there was any single organized immigration among Christians in Palestine;[40] instead, he suggests that there was 'rather spontaneous and gradual flight, culminating in the years 64-66'.[41] We may, however, suppose that Jesus' prediction could have inspired that later 'oracle'.[42] Some suggest that τὸ βδέλυγμα τῆς ἐρημώσεως (cf. Dan. 9.27; 11.31; 12.11— הַשִׁקּוּץ מְשֹׁמֵם) standing in the holy place (v. 15) points to the desecration of the temple by the Zealots in the winter of 67/68 CE.[43] Though this possibility is attractive, especially because the time suggested fits very well into what our text indicates, the Zealots' desecration, in fact, involved no strict idolatrous symbol at all which v. 15 indicates. Others suggest that τὸ βδέλυγμα τῆς ἐρημώσεως points to the appearance of the Roman standards in the temple at its actual destruction in 70 CE. Once again this possibility is not completely satisfactory, not only because the time suggested would be too late to allow escape from Jerusalem,[44]

---

39. See Eusebius, *Historia Ecclesiastica* 3.5.3; Epiphanius, *Panarion* 29.7.7-8, 30.2.7.

40. *New Testament Era: The World of the Bible from 500 BC to AD 100* (trans. D.E. Green; London: A. & C. Black, 1968), p. 216; cf. S.G.F. Brandon, *The Fall of Jerusalem and the Christian Church: A Study of the Effects of the Jewish Overthrow of AD 70 on Christianity* (London: SPCK, 2nd edn, 1957), pp. 172-73; G.R. Beasley-Murray, *Jesus and the Kingdom of God* (Exeter: Paternoster, 1986), pp. 330, 414 n. 82. For a different view, however, see Schürer, *History*, I, p. 498—it suggests 68 CE when the Zealots exercised 'their reign of terror' in Jerusalem. See J. Verheyden, 'The Flight of the Christian to Pella', *ETL* 66 (1990), pp. 368-84, for arguments and literature as regards the historicity of Christian flight to Pella.

41. *Era*, p. 216.

42. France, *Matthew*, p. 341; cf. also Blomberg, *Matthew*, pp. 358-59. See C. Koester, 'The Origin and Significance of the Flight to Pella Tradition', *CBQ* 51 (1989), pp. 90-106.

43. See Josephus, *War* 4.150-57: 'they transferred their insolence to the Deity and with polluted feet invaded the sanctuary... these wretches converted the temple of God into their fortress and refuge from any outbreak of popular violence, and made the Holy Place the headquarters of their tyranny'. Cf. Reicke, *Era*, p. 258; Schürer, *History*, I, pp. 496-97.

44. Carson, 'Matthew', p. 500. Cf. France, *Matthew*, p. 341—though he suggests that 'v. 16 speaks not of the city but of Judaea, which was to suffer savage devastation during and after the siege of Jerusalem', the extant evidence seems to suggest

but more importantly the fall of Jerusalem certainly did not happen in winter but in summer (9 Ab = August).[45] Moreover, there is no extant evidence which indicates any instant wholesale escape of Jews/Christians from Judaea into the mountains (cf. v. 16) in winter (cf. v. 20) immediately after the fall of Jerusalem. It is thus hard to believe that Matthew's text of vv. 15-28 was adjusted to the historical events of the Jewish War of 66–70 CE. In that case, even if we do not definitely deny the possibility of a post-70 dating of the Gospel, we are compelled to give more support to a pre-70 dating.[46] J.A.T. Robinson asks 'why warnings and predictions relating to the crisis in Judaea should have been produced or reproduced in such profusion *after* the events to which they referred' and concludes that 'I fail to see any motive for preserving, let alone inventing, prophecies long after the dust had settled in Judaea, unless it be to present Jesus as a prognosticator of uncanny accuracy' in which case Matthew along with other evangelists has 'defeated the exercise by including palpably unfulfilled predictions'.[47] R.D.A. Hare, after pointing out that 'there would be no point in praying about a past event' (cf. v. 20), concludes that the events of vv. 15-21 have, for Matthew, certainly 'not yet taken place'.[48] If we are to suppose nevertheless that Matthew wrote the Gospel after the fall of Jerusalem, a plausible explanation would be that Matthew was interested in preserving what Jesus had predicted regarding the fall of Jerusalem and in transmitting it to his community rather than in assimilating Jesus' prediction to what had happened.[49]

that there was no such immediate wholesale devastation throughout Judaea straight after the fall of Jerusalem, which would have compelled instant escape; see Josephus, *War* 6.237-7.118; cf. Reicke, *Era*, pp. 265-70, 283-317.

45. See Josephus, *War* 6.236-66; cf. Hare, *Matthew*, p. 277. F.D. Bruner's quotation from J.A. Bengel, *Gnomon of the New Testament*, I (2 vols.; Edinburgh: T. & T. Clark, 1877), p. 272, in his *Matthew. II. The Churchbook* (Dallas: Word Books, 1990) is interesting: 'Prayer helps; they prayed, and flight did *not* take place in winter'.

46. Cf. Reicke, 'Prophecy', pp. 121-34; Gundry, *Matthew*, pp. 481-83, 600, 603-604.

47. *Redating*, p. 25; cf. France, *Evangelist*, p. 85.

48. *Matthew*, p. 277—he, nevertheless, assumes a post-70 dating of the Gospel (see p. 2); he, therefore, attempts to explain the events depicted in vv. 15-21 in supernatural rather than natural terms (see p. 278), which is not very convincing.

49. It may be noteworthy here that Lk. 21.20 seems to have assimilated Jesus'

Now we need to ask some further questions regarding the saying of v. 20 in the light of its broader literary co-text. First of all, the speaker is obviously Jesus himself, even though the source of the saying is not definitely identifiable. The audience are the disciples in front of Jesus who are in Judaea (cf. vv. 1-4, 15, 20),[50] though the readers of the Gospel may be the community either within or outside Judaea who had lived in either the pre- or post-70 period. Those who are exhorted to pray are once again the disciples; and the flight referred to in v. 20 is the prospective flight by the same disciples, which the readers may either anticipate that they will participate in like the disciples (if the Gospel was written before 70 CE), or simply look back on as past history (if written after 70 CE)—in the latter case, they may have realized that events had not happened in the exact way described, perhaps because of the disciples' prayer.[51] Those who bring the persecution seem to be Gentiles, since the (non-Christian) Jews as well as the disciples are expected to flee (vv. 16-19).[52]

With this discussion of the literary co-text and historical context in mind, I will attempt to present my explanation of the additional phrase μηδὲ σαββάτῳ which may more satisfactorily fit into the co-text and context.

c. *My Proposal*

If the picture of Jesus depicted by Matthew is consistent in his Gospel (which is, though not required, highly probable for such a careful writer as Matthew), particularly in relation to Jesus' attitude to and understanding of the sabbath, the phrase μηδὲ σαββάτῳ in v. 20 must be explained in the light of Jesus' attitude to and understanding of the sabbath as depicted in 11.25–12.21. In view of the investigation in Chapter 4, it is beyond doubt that Jesus would not expect his disciples (listeners) to keep the sabbath more strictly than the contemporary Pharisees (cf. particularly 11.28-30; 12.3-7, 11-13). Matthew, then, who depicts Jesus like this,

---

prediction significantly to what had happened during the Jewish War of 66–70 CE (especially during the last four months).

50. Stanton's argument that 'With the additional phrase ἡ φυγὴ ὑμῶν, disciples, who include readers or listeners in the evangelist's day, are addressed directly' in his 'Pray', p. 203, is properly refuted by Wong, 'Sabbath', pp. 8-11; cf. also Gundry, *Matthew*, pp. 483, 668-69 n. 183.

51. We thus need to distinguish the world of the listeners and the world of readers here.

52. See Wong, 'Sabbath', pp. 8-14; *pace* Stanton, 'Pray', pp. 198-203.

would not expect his readers to keep the sabbath more strictly than the contemporary rabbis, either. On the historical level,[53] it is, in fact, highly improbable to suppose that any Christians would have kept the sabbath more strictly than non-Christian Jews, though some of them, at most, may have kept it equally strictly. Most rabbis, however, as we have seen in Chapter 2, allowed someone to save his or her life on the sabbath from immediate life-threatening danger, and, therefore, would have been ready to allow one to flee even on the sabbath.[54] Similarly, Hirsch's view that 'a Christian congregation fleeing on the Sabbath would have been as recognizable in Palestine as a spotted dog' is plausible only if the persecution came from Jews rather than Gentiles—a view which the broader co-text does not support as we have seen above. If, as I have suggested, the persecution came from Gentiles, most Jews as well as Christians would have fled even on the sabbath, and there is no possibility that the fleeing Christians could be 'as recognizable as a spotted dog'.[55]

It is highly important to note that Jesus' saying in v. 20, as a matter of fact, presupposes that the flight might have to take place even on the sabbath, as many scholars point out.[56] The immediate co-text of the phrase (i.e. vv. 19-20), as I pointed out above, 'speaks of external circumstances which will make flight difficult, not impossible'.[57] In that case the most plausible explanation is option 9 above. As Banks and others suggest, the problem posed by the sabbath when persecution happens is not the impossibility caused by Jewish-Christian principles of sabbath observance which, if they existed at all, may more readily allow one to flee than rabbinic principles, but the difficulty caused by Jewish implementation of sabbath regulations—for example, shutting the gates of the cities, suspension of services to travellers, difficulty in purchasing supplies, etc.[58] It is, of course, not easy to reconstruct the difficulty exactly. Nevertheless the Jewish regulations during the first century CE as we have observed in Chapter 2 illustrate well how difficult it would have been to flee on the sabbath when cities or even villages may have not

53. Both in Jesus' and Matthew's time.
54. This rules out options 1 and 8.
55. This rules out options 2, 4, 5, and 7.
56. Filson, *Matthew*, p. 255; Meier, *Matthew*, p. 284; Hare, *Matthew*, p. 272; *et al.*
57. Meier, *Matthew*, p. 284.
58. Banks, *Jesus*, p. 102; Gundry, *Matthew*, p. 483; France, *Matthew*, p. 341; *et al.* Cf. also Davies, *Matthew*, p. 168.

been operating their regular services. In a situation where Christians, the minority group, were surrounded by non-Christian Jews (i.e. the Jewish synagogues), the majority group, who still kept the general regulations of the sabbath faithfully, such regulations may surely have caused serious difficulties in sudden travelling and flight not only for Christians (cf. vv. 16, 20) but even for Jews themselves (cf. v. 16).

Matthew's inclusion of the additional phrase can then best be explained if Matthew wrote the Gospel before 70 CE in Palestine. In that case his community (the readers) would have easily identified themselves with the disciples (the listeners). The community, like the disciples, are exhorted to pray that their flight in the near future may happen neither in winter nor on the sabbath, because both season and day may cause extreme difficulties in their flight. If we nonetheless are to suppose that Matthew wrote the Gospel after 70 CE outside Palestine (e.g. in Syria), a plausible explanation for Matthew's inclusion of the additional phrase may be that Matthew's primary concern in including the phrase was to preserve what Jesus had exhorted, an exhortation which could still remind many members of his community of the Palestinian situation which they had personally experienced before they had left Palestine—a concern which, in fact, can be observed elsewhere in Matthew: for example especially, 5.23-24 (offering gifts at the altar[59]); 17.24-27 (paying the temple tax[60]);[61] etc. If, as I have supposed in Chapters 3 and 4, Matthew's community was in tension with the surrounding synagogues especially in relation to the rabbinic way of keeping the sabbath,[62] Jesus' exhortation regarding the sabbath in 24.20 may have made much sense to his community.

3. *Conclusions*

My explanation of the additional phrase(s) of 24.20 fits well not only into its immediate co-text but also into Matthew's overall stance on the

---

59. Note there could not have been any altar after the destruction of the temple, if Matthew wrote the Gospel after 70 CE.

60. Paying the temple tax could not be a current issue after the destruction of the temple, if Matthew wrote the Gospel after 70 CE. Cf. Robinson, *Redating*, pp. 104-105; Gundry, *Matthew*, p. 357. For an argument that 17.24-27 concerns the temple tax rather than secular taxes, see esp. Davies and Allison, *Matthew*, II, pp. 738-42.

61. Note both passages are unique to Matthew.

62. The two sabbath controversies as presented in Matthew may support such a possibility; note τὴν συναγωγὴν αὐτῶν.

law, and particularly on the sabbath, as I have investigated it in Chapters 3 and 4. If the disciples are ready to break Pharisaic sabbath regulations (12.1) and other 'tradition of the elders' (15.2), and if Jesus defends their behaviour (12.3-8; 15.3-20; cf. 12.11-13; 23.4, 16-26) against the Pharisees' accusations (12.2; 15.1-2), it is hard to suppose that Jesus expects his disciples to observe the Pharisaic sabbath regulations (e.g. Erub) more strictly than the Pharisees themselves. If most Pharisees and rabbis, as we have seen in Chapter 2, allowed one to save one's life on the sabbath from immediate life-threatening danger, and, therefore, would have been ready to allow one to flee even on the sabbath, Jesus and his disciples (= Christians) must have been more ready to allow themselves to flee even on the sabbath. This surely makes it necessary to explain the additional phrase as I have done above, as indicating not that flight on the sabbath was wrong in itself, but that it would be practically difficult. In that case, it is not right to argue that Matthew's community observed the sabbath simply on the grounds of 24.20,[63] and to interpret 12.1-14 in the light of such an understanding.

The presupposed difficulties of sabbath flight indicate the strict implementation of sabbath regulations by the Jews in the time of Jesus and/or of Matthew. This further confirms my previous conclusion that Matthew's community was surrounded by and confronted by the legalistic tendency which is represented by 'the Pharisees' in the Gospel.

I have pointed out that it is not likely that Matthew's text of 24.15-28 was adjusted to the historical events of the Jewish War of 66–70 CE. Furthermore, I have also shown that a pre-70 Palestine setting provides a best explanation for Matthew's inclusion of the additional phrase. If these two judgments are right, they seem to give more support to the possibility of the pre-70 date of the Gospel though they do not definitively rule out the possibility of the post-70 date.

---

63. *Contra* e.g. Hummel, *Auseinandersetzung*, p. 41; Hare, *Persecution*, p. 6; Gnilka, *Matthäusevangelium*, II, p. 323; *et al.*

Chapter 6

JESUS AND THE SABBATH IN MATTHEW'S GOSPEL:
COMPARATIVE STUDIES

In Chapter 4 I investigated the significance and implication of Jesus' fulfilment of the sabbath in Matthew by discussing the two main sabbath pericopes (12.1-8, 9-14) in the light of their immediate co-text as well as of the whole Gospel. In Chapter 5 I examined Matthew's additional phrase μηδὲ σαββάτῳ of 24.20 in the light of its immediate co-text and also of Matthew's overall stance on the law and particularly on the sabbath as I investigated it in Chapters 3 and 4. The remaining task now is to investigate the other synoptic sabbath-related passages in Mark and/or Luke which are, in Matthew, either absent altogether or present as non-sabbath passages,[1] then to provide explanation(s) as to why they are missing or present in different forms in Matthew. My investigation will be limited to certain issues which are more directly related to the purpose of this study, without attempting to present comprehensive studies of those passages.

1. *Jesus' Teaching and Healing on the Sabbath*
(Mark 1.21-34; Luke 4.31-41; cf. Matthew 4.13; 7.28-29; 8.14-17)

Most scholars attribute Mk 1.23-26,[2] 29-31,[3] 32-34[4] to tradition, and not

---

1.   That is, Mk 1.21-34 // Lk. 4.31-41 (cf. Mt. 4.13; 7.28-29; 8.14-17); Lk. 4.16-30 // Mk 6.1-6a (cf. Mt. 13.53-58); Lk. 13.10-17 (cf. Mt. 12.11); Lk. 14.1-6 (cf. Mt. 12.11); Lk. 23.56 (cf. Mt. 27.61; 28.1; cf. also Mk 16.1). In the synoptics the term σαββατον appears 44 times: Matthew—11; Mark—13; Luke—20. The whole list of those occurrences is found in Chart 1.

2.   Bultmann, *History*, p. 209; Schweizer, *Mark*, p. 50; Kuthirakkattel, *Beginning*, pp. 120-24; *et al.*

3.   E. Klostermann, *Das Markusevangelium* (HNT, 3; Tübingen: Mohr, 1950), p. 18; E. Lohmeyer, *Das Evangelium des Markus* (Kritisch-exegetischer Kommentar über das Neue Testament, 2; Göttingen: Vandenhoeck & Ruprecht, 1963), p. 40;

a few scholars suspect that at least some parts of Mk 1.21-22, 27-28 were also integral to the original tradition.[5]

A remote parallel of Mk 1.21 (// Lk. 4.31) is found in Mt. 4.13; but in the Matthean version neither synagogue visit nor sabbath is mentioned, and therefore the sabbath setting of the Markan and Lukan versions is lost. Though a word for word parallel with Mk 1.22 (// Lk. 4.32) is found in Mt. 7.28b-29,[6] the co-text of the latter is completely different from that of the former, and once again lacks the sabbath setting.[7] Mk 1.23-28 (// Lk. 4.33-37) has no parallel in Matthew. Mk 1.29-34 (// Lk. 4.38-41) has parallels in Mt. 8.14-17, but their co-texts are once again very dissimilar. Whereas in Mark and Luke the healing incident is preceded by Jesus' exorcism in the synagogue (Mk 1.23-28; Lk. 4.33-37) *on the sabbath* and followed by Jesus' private prayer (early the next morning) and the summary of his further teaching ministry in Galilee (Mk 1.35-39; Lk. 4.42-44; cf. Mt. 4.23), in Matthew the incident is preceded by the healing of a centurion's servant (8.5-13; cf. Lk. 7.1-10) and is followed by Jesus' conversation with a scribe and a disciple (8.18-22; cf. Lk. 9.57-60) and the calming of a storm (8.23-27; cf. Mk 4.35-41; Lk. 8.22-25). In the Matthean version the sabbath setting is completely missing. The second temporal phrase in Mk 1.32 (ὅτε ἔδυ ὁ ἥλιος; cf. Lk. 4.40) is particularly interesting, but it is absent in the Matthean version (cf. Mt. 8.16).

a. *Visiting the Synagogue on the Sabbath (Mark 1.21 par.; cf. Luke 4.16 par.)*
A number of synoptic passages witness that Jesus often visited the synagogue on the sabbath—Mk 1.21 (Lk. 4.31; cf. Mt. 4.13); Lk. 6.6 (// Mk 3.1 // Mt. 12.9); Mk 6.2 // Lk. 4.16 (Mt. 13.54); cf. Mk 1.39 // Mt. 4.23 //

Taylor, *Mark*, p. 178; Schweizer, *Mark*, pp. 53-54; Pesch, *Markusevangelium*, I, pp. 128-29; *et al.*

4.   Taylor, *Mark*, p. 180; Schweizer, *Mark*, p. 54 (vv. 32, 34a); Pesch, *Markusevangelium*, I, p. 133; *et al. Contra* Kuthirakkattel, *Beginning*, pp. 151-52.

5.   Taylor, *Mark*, p. 171; Cranfield, *Mark*, p. 71; cf. Kuthirakkattel, *Beginning*, pp. 120-24. Gundry, *Mark*, pp. 79-80, however, properly points out that 'Our lack of Mark's sources and the consequent and increasingly recognized difficulty of distinguishing between tradition and redaction leaves us in the lurch'.

6.   Except for the additions of οἱ ὄχλοι in v. 28b and αὐτῶν in v. 29. The second addition (...οὐκ ὡς οἱ γραμματεῖς αὐτῶν) is noteworthy—would this indicate the widening breach between Jesus and the Jewish establishment?. Cf. Mt. 12.9.

7.   Mt. 7.28b-29 functions as the conclusion of the Sermon on the Mount (chs. 5–7), and it has no clear temporal link at all.

Lk. 4.44; Mt. 9.35; Lk. 4.15; etc. On the grounds of this fact (especially on the grounds of Luke's presentation in Lk. 4.16), Bacchiocchi maintains that the evangelist sets Christ's practice before his readers as a model of sabbath keeping.[8] The significance of Jesus' visit to the synagogue on the sabbath, however, must not be exaggerated. Rordorf comments on the fact thus:

> This behaviour [= Jesus' visit to the synagogue on the sabbath] does not necessarily mean that Jesus was a zealous observer of the Jewish law or that he was very strict about the sabbath commandment. It stands to reason that Jesus used the opportunity to deliver his message in the synagogues where people were assembled on the sabbath.[9]

Rordorf's argument is certainly more cogent than that of Bacchiocchi, especially considering the fact that in all of the passages referred to above Jesus' visit to the synagogue is related to his preaching and teaching and sometimes to debates which have some teaching effects. More importantly, however, visiting the synagogue on the sabbath is, in fact, nowhere ordered in the Torah (or even in the whole Old Testament).[10] Jesus' visit to the synagogue then must at most be a matter of the custom (cf. Lk. 4.16) rather than of obedience to Torah. Many scholars assume that the phrase κατὰ τὸ εἰωθὸς αὐτῷ in Lk. 4.16 refers to the regularity of Jesus' synagogue attendance on the sabbath.[11] This assumption, however, is far from certain. Banks interestingly suggests that the phrase rather refers to Jesus' habit of teaching in the synagogue.[12] In the light of the immediately preceding verse (4.15: καὶ αὐτὸς ἐδίδασκεν

8.   Bacchiocchi, *Rest*, pp. 145-46.

9.   *Sunday*, pp. 67-68; see also Marshall, *Luke*, p. 181; Turner, 'Sabbath', p. 102; Pesch, *Markusevangelium*, I, p. 120.

10.   This is not, however, to deny that in the Old Testament the sabbath is frequently associated with cultic elements. Nevertheless, those cultic activities were centred in the temple (perhaps except for 2 Kgs 4.23), and there is no mention in the Old Testament which relates the sabbath with synagogue gathering; 'synagogue' is, of course, a post-Old Testament development anyway, nor does the Torah envisage such a gathering on the sabbath.

11.   E.g. P.J. Temple, 'The Rejection at Nazareth', *CBQ* 17 (1955), pp. 229-42, esp. p. 237; Bacchiocchi, *Sabbath*, p. 19; J.A. Fitzmyer, *The Gospel according to Luke (I–IX): Introduction, Translation, and Notes* (AB, 28; Garden City, NY: Doubleday, 1979), p. 530; E. Schweizer, *The Good News according to Luke* (trans. D.E. Green; London: SPCK, 1984), p. 88; C.F. Evans, *Saint Luke* (London: SCM Press, 1990), p. 268; *et al.*

12.   *Jesus*, p. 91.

ἐν ταῖς συναγωγαῖς αὐτῶν) and the only other use by Luke of the phrase[13] in reference to Paul's synagogue ministry (Acts 17.1-2: ὅπου ἦν συναγωγὴ τῶν Ἰουδαίων. κατὰ δὲ τὸ εἰωθὸς τῷ Παύλῳ εἰσῆλθεν πρὸς αὐτοὺς καὶ ἐπὶ σάββατα τρία διελέξατο αὐτοῖς ἀπὸ τῶν γραφῶν...),[14] Banks's suggestion seems more probable than the popular assumption.[15] We may then conclude that, while it is possible to suppose that Jesus, as a Jew, visited the synagogue on the sabbath to participate in the service there (probably, according to the contemporary Jewish *tradition*), even though the Torah does not require it (therefore, without *theological* reason), it is also possible (and probably more likely) that Jesus visited the synagogue on the sabbath in order to have teaching opportunities (that is, with *practical* purpose). At any rate, it is at least clear that Jesus' constant presence in the synagogue on the sabbath, as M.M.B. Turner concludes, 'provides little real evidence of *theological* commitment on behalf of Jesus...to Sabbath worship'.[16]

It is interesting to note that Matthew does not include any explicit mention that Jesus visits the synagogue *on the sabbath*. In 4.13 (cf. Mk 1.21; Lk. 4.31) he does not mention the synagogue visiting at all. In 13.54 (cf. Mk 6.2; Lk. 4.16) he simply mentions Jesus' teaching ministry in *their* synagogues without 'sabbath' reference. Even in 12.9 Matthew mentions Jesus' visit to *their* synagogue without explicitly mentioning, for example, 'on the same sabbath' (cf. Lk. 6.6: Ἐγένετο δὲ ἐν ἑτέρῳ σαββάτῳ), though, of course, this is implied from the co-text. Can we derive any significance from this fact? If the phrase was present in his version of 'common tradition', Matthew may well have omitted the

13. This is, in fact, the only other use of the same phrase in the whole New Testament.

14. See H. Schürmann, *Das Lukasevangelium*, I (HTKNT, 3/1; Freiburg: Herder, 1969), p. 227 n. 45; B. Chilton, *God in Strength* (Freistadt: Plöchl, 1979), pp. 134-35; *idem*, 'Announcement in Nazareth: An Analysis of Luke 4:16-21', in R.T. France and D. Wenham (eds.), *Gospel Perspectives*, II (Sheffield: JSOT Press, 1981), p. 153. Paul's synagogue ministry is amply witnessed in Acts (i.e. 9.20; 13.5, 14ff., 42ff.; 14.1; 17.2; 18.4, 19; 19.8).

15. Chilton, *God*, p. 135 n. 34, further points out that 'the report that Jesus "came" to Nazareth is not consistent with the view that he was resident there and entered the synagogue as an ordinary participant'; see also K.L. Schmidt, *Der Rahmen der Geschichte Jesu* (Berlin: Trowitzsch & Sohn, 1919), p. 39; Ellis, *Luke*, p. 97; *et al. Pace* Wilson, *Law*, pp. 23-24.

16. 'Sabbath', p. 102.

phrase simply because of the structure he adopted,[17] or he may have
simply presupposed that 'his readers would understand as a matter of
course that it must have been the Sabbath if Jesus was teaching in the
synagogue'.[18] It is, however, also possible to suppose that Matthew
omitted the phrase with some theological reasons. He may well have
refrained intentionally from using the phrase in order to avoid an unnecessary misunderstanding by the members in his community who had a
legalistic tendency—a misunderstanding that they were to worship on
the sabbath after the example of Jesus. Even if Mark and Luke did not
have any positive theological purpose in including those sabbath references, Matthew may have decided to omit them intentionally in the light
of the context of his community. At least one thing is very clear from
the above observation: Matthew is certainly not more conservative than
Mark or Luke in terms of the sabbath tradition, even if he was not
actually more liberal.

b. *Exorcism and Healing on the Sabbath (Mark 1.23-28 par., 29-31
par.)*
As regards the first incident (Mk 1.23-28 par.), one question which is significant for my inquiry is whether the act of exorcism was prohibited on
the sabbath in the time of Jesus. There is no first-hand material which explicitly witnesses the view of Jews in the first century CE (cf. Chapter 2).
Exorcism, in fact, is not mentioned either in the list of 39 categories of
work prohibited on the sabbath in *m. Šab.* 7.2 or in any other list of
works prohibited on the sabbath in the Tannaitic writings (e.g. *m. Beṣ.*
5.2). While it is assumed in the rabbinic literature that healing is prohibited on the sabbath, it is not clear that the same would be true of exorcism. The fact that Jesus did not face any outrage, for example, from the
Pharisees (cf. Mk 2.23-3.5 par.) or the ruler of the synagogue (cf. Lk.
13.10-17) for his exorcism (cf. Mk 1.27-28) may suggest that the act of
exorcism was not definitely designated as one of the prohibited acts
in the time of Jesus, and Jesus, therefore, did not commit any offence
against the Pharisaic halakhah at all. If this was not the case, however,
Carson's explanation is perceptive: 'Jesus' Sabbath practices were not
reviled by anyone at first, until opposition began to mount and *Jesus*

17.   Note the first part of his Gospel is significantly different in its order of
incidents both from Mark and Luke. See especially Davies and Allison, *Matthew*, I,
pp. 70-72.
18.   Gundry, *Matthew*, p. 282.

himself was reviled. At that point, the Sabbath legislation was used against Him, and attacks against Him were rationalized on the basis of the Halakah.'[19]

The second incident (Mk 1.29-31) raises a similar question: why is there no objection to Jesus' act of healing on the sabbath? Since the prohibition of healing on the sabbath is assumed, if not argued, in the various rabbinic writings (e.g. *m. Šab.* 14.3; 22.6; cf. *t. Šab.* 16.22), the absence of opposition may sound more striking than on the previous occasion. If, as some scholars suggest, the fever of the mother-in-law of Simon was so severe that it could threaten her life,[20] Jesus' healing would have been within the limits allowed by the Pharisees, because any Pharisees would have allowed one to heal in such a life-threatening situation (cf. *m. Yom.* 8.6). But more importantly, if the incident occurred in private at his disciple's home, probably only in the presence of his four disciples (cf. Mk 1.29) and Simon's household, the absence of opposition from the Pharisees or anyone else is not strange at all.

Many scholars rightly draw attention to the Christological and eschatological significance of these acts of Jesus (cf. especially Mk 1.24-27, 31).[21] Bacchiocchi, who characterizes the first act as 'the *spiritual* healing' and the second as 'the *physical* restoration', however, goes further and attempts to link the Christological and eschatological implications of these acts to the sabbath, on the basis of the Lukan version (4.33-39); he, therefore, argues that 'The meaning of the Sabbath as *redemption, joy* and *service*' are 'already present in an embryonic phase in these first healing acts of Christ'.[22] His argument may well be true for the Lukan version, though it depends heavily on his own interpretation of Lk. 4.16-21 which, as I will show in section 2, is highly questionable. As far as the

19. 'Sabbath', p. 59.

20. Cf. Gundry, *Mark*, p. 86: 'Her lying down instead of serving the men, especially the guests, show how severe the fever is...The immediacy of others' speaking to Jesus about the fever of Simon's mother-in-law and the historical present tense of λέγουσιν, "they speak", underline her plight'; cf. also Gnilka, *Markus*, I, p. 84. Davies and Allison, *Matthew*, II, p. 34, speculate that she may have suffered from 'malaria'.

21. See Taylor, *Mark*, p. 174; Bacchiocchi, *Sabbath*, pp. 29-30; Kuthirakkattel, *Beginning*, pp. 136-41, 144-48; *et al.* For the Jewish expectation that the messianic age will bring the destruction of evil power, see especially *1 En.* 55.4; 69.27; for other references, see Strack and Billerbeck, *Kommentar*, IV, p. 527.

22. *Sabbath*, pp. 29-30; quotation from p. 30; see also *idem*, *New Testament*, p. 62.

Markan version is concerned, however, it is extremely doubtful whether Mark really intended to relate the Christological and eschatological significance of Jesus' two acts particularly to the sabbath. As Carson points out, 'Mention of the day, in Mark at least, is related solely (and somewhat casually) to Jesus' entry into the synagogue to teach'.[23]

The remaining question now is, if these two incidents were present in his version of 'common tradition' in the sabbath co-text (which seems most probable), why did Matthew omit the first instance and put the second incident into a quite different co-text (i.e. 8.14-15 in its broader co-text, 8.1–9.34), which has no explicit link to the sabbath? G. Bornkamm once regarded this omission and modification as the evidence that 'the sabbath commandment has not lost its validity for Matthew'.[24] It is, however, extremely questionable to suppose that Matthew introduced these changes in order to maintain the validity of the sabbath commandment or to relieve Jesus of an apparent violation of the sabbath (cf. especially 12.10-13). As we have seen just above, Jesus, in fact, most probably did not violate the sabbath in the two incidents even according to the Pharisaic halakhah let alone according to the Torah and the Old Testament as a whole. Barth, therefore, concludes that the omission of the healing incident (Mk 1.21-28) in Matthew 'is not significant'.[25] Perhaps these changes may be once again best explained as arising from Matthew's distinctive order in the first half, and especially his favourite three triads structure of chs. 8–9.[26] By gathering the earlier miracles into three triads in Mt. 8.1–9.34, as Banks suggests, 'Matthew found both that one of the Marcan accounts had to be omitted', and that the implied reference to the sabbath (i.e. εὐθὺς ἐκ τῆς συναγωγῆς ἐξελθόντες of Mk 1.29) in the other 'was inappropriate'.

23.   'Sabbath', p. 59.

24.   G. Bornkamm, 'End-Expectation', in *idem, Tradition*, p. 31 n. 2; cf. also Kilpatrick, *Origins*, p. 116.

25.   'Law', p. 91 n. 1.

26.   Davies and Allison, *Matthew*, I, pp. 61-72, note that Matthean discourses and the narrative through ch. 12 characteristically feature tripartite structures. As one of the outstanding examples they (p. 67; see also pp. 101-102) quite convincingly demonstrate that 8.1–9.34 contains three sets of three; see also *idem, Matthew*, II, pp. 3, 6. In order to make the three sets of triads, however, they regard the two miracles in 9.18-26 as 'part of one indissoluble unit'; they also regard the evening healing incident (8.16) not as an independent miracle narrative but as a summary (cf. also 9.35) and an introduction to the formula quotation which immediately follows (8.17; cf. Isa. 53.4); thus they make the total number of miracles nine rather than eleven.

In that case, Banks's conclusion is probably right that 'Theological criteria...were absent' in these changes.[27]

c. *'That Evening, at Sundown' (Mark 1.32 par.)*
Mark's addition of ὅτε ἔδυ ὁ ἥλιος to ὀψίας δὲ γενομένης clarifies more exactly that the sabbath has come to the end in accordance with the Jewish way of reckoning days. From this fact, some might argue that Mark included the additional phrase in order to show not only that the people did not violate the sabbath by transporting their sick and demon-possessed but also that Jesus did not breach it by healings and exorcisms.[28] But such an argument is not convincing, not only because in 2.23–3.6, as we have seen already in Chapter 4, Mark, like Matthew, portrays Jesus as the Lord of the sabbath without trying to relieve him of the charge of violating it, but more importantly because in 1.23-31 Mark already explicitly depicts Jesus as performing both exorcism and healing on the sabbath. Mark is, thus, 'hardly concerned to exculpate the people and Jesus from breaking the Sabbath'.[29] Perhaps Mark's concern is rather with the fact that the people bring their sick and demon-possessed once the sabbath restrictions have been lifted with the sunset. The duality of the temporal phrases, whether or not Mark added any of them, and the introduction with an adversative δέ, as Gundry remarks, 'stress the alacrity with which the people bring their sick and demon-possessed once the Sabbath has ended'.[30] This may betray the situation that the ordinary Jews in the time of Jesus observed at least some of the sabbath regulations (e.g. carrying, travelling, healing) quite faithfully. Hence G.B. Caird comments on the Lukan version of the phrase

27. *Jesus*, p. 127 n. 2; cf. also Gundry, *Matthew*, p. 148.
28. Cf. Rawlinson, *Mark*, p. 18; Taylor, *Mark*, p. 180.
29. Gundry, *Mark*, p. 87.
30. *Mark*, pp. 87-88. Having said this, however, one needs to point out that double statements, temporal or local, are so typical of Mark (cf. esp. 1.35; 4.35; 13.11; 14.1, 12; 16.2) that it is doubtful whether they carry great significance whenever they appear; cf. Schweizer, *Mark*, p. 54. Taylor, *Mark*, p. 180, nevertheless, remarks: 'The phrase ὅτε ἔδυσεν ὁ ἥλιος defines the time more precisely as sunset. Thus, *as is often the case in Mk*, the double phrase is not so tautologous as it appears' (italics mine); cf. also Guelich, *Mark*, p. 65. For the double statements in Mark, see F. Neirynck, *Duality in Mark: Contributions to the Study of Markan Redaction* (BETL, 31; Leuven: Leuven University Press, 1972), pp. 94-96—he notes 68 occurrences of double statement, temporal or local, in Mark, of which 17 are retained in Matthew and 8 in Luke; cf. Kuthirakkattel, *Beginning*, p. 123 n. 35.

(4.40—δύνοντος δὲ τοῦ ἡλίου) thus: 'The crowds were more scrupulous than Jesus and waited until sunset when the sabbath ended, before taking advantage of his healing powers'.[31] Carson even suggests the possibility that 'they [Mark and Luke] are already implicitly criticizing Pharisaic regulations that keep people from Jesus'.[32]

It seems quite clear why Matthew does not retain Mark's second phrase (ὅτε ἔδυ ὁ ἥλιος) in 8.16, even if he found it in his version of 'common tradition'. Since Matthew has removed the sabbath setting from the preceding passage (i.e. 8.14-15), the present passage is not connected to the sabbath, either. The second phrase, thus, would have no point in Matthew's co-text, if it was originally added in order to clarify the end of the sabbath more precisely. It seems, therefore, extremely arbitrary to draw any theological significance from Matthew's omission of the second temporal phrase. Most probably Matthew drops the phrase simply because of the co-text he puts the present passage into. Having said this, however, the comparison of the two versions of the present story (that of Mk 1.32-34 [and Lk. 4.40-41] and that of Mt. 8.16-17) shows an interesting resultant effect that Matthew misses Mark's witness (though it may be implicit) that the ordinary Jews in the time of Jesus observed at least some of the sabbath regulations (e.g. carrying, travelling, healing) quite faithfully. Could Matthew have intended such a resultant effect? It is far from certain, but it is at least possible that he knowingly omitted the clause in order to avoid any unnecessary side-effects; he may, for example, have thought of the possibility that such a witness could have encouraged some members of his community to be legalistically bound to the rabbinic sabbath regulations—a tendency which probably was a real threat to his community.

d. *Conclusions*

From the above investigations we may draw some conclusions: (1) Mk 1.21-34 and Lk. 4.31-41 do not show any definite evidence that Jesus himself kept the sabbath faithfully either according to the halakhah or according to the Torah; Jesus' constant presence in the synagogue on the sabbath (Mk 1.21 par.; 6.2 par.; Lk. 6.6; etc.) was at most a matter of custom rather than of faithful obedience to halakhah or Torah. (2) The

31. *The Gospel of St Luke* (Pelican Gospel Commentaries; London: Penguin Books, 1963), p. 89.

32. 'Sabbath', p. 60. The burden of the Pharisaic regulations is more explicitly found in Mt. 11.28-30; 23.4.

passages also do not show any clear evidence that Jesus broke the sabbath commandment nor even the sabbath halakhah. (3) Jesus' behaviour on the sabbath in the passages nevertheless already reveals his understanding of the sabbath as clearly revealed in Mk 2.27, 28 par.; 3.4-5 par. (cf. also Mt. 12.5-6, 7, 11-12)—for example, τὸ σάββατον διὰ τὸν ἄνθρωπον ἐγένετο καὶ οὐχ ὁ ἄνθρωπος διὰ τὸ σάββατον (Mk 2.27), κύριός ἐστιν ὁ υἱὸς τοῦ ἀνθρώπου καὶ τοῦ σαββάτου (Mk 2.28), ἔξεστιν τοῖς σάββασιν ἀγαθὸν ποιῆσαι...(Mk 3.4; cf. Mt. 12.12). (4) The focus of the Markan (and probably Lukan) passages is not on the sabbath; these passages, therefore, do not demonstrate or even indicate a high theology of the sabbath at all. (5) Matthew's probable omissions of and modifications of the co-texts of the passages/ phrases in Mk 1.21-34 and Lk. 4.31-41 by no means show that Matthew is more conservative in respect of the sabbath; indeed, they may perhaps rather indicate that Matthew is more concerned about the legalistic tendency in his community—that is why he sometimes modifies the co-texts of and sometimes even omits certain passages/phrases which he thinks might unnecessarily encourage a legalistic observance of the sabbath.

2. *Jesus' Preaching in the Synagogue in Nazareth* *(Luke 4.16-30; Mark 6.1-6; Matthew 13.53-58)*

It is well recognized that Luke's way of presenting Jesus' first public ministry (4.14-15, 16-30; cf. Mk 6.1-6a; Mt. 13.53-58) is 'far more artistic and impressive'[33] than that of Mark (1.14-15) or Matthew (4.12-17), and most scholars agree that Lk. 4.16-30 is a programmatic preface to Jesus' whole public ministry.[34]

The nature and extent of the source(s) of Lk. 4.16-30 has been widely discussed but without any certainty or consensus, perhaps except for the

33. Evans, *Luke*, p. 266.
34. G. Bornkamm, *Jesus of Nazareth* (trans. I. McLuskey, F. McLuskey, and J.M. Robinson; London: Hodder & Stoughton, 1960), p. 75: 'the governing text of all Jesus' works'; H. Conzelmann, *The Theology of St Luke* (trans. G. Buswell; London: Faber & Faber, 1960), p. 221; F.W. Beare, *The Earliest Records of Jesus* (Oxford: Basil Blackwell, 1962), p. 46: 'a preview of the whole mission of Jesus'; D. Hill, 'The Rejection of Jesus at Nazareth (Luke iv 16-30)', *NovT* 13 (1971), p. 161: 'a programmatic preface to the public ministry'; Chilton, 'Announcement', pp. 150, 161; J.D. Kingsbury, *Conflict in Luke: Jesus, Authorities, Disciples* (Minneapolis, MN: Fortress Press, 1991), p. 44; *et al.*

notion that Mk 6.1-6a is at least a part of the source(s).[35] The historicity of Jesus' visit to the synagogue in Nazareth, however, is generally accepted,[36] though its place as the first act in the chronology of Jesus' ministry is seriously questioned. It is, in fact, doubtful whether Luke himself intended to present Jesus' visit to the synagogue in Nazareth as chronologically the first act of his public ministry.[37] Luke may well have had good reason to rearrange his material, without being strictly bound to its chronological order, for certain literary, and even more, theological purposes. As a 'programmatic preface', the passage indeed reflects many of the main themes of Luke–Acts: (1) the ministry of Jesus is the fulfilment of the Old Testament (vv. 18-19, 20—direct fulfilment of Isa. 61.1-2; 58.6; vv. 25-26, 27—typological fulfilment of 1 Kgs 17-18; 2 Kgs 5); (2) the last days, that is, the year of the Lord's favour (v. 19: ἐνιαυτὸν κυρίου δεκτόν), have now begun with the commencement of the ministry of Jesus (v. 21: σήμερον πεπλήρωται ἡ γραφὴ αὕτη ἐν τοῖς ὠσὶν ὑμῶν); (3) Jesus' eschatological ministry is characterized by the preaching of good news to the poor and the deliverance of the oppressed from their bondage (v. 18); (4) Jesus' allusion to the stories of Elijah and Elisha (vv. 25-27) paradigmatically anticipates the mission to the Gentiles by the church; (5) the rejection of Jesus by the people of Nazareth and Jesus' safe escape may well be 'a symbolic prophecy of the coming passion and resurrection of Jesus' (vv. 28-30).[38] My

35.   An extensive attempt to distinguish between redaction and tradition in Lk. 4.16-21 has been made by Chilton, 'Announcement', pp. 147-72. For other attempts, see Dibelius, *Tradition*, p. 110; Bultmann, *History*, pp. 31-32; H. Anderson, 'Broadening Horizons: The Rejection at Nazareth Pericope of Luke 4:16-30 in Light of Recent Critical Trends', *Int* 18 (1964), pp. 259-75; A.R.C. Leaney, *The Gospel according to St Luke* (BNTC; London: A. & C. Black, 2nd edn, 1966), pp. 50-54; P.D. Miller, 'Luke 4:16-21', *Int* 29 (1975), p. 418; Nolland, *Luke 1–9:20*, pp. 192-94; *et al.*

36.   See Anderson, 'Horizons', pp. 261-63; Hill, 'Rejection', pp. 170-80; Chilton, 'Announcement', pp. 147-72, esp. pp. 166-68; *et al.*; cf. Conzelmann, *Luke*, p. 34: 'There is no unrestrained symbolism in Luke; only what is in his opinion a historical event can possess genuine typological meaning'.

37.   Lk. 4.15 surely indicates that Jesus had already performed his teaching ministry (αὐτὸς ἐδίδασκεν ἐν ταῖς συναγωγαῖς αὐτῶν) before he came to Nazareth (cf. 4.16a—καὶ ἦλθεν εἰς Ναζαρά; cf. also 4.23 for his early activity in Capernaum); cf. Anderson, 'Horizons', pp. 273-74; Chilton, 'Announcement', pp. 150, 169 n. 8; *pace*, for example, Hill, 'Rejection', p. 172.

38.   See Marshall, *Luke*, p. 178.

investigation will be focused on vv. 16-21 which are more directly related to the present study.

a. *The Significance of Luke's Mention of the Sabbath in Luke 4.16-21*
Bacchiocchi, who assumes that Jesus habitually observed the sabbath simply on the basis of the phrase κατὰ τὸ εἰωθὸς αὐτῷ in Lk. 4.16, highlights the significance of Luke's mention of the sabbath in the co-text of 4.16-21. He first of all places a significant emphasis on the fact that in Luke the ministry of Christ begins on the sabbath. He goes on to assert that it is important to note that Jesus' inaugural Nazareth address on the sabbath day is delivered in the language of the messianic jubilee (or sabbatical year). He then argues that this messianic jubilee message carries a significant implication for the weekly sabbath. He asks: 'did Christ identify His mission with the Sabbath in order to make the day a fitting memorial of His redemptive activities?'[39] Not surprisingly his answer is affirmative.[40] Bacchiocchi's case, however, faces a number of serious problems.

Turner properly calls two of Bacchiocchi's fundamental arguments into question. Would Luke really have intended to connect messianic jubilee language with the weekly sabbath? Even if Luke did intend that, do we have any concrete evidence in the Gospel that he took the further step of coming to regard the weekly sabbath as *the* fitting memorial of Jesus' redemptive activities?[41] As for the second question, my answer is negative. Bacchiocchi, of course, attempts to build up his case mainly on the ground of Jesus' rhetorical question in Lk. 13.16 (ταύτην δὲ θυγατέρα 'Αβραὰμ οὖσαν, ἣν ἔδησεν ὁ σατανᾶς ἰδοὺ δέκα καὶ ὀκτὼ ἔτη, οὐκ ἔδει λυθῆναι ἀπὸ τοῦ δεσμοῦ τούτου τῇ ἡμέρᾳ τοῦ σαββάτου;).[42] The point of Jesus' rhetorical question, however, is by no means to demonstrate that the sabbath day is the most (still less only) appropriate time for such release but rather that such release, which would be permissible on all other days, may also be allowed on the

39.   Bacchiocchi, *Sabbath*, p. 21, quotation from p. 21.
40.   Cf. Bacchiocchi, *Sabbath*, pp. 25-26; *idem, New Testament*, pp. 63-64.
41.   Turner, 'Sabbath', p. 102.
42.   Bacchiocchi, *New Testament*, pp. 62-63; cf. W. Grundmann, *Das Evangelium nach Lukas* (THNT, 3; Berlin: Evangelische Verlagsanstalt, 1961), pp. 278-81; Caird, *St Luke*, pp. 107-108. Bacchiocchi also picks up some points from Lk. 4.31-39, but he acknowledges that the evidence found there is only 'embryonic', and so can not be a firm foundation.

sabbath. Would anyone assume that the sabbath is the most and only appropriate time for untying the ox or ass from the manger to lead it away to water it (cf. Lk. 13.15)? As for the first question, as Turner points out, 'Bacchiocchi's case is', once again, 'necessarily weakened by the observation that neither Isaiah 61 nor the Qumran *pesher* of it (11Q Melchizedek) actually mentions the *weekly* Sabbath'.[43] Even for Luke himself, the messianic jubilee language of Isa. 61 is surely much broader in its application than the weekly sabbath, as Luke's use of it in 7.22 shows.[44] Now if Luke gives no hint that the Isaiah passage chosen was *particularly* (if not *only*) applicable to the weekly sabbath, Turner goes on, and if Jesus uses the messianic jubilee language of Isa. 61 'to sum up his ministry', as in 7.22, and uses 'such language irrespective of the day of the week, then we have no reason for thinking that special significance attaches to the fact that Jesus' programmatic speech in Luke takes place *on a Sabbath*'. Most probably the mention of the sabbath in Lk. 4.16 'has the appearance of being merely incidental to a scene that has been elected to its programmatic position for other reasons'.[45]

Having said this, however, the above arguments do not deny that the sabbath, as we have seen in Chapters 1 and 4, was originally instituted as a sign of God's redemption for his people, nor that the jubilee also has a similar link with the notion of God's redemption, as the use of the jubilee language in Isa. 61.1-2 indicates (cf. Lev. 25; Deut. 15.2; cf. also 11QMelch.). Furthermore, I do not deny that the redemptive character of the sabbath, as we have seen in Chapter 4, has been fulfilled by Jesus, nor that Lk. 4.18-21 by adopting the jubilee language of Isa. 61.1-2 indicates the fulfilment of the eschatological aspect of the jubilee by Jesus' ministry.[46] One may therefore, perhaps, at most discern a remote and implicit link between the sabbath and the jubilee in their similar roles as signs for the eschatological redemption in the Old Testament. But I doubt whether, as far as Lk. 4.16-21 is concerned, there is any concrete

---

43.   'Sabbath', p. 102.

44.   It is extremely unlikely that the visit of the messengers from John the Baptist happened on the sabbath and that Luke had the notion of the sabbath in mind when he used the same language there.

45.   Turner, 'Sabbath', pp. 102-103.

46.   See Carson, 'Sabbath', pp. 71-72; A.T. Lincoln, 'Sabbath, Rest, and Eschatology in the New Testament', in Carson (ed.), *Lord's Day*, pp. 201-202. For a detailed discussion of this issue, see R.B. Sloan, *The Favorable Year of the Lord: A Study of the Jubilary Theology in the Gospel of Luke* (Austin, TX: Schola Press, 1977), esp. pp. 28-110.

evidence that Luke intended to assign a particular theological significance to the sabbath (for example, 'a fitting memorial of Jesus' redemptive activities', as Bacchiocchi puts it) by mentioning it in the co-text of
the programmatic announcement of Jesus' ministry (4.16-21).

b. *The Significance of Matthew's Omission of the Sabbath in Matthew
13.54*
Matthew's version of Lk. 4.16-30 is found in Mt. 13.53-58, which has a
much closer parallel in Mk 6.1-6a than in Lk. 4.16-30; Luke's account,
in fact, is considerably longer than the other two. This can be explained
by supposing that Matthew and Mark share similar versions of 'common tradition' for this section, whereas Luke either also shares a similar
version of 'common tradition' and combines it with material from
L *Sondergut* or uses a quite different version of 'common tradition'
which includes special material which is unique to it. From this point (or
from Mt. 14.1) Matthew's order is quite similar to that of Mark.[47] As is
usual, Matthew's present narrative (13.53-58) is shorter than that of
Mark.[48] Matthew may have freely abbreviated and rephrased the 'common tradition', whereas Mark may have rather faithfully preserved it.[49]

As was pointed out above, Matthew never explicitly states that it was
on the sabbath that Jesus visited the synagogue and taught there, and
13.54 is not an exception. If the clause γενομένου σαββάτου (Mk 6.2)[50]
was present in Matthew's version of 'common tradition', Matthew may
well have omitted it either 'in order to bring together "and having come
into his hometown" and "he began to teach"',[51] or because of his anticipation that his 'readers would understand as a matter of course that it

47. Except for, most obviously, Mk 6.7-13 (cf. Mt. 9.35; 10.1, 7-11, 14);
Mk 9.38-41 (cf. Mt. 10.41).
48. Matthew has 106 words, whereas Mark has 127 words; I owe this count to
Morris, *Matthew*, p. 364. If we exclude from the word-count Mt. 13.53a, which may
better be taken with the previous discourse section and has no direct parallel in Mark,
Matthew has only 98 words.
49. Cf. Davies and Allison, *Matthew*, II, p. 452; Hagner, *Matthew 1–13*, p. 404;
their comments, however, are based on the two-source hypothesis on which I am
more sceptical.
50. Luke has a rather different phrase—ἐν τῇ ἡμέρᾳ τῶν σαββάτων (4.16).
51. Gundry, *Matthew*, p. 282. Note καὶ ἀκολουθοῦσιν αὐτῷ οἱ μαθηταὶ
αὐτοῦ of Mk 6.1b is also absent in Matthew's version.

must have been the Sabbath if Jesus was teaching in the synagogue'.[52] Perhaps Matthew may have omitted it 'because the story does not involve a controversy concerning the observance of the sabbath'.[53] It is, however, also possible that Matthew refrained from using the clause intentionally in order not to cause any unnecessary misunderstanding that one must visit the synagogue and worship on the sabbath after the example of Jesus. Such an issue could have been a sensitive one, if Matthew's community was surrounded by Jewish synagogues which had meetings every sabbath probably as an expression of their faithfulness to the law and presumably accused Matthew's community of not observing the sabbath. In this connection Matthew's addition of the personal pronoun αὐτῶν after τῇ συναγωγῇ in Mt. 13.54 is once again highly significant. As in Mt. 12.9, by adding αὐτῶν to τῇ συναγωγῇ Matthew first of all highlights the gulf which had already developed between Jesus and the Jewish establishment (cf. especially, Mt. 12.14).[54] On its historical level αὐτῶν, of course, refers to the people of Nazareth (cf. Lk. 4.16). Nevertheless, Matthew may also have in mind to present their hostile reaction to Jesus (cf. Mt. 13.55-58) as typical of the hostile attitude of non-Christian Jewish synagogues around his community.[55]

As was pointed out above, even if Mark and Luke did not have any positive theological purpose in including the sabbath references in Mk 6.2 and Lk. 4.16, it may still be true that Matthew deliberately omitted it because of the context of his community. Once again, then, I may more or less repeat the previous conclusion that Matthew has neither a higher nor a more conservative view of the sabbath than Mark or Luke, even if he was not actually more liberal. Possibly Matthew's omission of the sabbath clause may witness his concern about the legalistic tendency within his community, and the addition of αὐτῶν may betray the irreconcilable breach between Matthew's community and the surrounding non-Christian Jewish synagogues.

---

52.   Gundry, *Matthew*, p. 282. Would this, therefore, demonstrate the Jewish character of Matthew's Gospel?

53.   Hagner, *Matthew 1–13*, p. 404.

54.   Cf. France, *Matthew*, p. 204. As a matter of fact, this is Jesus' last recorded teaching in a synagogue according to Matthew.

55.   Cf. Gundry, *Matthew*, p. 282; Harrington, *Matthew*, pp. 210-11. For a different view, however, cf. Hagner, *Matthew 1–13*, p. 405.

3. *Jesus' Further Healings on the Sabbath*
(Luke 13.10-17; 14.1-6; cf. Matthew 12.11-12; Mark 3.1-6)

Two sabbath controversy pericopes are unique to Luke, Lk. 13.10-17 and 14.1-6. In these pericopes Luke presents Jesus' further healings on the sabbath in the synagogue and at the house of a ruler respectively.

Scepticism about the unity and authenticity of the first pericope, as indicated in Bultmann's verdict that Lk. 13.10-17 is a 'variant on the theme of Sabbath healing...composed on the basis of an originally isolated saying (v. 15)' with 'the least skill in composition of all three Sabbath healing stories' (i.e. Mk 3.1-6 par.; Lk. 13.10-17; 14.1-6),[56] has been seriously challenged, and there is now no need to suppose the pericope to be a Lukan creation or to doubt its historicity, as Nolland in his recent commentary convincingly demonstrates.[57] Most probably the pericope may have come from L *Sondergut*.[58] Though some scholars attempt to distinguish tradition from redaction within this pericope, it seems impossible to be certain.[59] The narrative of this first pericope may be a 'pronouncement-story' occasioned by a healing incident.[60]

The second pericope, like the first one, is frequently treated as a variant of Mk 3.1-6 composed on the basis of an isolated saying (v. 5), but

---

56. *History*, pp. 12-13, 62; cf. also Lohse, 'σάββατον', pp. 25-26.

57. *Luke 9.21–18:34*, p. 723; see also, A. Plummer, *A Critical and Exegetical Commentary on the Gospel according to St Luke* (ICC; Edinburgh: T. & T. Clark, 5th edn, 1922), p. 341; Roloff, *Kerygma*, pp. 67-68; Turner, 'Sabbath', p. 106; J.A. Fitzmyer, *The Gospel according to Luke X–XXIV: Introduction, Translation, and Notes* (AB, 28a; Garden City, NY: Doubleday, 1985), pp. 1010-11; *et al.* Cf. W.L. Knox, *The Sources of the Synoptic Gospels*, II (2 vols.; Cambridge: Cambridge University Press, 1957), p. 78.

58. Turner, 'Sabbath', p. 106; Fitzmyer, *Luke X–XXIV*, p. 1010.

59. M.D. Hamm, 'The Freeing of the Bent Woman and the Restoration of Israel: Luke 13.10-17 as Narrative Theology', *JSNT* 31 (1987), p. 24.

60. Bultmann, *History*, pp. 12-13; Taylor, *Formation*, p. 69; R.F. O'Toole, 'Some Exegetical Reflections on Luke 13, 10-17', *Bib* 73 (1992), p. 89; *et al.* Hamm, 'Freeing', p. 40 n. 2, however, properly points out the limit of traditional form-criticism: 'their [= the form critics'] preoccupation with the sayings of Jesus have distracted subsequent commentators from taking seriously the *narrative* elements as an important vehicle of Luke's meaning'. J.B. Green, 'Jesus and a Daughter of Abraham (Luke 13.10-17): Test Case for a Lucan Perspective on Jesus' Miracles', *CBQ* 51 (1989), p. 648, therefore, even argues, though less convincingly, that the miracle and the controversy are deliberately juxtaposed in the narrative and it has, therefore, a balanced dual focus.

usually without offering firm evidence. As W. Grundmann and others point out, the narrative of the second pericope differs markedly in detail from that of Mk 3.1-6,[61] and this rather seems to argue for a distinct incident underlying each narrative. A number of scholars suspect that the pericope came from Q mainly on the basis of the seeming contacts between vv. 3b, 5 and Mt. 12.11-12,[62] while others think that it came from L *Sondergut*.[63] In the light of the differences in setting and content between Mt. 12.9-14 and Lk. 14.1-6, it is better to assign our pericope to L *Sondergut*. If it did come from Q material (rather than Q), then the pericope (especially, the saying in v. 5) seems to witness that Matthew and Luke use 'varying recensions' of Q material; this means that, as I.H. Marshall points out, we must be cautious in drawing conclusions about the evangelists' redactional activities from their use of Q material.[64]

a. *The Healing of the Crippled Woman (Luke 13.10-17)*

The first of the two unique sabbath healings in Luke (13.10-17) happens in 'one of the synagogues' (v. 10: ἐν μιᾷ τῶν συναγωγῶν). This healing (and teaching) incident is, in fact, Jesus' last recorded ministry in a synagogue according to Luke. R.F. O'Toole suggests a diptych structure of the pericope: (1) v. 10—introduction (the scene); (2) vv. 11-13—first panel of the diptych (Jesus' healing miracle and the woman's positive response); (3) vv. 14-17—second panel of the diptych (the ruler's opposition and Jesus' response). According to him, 'Luke develops and places more emphasis on the second panel (vv. 14-17)' than on the first (vv. 11-13).[65]

Most scholars observe a close link between the present pericope and the two parables which follow immediately (vv. 18-21; cf. especially οὖν

---

61.   Grundmann, *Lukas*, p. 291; see also Marshall, *Luke*, p. 578; Fitzmyer, *Luke X–XXIV*, p. 1039.

62.   H. Schürmann, *Traditionsgeschichtliche Untersuchungen zu den synoptischen Evangelien* (Düsseldorf: Patmos, 1968), p. 213; Marshall, *Luke*, p. 579.

63.   Manson, *Sayings*, pp. 188, 277; Fitzmyer, *Luke X–XXIV*, p. 1039; J.S. Kloppenborg, *Q Parallels: Synopsis, Critical Notes, and Concordance* (Sonoma, CA: Polebridge, 1988), p. 160.

64.   *Luke*, pp. 31, 579.

65.   'Reflections', pp. 85-90, 105; quotation from p. 105. Note vv. 14-17 have 106 words whereas vv. 11-13 have 44 words; he also points out that the second panel manifests a more elaborate style than the first.

of v. 18),[66] and O'Toole maintains that the parables provide 'an inter-pretative key' to the pericope.[67] In that case, since the theme of the two parables is the power of the kingdom of God which is at present pro-gressing, the pericope can be best understood as demonstrating how that power is working among God's chosen people (cf. θυγατέρα Ἀβραάμ in v. 16). It is worth noting here Luke's use of language in describing the woman's condition (vv. 11, 16) and Jesus' healing (vv. 12-13, 16). Firstly, the woman's condition, which seems to be a physical illness (cf. ἦν συγκύπτουσα καὶ μὴ δυναμένη ἀνακύψαι εἰς τὸ παντελές in v. 11) rather than a demon-possession (cf., however, πνεῦμα ἔχουσα ἀσθενείας in v. 11),[68] is identified as a problem of 'the bond of Satan' (cf. ἣν ἔδησεν ὁ σατανᾶς in v. 16). Secondly, Jesus' healing is regarded as 'loosing from the bond of Satan' (cf. λυθῆναι ἀπὸ τοῦ δεσμοῦ τούτου in v. 16).[69] This language of binding/loosing (vv. 12, 15-16) recalls the programmatic proclamation in Lk. 4.16-21 (esp. 4.18-19, 21), and thus suggests an eschatological character in our pericope. Our pericope then is perfectly in line with Jesus' statement in Lk. 11.20, εἰ δὲ ἐν δακτύλῳ θεοῦ [ἐγὼ] ἐκβάλλω τὰ δαιμόνια, ἄρα ἔφθασεν ἐφ᾽ ὑμᾶς ἡ βασιλεία τοῦ θεοῦ: the kingdom of Satan (i.e. the Satan-bound condition of the crippled woman—cf. v. 16) is being overcome by the kingdom of God through the powerful healing miracle of Jesus (cf. vv. 12-13, 16) who was anointed with the Holy Spirit by God (cf. Lk. 4.18; Acts 10.38). To this extent, our pericope is strongly related with the theme of the kingdom of God, and in the light of a wide agreement that sabbath observance was no longer a real issue for Luke and his readers,[70]

66. See Ellis, *Luke*, pp. 185-86; Hamm, 'Freeing', pp. 29-31; Green, 'Jesus', pp. 651-53; O'Toole, 'Reflections', pp. 90-100; *et al.*

67. 'Reflection', p. 91.

68. After the careful analysis of Luke's description of the woman's condition, J. Wilkinson, 'The Case of the Bent Woman in Luke 13:10-17', *EvQ* 49 (1977), pp. 195-205, medically diagnoses the woman's condition as *spondylitis ankylo-poietica* (an affliction of the spine which produces fusion or ankylosis of its joints); nevertheless, he does not fail to acknowledge that 'her condition is due to the activity of Satan as the primary cause of sin and disease' (p. 204). Cf. also J.D.M. Derrett, 'Positive Perspectives on two Lucan Miracles', *Downside Review* 104 (1986), pp. 274-77.

69. H.C. Kee, *Miracle in the Early Christian World: A Study in Socio-historical Method* (New Haven: Yale University Press, 1983), p. 204.

70. S.G. Wilson, *Luke and the Law* (SNTSMS, 50; Cambridge: Cambridge University Press, 1983), pp. 38-39; Schweizer, *Luke*, p. 222; Hamm, 'Freeing',

who may already quite possibly have kept Sunday as the day of worship (cf. Acts 20.7),[71] I suspect that the real focus of the pericope for Luke is more broadly on the presence of the kingdom of God rather than on the sabbath issue in particular.

Jesus' healing miracle, even though it is an expression of the presence of the kingdom of God, makes the ruler of the synagogue indignant (ἀγανακτῶν), because he thinks Jesus has breached the sabbath by his healing activity (v. 14). His preoccupation with the tradition made him unable to perceive the presence of the kingdom of God and accept Jesus as the bringer of that kingdom, and consequently made him unable to understand the true meaning of the sabbath. His attitude is indeed in sharp contrast with that of the woman, who receives the reign of God and praises him because of that (v. 13). The ruler's unresponsive attitude, as some suggest, may quite possibly be identified with the image of the unfruitfulness of the fig tree of the immediately preceding parable (vv. 6-9).[72]

In response to such opposition, Jesus points out that the ruler of the synagogue (and anyone present who agreed with him) would be ready to untie an ox or ass from the manger and to lead it away to water it (v. 15). In spite of their rigid restrictions on tying/untying (cf. *m. Šab.* 7.2; cf. also 15.1-2) and travelling (cf. CD 10.21; *m. 'Erub.* 4.1-2, 5, 11; *m. Sot.* 5.3), the ruler and his fellows do not consider the sabbath as an obstacle to letting their animal drink water (cf. CD 11.5-6; cf. also *m. 'Erub.* 2.1-4).[73] From this accepted practice, Jesus develops a further

p. 23; O'Toole, 'Reflections', p. 95; cf. Banks, *Jesus*, pp. 130-31; Tyson, 'Scripture', pp. 102-103.

71.   Lohse, 'Worte', p. 89; Rordorf, *Sunday*, pp. 196-205; Turner, 'Sabbath', pp. 128-33; O'Toole, 'Reflections', p. 95; *et al.* For a different view, however, see Bacchiocchi, *Sabbath*, pp. 101-11.

72.   See Hamm, 'Freeing', pp. 30-31; F.W. Danker, *Jesus and the New Age: A Commentary on St Luke's Gospel* (Philadelphia: Fortress Press, 2nd edn, 1988), pp. 260-61; Green, 'Jesus', pp. 651-52. It must be noted, however, that not a few scholars see a break between v. 9 and v. 10; cf. R.C. Tannehill, *The Narrative Unity of Luke–Acts: A Literary Interpretation* (Philadelphia: Fortress Press, 1986), pp. 240-42; Evans, *Luke*, p. 549.

73.   According to CD 11.5-6, even among the Essenes, who had a much stricter sabbath limit (1000 cubits) than that of the Pharisees (2000 cubits), 2000 cubits are allowed for bringing an animal to pasture; see above, Chapter 2. Roloff's claim that the rabbinic practice was more rigorous than is mentioned here, therefore, seems to

argument *a fortiori*, reasoning from the lesser to the greater, which is similar to that of Mt. 12.12a: if the sabbath cannot be an obstacle for the welfare of a mere animal which is bound for a few hours, it is wrong to use the sabbath as an obstacle to exercizing God's redemptive activity for the woman, the daughter of Abraham, who has been bound for eighteen years by Satan; if you allow yourselves to untie your animals even on the sabbath just as on the other six days of the week in order to lead them to water, how much more ought you to allow me to loose the woman from the bond of Satan even on the sabbath just as on the other six days of the week in order to lead her into the kingdom of God?

Jesus' argument here is based neither on the Pharisaic halakhah nor even on the law; it may rather be seen as reflecting his own authority as 'Lord of the sabbath' (cf. 6.5; cf. also Mt. 12.8) and also as the inaugurator of the kingdom of God (cf. 11.20). Furthermore, his healing activity, in which he takes the initiative (cf. v. 12),[74] is carried out on the one hand in accordance with his principle of the sabbath as already indicated in 6.9 (ἔξεστιν τῷ σαββάτῳ ἀγαθοποιῆσαι...ψυχὴν σῶσαι...; cf. Mt. 12.12b), and on the other hand as a concrete expression of the power of the kingdom of God (cf. vv. 16, 18-21). Thus both his argument and healing are further demonstrations of his authority as the Lord of the sabbath and as the inaugurator of the kingdom of God. The sabbath issue is thus dealt with in terms of (and, in fact, is subordinate to) Christology and eschatology.[75] The Christological and eschatological character of the pericope is thus well demonstrated by the pericope itself as well as by its co-text, that is, the two kingdom parables (vv. 18-21) and the parable of the barren fig tree (vv. 6-9). Even though the observance of the sabbath may not have been a live and sensitive issue for Luke, as it was for Matthew, once he is dealing with the issue, he certainly presents it, as Matthew does, in terms of Christology and eschatology.[76]

be unjustified (*Kerygma*, p. 67), and his argument against the authenticity of v. 15 loses its ground.

74. On the significance of Jesus' initiative, see Banks, *Jesus*, p. 130; Nolland, *Luke 9:21–18:34*, pp. 724-25.

75. It is once again quite similarly the case in 6.1-5, 6-11 and also in Mt. 12.1-8, 9-14; see above, Chapter 4. As Turner, 'Sabbath', pp. 103-104, maintains, Luke's omission of Mk 2.27 in his first sabbath controversy pericope (6.1-5) may show his concern for heightening the Christological comparison between David and Jesus; cf. Banks, *Jesus*, p. 120; Wilson, *Law*, pp. 34-35.

76. Cf. Wilson, *Law*, pp. 38-39; Hamm, 'Freeing', pp. 23-39; O'Toole,

Having said this, however, it is important to note here that there is no indication in Jesus' argument that the sabbath is a particularly appropriate day for such a healing, any more than that the sabbath is a particularly appropriate day for loosing animals from their manger to water them.[77] 'The argument', as Turner points out, 'is not that the Sabbath *is* a special day in this respect but precisely that it is *not*. The inbreaking kingdom, the loosing of Satan's captives, is no respecter of days.'[78]

b. *The Healing of the Man with Dropsy (Luke 14.1-6)*
The second of the two unique sabbath healings in Luke (14.1-6) happens 'at the house of a leader of the Pharisees' (v. 1: εἰς οἶκόν τινος τῶν ἀρχόντων [τῶν] Φαρισαίων). This is the last sabbath controversy pericope in Luke.

Luke's portrayal of Jesus having dinner at the house of a Pharisee here (similarly in 7.36; 11.37; cf. 13.31) may betray that Pharisaism was not such a live and a sensitive issue for Luke and his readers as, for example, for Matthew and his readers (cf. Excursus 2–3). This does not mean, however, that Luke is unaware of the Pharisees' antagonism

'Reflections', pp. 84-107. I cannot here attempt to present Luke's overall understanding of the sabbath. To do so properly I would need not only to investigate all the sabbath-related pericopes in depth but especially to do so in the light of his overall understanding of the law, which is obviously beyond my scope. Some helpful discussions, however, are found in Banks, *Jesus*, pp. 113-31, esp. pp. 128-31; Turner, 'Sabbath', pp. 100-57, esp. pp. 100-13; Wilson, *Law*, pp. 12-58, esp. pp. 31-39; Tyson, 'Scripture', pp. 89-104, esp. pp. 97-104; cf. also C.L. Blomberg, 'Law in Luke–Acts', *JSNT* 22 (1984), pp. 53-80. Some extracts from Turner's observations are worth quoting: 'Jesus' attitude to the Sabbath is clearly only one aspect of His attitude to the broader question of the law...In Him inheres the fulfillment of many strands of Old Testament hope; indeed the whole of the law, the prophets, and the psalms looked forward to his coming (24.44)...He appears to assert both its continuity and, in some areas, its discontinuity...Far from hallowing the Sabbath as a particularly appropriate day either for rest or for redemptive works, the Jesus of Luke's portrait continually subordinates the Sabbath to the demands of His own mission. Jesus' attitude to the law is entirely consistent with this; the law is being fulfilled but simultaneously transcended in His teaching and ministry, which together constitute the inauguration of a new covenant' (pp. 108-13). It is striking to note that, according to Turner's investigation, Luke's understanding of the sabbath and the law is quite similar to that of Matthew as I have discussed it in Chapters 3–5.

77.   See Turner, 'Sabbath', p. 107; Carson, 'Sabbath', p. 72. *Pace* Grundmann, *Lukas*, pp. 278-81; Bacchiocchi, *Sabbath*, p. 37.

78.   'Sabbath', p. 107.

against Jesus (e.g. 11.53-54). In the present pericope, as a matter of fact, the Pharisees quickly assume the role of opponents of Jesus rather than that of his followers (cf. vv. 1, 3-6; cf. also 6.7, 11; 15.2; 16.14; etc.).

To the unspoken challenge of the Pharisees (v. 1: αὐτοὶ ἦσαν παρατηρούμενοι αὐτόν),[79] Jesus responds with a question: ἔξεστιν τῷ σαββάτῳ θεραπεῦσαι ἢ οὔ; (v. 3).[80] It is striking that the Pharisees remain silent (v. 4: οἱ δὲ ἡσύχασαν) at his question,[81] since most probably the prohibition of healing on the sabbath is assumed by the Pharisees, if life is not in immediate danger. Even though we cannot be sure why they remain silent,[82] the implication of such silence after Jesus' forceful question is highly significant, especially when we take it together with a similar but more telling description of their inability to reply to another question from Jesus (v. 6: καὶ οὐκ ἴσχυσαν ἀνταποκριθῆναι πρὸς ταῦτα). In a relatively brief episode, such a double description of the silence of the opponents is remarkable. I, therefore, think it likely that Luke put such an impressive double response here intentionally, probably to highlight Jesus' authority over his opponents. Such a possibility becomes even stronger when we note that the initiative in the conversation is taken solely by Jesus, and the Pharisees in effect are not able to contribute a single word to it.

Though the Pharisees remained silent, Jesus must have known that his first question could not expect an affirmative response from them. Their silence is by no means that of agreement but that of having no other

---

79. Cf. also 6.7, where the Pharisees' intention of watching is explicitly stated—παρετηροῦντο δὲ αὐτὸν οἱ γραμματεῖς καὶ οἱ Φαρισαῖοι εἰ ἐν τῷ σαββάτῳ θεραπεύει, ἵνα εὕρωσιν κατηγορεῖν.

80. Even though a similar question is found in Mt. 12.10, there, unlike here, the question is raised by the Pharisees rather than Jesus (cf., however, v. 12b), and the form of the question there (εἰ ἔξεστιν τοῖς σάββασιν θεραπεῦσαι;), in fact, is quite different from that here.

81. A similar response is found in Mk 3.4 (οἱ δὲ ἐσιώπων), though there a different verb is used (Luke, however, does not have this response in its parallel [i.e. Lk. 6.9]; cf. also Mt. 12.12). But the preceding question in Mk 3.4 (and also in Lk. 6.9) is significantly different from that in here—i.e. 'saving life or killing' rather than 'healing or not', and the Pharisaic response to the one would be quite opposite to that to the other.

82. For various explanations, see, for example, Danker, *Jesus*, p. 268; Nolland, *Luke 9.21–18.34*, p. 746—he suggests, 'It is one thing to criticize Jesus for healing on the sabbath; it is another thing to take responsibility oneself for denying restoration to a needy person'.

choice before an authoritative figure. Even though he presumably recognizes their uncomfortable silence, Jesus carries on his healing ministry. His healing is thus an outright challenge to the authority of the Pharisaic halakhah, and thus has a highly provocative character. He performs healing not with the approval of the Pharisees but rather on his own authority as 'the Lord of the sabbath' as he himself has proclaimed in Lk. 6.5. Furthermore his healing is a kind of acted statement that 'it is lawful to heal on the sabbath' (cf. v. 3; cf. also 6.9). His first question and healing is to this extent anti-halakhic (rather than halakhic) and has a highly Christological character.

After healing the man with dropsy, Jesus raises the second question to the Pharisees: τίνος ὑμῶν υἱὸς ἢ βοῦς εἰς φρέαρ πεσεῖται, καὶ οὐκ εὐθέως ἀνασπάσει αὐτὸν ἐν ἡμέρᾳ τοῦ σαββάτου; (v. 5).[83] On the surface this question, unlike the first one (v. 3), seems to have no significant relevance to his healing activity (v. 4) and, therefore, sounds out of place. Is there, however, some more subtle link between Jesus' second question and his healing, which may make Jesus' argument effective?

The basic assumption of his question is that the Pharisees in front of him will *immediately* (εὐθέως) pull their son or ox out of water even on the sabbath if he/it falls into a well. Such a practice must have been allowed by most of the first-century Jews, especially in the case of a human being (cf. CD 11.16-17; 4Q251 2.6-7).[84] In that case, to Jesus' second question, unlike to the first one, the Pharisees would not raise any objection. But they could still raise an objection to Jesus' healing of the man (v. 4), since (in their judgment) he was presumably not in such an urgent situation. It seems, however, to be exactly against this seemingly obvious presumption that Jesus raises a question. Jesus, unlike the Pharisees, apparently thinks that the man with dropsy is indeed in an *urgent* situation like a son or an ox fallen into a well! In that case the

83. Although a similar question is found in Mt. 12.11, the sentence structure, content (e.g. υἱὸς ἢ βοῦς / πρόβατον; φρέαρ / βόθυνον; lack of εὐθέως in Matthew; etc.) and vocabulary (only 3 [or more precisely just one] words out of 17 [22 in Matthew] are identical in both questions—i.e. ὑμῶν[?], εἰς, καί[?]) of the two forms of question differ from each other significantly, and I doubt whether the two sayings came from exactly the same source. If the two sayings nevertheless came from a common source (i.e. Q material), then the sayings seem to witness that Matthew and Luke use varying recensions of Q material; cf. Marshall, *Luke*, p. 31; Turner, 'Sabbath', p. 107.

84. On the case of an animal, see *b. Šab.* 128b. For an extreme view, however, see CD. 11.13-14; 4Q251 2.5-6.

underlying contact between Jesus' question and his healing becomes clear: both of them are in an *urgent* situation, and they need *immediate* rescue. The interpretive key, then, lies in the word εὐθέως of v. 5. On what ground, however, does Jesus (and Luke) regard the man with dropsy to be in such an urgent situation? In the text itself we cannot find any definite clue for this question. In this connection the observation of the co-text of our pericope can be fruitful.

The present pericope is followed by two precepts (vv. 7-11, 12-14) and a concluding parable (vv. 15-24). The unity of vv. 1-24 is well recognized by many,[85] and Fitzmyer and others suggest that the pericope is used as a means to introduce the following table discourses.[86] The general theme of vv. 1-24 is criticism of the Pharisees. All four pericopes in the unit belong to the same setting, that is, Jesus being at table with the Pharisees (and the lawyers); apart from the healing pericope all the remaining three discourses in this section, in fact, concern a banquet or a dinner. E.E. Ellis interestingly suggests that the introductory episode (vv. 1-6) is applied by the concluding parable, the parable of the great banquet (vv. 15-24), as is the case elsewhere in Luke.[87] If his suggestion is acceptable, the point of application of the present pericope in the parable may be as follows: as the banquet of the kingdom of God is already prepared and the invitation to the banquet and response to it has an urgent character, so the exercise of the healing power of the kingdom of God and experience of it is urgent; as the poor, the maimed, the blind, and the lame who accept the invitation are finding their way into the banquet (instead of the long-invited guests who fail to see the urgency of the call to the banquet), the man with dropsy who is ready to accept Jesus' eschatological healing is experiencing the power of the kingdom of God (instead of the Pharisees who fail to see the urgent need of the man with dropsy for this eschatological healing). This application is, of course, by no means self-evident from the text itself. Nevertheless, the co-text of the pericope strongly indicates the possibility of such an application. If such an application is acceptable, Jesus' argument

85. Ellis, *Luke*, p. 192; Banks, *Jesus*, p. 129; Marshall, *Luke*, pp. 577-78; Turner, 'Sabbath', p. 108; Fitzmyer, *Luke X–XXIV*, p. 1038; Evans, *Luke*, p. 568; *et al.*

86. Fitzmyer, *Luke X–XXIV*, p. 1038; see also J.M. Creed, *The Gospel according to St Luke: The Greek Text with Introduction, Notes, and Indices* (London: Macmillan, 1930), p. 188; Evans, *Luke*, p. 568.

87. Ellis, *Luke*, p. 192; on other cases, see p. 179.

in his second question after his highly Christological healing activity is effective enough to show the eschatological significance of his sabbath healing ministry. Such an argument by Jesus may look extraordinary from a Pharisaic viewpoint.[88] His argument, however, is not meant to be halakhic. The Pharisaic halakhah, of course, is used but only rhetorically. The ultimate foundation of his argument is thus not on the Pharisaic halakhah itself but rather on his own authority as the one who exercises the eschatological healing power even on the sabbath because he is also the Lord of the sabbath. To this extent his healing, in the light of the second question, has implicitly an eschatological as well as a Christological character.

In short, from the above investigations of the pericope, one may conclude with some confidence that (1) the whole pericope portrays the authority of Jesus over the Pharisees and their halakhah as the Lord of the sabbath (and also as the one who exercises the eschatological healing power), and thus it has a highly Christological character; (2) Jesus' healing and his argument in the second question can be best understood in terms of the urgency of experiencing Jesus' own eschatological power of healing, and thus has (though implicitly) an eschatological character; (3) these points further support the previous conclusion that even though for Luke the question of the sabbath may be neither a live nor a sensitive issue, he, in fact, uses it as a springboard to bring the discussion to the heart of the matter, that is, Christology and eschatology.

c. *The Significance of the Absence of Luke 13.10-17, 14.1-6 in Matthew*
Does the absence of Luke's two unique pericopes in Matthew throw any light on Matthew's understanding of the sabbath? If it does, can we clarify it?[89]

As I mentioned above, Lk. 13.10-17 almost certainly comes from L *Sondergut*, though we cannot exclude completely the possibility that it

---

88.   In fact, they seem to fail to understand what Jesus is arguing for here, as their question in v. 15 indicates. As a matter of fact, their silent response in v. 6 does not necessarily imply their understanding but simply their inability to raise objections to Jesus' question and healing.

89.   The fundamental problem lying behind these questions is that we cannot be sure about the source(s) of the Lukan pericopes, and that without settling the source-problem we cannot reach a definite conclusion about the questions. My investigation in this section will, therefore, necessarily bring forward more than one possible conclusion according to the more probable but not yet certain hypotheses concerning the source(s).

comes from Q material or even from Mk 3.1-6. Lk. 14.1-6 probably comes from L *Sondergut*, but Q material still remains an equally possible candidate for its source.

If both pericopes came from L *Sondergut*, the significance of the absence of them in Matthew is minimal, if there is any. If one (Lk. 14.1-6 would be the more possible candidate) or both of the two, however, came from Q material, the subsequent question is why Matthew omitted it/them. One possible explanation is Matthew's characteristically economic and systematic style of writing.[90] Since the pericope(s) are more or less similar to that in Mt. 12.9-14 in theme (i.e. Jesus' healing on the sabbath), Matthew may have drawn the basic elements of the stories which he had in front of him and put them together in one pericope (i.e. 12.9-14). In that case Mt. 12.11-12 compensates for his omission of other stories elsewhere. Such a practice by Matthew is in contrast with Luke's way of dealing with his material, since Luke more or less faithfully reproduced presumably all the sabbath healing stories that he had in front of him. This reflects his tendency generally to preserve and reproduce the tradition 'more or less intact as it came to him'.[91] In that case C.F. Evans's suggestion that the repeated appearance of the sabbath healing story (exactly three times) 'shows the importance Luke attached to the subject'[92] is not very convincing. It becomes still less convincing when we recall the conclusions above that the focus of the sabbath healing stories in Luke is more on the theme of the presence of the kingdom of God than on sabbath observance (at least in the case of the last two pericopes), and that for Luke the question of the sabbath was most likely neither a live nor a sensitive issue.

Unlike Luke, however, for Matthew and his community the sabbath was most probably a live and sensitive issue (cf. Chapter 4). In that case, another explanation, which is not necessarily unrelated to the previous one, is possible: Matthew omitted the pericope(s) because of his concern about his context, in which the sabbath issue must be dealt with very carefully. We have already seen that Matthew quite possibly omitted all

90. On his characteristic style of writing, see especially France, *Evangelist*, pp. 123-65; Davies and Allison, *Matthew*, I, pp. 72-96.

91. See Banks, *Jesus*, pp. 128-31 (quotation from p. 128); cf. also C.F.D. Moule, 'The Christology of Acts', in L.E. Keck and J.L. Martyn (eds.), *Studies in Luke–Acts* (Philadelphia: Fortress Press, 1966), pp. 181-82; I.H. Marshall, *Luke: Historian and Theologian* (Exeter: Paternoster, 1970), pp. 216ff.

92. *Luke*, p. 568.

the sabbath references in relation to Jesus' visit to the synagogue and the 'at sundown' reference in order to avoid providing unnecessary support to the members in his community who had a legalistic tendency. A similar explanation may be possible for the present case. In such a sensitive situation repeating the sabbath healing stories could cause an unnecessary misunderstanding by those conservative members—a mis-understanding that Jesus attached a great importance to the sabbath or that he hallowed the sabbath as a specially suitable day for healing, as even a number of modern interpreters of Luke suggest on the basis of his repeated inclusion of the sabbath healing stories.[93] After all, Matthew, in comparison with Luke, is by no means more conservative in terms of the sabbath; on the contrary, he had great concern about the legalistic and conservative tendency in his community in relation to the sabbath issue.

Even though the contexts of the two evangelists were thus far differ-ent, it is interesting, however, to note that both evangelists present the sabbath in terms of Christology and eschatology. In all the sabbath peri-copes which I have discussed so far,[94] the ultimate issue for both evan-gelists is not the sabbath but the Christ who is the Lord of the sabbath (Mt. 12.8; Lk. 6.5), the fulfilment of the law (Mt. 5.17; Lk. 24.44), and the inaugurator of the kingdom of God (Mt. 5.20; 12.28; Lk. 11.20).

4. *The Sabbath Rest of the Women from Galilee* *(Luke 23.56; cf. Mark 16.1; Matthew 27.61–28.1)*

The last text to be investigated in these comparative studies is Lk. 23.56, which is once again unique to Luke. The pericopes to which Lk. 23.56 belongs (i.e. Lk. 23.50-56a; 23.56b–24.12) may have come from 'com-mon tradition' with some additions from L *Sondergut*.[95] Lk. 23.56 itself

---

93. See, for example, for the latter case, Grundmann, *Lukas*, pp. 278-81; Bacchiocchi, *Sabbath*, p. 37, and for the former, Evans, *Luke*, p. 568.

94. As a matter of fact, I have now discussed practically all the sabbath-related pericopes in the synoptic Gospels apart from Lk. 23.56 which I will discuss in the next section. Though Mk 2.23–3.6 and Lk. 6.1-11 are not directly discussed sepa-rately, the crucial issues involved were discussed in Chapter 4 when I investigated the central pericopes (that is, their parallels in Matthew).

95. On the sources of these pericopes, see Grundmann, *Lukas*, pp. 436, 439; V. Taylor, *The Passion Narrative of St Luke* (Cambridge: Cambridge University Press, 1972), pp. 99-109; Fitzmyer, *Luke X–XXIV*, pp. 1523-25, 1533-43; Taylor also detects some contacts with Johannine tradition.

probably came from L *Sondergut*,[96] though the possibility of Luke's redaction cannot be entirely ruled out.[97] An intimate relation between Lk. 23.56b and 24.1(-12) is well recognized by a number of scholars (cf. especially the μέν...δέ construction in 23.56b–24.1).[98] We should, then, take Lk. 23.56a as the conclusion of the preceding story (i.e. the burial of Jesus) and 23.56b as the beginning of the following story (i.e. the empty tomb found by the women).[99] There is no compelling reason to doubt the general historicity of the two stories.[100]

According to the later Mishnaic tradition (*m. Šab.* 23.5), the Jews were allowed to 'make ready [on the Sabbath] all that is needful for the dead, and anoint it and wash it...' It is, however, not clear whether that was also the case during the first century CE in Jerusalem. Luke's presentation of the women's behaviour in Lk. 23.56[101] rather seems to indicate that a stricter view was in force during that period.[102] In any case, Luke clearly portrays the women as keeping the sabbath 'according to the commandment' (κατὰ τὴν ἐντολήν; cf. Exod. 20.8-10; Deut. 5.12-15). If his portrayal is historically reliable, it is interesting to note that the women were still faithful to the sabbath commandment. While there is nothing unusual in the women's observance of the sabbath commandment, it nonetheless suggests, as discussed above, that they had not fully understood the implication that Jesus had fulfilled the sabbath and become the Lord of the sabbath. This is probably because they lived in a distinctive period when much of Jesus' redemptive work (e.g.

96.   Grundmann, *Lukas*, p. 436; Taylor, *Passion*, pp. 101-109.

97.   Evans, *Luke*, p. 883.

98.   Marshall, *Luke*, p. 881; Fitzmyer, *Luke X–XXIV*, p. 1543; Evans, *Luke*, p. 883.

99.   Marshall, *Luke*, p. 881; Taylor, *Passion*, p. 103; Fitzmyer, *Luke X–XXIV*, p. 1543; cf. also Nolland, *Luke 18.35–24.53*, p. 1162—he suggests that 'v 56b is really a transitional pause between 23:50-56a and 24:1-12'.

100.   Schweizer, *Mark*, p. 361; Ellis, *Luke*, pp. 273-76.

101.   For various attempts to explain the seeming discrepancy between Lk. 23.56a and Mk 16.1, see, for example, Leaney, *Luke*, p. 288; Rordorf, *Sunday*, p. 121; Marshall, *Luke*, p. 881; Turner, 'Sabbath', pp. 105-106; R.E. Brown, *The Death of the Messiah*, II (2 vols.; London: Geoffrey Chapman, 1994), p. 1257.

102.   Cf. Fitzmyer, *Luke X–XXIV*, p. 1530; Nolland, *Luke 18:35-24:53*, p. 1166; cf. also Brown, *Death*, p. 1258—he, however, sees *m. Šab.* 8.1 behind the women's behaviour. For some different understandings of the women's behaviour in Lk. 23.56 in the light of *m. Šab.* 23.5, see J. Jeremias, *The Eucharistic Words of Jesus* (trans. N. Perrin; London: SCM Press, 2nd edn, 1966), pp. 74-75; Marshall, *Luke*, p. 883; Evans, *Luke*, p. 884.

resurrection, ascension as well as his second coming) was still waiting for its accomplishment; or because, if they did grasp the theological meaning of Jesus' fulfilment of the sabbath, it took time for them to draw from the theological meaning its implication for their practice in relation to the sabbath.

Some might argue that Luke's unique portrayal of the women as faithful observants of the sabbath commandment demonstrates Luke's high view of the sabbath.[103] Considering, however, that Luke, like Matthew and Mark, elsewhere puts the sabbath under the authority of Jesus who is the Lord of the sabbath (cf. especially 6.5) and also even under the need of various people, it is rather unlikely that this is the case here. Luke's inclusion of the unique portrayal may be better explained by supposing that Luke, as elsewhere, more or less faithfully reproduced his source which may originally have included this feature. This explanation is in line with the conclusion above that Luke is less sensitive and careful in presenting the sabbath material, probably because the sabbath was no longer a real issue for him and his reader. Perhaps, as some suggest, Luke may have included the portrayal (especially, κατὰ τὴν ἐντολήν) intentionally in order to make a structural balance with the descriptions of the figures involved in Jesus' birth and youth (e.g. Jesus' parents, Simeon, Anna; cf. Lk. 2.22-24, 25, 37, 41-42) who are also portrayed as being loyal to the law.[104] In doing this Luke may well have intended to put Jesus' life in the continuing line of the Old Testament— his life, from his birth to his death, was carried out in full contact with the Old Testament, but not for its own sake but to fulfil it (cf. Lk. 24.44). Finally, it may be noteworthy that there is no further positive portrayal of the disciples' observance of the sabbath beyond this point (i.e. Jesus' resurrection) either by Luke or by any other Gospels or books in the New Testament.[105]

If Lk. 23.56 came from L *Sondergut* or from Luke himself, the significance of its absence in Matthew is minimal, if any. Even if it came from Q material, however, it is not difficult to explain why Matthew omitted it. Unlike for Luke, since the sabbath was most probably a live and sensitive issue for Matthew and his community, Matthew may well have

---

103. E.g. Bacchiocchi, *New Testament*, p. 89.

104. Cf. Marshall, *Luke*, p. 883; Brown, *Death*, p. 1287.

105. Cf. F. Godet, *A Commentary on the Gospel of St Luke*, II (2 vols.; trans. E.W. Shelders; Edinburgh: T. & T. Clark, 1887, 1889), p. 343; Schweizer, *Luke*, p. 364.

omitted the passage, once again in order to avoid encouraging those members of his community who had a legalistic tendency to observe the sabbath scrupulously as an expression of their loyalty to the commandment (the very attitude which Jesus has refuted in Mt. 12.1-8 par., 9-14 par.; cf. also Lk. 13.10-17; 14.1-6).

5. *Conclusions*

In this chapter I have investigated all the sabbath-related passages in Mark and/or Luke which are, in Matthew, either absent altogether or present as non-sabbath passages. The main aim of the investigations of those passages has obviously been to provide explanation(s) for why they are missing or present in different forms in Matthew, though I have also reached some additional conclusions about the significance and implication of those Markan and/or Lukan passages in their own right. The following is the summary of what I have concluded.

1) Jesus' constant presence in the synagogue on the sabbath (Mk 1.21 par.; 6.2 par.; Lk. 6.6; etc.) was at most a matter of custom rather than of obedience to Torah, and, therefore, 'provides little real evidence of *theological* commitment on behalf of Jesus...to Sabbath worship'.[106]

2) Jesus' exorcism and healing on the sabbath in Mk 1.21-34 and Lk. 4.31-41 already betrays his understanding of the sabbath in the light of his fulfilment of it, as clearly revealed in Mk 2.27, 28 par.; 3.4-5 par. (cf. also Mt. 12.5-6, 7, 11-12).

3) It is highly unlikely that Luke intended to assign any theological significance to the sabbath (for example, 'a fitting memorial of Jesus' redemptive activities', as Bacchiocchi puts it) by mentioning it in the cotext of the programmatic announcement of Jesus' ministry (Lk. 4.16-21).

4) Though Mk 1.32 par. and Lk. 23.56 respectively indicate that the ordinary Jews in the time of Jesus and also even some of his disciples before his resurrection observed the sabbath according to the tradition and/or the commandment, such a fact by no means affirms that Jesus expected them to do so. My investigations in Chapters 4, 5 and 6 as a whole rather steer the verdict in the opposite direction.

5) For Luke and his readers, unlike for Matthew, the sabbath was probably neither a live nor a sensitive issue, and Luke therefore seems to have much more freedom in presenting the sabbath material than Matthew. He seems to reproduce his source more or less faithfully.

106. Turner, 'Sabbath', p. 102.

6) The focus of most sabbath passages in Mark and Luke (e.g. Mk 1.21-34 par.; Lk. 4.16-21; 13.10-17; 14.1-6) is, as in Mt. 12.1-8 par., 9-14 par., more on Christology and eschatology than on the sabbath itself. Even though the observance of the sabbath may be, unlike for Matthew, neither a live nor a sensitive issue for Luke, once he is dealing with the issue, he also presents it, like Matthew (and also Mark), in terms of Christology and eschatology.

7) It is thus extremely doubtful whether any of the Markan and Lukan (as well as Matthean) sabbath passages implies or even demonstrates a high view of the sabbath.

8) Matthew's probable omissions or modifications of the Markan and/or Lukan sabbath passages by no means show that Matthew is more conservative than Mark or Luke in respect of the sabbath. They witness instead that Matthew is much more careful in presenting the sabbath material than Mark or Luke, most probably because the sabbath was still a live and sensitive issue for his community: since he was deeply concerned about the legalistic observance of the sabbath in his community, he sometimes modifies or even omits certain sabbath passages or phrases which he thinks might unnecessarily encourage such a legalistic tendency.

9) From the above investigations and observations, we can note that in the presentations of the sabbath material in Matthew, Mark and Luke there are significant similarities (e.g. Christological and eschatological focus, no high view of the sabbath, criticisms against Pharisaic way of keeping the sabbath) as well as outstanding differences (e.g. Matthew's greater care in presenting the sabbath material than Luke and Mark; unique passages/phrases in each Gospel). The similarities may be best explained by the common origin of their sabbath materials (from common tradition, Q material, M *Sondergut*, or L *Sondergut*) which is most likely Jesus' teaching itself,[107] while the differences can be explained by the different literary style and structure of each Gospel and more importantly by the different contexts of writing which may have led each evangelist to have much or little focus on and concern about certain issues.

---

107. We have already seen on various occasions the unlikeliness of the creation of sabbath controversy materials by the early Christian communities. See above, for example, Chapter 4, section 3. Cf. also, Pesch, *Markusevangelium*, I, p. 183.

Chart 1
Sabbath References in the Synoptic Gospels[108]

Matthew (11)	Mark (13)	Luke (20)
	1.21-34	*4.31-41*
(4.13)-noS	1.21	4.31
(8.16)-noS	(1.32)-sunset	(4.40)-sunset
12.1-8	*2.23-28*	*6.1-5*
12.1	2.23	6.1
12.2	2.24	6.2
12.5 (×2)	–	–
–	2.27 (×2)	–
12.8	2.28	6.5
12.9-14	*3.1-6*	*6.6-11*
(12.9)-noS	(3.1)-noS	6.6
12.10	3.2	6.7
12.11	–	(13.15; 14.5)
12.12	3.4	6.9
(13.53-58)	*6.1-6*	*4.16-30*
(13.54)-noS	6.2	**4.16**
		13.10-17
–	–	13.10
–	–	13.14 (×2)
(12.11)	–	13.15
–	–	13.16
		14.1-6
–	–	14.1
–	–	14.3
(12.11)	–	14.5
–	–	18.12 (week)

108. Non-synoptic sabbath references in the New Testament are as follows: Jn 5.1-18 (esp. v. 17); 7.22-23; 9.1-41 (esp. v. 4); Acts 1.12; 13.5, 14, (27), 42, 44; 15.21; 16.13; 17.2; 18.4; (20.7); (Rom. 14.5-8); (1 Cor. 16.2); (Gal. 4.10); Col. 2.16; Heb. 4.1-11.

The following are 'first day'/'Lord's day' references: Acts 20.7—first day of the week; 1 Cor. 16.2—first day of the week; Rev. 1.10—ἐν τῇ κυριακῇ ἡμέρᾳ.

24.20	(13.18)-noS	*(21.23)-noS*
27.57-noS	15.42 (+DP)	(23.54)
–	(15.42)	23.54 (+DP)
–	–	**23.56** (rest)
[27.62] (DP) (vv. 62-66)	–	–
28.1	16.1	*24.1-noS*
28.1 (week)	16.2 (week)	24.1 (week)
28.9-noS	16.9 (week)	*24.10-noS*

Comments on Chart 1
1. **bold**—passages/verses which are the main objects of my exegetical studies
2. (verse)—an indirect parallel in a different co-text
3. 'noS'—no σάββατον appearance
4. 'week'—the term σάββατον is used in the meaning of the 'week' rather than the 'sabbath'
5. *italic*—no parallel of the term, phrase, or clause, though the co-text is same
6. 'DP'—the day of Preparation
7. [verse]—no σάββατον material, but related to the sabbath

Chapter 7

JESUS AND THE SABBATH IN MATTHEW'S GOSPEL:
ITS SIGNIFICANCE AND INFLUENCE IN THE EARLY CHURCH

It is frequently argued that the influence of Matthew's Gospel on the
'Apostolic Fathers',[1] the earliest extant non-canonical writings, was
greater than that of any other Gospel.[2] If so, it is appropriate to compare
and/or contrast Matthew's treatment of the sabbath in the light of Jesus'
fulfilment of it with their treatment of the sabbath (and also of the Lord's
day/the eighth day etc., which frequently appears as a related issue).
Such a comparison may be expected (i) to enable us to evaluate how
Matthew's treatment of the sabbath was adopted, adapted or overlooked

1.   The term 'Apostolic Fathers' is defined by F.L. Cross and E.A. Livingstone
(eds.), *The Oxford Dictionary of the Christian Church* (Oxford: Oxford University
Press, 2nd rev. edn, 1983), p. 76, thus: 'The title given since the later 17th cent. to
those Fathers of the age immediately succeeding the New Testament period whose
works in whole or in part have survived'. Unless otherwise stated, the texts come
from K. Lake (trans.), *Apostolic Fathers* (2 vols.; LCL; London: Heinemann, 1912,
1913). A useful collection of the sabbath and Lord's day texts with German
translations is found in W. Rordorf, *Sabbat und Sontag in der Alten Kirche* (Zürich:
Theologischer Verlag, 1972). Other translations are also found in A. Roberts and
J. Donaldson (eds.), *The Ante-Nicene Fathers*, I (Grand Rapids: Eerdmans, repr.
1973); J.A. Kleist, *The Didache, Barnabas, St Polycarp, Papias, Diognetus*
(London: Longmans, Green, 1948); C.C. Richardson, *Early Christian Fathers* (New
York: Macmillan, 1953); *et al.*, to which frequent references will be made whenever
it is required.
2.   E.g. E. Massaux, *The Influence of the Gospel of Saint Matthew on Christian
Literature before Saint Irenaeus* (3 vols.; trans. N.J. Belval and S. Hecht; NGS, 5/1-
3; Macon, GA: Mercer University Press, 1990–93); Luz, *Matthew 1–7*, pp. 92-93.
For a sceptical view, however, see, for example, H. Köster, *Synoptische Überlieferung bei den Apostolischen Vätern* (Berlin: Akademie-Verlag, 1957). A brief but
useful survey of the differing views of this issue is found in F. Neirynck, 'Preface to
the Reprint', in Massaux, *Influence*, I, pp. xi-xix. The probability of such an argument will be discussed in due course in the following sections of this chapter.

by them, and (ii) to validate further some aspects of our understanding of Matthew's treatment as we have investigated it in the previous chapters. The sabbath/Lord's day references in the Apostolic Fathers, however, are surprisingly scanty, and, as a matter of fact, only four references are found in four writings (Ignatius, *Magn.* 9.1; *Barn.* 15; *Did.* 14.1; *Diogn.* 4.1-3).[3] Nor do any of these references (except perhaps *Diogn.* 4.3) directly reflect any of Matthew's sabbath references. Moreover, since the picture of the Christian world at the beginning of the second century as well as of the origins (i.e. authors, dates, and places) of those writings (except probably for Ignatius's *Letter to the Magnesians*) is so obscure, our discussion must necessarily be tentative. It may seem, then, that this investigation will involve many difficulties but pay few dividends;[4] but in fact we shall find that some positive results emerge.

1. *Ignatius*

In spite of at least three recent attempts to challenge the modern consensus[5] concerning the authenticity of Ignatius's letters,[6] most scholars[7]

---

3.   Apart from these occurrences, two interesting references to ἡ κυριακή appear in the *Gospel of Peter* (9.35; 12.50), which may well stem from the time of the Apostolic Fathers; see Brown, *Death*, II, pp. 1341-48. Though these uses of ἡ κυριακή in place of μία (τῶν) σαββάτων ('the first day of the week') used in the Resurrection narratives of the canonical gospels (Mt. 28.1 par.; cf. Jn 20.1) do show that by the time the *Gospel of Peter* was written the term was used to refer to Sunday (or at least the Easter Sunday; see R. Bauckham, 'The Lord's Day', in Carson [ed.], *Lord's Day*, p. 229), they do not carry any significant theological weight in the context; I will therefore leave them aside in this study.

4.   Cf. C. Trevett, 'Approaching Matthew from the Second Century: The Underused Ignatian Correspondence', *JSNT* 20 (1984), p. 65.

5.   The consensus was established especially by T. Zahn, *Ignatii et Polycarpi Epistulae, Martyria, Fragmenta* (Leipzig: Hinrichs, 1876) and J.B. Lightfoot, *The Apostolic Fathers*. II. *S. Ignatius, S. Polycarp* (3 vols.; London: Macmillan, 1889).

6.   R. Weijenborg, *Les lettres d'Ignace d'Antioche* (Leiden: Brill, 1969); *idem*, 'Is Evagrius Ponticus the Author of the *Longer Recension* of the Ignatian Letters?', *Antonianum* 44 (1969), pp. 339-47; J. Rius-Camp, *The Four Authentic Letters of Ignatius, The Martyr* (Rome: Pontificium Institutum Orientalium Studiorum, 1979); R. Joly, *Le dossier d'Ignace d'Antioche* (Brussels: Editions de l'université, 1979); cf. also H. Delafosse, 'Nouvel examen des lettres d'Ignace d'Antioche', *Revue d'histoire et de littérature religieuse* 8 (1922), pp. 303-37, 477-533.

7.   E.g. C.P.H. Bammel, 'Ignatian Problems' *JTS* 33 (1982), pp. 62-97; W.R. Schoedel, *Ignatius of Antioch* (Hermeneia; Philadelphia: Fortress Press, 1985),

remain confident about the authenticity of the seven letters[8] of the 'middle recension'.[9] If these letters are authentic, the date is generally agreed to be somewhere between 100–118 CE.[10]

On his way to martyrdom in Rome, Ignatius, the bishop of Antioch in Syria, wrote seven letters, four from Smyrna and three from Troas. One of these letters, the *Letter to the Magnesians*, includes a brief but problematic reference to sabbath observance: Εἰ οὖν οἱ ἐν παλαιοῖς πράγμασιν ἀναστραφέντες εἰς καινότητα ἐλπίδος ἦλθον, μηκέτι σαββατίζοντες, ἀλλὰ κατὰ κυριακὴν [ζωὴν] ζῶντες, ἐν ᾗ καὶ ἡ ζωὴ ἡμῶν ἀνέτειλεν δι᾽ αὐτοῦ καὶ τοῦ θανάτου αὐτοῦ...(9.1). The first problem is raised by the difference between the Greek and Latin texts: (i) the Greek reading—κατὰ κυριακὴν ζωὴν ζῶντες; (ii) the Latin reading—*secundum Dominicam viventes*. As most scholars (except for some Seventh-day Adventist scholars[11]) suggest,[12] various (linguistic and

pp. 5-7; C. Trevett, *A Study of Ignatius of Antioch in Syria and Asia* (Lampeter: Edwin Mellen Press, 1992), pp. 9-15; cf. also V. Corwin, *St Ignatius and Christianity in Antioch* (New Haven: Yale University Press, 1960), pp. 3-10.

8. Letters to the Ephesians, Magnesians, Trallians, Romans, Philadelphians, Smyrnaeans, and Polycarp, the bishop of Smyrna.

9. On the three recensions of Ignatius's letters, see esp. F. Guy, '"The Lord's Day" in the Letter of Ignatius to the Magnesians', *AUSS* 2 (1964), pp. 2-6; Schoedel, *Ignatius*, pp. 3-4; cf. also Lightfoot, *Ignatius*, II, pp. 3-7; Lake, *Fathers*, I, pp. 167-69; *et al.*

10. See, esp. Lightfoot, *Ignatius*, II, pp. 435-72; cf. also Lake, *Fathers*, I, p. 166; R.E. Brown and J.P. Meier, *Antioch and Rome* (London: Geoffrey Chapman, 1983), p. 77 (108–117 CE); Schoedel, *Ignatius*, p. 5, esp. n. 30; *et al.*

11. E.g. R.A. Kraft, 'Some Notes on Sabbath Observance in Early Christianity', *AUSS* 3 (1965), pp. 27-28; R.B. Lewis, 'Ignatius and the "Lord's Day"', *AUSS* 6 (1968), pp. 46-59; Bacchiocchi, *Sabbath*, pp. 214-16—his argument here is most disappointing, because he dismisses the obvious counter-evidence in 'the long recension' (i.e. 'let every friend of Christ keep the Lord's Day as a festival, the resurrection-day...', quotation from Roberts and Donaldson, *Fathers*, I, p. 63), while he makes use of the same recension to support his further argument that the 'sabbatizing' which Ignatius condemns 'could hardly be the repudiation of the Sabbath as a day'. Their arguments in general are more or less strained, as Schoedel, *Ignatius*, p. 123 n. 3 points out. For similar but more balanced treatments of the issue, see Guy, 'Magnesians', pp. 1-17; K.A. Strand, 'Another Look at "Lord's Day" in the Early Church and in Rev. I.10', *NTS* 13 (1967), pp. 178-79.

12. E.g. Zahn, *Ignatii*, pp. 36-38; Lightfoot, *Ignatius*, II, pp. 129-30; Lake, *Fathers*, I, pp. 204-205 (but without a comment on the variant reading); C.K. Barrett, 'Jews and Judaizers in the Epistles of Ignatius', in R. Hamerton-Kelly and R. Scroggs (eds.), *Jews, Greeks and Christians: Religious Cultures in Late Antiquity*

co-textual as well as textual) factors favour the Latin reading and, there-fore, the omission of ζωήν. Even if ζωήν is an original part of the text, however, the translation 'living a life in accordance with the Lord's day'[13] seems more natural than the alternative translation 'living accord-ing to the Lord's life', especially in the light of the preceding counter-part clause (μηκέτι σαββατίζοντες) and also of the following clause.[14] My translation of the whole sentence then is as follows: 'If then those who walked in old customs came to newness of hope, no longer keeping the sabbath, but living [a life] in accordance with the Lord's day, on which also our life arose through him and his death...'

Once we have adopted this translation, however, the interpretation of the text (9.1) still remains problematic, especially in relation to (i) the ref-erent of those who [previously] walked in old customs [but now] came to newness of hope; (ii) the precise meaning of 'no longer keeping the sabbath, but living in accordance with the Lord's day'. Since 9.1 is closely linked with its immediate co-text (8.1–10.3;[15] note οὖν in 9.1), a proper interpretation of it requires a careful consideration of the co-text. The flow of argument in 8.1–10.3 as I understand it, and my interpre-tation of 9.1 in that flow, is as follows:

1) The key issue for Ignatius now is 'Judaism'[16] which is on the one

---

(Leiden: Brill, 1976), p. 238; Schoedel, *Ignatius*, p. 123, esp. n. 3.

13. This translation is possible by treating ζωήν as a cognate accusative; see Guy, 'Magnesians', pp. 15-16; Bauckham, 'Lord's Day', p. 247 n. 29.

14. Cf. Bauckham, 'Lord's Day', p. 228; he offers a useful discussion of the usage of κυριακή with or without ἡμέρα with the meaning 'the Lord's day' (= Sunday) in the same article, pp. 222-50. For a discussion of the two possible translations, see Guy, 'Magnesians', pp. 12-15—his position is, however, neutral.

15. *Magn.* 8.1-10.3 clearly constitutes a thematic block (i.e. on Judaism and Christianity). Up to 7.2 the theme is unity under the authority of the bishop, and 11.1–15.1 constitutes the closing and farewell.

16. Various views as regards the identities of Ignatius's opponents have been proposed, and good surveys of those views are found in Barrett, 'Ignatius', pp. 220-30; Trevett, *Study*, pp. 150-52. The central question of those various views is whether the opponents are two (or more) different groups (i.e. the Judaizers and the docetists) or a single group with double (or multiple) characters. After an extensive and thorough investigation, Trevett carefully and convincingly concludes that 'in my view Ignatius's descriptions of the errors leave the balance of probability on the side of two, separate ones (and not just two,...), though he may indeed have known that in some places, at some times, a more syncretistic phenomenon had existed' (see her *Study*, p. 152; cf. also Bammel, 'Problems', p. 83). Trevett, *Study*, p. 86, also points out that Ignatius was particularly concerned about the presence of Judaizing

hand identified with 'strange doctrines' and 'old fables' which are profit-
less (cf. 1 Tim. 1.4; 4.7; Tit. 1.14) and on the other contrasted with
'grace' (8.1).

2) The Old Testament 'prophets', who lived according to Jesus Christ
and were therefore persecuted, were inspired by Jesus' 'grace' so that
they must persuade 'the disobedient' to believe in Jesus Christ who is
God's 'Word' (8.2). The Old Testament 'prophets', 'Jesus' and his
'grace' are thus distinct from 'Judaism' and indeed contrasted with it;
and 'the disobedient' may refer to the early Jewish Christians who had
believed in Jesus on the ground of the Old Testament prophets' witness
to him.

3) The early Jewish Christians (not the Old Testament prophets)[17] no
longer kept the sabbath but lived in accordance with the Lord's day
(9.1a). Sabbath observance is thus brought forward as a characteristic
feature of Judaism which the converted Jewish Christians were expected
to give up; and living in accordance with the Lord's day is characterized
as a distinctive feature of Christian life.

4) Like the early Jewish Christians, *we* (= Ignatius and his contemporary Christians, especially the Magnesians) [also live in accordance with
the Lord's day],[18] on which 'our life arose through him and his death'
(9.1b). In the light of this clause, we may suppose that the clause 'living
in accordance with ($\kappa\alpha\tau\acute{\alpha}$) the Lord's day' refers not to observing the
day as a rest day[19] but to observing the day by worshipping the Lord
who was raised on that day from death and by celebrating their participation in his resurrection quite possibly through eucharist (cf. 4.1;

Christians in Magnesia who were 'a group distinct from docetists', and that 'the
docetists were in fact not active within the community Ignatius was addressing in
Magnesia' (cf. *Magn.* 11-12). I will adopt Trevett's conclusions in the subsequent
discussions.

17. See Lightfoot, *Ignatius*, II, p. 128; Schoedel, *Ignatius*, p. 123—he properly
points out that 'It would be unnatural to attribute to the "most divine prophets" as
described in *Mag.* 8.1-2 the need for conversion referred to here' (cf. also n. 2); cf.
Rordorf, *Sunday*, pp. 139-40; Bauckham, 'Post-Apostolic Church', pp. 260-61.
Pace Lewis, 'Ignatius', p. 50; Strand, 'Lord's Day', p. 178; Bacchiocchi, *Sabbath*,
p. 215.

18. This seems to be presupposed in Ignatius's argument; note the change of
personal pronoun from the third person to the first, but without break of thought.

19. Rordorf, *Sunday*, pp. 154-58, properly points out the impracticability of
keeping the Lord's day (= Sunday) as a day of rest in the second century; cf. also
Bauckham, 'Post-Apostolic Church', p. 274.

cf. also Ignatius, *Phld.* 7.1-8.2; *Did.* 14.1; *Barn.* 15.9; Justin, *First Apology* 67.7).[20]

5) The 'mystery' of *our* participation in Jesus' death and resurrection, *our* 'faith', and *our* 'suffering' helps *us* to become 'disciples of Jesus Christ' who is 'our only teacher' (9.1c; cf. Mt. 23.8). The ultimate concern of Ignatius's argument thus seems to be focused on strengthening the Magnesians in their discipleship (cf. also 10.1).

6) Not only *we* are disciples of Jesus Christ but even the Old Testament prophets were his 'disciples in the Spirit'; they indeed looked forward to Jesus Christ as their teacher, and, therefore, when Jesus came [and fulfilled their expectation] he raised [not only *us* but also] them from the dead (9.2).[21] Once again Ignatius turns to the relation between Jesus and the Old Testament prophets. His implicit argument may be that it is not Judaism and Judaizers, who keep the sabbath, but Jesus and his disciples (= Christians), who live in accordance with the Lord's day, who are in the continuing line of the Old Testament, because Jesus was the ultimate goal of Old Testament prophecy.

7) Finally, a concluding exhortation in relation to Judaism and Judaizers follows, in which Judaism (= the evil leaven grown old and sour) is once again contrasted with Christ (= the new leaven) and Christianity (10.1-3).

If my overview of 8.1–10.3 and interpretation of 9.1 in the light of it is right, one may make the following observations: (i) it is striking that Ignatius brings forward sabbath observance as a characteristic feature of Judaism which even Jewish Christians are expected to give up; (ii) it is interesting to note that Ignatius mentions the Lord's day in connection with the sabbath, though he may not have considered the day as a day of rest and still less as the Christian sabbath (as large parts of the Christian church since the Middle Ages understood it);[22] (iii) it should be pointed out that, even though the Lord's day is referred to as a kind of badge of Christian identity, the real focus of Ignatius's argument seems to be on strengthening the Magnesians in their discipleship and on

---

20. See Rordorf, *Sunday*, pp. 210-11; Barrett, 'Ignatius', pp. 224, 236.

21. Might this be, however, a reflection of Mt. 27.52? In that case, my interpretive suggestion in the square bracket (i.e. 'not only us but also') must be given up.

22. For the development of the idea of the Lord's day as the Christian sabbath, see esp. Bauckham, 'Post-Apostolic Church', pp. 275-98; *idem*, 'Sabbath and Sunday in the Medieval Church in the West', in Carson (ed.), *Lord's Day*, pp. 300-309.

pointing out the fact that Jesus Christ is the continuation of the Old Testament and perhaps its ultimate fulfilment; (iv) I suspect that the Judaizers who are supposed to deny Christ's grace (8.1; cf. 10.2-3) were, as C. Trevett suggests after her thorough investigation, 'overly-legalistic'.[23] What would be, then, the implications of these points observed above for this study?

The crucial question is whether Ignatius knew Matthew and used it in his writings as a source. Opinions are still widely divided among scholars. Most scholars, however, seem to agree that Ignatius at least shared a common source with Matthew's Gospel,[24] if not the Gospel itself.[25] In relation to our text itself (*Magn.* 9.1a), however, it is not easy to judge its link with the Matthean sabbath references, since it is neither a direct quotation of nor even an allusion to those references. Nevertheless, considering that its immediate co-text betrays remarkable reflections of the Matthean type of teaching regarding the Pharisees and the prophets (e.g. *Magn.* 8.2 // Mt. 23.29, 34; cf. also Mt. 5.11-12; *Magn.* 9.1c // Mt. 23.10; *Magn.* 9.2 // Mt. 27.52), I suspect that *Magn.* 9.1a could well be a reflection of the two Matthean pericopes regarding the sabbath controversies between Jesus and the Pharisees. Ignatius may well have identified the Judaizers' sabbath observance in his own time with the Pharisees' stringent attitude to the sabbath in the controversies, and, since the Pharisees' attitude was refuted by Jesus, Ignatius may have condemned the Judaizers' sabbath observance altogether. In that case, Ignatius may have understood the practical implication of Jesus' fulfilment of the sabbath for Christians as giving up sabbath observance altogether, especially when sabbath observance endangers the centrality

---

23. Trevett, *Study*, p. 177; cf. also P.J. Donahue, 'Jewish Christianity in the letters of Ignatius of Antioch', *VC* 32 (1978), pp. 81-93.

24. E.g. Köster, *Überlieferung*, pp. 24-61; J. Smit Sibinga, 'Ignatius and Matthew', *NovT* 8 (1966), pp. 263-83; D.A. Hagner, 'The Sayings of Jesus in the Apostolic Fathers and Justin Martyr', in D. Wenham (ed.), *Gospel Perspectives*, V (Sheffield: JSOT Press, 1984), pp. 240, 263 n. 31; Trevett, 'Matthew', pp. 62-64.

25. There are, however, not a few scholars who see the Gospel itself as a source of Ignatius; for example, B.H. Streeter, *The Four Gospels: A Study of Origins* (London: Macmillan, 1924), pp. 504-507; Massaux, *Influence*, I, p. 96; C.C. Richardson, *The Christianity of Ignatius of Antioch* (New York: AMS Press, 1967), pp. 60, 103 n. 105; W.G. Kümmel, *Introduction to the New Testament* (trans. H.C. Kee; London: SCM Press, 2nd edn, 1975), p. 119, esp. n. 61; W.-D. Köhler, *Die Rezeption des Matthäusevangeliums in der Zeit vor Irenäus* (WUNT, 2/24; Tübingen: Mohr, 1987), pp. 73-96.

of Jesus Christ in Christian faith as presumably he believed was the case among the Magnesians (cf. *Magn.* 9.1; 10.2-3).[26] As so much, however, depends on conjectures and presuppositions, any definite conclusion seems unlikely. Nevertheless, if my reconstruction of Ignatius's interpretation and contextualization of Matthew's treatment of the sabbath in the light of Jesus' fulfilment of it is plausible, this helps us to reinforce the tentative conclusion in Chapter 4 on the practical implication of Jesus' teaching regarding the sabbath as presented in Matthew, since most probably Ignatius was a person who may have lived not far away from Matthew and his community in terms of time gap (less than one generation, and some scholars even suggest only one decade), geography (Matthew—Syria or Palestine; Ignatius—Antioch in Syria; Magnesia in Asia Minor) and problem (i.e. the legalistic tendency). He could, therefore, have more or less directly experienced or at least had contact with the context which Matthew had been faced with and the manner in which Matthew had dealt with the context. In other words, he was a person who could have reflected Matthew's intention in his Gospel, and/or more importantly the impact of Matthew's Gospel in his community during the subsequent two or three decades since the Gospel had been written, *more closely than anyone else* even among the Apostolic Fathers (perhaps apart from the author of the *Didache*).

Having said this, however, I should also point out that there are significant differences between Ignatius and Matthew in their treatments of the sabbath: (i) Whereas in Matthew sabbath observance itself is not clearly condemned (note, however, that the sabbath is downplayed in comparison with the temple and Jesus and perhaps even with human need), in Ignatius sabbath observance is condemned outright without any explanation or reservation. This difference, however, may be explained by their different contexts. Perhaps the legalistic tendency faced by Ignatius was much more severe than that faced by Matthew and Ignatius may have needed more outright negative instruction than Matthew needed.[27] We may, however, also need to consider more

---

26. Could Ignatius have been also influenced by Paul's rebuke in Gal. 4.10 (cf. also Col. 2.16-17)? As regards the possibility of Ignatius's acquaintance with Pauline letters, see Massaux, *Influence*, I, pp. 105-16, esp. p. 105; Corwin, *Ignatius*, pp. 66-67.

27. Furthermore, we may suppose that Ignatius did not face a delicate tension between the church and the synagogue, which Matthew may still have faced and which may have prevented him from giving outright negative instruction.

seriously the difference of genre between the two writings. Ignatius, writing a letter, may have been able to reflect his own concern about the problem of his readers in his writing directly and explicitly, while Matthew, writing not a letter but a Gospel, may have been restricted from putting his own context into his writing explicitly (note he is writing a story of Jesus not of himself or his community).

(ii) Whereas in Matthew there is no direct or even indirect connection between the sabbath and the Lord's day, in Ignatius such a connection is readily made. As far as Jesus' teaching as presented not only in Matthew but also in Mark and Luke (and even in John) is concerned, the sabbath is indeed not linked with the Lord's day at all. Indeed apart from Rev. 1.10 (and perhaps also *Did.* 14.1) the use of κυριακή in *Magn.* 9.1 is, the first appearance of the term in the meaning of the 'Lord's day' in the extant Christian literature. Regardless of when and where the observance of the Lord's day as a day of worship (not as a day of rest) originated,[28] Ignatius's connection of the two days is highly significant, because, even though, as pointed out just above, the connection has no biblical basis, his way of linking the two days without any explanation in *Magn.* 9.1 seems to reveal that the Lord's day was already conceived in conjunction with the sabbath, if not as a substitute for it. From this we may deduce that the two days were readily connected at an earlier stage of the Christian church and by the time of Ignatius the connection of the two was more or less taken for granted.[29]

It should be noted, however, that Ignatius's way of putting the Lord's day more or less in opposition to the sabbath seems to have paved the way for another legalistic tendency towards keeping the Lord's day as a day of rest (or as the Christian sabbath) as well as a day of worship, a tendency which, according to my argument above, Jesus himself and the evangelists would have severely criticized and fought against. While Ignatius himself probably did not intend and would have fought against a legalistic understanding of the Lord's day,[30] by connecting the Lord's

28. Bauckham suggests Palestinian origin during the earlier part of the first century CE; see his 'Lord's Day', pp. 222-50, esp. pp. 236-40.

29. Could Paul have had in mind the Lord's day in opposition to the sabbath when he wrote Rom. 14.5: Ὅς μὲν [γαρ] κρίνει ἡμέραν παρ' ἡμέραν? Though we cannot be sure, this possibility cannot be absolutely excluded; see C.E.B. Cranfield, *The Epistle to the Romans*, II (2 vols.; Edinburgh: T. & T. Clark, 1975, 1979), pp. 690-99, 705. For a sceptical view, however, see, for example, J.D.G. Dunn, *Romans 9–16* (WBC, 38b; Dallas: Word Books, 1988), pp. 805-806.

30. Note as I have pointed out above, his overall focus in *Magn.* 8.1–10.3 is on

day directly with the sabbath he may have inadvertently encouraged such a tendency.

2. *The* Letter of Barnabas

The writer of the document known as the *Letter of Barnabas* is generally supposed to have been an Alexandrian Jew[31] but most certainly not the Barnabas of the New Testament, a companion of Paul.[32] The letter is dated roughly to 100–132 CE.[33] J.C. Paget interestingly places the letter 'in Alexandria/Egypt before the outbreak of the so-called Trajanic revolt in 115', up to when Jews were much more numerous than Christians in that area, and could not possibly have been ignored by Christians, 'particularly as many Christians probably hailed from a Jewish background'.[34] Paget's suggestion is probable, especially if we accept that the letter was written in opposition to Judaism which was a real threat to Barnabas and his readers in Alexandria.[35]

contrasting (probably legalistic) Judaism with Christianity (which by implication must not be legalistic) and strengthening the Magnesians in their discipleship.

31. The reason for the suggested Alexandrian origin is mainly twofold: (i) the extensive use of allegorical interpretation by the writer, which was so popular in Alexandrian thought; (ii) the early recognition of the letter (even as a canonical writing) among the Alexandrian Fathers (esp. by Clement of Alexandria).

32. See, for example, J. Quasten, *Patrology*, I (3 vols.; Utrecht: Spectrum, 1950), p. 89.

33. Most scholars seem to agree that the letter was written before the beginning of the Bar Kochba insurrection in 132 CE, mainly on the basis of ch. 16; cf. R.A. Kraft, *The Apostolic Fathers: A New Translation and Commentary*. III. *Barnabas and the Didache* (5 vols.; ed. R.M. Grant; New York: Thomas, Nelson & Sons, 1965), pp. 42-43; W.H. Shea, 'The Sabbath in the Epistle of Barnabas', *AUSS* 4 (1966), p. 149, esp. n. 2. For earlier date (i.e. before 100 CE), however, see J.B. Lightfoot, *The Apostolic Fathers*, part I: *S. Clement of Rome* (2 vols.; London: Macmillan, 1890), pp. 503-12; A.L. Williams, 'The Date of the Epistle of Barnabas', *JTS* 34 (1933), pp. 337-46, esp. p. 344 (mainly on the basis of *Barn*. 4.4-5).

34. J.C. Paget, *The Epistle of Barnabas* (Tübingen: Mohr, 1994), p. 56.

35. On the identity of Barnabas's opponents, see Paget, *Barnabas*, pp. 51-66, who properly criticizes some sceptical views about the anti-Jewish character of the letter—e.g. A. Harnack, *Die Chronologie der altchristilichen Literatur bis Eusebius* (Leipzig: Hinrichs, 1897), p. 414; H. Windisch, *Der Barnabasbrief* (Tübingen: Mohr, 1920), pp. 322-23; K. Wengst, *Didache (Apostellehre). Barnabasbrief. Zweiter Klemensbrief. Schrift an Diognet* (Munich and Darmstadt: Wissenschaftliche Buchgesellschaft, 1984), pp. 112-14; *et al.* For those who see the threat of Judaism as real, see Kleist, *Didache*, pp. 31-32; Bacchiocchi, *Sabbath*, p. 218; *et al.* On the

The letter has 21 chapters altogether and is divided into two main parts: (i) chs. 1–17—an allegorical interpretation of the Old Testament law/covenant; (ii) chs. 18–21—'Two Ways', that is, a manual of Christian morality. In the first part Barnabas deals with the major tenets of Judaism: (i) sacrificial system (chs. 2, 5, 7, 8, 12); (ii) fasts (ch. 3); (iii) the covenant (chs. 4, 13, 14); (iv) the promised land (ch. 6); (v) circumcision (ch. 9); (vi) food laws (ch. 10); (vii) the sabbath (ch. 15); (viii) the temple (ch. 16). Over against the Jewish literalistic understanding of these tenets, Barnabas presents his allegorical interpretation of them as the true understanding of the Old Testament. He claims that Jews lost their covenant with God, soon after Moses received it, by turning to idols at Sinai (cf. 4.7-8), and now the covenant is transmitted to Christians through Christ (cf. 14.5) who is the fulfilment of the various Old Testament types (i.e. fasting, the scapegoat, a heifer, etc.; cf. especially, chs. 7–8).

Since the sabbath was one of the hallmarks of Judaism, it is not surprising at all that Barnabas discusses the issue in a whole chapter (ch. 15). The flow of Barnabas's argument in the chapter is as follows:

1) The sabbath commandment which is one of the ten commandments (ἐν τοῖς δέκα λόγοις) is enjoined by the Lord in the Old Testament (vv. 1-2; cf. Exod. 20.8; Deut. 5.12; cf. also Ps. 23.4). Barnabas recognizes the authority of the Old Testament; he may be anti-Judaistic, but is certainly not anti-Old Testament.

2) God, in fact, speaks of the sabbath in his creation story (v. 3; cf. Gen. 2.2); in that story 'six days' refers to 'six thousand years', for 'a day with him means a thousand years' (cf. Ps. 89.4 [LXX]; cf. also *Jub.* 4.30; 2 Pet. 3.8); in six thousand years, everything will be completed, and the last thousand years (= the seventh day) will arrive when God's Son comes, and destroys the time of the evil one and brings the true rest (vv. 4-5). Barnabas interprets the sabbath eschatologically (and also Christologically) but solely by means of allegorical interpretation.

3) At present nobody can keep the sabbath holy as God demands (v. 6); but when Jesus comes and makes us holy, we will be able to keep the sabbath holy (v. 7). According to these two verses alone, the fulfilment of the sabbath for Barnabas sounds purely futuristic.[36]

relation between Judaism and Christianity in Alexandria in the period 70–135 CE, see L.W. Barnard, *Studies in the Apostolic Fathers and their Background* (Oxford: Blackwell, 1966), pp. 41-55, esp. pp. 51-55.

36. Shea, 'Barnabas', p. 156, therefore, claims that whereas 'almost all of these items of the faith [i.e. the sacrificial system, the covenant, circumcision, etc.; see

4) God declares that the present sabbaths are not acceptable to him (cf. Isa. 1.13); instead, God has made another day, that is, the eighth day, which is the beginning of another world; therefore, 'we celebrate with gladness' the eighth day, on which Jesus 'rose from the dead, and was made manifest, and ascended into heaven' (vv. 8-9). Though the interpretation of these two verses in the light of the whole chapter/letter is notoriously difficult,[37] as C.K. Barrett properly points out, 'the only point that Barnabas really wanted to make' by adding the statement on the eighth day (i.e. vv. 8-9) is that 'the Jews with their sabbath are in the wrong, the Christians with their Sundays are in the right'.[38] Barnabas is less ambiguous than Ignatius about how and why Christians kept the eighth day: (i) they had cheerful celebrations on the eighth day, which may most likely refer to Sunday worship; (ii) they kept it because the eighth day is the day of Jesus' resurrection, manifestation, and ascension (ἀνέβη εἰς οὐρανούς).[39]

For my purpose, the following points may be made: (i) for Barnabas the Old Testament is still authoritative, though Jewish literalistic interpretation of it cannot be acceptable; (ii) nevertheless his extremely fanciful and sometimes allegorical interpretation of the sabbath passages in the Old Testament (usually without considering their co-texts) results in a too negative view of the (literal) sabbath (let alone of the Jewish observance of it[40]) which cannot be fully in line either with the Old Testament

pp. 154-55] receive their fulfillment in the present Christian era...the Sabbath is exclusively future in application'. But Barnabas may have had the present application of the sabbath in mind when he explains Christian celebration of the Lord's day in vv. 8-9, though, in that case, his argument there may be inconsistent with that in v. 6; cf. Bauckham, 'Post-Apostolic Church', pp. 263-64.

37. Mainly because of the unclear relation between the seventh day and the eighth day; see Kraft, *Barnabas*, pp. 28-29, 128-29. Some scholars, therefore, classify Barnabas as premillennialist (e.g. Kleist, *Didache*, p. 179 n. 161; Shea, 'Barnabas', pp. 166-67; Rordorf, *Sunday*, pp. 93-94), whereas others classify him as amillennialist (e.g. Bauckham, 'Post-Apostolic Church', p. 263; Paget, *Barnabas*, p. 170).

38. C.K. Barrett, 'The Eschatology of the Epistle to the Hebrews', in W.D. Davies and D. Daube, *The Background of the New Testament and its Eschatology* (Cambridge: Cambridge University Press, 1956), p. 370.

39. Kleist, *Didache*, p. 180 n. 162, rightly points out the problem of Barnabas's use of the term 'the eighth day' in two entirely different senses: (i) the day of eternity; (ii) the first day of the week.

40. Barnabas's rejection of the Jewish observance is much more definite and explicit than that of Ignatius. Barnabas's argument against the sabbath observance is well summarized by Bauckham, 'Post-Apostolic Church', p. 265: 'The Jewish

or even with Jesus' understanding of it as presented, for example, in Matthew, according to the investigations above; (iii) his understanding of the sabbath, however, is interestingly focused on eschatology and Christology, which might be a vague reflection of the general tendency to relate the sabbath to Christ, even if his interpretive method may seem unskilful and probably even unacceptable from our perspective (if, however, he is writing his letter in Alexandria for the people there, such a method could be expected to communicate well in that context); (iv) for Barnabas the fulfilment of the sabbath may be a matter of the future, though he links the sabbath with the Christian celebration of the eighth day (especially in relation to its fulfilment; cf. v. 8: ἀλλὰ ὃ πεποίηκα, ἐν ᾧ καταπαύσας τὰ πάντα ἀρχὴν ἡμέρας ὀγδόης ποιήσω, ὅ ἐστιν ἄλλου κόσμου ἀρχήν) and gives the impression that the eighth day celebration [worship] has some kind of relationship with the fulfilment of the sabbath;[41] (v) according to Barnabas, Christians worshipped on Sunday instead of the sabbath, because it is not only the day signifying 'the beginning of another world' but also the day of Jesus' resurrection, manifestation, and ascension; his connection of the sabbath with Sunday is thus more direct than that of Ignatius and confirms the suggestion above that by the time of Ignatius and Barnabas the connection of the two days was more or less taken for granted. What would these findings, then, contribute to this study?

The crucial question is whether Barnabas knew Matthew and used it in his writing as a source. Opinions are once again widely divided among scholars. There are certain indications which suggest Barnabas's use of or acquaintance with Matthew's Gospel or at least a source of the Gospel.[42] In relation to our text (ch. 15), however, it is extremely difficult to judge its link with the Matthean sabbath passages, since in ch. 15 neither direct quotation nor even allusion to those passages is found. We

practice of the Sabbath was not obedience but disobedience to God, and therefore Christians, the true heirs of the covenant, must not observe the Sabbath'; as Bauckham properly points out, 'the purely negative evaluation of the Jewish Sabbath in the context of a wholesale condemnation of Judaism is characteristic of the Fathers'.

41. On this point, see Bauckham, 'Post-Apostolic Church', p. 263—he is, however, rather cautious to interpret the eighth day as the fulfilment of the sabbath.

42. E.g. *Barn.* 4.14 // Mt. 22.14 and 20.16; *Barn.* 5.9 // Mt. 9.13 (cf. Mk 2.17); *Barn.* 5.12 // 26.31 (cf. Mk 14.27; Zech. 13.7); *Barn.* 7.9b // Mt. 26.63-64 and 27.28-31. For further possible or doubtful contacts, see Massaux, *Influence*, I, pp. 59-74; Köster, *Überlieferung*, pp. 4-23; Köhler, *Rezeption*, pp. 111-23; *et al.*

may only detect certain remote contacts in terms of some theological similarities in their understandings of the sabbath: (i) as in Matthew, the authority of the Old Testament is well recognized in Barnabas, though Barnabas's use of Old Testament passages (cf. vv. 1-2, 3, 4, 5, 6, 8) is quite different from Jesus' use of the Old Testament in Matthew 12 (cf. vv. 3-4, 5-6, 7); (ii) as in Matthew the Pharisees' attitude to the sabbath is criticized, so in Barnabas the Jewish observance of the sabbath is rejected;[43] (iii) as in Matthew, the sabbath is viewed in terms of Christology and eschatology in Barnabas. One may need to comment here that Barnabas's Christological and eschatological understanding is not irrelevant to his outright rejection of the observance of the sabbath. Perhaps, if he knew Matthew's Gospel and especially Matthew's sabbath controversy pericopes, Barnabas, like Ignatius, may have understood the practical implication of Jesus' fulfilment of the sabbath for Christians as rejecting sabbath observance altogether, especially when the various Jewish practices endanger the centrality of Jesus Christ in Christian faith, as presumably Barnabas believed was the case among the Alexandrians. If this reconstruction is plausible, this once again may help us to reinforce the tentative conclusions on the practical implication of Jesus' teaching regarding the sabbath in Matthew.

Having said this, however, we cannot fail to note that there are clear differences between Barnabas and Matthew in their treatments of the sabbath: (i) unlike Matthew, Barnabas interprets the Old Testament passages extremely fancifully and sometimes allegorically; such an imaginative/allegorical interpretation by Barnabas results in an extremely negative understanding of the literal (Old Testament) weekly sabbath, an understanding which Matthew (and probably Jesus as well) may not have shared; (ii) unlike Matthew, Barnabas seems to betray a too futuristic view of the fulfilment of the sabbath; (iii) unlike in Matthew, the eighth day (= Sunday, the Lord's day) is, in Barnabas, directly linked with the sabbath and even replaces its role as a day of worship. From the final point we may once again deduce that the two days (i.e. the sabbath and the eighth [Lord's] day) were readily connected at an earlier stage of the Christian church and by the time of Barnabas (and

---

43. This similarity, however, betrays clear differences as well, since, for example, whereas Barnabas rejects outright the Jewish observance of the sabbath, Jesus' criticism in Matthew is limited only to the Pharisees' legalistic attitude to the sabbath at least on its surface.

Ignatius) the connection of the two was more or less taken for granted.[44] It should be once again noted, however, that his way of putting the eighth day in opposition to the sabbath (together with Ignatius's linking the Lord's day with the sabbath) seems to have paved the way for another legalistic tendency towards keeping Sunday as a day of rest as well as a day of worship, a tendency which not only neither Matthew nor Jesus would have condoned but even Barnabas himself probably did not intend and would not have approved of.

All in all, the contact between Barnabas and Matthew, especially in their sabbath materials, is too vague, and it seems unwise to draw any definite conclusions about Matthew's influence (positive or negative) on Barnabas, possibly apart from the above general observations regarding the consequent abandonment of the sabbath and the Christological and eschatological understanding of the sabbath.

3. *The* Didache

Even though none of the issues regarding the authorship, date, provenance and character of the *Didache*, in spite of an enormous amount of literature on them, have been resolved conclusively,[45] for my purposes it suffices to adopt the following position which reflects the majority view in current *Didache* scholarship: the *Didache* was composed and/or compiled possibly towards the end of the first century, but more probably in the early second century,[46] in Syria or Palestine[47] (rather than in

44. In Barnabas the eighth day [= the Lord's day] is more clearly identified than in Ignatius as a day of worship which celebrates Jesus' resurrection on that day and even carries eschatological significance as well. This may betray that the eighth day [= the Lord's day] came to have significance as a day of worship because it was related with Jesus' resurrection.

45. All those issues indeed still remain as a 'riddle' or an 'enigma' (cf. the titles of F.E. Vokes, *The Riddle of the Didache* [London: SPCK, 1938] and S. Giet, *L'énigme de la Didaché* [Paris: Ophrys, 1970]). For a detailed summary of various scholarly suggestions on the issues of date and provenance, see C.N. Jefford, *The Sayings of Jesus in the Teaching of the Twelve Apostles* (SupVC, 11; Leiden: Brill, 1989), pp. 3-17; cf. also Massaux, *Influence*, I, pp. 3-6. For a summary of scholarly views on the literary character of the *Didache*, see I.H. Henderson, '*Didache* and Orality in Synoptic Comparison', *JBL* 111 (1992), pp. 284-91.

46. The vast majority of scholars agree that the *Didache* was written before the middle of the second century; see Jefford, *Sayings*, pp. 3-17—Jefford himself suggests 80–100 CE (p. 145); cf. also *idem*, 'Did Ignatius of Antioch Know the *Didache*?', in C.N. Jefford (ed.), *The Didache in Context: Essays on its Text,*

Alexandria[48]) where Matthew's Gospel was probably known and accepted as authoritative;[49] the Didachist(s) thus most probably knew Matthew's Gospel and used it as a source.[50]

The *Didache* may be roughly divided into three sections: (i) the 'Two Ways' (chs. 1–6); (ii) the definitions of rituals (chs. 7–10) and establishment of ecclesiastical offices (chs. 11–15); (iii) the little apocalypse (ch. 16). The Lord's day reference (but not in connection with the sabbath!) is found in the latter half of the second section, 14.1—Κατὰ κυριακὴν δὲ κυρίου συναχθέντες κλάσατε ἄρτον καὶ εὐχαριστήσατε, προεξομολογησάμενοι τὰ παραπτώματα ὑμῶν, ὅπως καθαρὰ ἡ θυσία ὑμῶν ᾖ.[51] κατὰ κυριακὴν δὲ κυρίου may be translated either

History and Transmission (NovTSup, 77; Leiden: Brill, 1995), p. 331. *Pace* Vokes, *Riddle*, pp. 129-76 (the end of the second / the beginning of the third century); Kraft, *Barnabas*, pp. 72-77 (not earlier than mid-second century).

47. Most of the French scholars and many British/American scholars prefer Syria or Palestine to Alexandria; see the summary in Jefford, *Sayings*, pp. 3-17 —Jefford himself (*Sayings*, p. 145) suggests the city of Antioch, in which he supposes Matthew's Gospel was written and of which Ignatius was the bishop.

48. As the summary in Jefford, *Sayings*, pp. 3-17, shows, a number of German scholars and some British/American scholars suggest Egypt/Alexandria as the provenance of the *Didache*. The similarity between *Did.* 1–5 and *Barn.* 18–20, which is a major ground for such a view, does not necessarily suggest the same provenance for the two documents; the similarity may be explained by supposing a common source upon which both the *Didache* and Barnabas were dependent; cf. Jefford, *Sayings*, pp. 22-90.

49. Cf. J.M. Court, 'The Didache and St Matthew's Gospel', *SJT* 34 (1981), pp. 111-14; Jefford, *Sayings*, pp. 143-45. Massaux, *Influence*, III, pp. 145, 155, and some others suggest that τὸ εὐαγγέλιον throughout the *Didache* (cf. 8.2; 11.3; 15.3, 4) is to be considered as a reference to Matthew's Gospel itself; for a different view, however, see J. Draper, 'The Jesus Tradition in the Didache', in Wenham (ed.), *Perspectives*, V, pp. 283-84.

50. See, most recently, C.M. Tuckett, 'Synoptic Tradition in the Didache', in J.-M. Sevrin (ed.), *The New Testament in Early Christianity / La réception des écrits néo-testamentaires dans le christianisme primitif* (Louvain: Louvain University Press, 1989), pp. 197-230; Jefford, '*Didache*', pp. 330-51; *el al. Pace* Draper, '*Didache*', pp. 269-87; W. Rordorf, 'Does the Didache Contain Jesus Tradition Independently of the Synoptic Gospels?', in H. Wansbrough (ed.), *Jesus and the Oral Gospel Tradition* (JSNTSup, 64; Sheffield: JSOT Press, 1991), pp. 394-423.

51. There is no serious textual problem apart from προεξομολογησάμενοι (Codex Hierosolymitanus 54 [H] has προσεξομολογησάμενοι instead—cf. also the texts edited by Bryennois, Rordorf-Tuilier, Wengst) and ὑμῶν (H has ἡμῶν instead). Even though J.-P. Audet, *La Didaché: Instructions des apôtres* (Paris: Gabalda,

'according to the Lord's day of the Lord' or 'on the Lord's own day', and most probably refers to Sunday.[52] If so, our text shows more clearly than Ignatius and Barnabas what Christians did on Sunday (= the Lord's day, the eighth day)—they worshipped the [risen][53] Lord by participating in the eucharist. The Didachist seems to take the Sunday eucharist for granted and, without any argument for such a practice, just gives instructions on how to participate in it (i.e. a proper preparation for it— προεξομολογησάμενοι τὰ παραπτώματα ὑμῶν, ὅπως καθαρὰ ἡ θυσία ὑμῶν ᾖ). It seems then highly probable that by the Didachist's time the Lord's day worship was well established at least in his or her community.

As far as the primary purpose of this study is concerned, however, no immediate positive contribution is found in our text alone—there is no explicit reference to the sabbath in the text. Nevertheless, the co-text does seem to offer a clue which may link our text with the sabbath. In 13.3 the Didachist identifies the Christian prophets in his or her community and their payment with the 'high priests' (οἱ ἀρχιερεῖς ὑμῶν) and the 'first fruit' (ἡ ἀπαρχή) respectively (cf. Num. 18.12; Deut. 18.3-5). In 14.2 the Didachist once again identifies the 'eucharist' with a 'sacrifice' (cf. Mt. 5.23-24). If the Didachist readily pictures these New Testament figures by employing their Old Testament counterparts,[54] he or she may well also have had the sabbath in mind as an Old Testament counterpart of the 'Lord's day'. Since the Didachist is talking about the

---

1958), pp. 72-73, 240, presents a reconstructed reading Καθ' ἡμέραν δὲ κυρίου in place of Κατὰ κυριακὴν δὲ κυρίου, his reconstruction is far from convincing because it is based on the Georgian Version, whose reliability is seriously questioned (cf. for example, Vokes, *Riddle*, pp. 11-12; Jefford, *Sayings*, p. 9); not surprisingly, most scholars ignore his suggestion—cf. most recently, K. Niederwimmer, 'Der Didachist und seine Quellen', in Jefford (ed.), *Didache*, p. 34.

52. See Rordorf, *Sunday*, pp. 209-10; Bauckham, 'Lord's day', pp. 227-28; cf. A. Cody, 'The *Didache*: An English Translation', in Jefford (ed.), *Didache*, p. 13: 'on every Sunday of the Lord'. Bacchiocchi's translation, 'according to the sovereign doctrine of the Lord' (*Sabbath*, p. 114 n. 73—he adopts the suggestion by J.B. Thibaut, *La Liturgie romaine* [Paris: Rue Bayard, 1964], pp. 33-34), is far from convincing; his view is criticized by Bauckham, 'Lord's Day', pp. 227-28; cf. Audet, *Didachè*, pp. 72-73, 459-61.

53. Cf. the Apostolic Constitution 7.30.1: τὴν ἀναστάσιμον τοῦ κυρίου ἡμέραν, τὴν κυριακὴν φαμεν.

54. They are neither allegorical nor typological (still less literal) counterparts but, as Court, 'Didache', pp. 116-18, suggests, spiritually interpreted counterparts.

weekly celebration of the eucharist, he or she may well have regarded this weekly eucharist as a spiritualized substitute for the weekly (that is, sabbath) temple sacrifice. If that was the case, the Didachist may have already presupposed (and so does not need to spell out) that the Lord's day on which the eucharist is celebrated is a spiritualized substitute for the sabbath on which the temple service and synagogue worship is carried on.[55] If so, *Did.* 14.1 may be a further indication that Christians were indeed expected to substitute the Lord's day celebration for the sabbath observance (especially its worship aspect) (cf. *Magn.* 9.1; *Barn.* 15.8-9) by the beginning of the second century at least in Syria and/or Palestine (and also in Alexandria), and that quite probably many Christians did in fact substitute the former for the latter by that time in those districts. We may then suppose that the Didachist and his or her community, if they, as I have assumed, knew Matthew's Gospel and if the Gospel had authority over them, may have interpreted Jesus' fulfilment of the sabbath as presented in Matthew in such a way that they gave up the sabbath observance altogether and substituted the Lord's day celebration for it. But this was probably not on the basis of theological appropriateness (e.g. a typological substitution) but rather for the sake of practical/pastoral appropriateness.[56] This substitution, however, together with that of Ignatius and of Barnabas, may have paved the way for another legalistic tendency of keeping the Lord's day as the Christian sabbath, whatever the Didachist's own intention. To be sure, however, all these suggestions depend heavily upon various hypotheses and conjectures, and we have no basis for being too definite concerning how Jesus' fulfilment of the sabbath as presented in Matthew was understood and applied by the Didachist and his or her community.

4. *The* Letter to Diognetus

While the authorship, date and provenance of the *Letter to Diognetus* remain an enigma, I accept the view of a number of scholars that the

---

55. Cf. Court, 'Didache', p. 118; Jefford, *'Didache'*, pp. 347-48. Cf. also the Didachist's instruction on the Christian fasting days (i.e. Wednesdays and Fridays) which substitute for the Jewish (= the hypocrites, ὑποκριταί) fasting days (i.e. Mondays and Thursdays) in 8.1.

56. This may also be the case in the other identifications in chs. 13–14 (e.g. the Christian prophets with the high priests, the payment for the prophets with the first fruit, and the eucharist with the sacrifice).

letter (at least chs. 1–10)[57] was most probably written in the early second century in Asia Minor or Syria.[58] The *Letter to Diognetus* is an apologetic tract by an unknown writer addressed to a highly educated pagan. The letter answers the questions raised by the pagan regarding the late origin of Christianity (ch. 1), the pagan gods (ch. 2), the difference between Judaism and Christianity (chs. 3–4), Christian life (chs. 5–6), the divine origin of Christianity (chs. 7–9), thorough knowledge of God (ch. 10), the mysteries of the Father (chs. 11–12).

It is in ch. 4 that an interesting argument against the Jewish sabbath observance appears: τὸ δὲ καταψεύδεσθαι θεοῦ ὡς κωλύοντος ἐν τῇ τῶν σαββάτων ἡμέρᾳ καλόν τι ποιεῖν, πῶς οὐκ ἀσεβές; (4.3). This argument is particularly significant for our study, because the clause κωλύοντος ἐν τῇ τῶν σαββάτων ἡμέρᾳ καλόν τι ποιεῖν reminds us of Jesus' saying in Mt. 12.12 (ὥστε ἔξεστιν τοῖς σάββασιν καλῶς ποιεῖν). The author of the letter assumes that Jews of his time refrained from doing a good deed on the sabbath,[59] and he criticizes such an observance of the sabbath by Jews as 'superstition' (cf. 4.1: τὴν περὶ τὰ σάββατα δεισιδαιμονίαν), and as distorting God's will for the sabbath (τὸ δὲ καταψεύδεσθαι θεοῦ ὡς κωλύοντος...πῶς οὐκ ἀσεβές; cf. also 4.6: ἀπάτη). He also affirms that Christians of his time gave up this Jewish sabbath observance, when he says in his concluding statement (4.6) that τῆς μὲν οὖν κοινῆς εἰκαιότητος καὶ ἀπάτης καὶ τῆς Ἰουδαίων πολυπραγμοσύνης καὶ ἀλαζονείας ὡς ὀρθῶς ἀπέχονται Χριστιανοί ('the Christians do rightly in abstaining from the general silliness and deceit and fussiness and pride of the Jews').

---

57. At the end of ch. 10 the Strassburg MS (destroyed in 1870) shows a lacuna with a marginal note 'here the copy had a break', and most scholars suspect that chs. 11–12 did not belong to the original letter.

58. Cf. P. Andriessen, 'The Authorship of the *Epistula ad Diognetum*', *VC* 1 (1947), pp. 129-36 (123–24/129 CE, Asia Minor); Kleist, *Didache*, pp. 131-32; Richardson, *Fathers*, pp. 206-10 (129 CE [?], Asia Minor); L.W. Barnard, 'The *Epistula ad Diognetum*: Two Units from One Author?', *ZNW* 56 (1965), pp. 130-37; *idem*, *Studies*, pp. 171-73 (100–130 CE, Ephesus, Antioch, Alexandria); W.H.C. Frend, *Martyrdom and Persecution in the Early Church: A Study of Conflict from the Maccabees to Donatus* (Oxford: Blackwell, 1965), p. 202 n. 11 (120–150 CE); *idem*, *The Rise of Christianity* (London: Darton, Longman & Todd, 1984), pp. 236, 261 n. 24 (not later than 150 CE). There are, however, some scholars who suggest later dates—e.g. R.H. Connolly, 'The Date and Authorship of the Epistle to Diognetus', *JTS* 36 (1935), pp. 347-53 (the latter half of second–third century).

59. Cf. *t. Šab.* 16.22.

While it is almost certain that the writer of the letter knew Johannine literature and used it in his writing,[60] it is by no means clear whether the writer knew and used Matthew's Gospel. Perhaps our reference (4.3) may be a remote reflection of Jesus' saying as preserved in Matthew.[61] If the assumption that the letter was written in the early second century in Asia Minor or Syria is correct, it seems more likely that the writer was acquainted with Matthew's Gospel than that he was not. If the writer did know Matthew's Gospel (and particularly the sabbath controversy pericopes) and had in mind Jesus' saying in Mt. 12.12 when he wrote 4.3,[62] his affirmation that Christians abstain from observing the sabbath (at least in the Jewish way) can be quite significant for this study. Perhaps, the writer of the letter may have understood, like Ignatius, the practical implication of Jesus' fulfilment of the sabbath for Christians as giving up sabbath observance altogether, especially when sabbath observance (with other Jewish practices such as food laws, circumcision, fasting, feast of the new moon, and sacrifices; cf. 4.1, 4-6)[63] endangers the distinctiveness of Christianity from Judaism. This is, however, by no means saying that the writer was solely influenced by Matthew. We may rather suggest that Matthew's sabbath pericopes could have been one of various factors which influenced the writer's negative view regarding sabbath observance. If so, this may once again, though remotely, help us to reinforce the tentative conclusion on the practical implication of Jesus' teaching regarding the sabbath as presented in Matthew. To be sure, however, my suggestions above depend heavily upon indefinite assumptions (especially regarding the origin of

---

60. *Diogn.* 6.3 with Jn 16.19; 17.14-16; 18.36; *Diogn.* 7.2 with Jn 1.1-3; *Diogn.* 7.4-5 with Jn 3.17; 12.47; *Diogn.* 8.5 with Jn 1.18; 1 Jn 4.12; etc.; see Barnard, *Didache*, pp. 170-71; Richardson, *Fathers*, pp. 207-208 n. 3.

61. Note Mk 3.4 and Lk. 6.9 have ἀγαθὸν ποιῆσαι and ἀγαθοποιῆσαι respectively, whereas Mt. 12.12 has καλῶς ποιεῖν; *Diogn.* 4.3 (καλόν τι ποιεῖν) is much more similar to the Matthean form than to the Markan and Lukan forms.

62. His criticism of the Jewish sabbath observance as misrepresenting God's will for the sabbath (cf. 4.1, 3, 6) is indeed in line with Jesus' argument against the Pharisees' attitude towards and observance of the sabbath in Mt. 12.1-14, esp. vv. 7, 11-12. See above the discussions of those verses in Chapter 4.

63. The list of Jewish practices and the writer's attitude to them make one suspect Pauline influence as well; cf. Col. 2.16; Gal. 4.10-11. Note the writer's argument in ch. 2 (Christian God vs. pagan gods) reminds us of Paul's argument in Gal. 4.8-9 which precedes his criticism against observance of days, months, seasons, and years as we find also in *Diogn.* chs. 2–4.

the letter) and conjectures, and again we cannot be too definite concerning how Jesus' fulfilment of the sabbath as presented in Matthew was understood and applied by the writer of the letter and his fellow Christians.

5. *Conclusions*

In this chapter I have investigated all the sabbath and/or Lord's day (= Sunday, the eighth day) related passages in the Apostolic Fathers. The object of the investigations of those four passages has obviously been to evaluate how Matthew's treatment of the sabbath was adopted, adapted or overlooked in them and also to validate further some aspects of my understanding of Matthew's treatment as developed in the previous chapters, though we have also reached some additional conclusions especially concerning the Lord's day in connection with the sabbath.

Disappointingly, we have observed that no direct quotation of or even clear allusion to the Matthean sabbath references is found in any of the four sabbath passages (except perhaps *Diogn.* 4.3). The focus of the investigations therefore has been directed to the points of similarity and/ or difference between Matthew's treatment and that of the Apostolic Fathers, with an expectation that those points may enable us to evaluate Matthew's influence (or impact) on those Apostolic Fathers and their writings. Disappointingly again, the results of the investigations are not very definite, especially because the origins (i.e. authors, dates, and places) of those writings (except probably for *Magn.* 9.1) are not at all certain. Nevertheless, those results are still quite significant for building up a picture of how Jesus' fulfilment of the sabbath as presented in Matthew was understood and applied among the communities which most probably directly inherited Matthew's Gospel (or at least the tradition of it) and accepted it as authoritative.

The points of similarity are as follows: (1) For Ignatius and Barnabas (and also for the Didachist), as for Matthew, the Old Testament is still authoritative, and its role is looking forward to Jesus Christ (7.1-3; cf. *Magn.* 8.2; 9.2; *Barn.* 15.1-3; cf. also *Did.* chs. 13–14); for them Jesus must have been understood as the fulfilment of the Old Testament and therefore also of the sabbath (cf. especially, *Barn.* 15.3-5). (2) Ignatius and Barnabas, like Matthew, understand the sabbath in terms of eschatology and Christology. (3) Ignatius, Barnabas, and the writer of the *Letter to Diognetus*, like Matthew, criticize or even condemn the legalistic, literalistic (cf. especially *Barn.* 15), and/or superstitious (cf. especially

Diogn. 4.1) observance of the sabbath by the Jews.

If they (or at least some of them) were acquainted with and used Matthew's Gospel (especially Matthew's sabbath controversy pericopes), the above points show how they adopted Matthew's treatment of the sabbath in their own treatments. Significantly enough, Ignatius, Barnabas, and the writer of the *Letter to Diognetus* explicitly, and the Didachist implicitly, reject or even condemn sabbath observance altogether. Such outright rejections, in spite of their recognition of the authority of the Old Testament, may well derive from their understanding of the sabbath in eschatological and Christological terms as well as their critical view of Judaism. We can draw then a quite probable conclusion on the basis of the above cumulative witnesses that the Apostolic Fathers referred to above may have understood the practical implication of Jesus' fulfilment of the sabbath for Christians (or at least for their communities/readers) as giving up sabbath observance altogether, especially when sabbath observance, together with other Jewish practices (e.g. circumcision, fasting, etc.), endangers the centrality of Jesus Christ in Christian faith. If this conclusion is reliable, it supports my tentative conclusion on the practical implication of Jesus' teaching regarding the sabbath as presented in Matthew.[64] The Apostolic Fathers may have made explicit in their writings what had been implicit in Matthew.

Having said this, however, there are also significant differences: (1) While in Matthew the literal sabbath is not rejected outright (even though it *is* downplayed in comparison with the temple and Jesus), in Barnabas (and implicitly in Ignatius and the *Letter to Diognetus*) the literal sabbath itself is rejected, let alone sabbath observance. (2) Unlike Matthew, Barnabas and perhaps the Didachist adopt the allegorical and 'spiritual' interpretation of the sabbath respectively. (3) Unlike Matthew, Barnabas betrays a too futuristic view of the fulfilment of the sabbath. (4) Unlike in Matthew (and any other New Testament books[65]), in Ignatius and Barnabas (and implicitly in the *Didache*), the Lord's (or

---

64. One thing that is certain is that there is no counter-evidence against my conclusion in Chapter 4 (that is, any kind of statement which encourages or at least approves of sabbath observance), at least in the writings of the Apostolic Fathers.

65. Cf., however, Acts 20.7; 1 Cor. 16.1-2; for various discussions of these passages, see especially Rordorf, *Sunday*, pp. 193-205; Jewett, *Lord's Day*, pp. 56-72; Bacchiocchi, *Sabbath*, pp. 90-111; Beckwith and Stott, *Day*, pp. 30-42; Turner, 'Sabbath', pp. 128-33; D.R. De Lacey, 'The Sabbath/Sunday Question and the Law in the Pauline Corpus', in Carson (ed.), *Lord's Day*, pp. 184-86.

eighth) day is readily linked with and even substituted for the sabbath as a day for worship.[66]

If Matthew's Gospel was known to and used by them, the above differences may have been various attempts to adapt Matthew's treatment of the sabbath in their particular contexts, though most of them may not have been adopted either by Matthew or by Jesus himself.[67] The problem for those adaptations was that, even though they properly emphasized the aspect of discontinuity in Jesus' fulfilment of the sabbath, they overlooked and failed to emphasize the aspect of continuity in Jesus' fulfilment of the sabbath in terms of Jesus' redemption, and as a result of that they failed to direct attention to Jesus' redemptive work as the true fulfilment of the sabbath but rather put the Lord's (or eighth) day in opposition to the sabbath as a day for worship (but not as a day of rest). These attempts at adaptation then may be examples of poor contextualization of biblical texts into a particular context, which in consequence could produce unexpected and unnecessary side effects. Thus, for instance, to take the last point (point 4 above), by putting the Lord's day more or less in opposition to the sabbath, not because they could see any concrete *theological link* between the two but probably rather because they felt a *practical need* to have another day which could substitute for the Jewish worship day, Ignatius, Barnabas, and perhaps *Didache*, paved the way for another legalistic tendency towards keeping the Lord's day as a day of rest as well as a day for worship, a tendency which they may not have intended or even anticipated. To be sure, they may not have intended to institute the Lord's (or eighth) day as a day of rest, and still less to encourage Christians to keep the day legalistically—they, in fact, might have sharply criticized such a tendency if they had faced it. They are nevertheless, regardless of their intention, partly responsible for today's tendency to regard the Lord's day just as a continuation of (or substitute for) the Old Testament sabbath without proper understanding of the aspects of continuity and discontinuity in Jesus' fulfilment of the sabbath in terms of his redemption, so that the Lord's day is kept legalistically as a day of rest as well as a day for worship.

Finally, we have reached an additional conclusion that, regardless of when and where the observance of the Lord's day as a day of worship

66. Note, however, not as a day of rest.

67. For example, especially Barnabas's employment of the allegorical way of interpretation.

originated, the tendency to conceive the Lord's day in conjunction with the sabbath must have appeared very early (probably not on biblical and theological grounds but from the practical and pastoral need[68]) and by the time of Ignatius and Barnabas the connection of the two days was more or less taken for granted. Quite possibly, as Ignatius, Barnabas and the Didachist indicate, the Jewish sabbath worship was replaced (or at least in the process of replacement) with the Christian Lord's day worship at least in their communities, and this Lord's day worship through the celebration of the eucharist, from its very start, may have had a close relation to Jesus' resurrection which had happened on the first day of the week.

68. That is, to battle against the legalistic tendency to keep the sabbath in the Jewish way. In order to do this more effectively they may have needed to put the Christian eucharistic celebration on the Lord's day, whose origin may have had a theological basis as the day of Jesus' resurrection, in opposition with the Jewish sabbath worship.

Chapter 8

JESUS AND THE SABBATH IN MATTHEW'S GOSPEL:
SUMMARY AND CONCLUSIONS

In this final chapter I will first recapitulate the various conclusions that have been reached in the previous chapters, then attempt to draw out the theological significance and practical implication of Jesus' fulfilment of the sabbath for Matthew and his community.

1. *Summary*

As a background study, I investigated the sabbath materials in the Old Testament and Jewish (and some Graeco-Roman) literature to the first century CE. From the investigation of the Old Testament materials, the following conclusions have been drawn: (1) God's rest on the seventh day in creation provides the etiology of the sabbath in the sense that it creates a rhythm which is to affect the whole creation (cf. Gen. 2.2-3; Exod. 20.8-11; 31.12-27). The ultimate purpose of the seventh day, however, goes beyond the institution of a weekly sabbath. I suggested that God's rest on the seventh day has an eschatological significance. (2) Most of the Old Testament sabbath materials presuppose, or assert, the holiness of the sabbath, because God is Lord of the sabbath (cf. Exod. 31.13-15; Isa. 58.13-14; Ezek. 20.12-20; 44.24; etc.). (3) A number of Old Testament sabbath references carry a covenantal overtone, and in two places the sabbath is called the sign of the eternal covenant (Exod. 31.13; Ezek. 20.12). In at least one place the covenant blessing promised for those who keep the sabbath holy is related to the messianic kingdom (Jer. 17.25-26; cf. Isa. 66.23). In some places legalistic observance of the sabbath without appreciation of its covenantal character is rejected by YHWH (Isa. 1.13; Hos. 2.13; Amos 8.5). (4) Though there are some signs of humanitarian concern in the sabbath commandments (Exod. 23.12; Deut. 5.15; etc.), in every case the primary concern is, in fact, not humanitarian or social as such but rather theological. (5) Though there are a few specific regulations of sabbath activity in the Old Testament (Neh. 10.32; 13.15-22; Jer. 17.19-27; etc.), their proportion in relation to the whole range of material on the sabbath in the Old Testament suggests a very different perspective as compared with later preoccupation with exceedingly detailed casuistic regulations, for example, in the Mishnah. (6) In a number of places the sabbath is associated with cultic elements. Considering the holiness of and God's Lordship of the sabbath, it would be natural that the sabbath provided an occasion for festal gathering in remembrance of their covenant relationship with God the creator and deliverer (from Egypt and Babylon).

From my investigating post-biblical Jewish (and some Graeco-Roman) literature the following conclusions have been drawn: (1) Through the centuries up to the first century CE, on the one hand, the rather general sabbath laws in the Old Testament were developed in the direction of an increasingly more specific and meticulous casuistry, and on the other hand, at least some of the sabbath regulations had moved towards leniency. Probably both developments were the result of attempts to render the sabbath law more applicable and practicable. In spite of the movement towards leniency, however, the growing number of more specific and meticulous regulations must inevitably have made the sabbath law more burdensome and directed the concern of the people away from *why* they should keep it to *how* they should keep it. (2) The recognition of the covenantal significance of the sabbath in post-biblical Jewish literature (perhaps apart from *Jubilees*; cf. *Jub.* 2.17-33) is strikingly weak as compared with that of the Old Testament. The holiness of the sabbath, however, is more widely recognized (*Jub.* 2.25; CD 3.14; 11.14-15; Philo, *Op. Mund.* 89-128; etc.), though in rabbinic literature this concern is once again not clearly expressed. (3) A number of Jewish sabbath references present the sabbath as a festival day to be celebrated. In many references, it is presupposed or prescribed that on the sabbath Jews offered the sacrifices in the temple and gathered in the synagogue in order, for example, to learn the torah and/or share communal meals (Josephus, *Life* 277-279; Philo, *Leg. All.* 156; etc.). (4) From the above observations I concluded that well before the first century CE the sabbath was established as one of the central characteristics of the Jewish religion, that there were various positions regarding the sabbath,[1] and

---

1. Probably because of differing contexts as well as differing theological perspectives.

that among those various trends the Pharisees and the first-century rabbis are outstanding in their extremely meticulous casuistry, in their movement towards greater leniency, and in their lack of emphasis on the covenantal significance of the sabbath.

Since the sabbath controversies in Mt. 12.1-14 appear to be closely related to Matthew's overall understanding of the law in relation to Jesus, I attempted first to present this overall understanding in the Gospel thus: (1) The programmatic pericope Mt. 5.17-20 is of crucial importance for the understanding of the law in Matthew's Gospel. (2) In 5.17 Matthew assigns the law a prophetic role in a limited period of salvation-history, which is now fulfilled by Jesus; the fulfilment of the law by Jesus includes the elements of 'continuity' and 'discontinuity', and this characteristic of fulfilment creates a genuine tension. (3) According to 5.18 the law has its validity for a limited period of salvation-history, the end of which has already been inaugurated by Jesus' first eschatological coming but awaits its consummation in his second coming. (4) According to 5.19 to obey or to set aside the slightest details of the law seen in the light of Jesus' fulfilment will determine one's status in the consummated kingdom—a warning against an antinomian tendency. (5) In 5.20 the greater righteousness which the disciples are expected to possess is presented as the criterion for entering the consummated kingdom—a warning against a legalistic tendency. According to Matthew's presentation in vv. 19 and 20, Jesus' warning against legalism (v. 20—i.e., exclusion from the kingdom) is much more severe than that against antinomianism (v. 19—i.e., the lowest status in the kingdom). (6) The six antitheses of 5.21-48 and other Matthean law-related passages (7.12; 9.13; 15.1-20; 19.16-21; 22.40; 23.1-36; etc.) confirm my conclusions above regarding 5.17-20. (7) These passages also show that the greater righteousness involves not only extending the scope of the law but also proceeding towards the higher and deeper level of godly life, and that the love commandment is the centre of the greater righteousness, but it is by no means all that it entails.

In the light of these background and preliminary investigations, I presented my understanding of the two sabbath controversy pericopes as follows.

The preceding pericope (11.25-30) prepares the way for the following sabbath controversy pericopes effectively; in particular the discussion of the fulfilment of the sabbath by Jesus is anticipated by the introduction of the notion of rest (v. 29) in a Christological and eschatological setting.

The real issue in the first controversy pericope (12.1-8) is not the question of the interpretation of the sabbath law as such; what is really asserted is rather that someone dramatically significant is present who is greater than David and the temple and that he is none other than the Son of man, who is the Lord of the sabbath, since he has fulfilled the sabbath by providing the eschatological rest (i.e., redemption) which is the ultimate goal of the sabbath. By piling up Jesus' first three responses (vv. 3-4, 5-6, 7) to the Pharisees' accusation (v. 2), which are all grounded upon the Old Testament in different ways, Matthew has already produced an extremely powerful argument. For Matthew, however, all these answers, in some sense, function as a preparation for the final response, the climax of the story, which pronounces Jesus' Lordship over the sabbath (v. 8). Jesus' authority which has already been the focus of the previous responses finds its culminating expression in the final pronouncement of his Lordship, which not only functions as the final response to the Pharisees' accusation but also adds another important dimension by injecting a high Christological note in the flow of the Gospel story as a whole.

The second controversy pericope (12.9-14) is closely linked with the first one, especially in the sense that Jesus' pronouncement in v. 8 extends its effect into the present pericope and that the Pharisees' reaction in v. 14 is to be seen as the reaction to Jesus' argument in vv. 3-8 as well as his argument and healing in vv. 11-13. The question raised by the Pharisees at the beginning (v. 10) is answered by Jesus (vv. 11-12) culminating in his pronouncement of the principle for the sabbath (v. 12b). These are some outstanding features of this pericope: (1) the Pharisees' antagonistic and unmerciful character is strikingly contrasted with Jesus' mercifulness (cf. also 11.29; 12.7, 19-20); (2) the legal issue ultimately gives way to Christology; (3) the healing miracle, even if not the focus of the pericope, still witnesses to Jesus as the messiah who brings wholeness of life to those who are under a bodily burden as a concrete sign of his messianic redemption, the ultimate goal of the sabbath; (4) the Pharisees' plan to kill Jesus in the face of his messianic ministry seems to anticipate that it is the messiah's fate to be killed by his opponents simply because of his messiahship (cf. 16.21; chs. 26–27).

The formula quotation with its introductory pericope (12.15-21) effectively confirms the Christological nature of the two preceding sabbath controversy pericopes by revealing their fulfilling aspects even more clearly. In particular Matthew's quotation of Isa. 42.1-4 introduced by the fulfilment formula endorses the claim that Jesus' proclamations regarding the sabbath and his healing on the sabbath are essential aspects of the fulfilment of the servant's mission as revealed in the Servant Song.

In the light of such an understanding of the sabbath pericopes I investigated another Matthean sabbath reference which is very short (24.20). After surveying various views presented to date, I concluded that the additional phrase μηδὲ σαββάτῳ is to be explained as indicating not that flight on the sabbath was wrong in itself, but that it would be practically difficult, and that it is therefore not right to argue that Matthew's community observed the sabbath simply on the grounds of 24.20.

Since Matthew's Gospel does not stand alone but is related to the other synoptic Gospels in some ways, without a discussion of the non-Matthean synoptic sabbath-related passages this investigation cannot be complete. I therefore investigated the other synoptic sabbath-related passages in Mark and/or Luke which are, in Matthew, either absent altogether or present as non-sabbath passages, and attempted to explain why they are missing or present in different forms in Matthew. These are the more important conclusions from the investigation: (1) For Luke and his readers, unlike for Matthew, the sabbath was probably neither a live nor a sensitive issue, and Luke therefore seems to have much more freedom in presenting the sabbath material than Matthew. (2) The focus of most sabbath passages in Mark and Luke (Mk 1.21-34 par.; Lk. 4.16-21; 13.10-17; 14.1-4) is, as in Mt. 12.1-8 par., 9-14 par., more on Christology and eschatology than on the sabbath itself. (3) It is thus extremely doubtful whether any of the Markan and Lukan (as well as Matthean) sabbath passages implies or even demonstrates a view which, in addition to recognizing the theological significance of the sabbath, even emphasizes the practical observance of it. (4) Matthew's probable omissions or modifications of the Markan and/or Lukan sabbath passages by no means show that Matthew is more conservative than Mark or Luke in respect of the sabbath. They rather witness that Matthew is much more careful in presenting the sabbath material than Mark or Luke, most probably because the sabbath was still a live and sensitive issue for his community. (5) In presenting the sabbath materials, Matthew, Mark and Luke show significant similarities[2] as well as

---

2. E.g. Christological and eschatological focus, criticism against Pharisaic way of keeping the sabbath, etc.

differences.[3] The similarities may be best explained by the common origin of their sabbath materials which is most likely Jesus' teaching itself, while the differences can be explained by the different literary style and structure of each Gospel and more importantly by the different context of each writing.

As an attempt to evaluate how Matthew's treatment of the sabbath was adopted, adapted or overlooked by the early church and to validate further some aspects of our understanding of Matthew's treatment as developed in the previous chapters, I investigated four passages in the Apostolic Fathers which relate to the sabbath/Lord's day. Since no direct quotation of or even clear allusion to the Matthean sabbath references is found in any of those writings, and since the origins of them (except probably for *Magn.* 9.1) are not at all certain, we cannot expect any definite conclusions. Nevertheless, the following are some significant conclusions: (1) Whether or not those Apostolic Fathers (or at least some of them) were acquainted with and made direct use of Matthew's Gospel (especially Matthew's sabbath controversy pericopes), their outright rejections of sabbath observance, in spite of their recognition of the authority of the Old Testament, may well derive from their understanding of the sabbath in eschatological and Christological terms as well as from their critical view of Judaism. They may then have understood the practical implication of Jesus' fulfilment of the sabbath for Christians as giving up sabbath observance altogether, especially when sabbath observance endangers the centrality of Jesus in Christian faith. (2) Many of their attempts to adapt Matthew's treatment of the sabbath in their particular contexts may be examples of poor contextualization, especially because, though they properly emphasized the aspect of discontinuity in Jesus' fulfilment of the sabbath, they overlooked and failed to emphasize the aspect of continuity in Jesus' fulfilment of the sabbath in terms of Jesus' redemption, and they consequently failed to direct attention to Jesus' redemptive work as the true fulfilment of the sabbath but rather put the Lord's (or eighth) day in opposition to the sabbath. Their misplacement of focus on another day instead of on Jesus himself and his redemption may have paved the way for another unhealthy tendency towards keeping the Lord's day legalistically as a day of rest as well as a day for worship without proper understanding of the aspects of

---

3. E.g. Matthew's greater care in presenting the sabbath material than Luke and Mark, etc.

continuity and discontinuity in Jesus' fulfilment of the sabbath in terms of his redemption.

2. The Theological Significance of Jesus' Fulfilment of the Sabbath for Matthew

In the light of the background, preliminary and exegetical investigations in Chapters 1–7, I will now briefly restate but with more confidence the theological significance of Jesus' fulfilment of the sabbath for Matthew as I have clarified it in Chapter 4.

First, Jesus' fulfilment of the sabbath as shown in Mt. 11.25–12.21 is nothing else but the fulfilment of God's original intention and ultimate goal for the sabbath as revealed in the Old Testament. As we have seen in Chapter 1, the sabbath is a reflection of the blessing of the seventh day which has its ultimate purpose in the eternal/eschatological rest for God's people. This rest is implied in God's rest after his creation which has no end (Gen. 2.2-3; Exod. 20.8-11) and is also exemplified in his deliverance of Israel from Egypt (Deut. 5.12-15). The sabbath command-ment thus was not given as a burden in its origin but as an expression of God's covenantal blessing. But this original intention and ultimate pur-pose were frequently forgotten or seriously distorted throughout the history of Israel, as some Old Testament passages indicate (e.g. Isa. 1.13; Hos. 2.13; Amos 8.5). By the time of Jesus the emphasis on the covenan-tal significance of the sabbath was strikingly weakened, and instead the rather general sabbath-related rules in the Old Testament had been developed in the direction of an increasingly meticulous casuistry. Though some sabbath regulations had moved towards leniency, the growing number of more specific and meticulous regulations must inevitably have made sabbath observance more burdensome and direct-ed the concern of the people away from *why* they should keep it to *how* they should keep it—an undesirable development towards legalistic observance of the sabbath. The sabbath which had been originally instituted as an expression of God's covenantal blessing thus became a burdensome institution (cf. Mt. 11.28). In such a situation Jesus came to recover the original intention and fulfil the ultimate goal for the sabbath as revealed in his invitation (11.28-30), teaching (especially, 12.3-7, 11-12), healing (12.13) and proclamation (12.8, 12b) as the Lord of the sabbath.

Secondly, Jesus' fulfilment of the sabbath as revealed in Mt. 11.25–

12.21 is a good example of what Jesus' saying in Mt. 5.17-20 signifies, and this example is in harmony with other examples in the Gospel which I examined in Chapter 3. Jesus, the Son of man, has come not to abolish the sabbath but to fulfil it. Jesus' fulfilment of the sabbath, like that of other laws, has the elements of both 'continuity' in the sense that Jesus' redemption fulfils the ultimate goal of the sabbath and 'discontinuity' in the sense that the sabbath is no longer the same after Jesus' fulfilment but is transcended by that fulfilment. Since the disciples are now partici-pating in the eschatological rest (= redemption), they are no longer obliged to keep the Old Testament sabbath law in the same way as the people in the Old Testament period did. This is strongly implied in 12.5-6: if the priests are not obliged to keep the sabbath as far as they are in the temple, the disciples are still less obliged to keep the sabbath because they are with Jesus who is greater than the temple. Such an implication can be even further extended in Matthew. If the temple, which is greater than the sabbath (12.6), ceases to function in its role as type after Jesus' fulfilment of it (ch. 24; 27.51), the sabbath can even more easily cease to function in its role as sign/type after Jesus' fulfil-ment of it. It is, of course, still not spelled out explicitly how this trans-cendental character in Jesus' fulfilment of the sabbath should affect the way the disciples relate themselves to the sabbath. But the Apostolic Fathers seem to have perceived it as implying the abandonment of the sabbath observance all together, as we have seen in Chapter 7.

Thirdly, Jesus' fulfilment of the sabbath as revealed in 11.25–12.21, like other aspects of his fulfilment, involves the eschatological tension— that is, the sabbath is *already* fulfilled by Jesus' ministry but it is *still* looking forward to its consummation at the close of the age (cf. 28.20). Jesus is already the Lord of the sabbath (12.8), by fulfilling the sabbath, that is, by providing the eschatological rest (= redemption). Nevertheless, the eschatological rest Jesus provides has also a futuristic element—Jesus' Lordship over the sabbath is not yet recognized by many Jews as well as by most Gentiles, and more importantly Jesus' proclamation of justice to the Gentiles is not yet completed (12.18, 20-21; cf. also 28.19-20).

All in all, the sabbath in Matthew, like the law in general, is to be understood in a context of fulfilment, eschatology and Christology—that is, in a context of salvation-history.[4]

4.	Cf. Meier, *Law*, pp. 88-89.

3. *The Practical Implication of Jesus' Fulfilment of the Sabbath for Matthew and his Community*

For Matthew's community, through their confrontation with non-Christian Jews, Jesus' relation to the Old Testament law (including the sabbath law) and also their relation to it must have been a live issue. In this context, two opposite tendencies (i.e., legalistic and antinomian) could have coexisted within the Christian movement and both of them may have been real threats to the community. In such a situation, Matthew presents a foundational principle regarding Jesus' relation to the law in 5.17-20 with appropriate warnings against the two dangers—that is, legalism (v. 20) and antinomianism (v. 19). In 11.25–12.21 Matthew has attempted to apply this principle for the sabbath law, one of the crucial issues of his day. I have already pointed out that for Matthew Jesus' fulfilment of the sabbath, as of other laws, involves the elements of both 'continuity' and 'discontinuity'. What practical implication, however, would this double continuity–discontinuity character have had for his community?

Though we cannot be sure, some groups in Matthew's community may still have kept the sabbath, while others did not. If there were, as there may have been, some people in the community who still observed the sabbath legalistically, Matthew's message for them must have been clear and strong: Turn your attention to the significance of Jesus' fulfilment of the sabbath, especially to the element of discontinuity in that fulfilment, since the sabbath remains no longer the same after Jesus' fulfilment but rather is transcended by his fulfilment of it. For other groups who may have disregarded or even condemned the observance of the sabbath, Matthew may at most have reminded them that the sabbath commandment itself is not such a bad thing as they supposed, provided that their focus is on Jesus himself and his redemption. If this was the case, Matthew's treatment of the sabbath is once again in line with that of the law in general in 5.17-20, where Jesus' warning against legalism is much more severe than that against antinomianism. For Matthew, the sabbath is perpetual only until its fulfilment, like the temple (ch. 24; cf. 12.6) and accordingly the priesthood and sacrifices. After Jesus' fulfilment of the sabbath, the function of the sabbath as the sign/type is replaced by Jesus' redemption, the antitype of the sabbath, and thus is no longer required. Matthew may then have had enough reason even to encourage his community to give up sabbath observance and instead to focus on Jesus, the Lord of the sabbath, and on his redemption, the ultimate goal of the sabbath. Such advice may even have been necessary especially if the community had to face the danger of legalism within it and also the threat of casuistic Pharisaism outside it, both of which endangered the true meaning and significance of Jesus' fulfilment of the sabbath. To be sure this suggestion has to some extent gone beyond what is clearly indicated in 11.25–12.21. Nevertheless, in the light of 5.17-20 and other law-related passages in the Gospel, the general character of Matthew's community as I have assumed and observed it, the plot of the Gospel, and especially the witnesses of the Apostolic Fathers, I am now quite confident that it is not far from the truth.

BIBLIOGRAPHY

1. *Editions and Translations Used*

Aland, K., *et al.* (eds.), *Novum Testamentum Graece* (Stuttgart: Deutsche Bibelgesellschaft, 27th edn, 1993).

Aland, K. (ed.), *Synopsis Quattuor Evangeliorum. Locis parallelis evangeliorum apocryphorum et patrum adhibitis edidit* (Stuttgart: Deutsche Bibelgesellschaft Stuttgart, 13th edn, 1985).

Boyle, I., *Eusebius' Ecclesiastical History* (repr.; Grand Rapids: Baker, 1955).

Charles, R.H., *The Book of Jubilees* (London: A. & C. Black, 1902).

Charlesworth, J.H. (ed.), *The Old Testament Pseudepigrapha* (2 vols.; Garden City, NY: Doubleday, 1983, 1985).

Colson, F.H., *et al.*, *Philo* (10 vols.; LCL; London: Heinemann, 1929–62).

Danby, H., *The Mishnah: Translated from the Hebrew with Introduction and Brief Explanatory Notes* (Oxford: Oxford University Press, 1933).

Davies, P.R., *The Damascus Covenant* (JSOTSup, 25; Sheffield: JSOT Press, 1982).

Dupont-Sommer, A., *The Essene Writings from Qumran* (trans. G. Vermes; Oxford: Blackwell, 1961).

Eisenman, R., and M. Wise, *The Dead Sea Scrolls Uncovered: The First Complete Translation and Interpretation of 50 Key Documents Withheld for Over 35 Years* (Shaftesbury: Element, 1992).

Epstein, I. (ed.), *The Babylonian Talmud* (35 vols.; London: Soncino Press, 1935–52).

Kleist, J.A., *The Didache, Barnabas, St Polycarp, Papias, Diognetus* (London: Longmans, Green, 1948).

Lake, K., *Apostolic Fathers* (2 vols.; LCL; London: Heinemann, 1912, 1913).

Lauterbach, J.Z., *Mekilta de Rabbi Ishmael: A Critical Edition on the Basis of the MSS and Early Editions with an English Translation, Introduction and Notes* (3 vols.; Philadelphia: Jewish Publication Society, 1933–35).

Lohse, E., *Die Texte aus Qumran* (Munich: Kösel-Verlag, 1964).

Maier, J., *The Temple Scroll: An Introduction, Translation and Commentary* (JSOTSup, 34; Sheffield: JSOT Press, 1985).

Martínez, F.G., *The Dead Sea Scrolls Translated: The Qumran Texts in English* (trans. W.G.E. Watson; Leiden: Brill, 1994).

Neusner, J., *The Rabbinic Traditions about the Pharisees before 70* (3 parts; Leiden: Brill, 1971).

Neusner, J., *et al.* (eds.), *The Tosefta* (6 vols.; New York: Ktav, 1977–86).

Rabin, C., *The Zadokite Documents. I. The Admonition. II. The Laws. Edited with a Translation and Notes* (Oxford: Oxford University Press, 2nd edn, 1958).

Rahlfs, A. (ed.), *Septuaginta* (2 vols.; Stuttgart: Deutsche Bibelgesellschaft Stuttgart, 1935, 1979).

Richardson, C.C. (ed.), *Early Christian Fathers* (New York: Macmillan, 1953).

Roberts, A., and J. Donaldson (eds.), *The Ante-Nicene Fathers* (10 vols.; Grand Rapids: Eerdmans, repr. 1973 [1885–87]).

Rordorf, W., *Sabbat und Sontag in der Alten Kirche* (Zürich: Theologischer Verlag, 1972).

Schaff, P. (ed.), *The Nicene and Post-Nicene Fathers* (28 vols.; Grand Rapids: Eerdmans, repr. 1956 [1886–88]).

Sparks, H.F.D. (ed.), *The Apocryphal Old Testament* (Oxford: Oxford University Press, 1984).

Stern, M., *Greek and Latin Authors on Jews and Judaism* (3 vols.; Jerusalem: Israel Academy of Sciences and Humanities, 1976–84).

Thackeray, H.St.J., *et al.*, *Josephus* (10 vols.; LCL; London: Heinemann, 1926–65).

Vermes, G., *The Dead Sea Scrolls in English* (Sheffield: JSOT Press, 3rd edn, 1987).

Whittaker, M., *Jews and Christians: Graeco-Roman Views* (CCWJCW, 6; Cambridge: Cambridge University Press, 1984).

2. *Reference Works*

Balz, H., and G. Schneider (eds.), *Exegetical Dictionary of the New Testament* (3 vols.; Edinburgh: T. & T. Clark, 1990–93).

Cross, F.L., and E.A. Livingstone (eds.), *The Oxford Dictionary of the Christian Church* Oxford: Oxford University Press, 2nd rev. edn, 1983).

Galling, K., *et al.* (eds.), *Die Religion in Geschichte und Gegenwart* (Tübingen: Mohr, 3rd edn, 1958).

Green, J.B., *et al.* (eds.), *Dictionary of Jesus and the Gospels* (Leicester: IVP, 1992).

Kittel, G., and G. Friedrich (eds.), *Theological Dictionary of the New Testament* (9 vols.; trans. G.W. Bromiley; Grand Rapids: Eerdmans, 1964–74).

3. *General Works*

Ackroyd, P.R., *The Chronicler in his Age* (JSOTSup, 101; Sheffield: JSOT Press, 1991).

Aichinger, H., 'Quellenkritische Untersuchung der Perikope vom Ährenraufen am Sabbat. Mk 2,23-28 par Mt 12,1-8 par Lk 6,1-5', in A. Fuchs (ed.), *Jesus in der Verkündigung der Kirche* (SNTU, a1; Freistadt: Plöchl, 1976), pp. 110-53.

Albeck, C., *Einführung in die Mischna* (Berlin: de Gruyter, 1971).

Albright, W.F., and C.S. Mann, *Matthew: A New Translation with Introduction and Commentary* (AB, 26; New York: Doubleday, 1971).

Allen, L.C., *Ezekiel 20–48* (WBC, 29; Dallas: Word Books, 1990).

Allen, W.C., *A Critical and Exegetical Commentary on the Gospel according to Saint Matthew* (ICC; Edinburgh: T. & T. Clark, 3rd edn, 1912).

Allison, D.C., *The New Moses: A Matthean Typology* (Edinburgh: T. & T. Clark, 1993).

—'Two Notes on a Key Text: Matthew 11.25-30', *JTS* 39 (1988), pp. 477-85.

Anderson, H., 'Broadening Horizons. The Rejection at Nazareth Pericope of Luke 4.16-30 in Light of Recent Critical Trends', *Int* 18 (1964), pp. 259-75.

Anderson, J.C., *Matthew's Narrative Web: Over, and Over, and Over Again* (JSNTSup, 91; Sheffield: JSOT Press, 1994).

Andreasen, N.-E.A., *The Old Testament Sabbath. A Tradition-Historical Investigation* (SBLDS, 7; Missoula, MT: Society of Biblical Literature, 1972).

Andriessen, P., 'The Authorship of the *Epistula ad Diognetum*', *VC* 1 (1947), pp. 129-36.

Aquinas, T., *Summa Theologica* (5 vols.; New York: Benziger Brothers, repr. 1948).

Attridge, H.W., 'Josephus and his Works', in M.E. Stone (ed.), *The Literature of the Jewish People in the Period of the Second Temple and the Talmud*. II. *Jewish Writings of the Second Temple Period* (CRINT, 2; Assen: Van Gorcum, 1984), pp. 185-232.

Audet, J.-P., *La Didaché: Instructions des apôtres* (Paris: Gabalda, 1958).

Bacchiocchi, S., *Divine Rest for Human Restlessness* (Rome: Pontifical Gregorian University Press, 1980).

—*From Sabbath to Sunday: A Historical Investigation of the Rise of Sunday Observance in Early Christianity* (Rome: Pontifical Gregorian University Press, 1977).

—'Remembering the Sabbath: The Creation-Sabbath in Jewish and Christian History', in T.C. Eskenazi, *et al.* (eds.), *The Sabbath in Jewish and Christian Traditions* (New York: Crossroad, 1991), pp. 69-97.

—*The Sabbath in the New Testament* (Berrien Springs, MI: Biblical Perspectives, 2nd edn, 1990).

Bacon, B.W., *Studies in Matthew* (London: Constable, 1930).

Baltensweiler, H., 'Die Ehebruchsklauseln bei Matthäus. Zu Matth. 5,32; 19,9', *TZ* 15 (1959), pp. 340-56.

Bammel, C.P.H., 'Ignatian Problems', *JTS* 33 (1982), pp. 62-97.

Banks, R., *Jesus and the Law in the Synoptic Tradition* (SNTSMS, 28; Cambridge: Cambridge University Press, 1975).

Barnard, L.W., 'The *Epistula ad Diognetum*: Two Units from One Author?', *ZNW* 56 (1965), pp. 130-37.

—*Studies in the Apostolic Fathers and their Background* (Oxford: Blackwell, 1966).

Barr, J., *The Semantics of Biblical Language* (Oxford: Oxford University Press, 1961).

Barrett, C.K., 'The Eschatology of the Epistle to the Hebrews', in W.D. Davies and D. Daube (eds.), *The Background of the New Testament and its Eschatology* (Cambridge: Cambridge University Press, 1956), pp. 363-93.

—'Jews and Judaizers in the Epistles of Ignatius', in R. Hamerton-Kelly and R. Scroggs (eds.), *Jews, Greeks and Christians: Religious Cultures in Late Antiquity* (Leiden: Brill, 1976), pp. 220-44.

Barth, G., 'Matthew's Understanding of the Law', in G. Bornkamm, G. Barth and H.J. Held, *Tradition and Interpretation in Matthew* (trans. P. Scott; London: SCM Press, 1963), pp. 58-164.

Bauckham, R., 'The Lord's Day', in D.A. Carson (ed.), *From Sabbath to Lord's Day: A Biblical, Historical, and Theological Investigation* (Grand Rapids: Zondervan, 1982), pp. 221-50.

—'Sabbath and Sunday in the Medieval Church in the West', in Carson (ed.), *Lord's Day*, pp. 300-309.

—'Sabbath and Sunday in the Post-Apostolic Church', in Carson (ed.), *Lord's Day*, pp. 251-98.

—'Sabbath and Sunday in the Protestant Tradition', in Carson (ed.), *Lord's Day*, pp. 311-41.

Bauer, D.R., *The Structure of Matthew's Gospel* (JSNTSup, 31; Sheffield: JSOT Press, 1988).

Beare, F.W., *The Earliest Records of Jesus* (Oxford: Blackwell, 1962).

—*The Gospel according to St Matthew: A Commentary* (Oxford: Blackwell, 1981).

—'The Sabbath was Made for Man', *JBL* 79 (1960), pp. 130-36.

Beasley-Murray, G.R., *Jesus and the Kingdom of God* (Exeter: Paternoster, 1986).

Beckwith, R.T., and W. Stott, *This is the Day: The Biblical Doctrine of the Christian Sunday in its Jewish and Early Church Setting* (London: Marshall, Morgan & Scott, 1978).

Bertram, G., 'κρεμάννυμι', *TDNT*, III, pp. 915-21.

—'νήπιος', *TDNT*, IV, pp. 912-23.

Betz, H.D., *Essays on the Sermon on the Mount* (Philadelphia: Fortress Press, 1985).

—'The Logion of the Easy Yoke and of Rest', *JBL* 86 (1967), pp. 10-24.

Bilde, P., *Flavius Josephus between Jerusalem and Rome* (JSPSup, 2; Sheffield: JSOT Press, 1988).

Black, M., 'The Aramaic Spoken by Christ and Luke 14[5]', *JTS* 1 (1950), pp. 60-62.

Blomberg, C.L., 'Law in Luke–Acts', *JSNT* 22 (1984), pp. 53-80.

—*Matthew* (NAC; Nashville: Broadman, 1992).

Borg, M.J., *Conflict, Holiness and Politics in the Teachings of Jesus* (New York and Toronto: Edwin Mellen Press, 1984).

Borgen, P., 'Philo of Alexandria', in M.E. Stone (ed.), *The Literature of the Jewish People in the Period of the Second Temple and the Talmud*. II. *Jewish Writings of the Second Temple Period* (CRINT, 2; Assen: Van Gorcum, 1984), pp. 233-82.

Bornkamm, G., 'End-expectation and Church in Matthew', in G. Bornkamm, G. Barth and H.J. Held, *Tradition and Interpretation in Matthew* (trans. P. Scott; London: SCM Press, 1963), pp. 15-51.

—*Jesus of Nazareth* (trans. I. McLuskey, F. McLuskey and J.M. Robinson; London: Hodder and Stoughton, 1960).

Botterweck, G.J., 'Der Sabbat im Alten Testament', *Theologische Quartalschrift* 134 (1954), pp. 134-47, 448-457.

Brandon, S.G.F., *The Fall of Jerusalem and the Christian Church: A Study of the Effects of the Jewish Overthrow of A.D. 70 on Christianity* (London: SPCK, 2nd edn, 1957).

Branscomb, B.H., *Jesus and the Law of Moses* (London: Hodder & Stoughton, 1930).

Braun, H., *Spätjüdisch-häretischer und frühchristlicher Radikalismus* (2 vols.; Tübingen: Mohr, 1957).

Braun, R., *1 Chronicles* (WBC, 14; Waco, TX: Word Books, 1986).

Brockington, L.H. (ed.), *Ezra, Nehemiah and Esther* (London: Nelson, 1969).

Broer, I., 'Die Antithesen und der Evangelist Matthäus', *BZ* 19 (1975), pp. 50-63.

—*Freiheit vom Gesetz und Radikalisierung des Gesetzes* (SBS, 98; Stuttgart: Verlag Katholisches Bibelwerk, 1980).

Brooks, S.H., *Matthew's Community: The Evidence of his Special Sayings Material* (JSNTSup, 16; Sheffield: JSOT Press, 1987).

Brown, R.E., *The Death of the Messiah: A Commentary on the Passion Narratives in the Four Gospels* (2 vols.; The Anchor Bible Reference Library; London: Geoffrey Chapman, 1994).

Brown, R.E., and J.P. Meier, *Antioch and Rome* (London: Geoffrey Chapman, 1983).

Bruner, F.D., *Matthew*. I. *The Christbook*. II. *The Churchbook* (2 vols.; Dallas: Word Books, 1987, 1990).

Büchsel, F., 'λύω', *TDNT*, IV, pp. 335-56.

Budd, P.J., *Numbers* (WBC, 5; Waco, TX: Word Books, 1984).

Bultmann, R., *The History of the Synoptic Tradition* (trans. J. Marsh; Oxford: Blackwell, 1963).

—*Theology of the New Testament* (2 vols.; trans. K. Grobel; London: SCM Press, 1952, 1955).

Caird, G.B., *The Gospel of St Luke* (Pelican Gospel Commentaries; London: Penguin Books, 1963).

Calvin, J., *Institutes of the Christian Religion* (2 vols.; ed. J.T. McNeill; trans. F.L. Battles; LCC, 20, 21; Philadelphia: Westminster, 1960).

Caragounis, C.C., *The Son of Man: Vision and Interpretation* (Tübingen: Mohr, 1986).

Carlston, C., 'The Things that Defile', *NTS* 15 (1968/69), pp. 75-96.

Carroll, R.P., *Jeremiah 1–25* (OTL; London: SCM Press, 1986).

Carson, D.A., 'Jesus and the Sabbath in the Four Gospels', in *idem* (ed.), *From Sabbath to Lord's Day: A Biblical, Historical, and Theological Investigation* (Grand Rapids: Zondervan, 1982), pp. 57-97.

—'The Jewish Leaders in Matthew's Gospel: a Reappraisal', *JETS* 25 (1982), pp. 161-74.

—'Matthew', in F.E. Gaebelein (ed.), *The Expositor's Bible Commentary*, VIII (12 vols.; Grand Rapids: Zondervan, 1984), pp. 1-599.

Casey, M., 'Culture and Historicity: The Plucking of the Grain (Mark 2.23-28)', *NTS* 34 (1988), pp. 1-23.

Cassuto, U., *A Commentary on the Book of Genesis*. I. *From Adam to Noah* (Jerusalem: Magnes Press, 1961).

Charette, B., '"To Proclaim Liberty to the Captives": Matthew 11.28-30 in the Light of OT Prophetic Expectation', *NTS* 38 (1992), pp. 290-97.

Charlesworth, J.H., *Jesus within Judaism: New Light from Exciting Archaeological Discoveries* (London: SPCK, 1988).

Childs, B.S., *Exodus* (OTL; London: SCM Press, 1974).

—*Introduction to the Old Testament as Scripture* (London: SCM Press, 1979).

Chilton, B., 'Announcement in Nazareth: An Analysis of Luke 4.16-21', in R.T. France and D. Wenham (eds.), *Gospel Perspectives*. II. *Studies of History and Tradition in the Four Gospels* (Sheffield: JSOT Press, 1981), pp. 147-72.

—*God in Strength* (Freistadt: Plöchl, 1979).

Christensen, D.L., *Deuteronomy 1–11* (WBC, 6a; Dallas: Word Books, 1991).

Clines, D.J.A., *Ezra, Nehemiah, Esther* (NCB; London: Marshall, Morgan & Scott, 1984).

Cody, A., 'The *Didache*: An English Translation', in C.N. Jefford (ed.), *The Didache in Context: Essays on its Text, History and Transmission* (NovTSup, 77; Leiden: Brill, 1995), pp. 3-14.

Cohn, S.S., 'The Place of Jesus in the Religious Life of his Day', *JBL* 48 (1929), pp. 82-108.

Cohn-Sherbok, D.M., 'An Analysis of Jesus' Arguments concerning the Plucking of Grain on the Sabbath', *JSNT* 2 (1979), pp. 31-41.

Collins, R.F., 'Matthew's ἐντολαί. Towards an Understanding of the Commandments in the First Gospel', in F. van Segbroeck, *et al.* (eds.), *The Four Gospels 1992:*

Festschrift Frans Neirynck, II (3 vols.; BETL, 100; Leuven: Leuven University Press, 1992), pp. 1325-48.

Connolly, R.H., 'The Date and Authorship of the Epistle to Diognetus', *JTS* 36 (1935), pp. 347-53.

Conzelmann, H., *The Theology of St Luke* (trans. G. Buswell; London: Faber & Faber, 1960).

Cope, O.L., *Matthew: A Scribe Trained for the Kingdom of Heaven* (CBQMS, 5; Washington, DC: The Catholic Biblical Association of America, 1976).

Corwin, V., *St Ignatius and Christianity in Antioch* (New Haven: Yale University Press, 1960).

Cotterell, P., and M. Turner, *Linguistics and Biblical Interpretation* (London: SPCK, 1989).

Court, J.M., 'The Didache and St Matthew's Gospel', *SJT* 34 (1981), pp. 109-20.

Craigie, P.C., *The Book of Deuteronomy* (NICOT; Grand Rapids: Eerdmans, 1976).

Cranfield, C.E.B., *The Epistle to the Romans* (2 vols.; ICC; Edinburgh: T. & T. Clark, 1975, 1979).

—*The Gospel according to St Mark* (Cambridge Greek Testament Commentary; Cambridge: Cambridge University Press, 1977 [1959]).

Creed, J.M., *The Gospel according to St Luke: The Greek Text with Introduction, Notes, and Indices* (London: Macmillan, 1930).

Crossan, J.D., *The Historical Jesus: The Life of a Mediterranean Jewish Peasant* (Edinburgh: T. & T. Clark, 1991).

Cullmann, O., *The Christology of the New Testament* (trans. S.C. Guthrie and C.A.M. Hall; London: SCM Press, 2nd edn, 1963).

Dalman, G., *Jesus-Jeshua: Studies in the Gospels* (trans. P.L. Levertoff; London: SPCK, 1929).

Danker, F.W., *Jesus and the New Age: A Commentary on St Luke's Gospel* (Philadelphia: Fortress Press, 2nd edn, 1988).

Daube, D., *The New Testament and Rabbinic Judaism* (London: Athlone Press, 1956).

—'The Responsibilities of Master and Disciples in the Gospels', *NTS* 19 (1972), pp. 1-15.

Dautzenberg, G., 'Ist das Schwurverbot Mt 5,33-37; Jak 5,12 ein Beispiel für die Torakritik Jesu?', *BZ* 25 (1981), pp. 47-66.

Davies, M., *Matthew* (Readings: A New Biblical Commentary; Sheffield: JSOT Press, 1993).

Davies, W.D., '"Knowledge" in the Dead Sea Scrolls and Matthew 11.25-30', in *idem, Origins*, pp. 119-44.

—'Matthew 5:17, 18', in *idem, Christian Origins and Judaism* (London: Darton, Longman & Todd, 1962), pp. 31-66.

—*The Setting of the Sermon on the Mount* (Cambridge: Cambridge University Press, 1964).

Davies, W.D., and D.C. Allison, *A Critical and Exegetical Commentary on the Gospel according to Saint Matthew* (2 vols.; ICC; Edinburgh: T. & T. Clark, 1988 [vol. I], 1991 [vol. II]).

Delafosse, H., 'Nouvel examen des lettres d'Ignace d'Antioche', *Revue d'histoire et de littérature religieuse* 8 (1922), pp. 303-37, 477-533.

Delling, G., 'τρεῖς κτλ', *TDNT*, VIII, pp. 216-25.

Derrett, J.D.M., 'Christ and the Power of Choice (Mark 3,1-6)', *Bib* 65 (1984), pp. 168-88.

—'Judaica in St Mark', in *idem, Studies in the New Testament*, I (Leiden: Brill, 1977), pp. 85-100.

—'Positive Perspectives on two Lucan Miracles', *Downside Review* 104 (1986), pp. 272-87.

Deutsch, C., *Hidden Wisdom and the Easy Yoke: Wisdom, Torah and Discipleship in Matthew 11.25-30* (JSNTSup, 18; Sheffield: JSOT Press, 1987).

—'Wisdom in Matthew: Transformation of a Symbol', *NovT* 32 (1990), pp. 13-47.

Dibelius, M., 'Die Bergpredigt' (1937, 1940), in *idem, Botschaft und Geschichte* (Tübingen: Mohr, 1953), pp. 79-174.

—*From Tradition to Gospel* (trans. B.L. Woolf; London: Ivor Nicholson & Watson, 1934).

Dillard, R.B., *2 Chronicles* (WBC, 15; Waco, TX: Word Books, 1987).

Donahue, P.J., 'Jewish Christianity in the Letters of Ignatius of Antioch', *VC* 32 (1978), pp. 81-93.

Draper, J., 'The Jesus Tradition in the Didache', in D. Wenham (ed.), *Gospel Perspectives*, V (Sheffield: JSOT Press, 1984), pp. 269-87.

Dressler, H.H.P., 'The Sabbath in the Old Testament', in D.A. Carson (ed.), *From Sabbath to Lord's Day: A Biblical, Historical, and Theological Investigation* (Grand Rapids: Zondervan, 1982), pp. 21-41.

Driver, G.R., *The Judaean Scrolls: The Problem and a Solution* (Oxford: Blackwell, 1965).

Dunn, J.D.G., 'Mark 2.1–3.6: A Bridge between Jesus and Paul on the Question of the Law', in *idem, Jesus, Paul and the Law: Studies in Mark and Galatians* (London: SPCK, 1990), pp. 10-36.

—'Pharisees, Sinners, and Jesus', in *idem, Law*, pp. 61-88.

—*Romans 9–16* (WBC, 38b; Dallas: Word Books, 1988).

Durham, J.I., *Exodus* (WBC, 3; Waco, TX: Word Books, 1987).

Edwards, R.A., *Matthew's Story of Jesus* (Philadelphia: Fortress Press, 1985).

Eichrodt, W., *Ezekiel* (trans. C. Quin; OTL; London: SCM Press, 1970).

Ellis, E.E., *The Gospel of Luke* (NCB; London: Marshall, Morgan & Scott, 2nd edn, 1974).

Evans, C.F., *Saint Luke* (London: SCM Press, 1990).

Fensham, F.C., *The Books of Ezra and Nehemiah* (NICOT; Grand Rapids: Eerdmans, 1982).

Fenton, J.C., *The Gospel of St Matthew* (Pelican Gospel Commentaries; London: Penguin Books, 1963).

Filson, F.V., *A Commentary on the Gospel according to St Matthew* (BNTC; London: A. & C. Black, 1960).

Finkelstein, L., *The Pharisees: The Sociological Background of their Faith* (2 vols.; Philadelphia: Jewish Publication Society, 3rd edn, 1962).

Fitzmyer, J.A., *The Gospel according to Luke: Introduction, Translation, and Notes* (2 vols.; AB, 28-28a; Garden City, NY: Doubleday, 1979, 1985).

—'The Matthean Divorce Texts and Some New Palestinian Evidence', *Theological Studies* 37 (1976), pp. 197-226.

Fohrer, G., *Die Hauptprobleme des Buches Ezechiel* (Berlin: Töpelmann, 1952).

—*Introduction to the Old Testament* (trans. D. Green; London: SPCK, 1968).

France, R.T., *The Gospel according to Matthew: An Introduction and Commentary* (TNTC; Leicester: IVP, 1985).

—*Jesus and the Old Testament: His Application of Old Testament Passages to Himself and his Mission* (London: Tyndale Press, 1971).

—*Matthew: Evangelist and Teacher* (Exeter: Paternoster, 1989).

Frankemölle, H., *Yahwe-Bund und Kirche Christi: Studien zur Form- und Traditions-geschichte des 'Evangeliums' nach Matthäus* (NTAbh, NS 10; Münster: Aschendorff, 2nd edn, 1984).

Frend, W.H.C., *Martyrdom and Persecution in the Early Church: A Study of Conflict from the Maccabees to Donatus* (Oxford: Blackwell, 1965).

—*The Rise of Christianity* (London: Darton, Longman & Todd, 1984).

Freyne, S., *Galilee from Alexander the Great to Hadrian: A Study of Second Temple Judaism* (Wilmington, DE: Glazier/Notre Dame University Press, 1980).

—*Galilee, Jesus and the Gospels: Literary Approaches and Historical Investigations* (Dublin: Gill & Macmillan, 1988).

Friedlander, G., *The Jewish Sources of the Sermon on the Mount* (New York: KTAV, 1969).

Garland, D.E., *The Intention of Matthew 23* (NovTSup, 52; Leiden: Brill, 1979).

Gärtner, B., *The Temple and the Community in Qumran and the New Testament: A Comparative Study in the Temple Symbolism of the Qumran Texts and the New Testament* (SNTSMS, 1; Cambridge: Cambridge University Press, 1965).

Gerhardsson, B., *The Gospel Tradition* (ConBNT, 15; Lund: Gleerup, 1986).

—*Memory and Manuscript: Oral Tradition and Written Transmission in Rabbinic Judaism and Early Christianity* (trans. E.J. Sharpe; ASNU, 22; Lund: Gleerup, 2nd edn, 1964).

—*The Mighty Acts of Jesus according to Matthew* (Lund: Gleerup, 1979).

Gese, H., 'Das Gesetz', in *idem, Zur biblischen Theologie* (Münich: Kaiser, 1977), pp. 55-84.

Giet, S., *L'énigme de la Didaché* (Paris: Ophrys, 1970).

Gnilka, J., *Das Evangelium nach Markus* (2 vols.; EKKNT, 2; Zürich: Benziger Verlag, 1980).

—*Das Matthäusevangelium* (2 vols.; HTKNT, 1; Freiburg: Herder, 1986, 1988).

Godet, F., *A Commentary on the Gospel of St Luke* (2 vols.; trans. E.W. Shelders; Edinburgh: T. & T. Clark, 1887, 1889).

Golb, N., 'Who Hid the Dead Sea Scrolls?', *Biblical Archaeologist* 48 (1985), pp. 68-82.

Goldberg, A., 'The Mishna—A Study Book of Halakha', in S. Safrai (ed.), *The Literature of the Jewish People in the Period of the Second Temple and the Talmud. III. The Literature of the Sages. Midrash, Mishnah, Talmud.* Part I. (CRINT, 2; Assen: Van Gorcum, 1987), pp. 211-62.

Goppelt, L., 'Das Problem der Bergpredigt', in *idem, Christologie und Ethik* (Göttingen: Vandenhoeck & Ruprecht, 1968), pp. 27-43.

—*Theology of the New Testament* (2 vols.; ed. J. Roloff; trans. J.E. Alsup; Grand Rapids: Eerdmans, 1981).

Gordon, R.P., *1 & 2 Samuel* (Exeter: Paternoster, 1986).

Gould, E.P., *A Critical and Exegetical Commentary on the Gospel according to St Mark* (ICC; Edinburgh: T. & T. Clark, 1896).

Goulder, M.D., *Midrash and Lection in Matthew* (London: SPCK, 1974).

Gowan, D.E., *Bridge between the Testaments* (Allison Park, PA: Pickwick, 1986).

Gray, J., *1 & 2 Kings* (OTL; London: SCM Press, 3rd edn, 1977).

Green, H.B., *The Gospel according to Matthew* (New Clarendon Bible; Oxford: Oxford University Press, 1975).

Green, J.B., 'Jesus and a Daughter of Abraham (Luke 13:10-17): Test Case for a Lucan Perspective on Jesus' Miracles', *CBQ* 51 (1989), pp. 643-54.

Grindel, J., 'Matthew 12,18-21', *CBQ* 29 (1967), pp. 110-15.

Grundmann, W., *Das Evangelium nach Lukas* (THNT, 3; Berlin: Evangelische Verlagsanstalt, 1961).

—*Das Evangelium nach Markus* (THNT, 2; Berlin: Evangelische Verlagsanstalt, 7th edn, 1977).

—*Das Evangelium nach Matthäus* (THNT, 1; Berlin: Evangelische Verlagsanstalt, 1968).

Guelich, R.A., *Mark 1–8.26* (WBC, 34a; Dallas: Word Books, 1989).

—*Sermon on the Mount* (Waco, TX: Word Books, 1982).

Gundry, R.H., *Mark: A Commentary on his Apology for the Cross* (Grand Rapids: Eerdmans, 1993).

—*Matthew: A Commentary on his Literary and Theological Art* (Grand Rapids: Eerdmans 2nd edn, 1994 [1982]).

—'A Responsive Evaluation of the Social History of the Matthean Community in Roman Syria', in D.L. Balch (ed.), *Social History of the Matthean Community: Cross-Disciplinary Approaches* (Minneapolis, MN: Fortress Press, 1991), pp. 62-67.

—*The Use of the Old Testament in St. Matthew's Gospel with Specific Reference to the Messianic Hope* (NovTSup, 18; Leiden: Brill, 1967).

Gutbrod, W.H., 'νόμος', *TDNT*, IV, pp. 1036-91.

Guy, F., '"The Lord's Day" in the Letter of Ignatius to the Magnesians', *AUSS* 2 (1964), pp. 1-17.

Haenchen, E., *Der Weg Jesu: Eine Erklärung des Markus-Evangeliums und der kanonischen Parallelen* (Berlin: Töpelmann, 1966).

Hagner, D.A., *Matthew 1–13* (WBC, 33a; Dallas: Word Books, 1993).

—'The Sayings of Jesus in the Apostolic Fathers and Justin Martyr', in D. Wenham (ed.), *Gospel Perspectives*, V (Sheffield: JSOT Press, 1984), pp. 233-68.

Hahn, F., 'Die Bildworte vom neuen Flicken und vom jungen Wein', *EvT* 31 (1971), pp. 357-75.

Hamerton-Kelly, R.G., 'Attitudes to the Law in Matthew's Gospel: a Discussion of Matthew 5.18', *Biblical Research* 17 (1972), pp. 19-32.

Hamilton, V.P., *The Book of Genesis: Chapters 1–17* (NICOT; Grand Rapids: Eerdmans, 1990).

Hamm, M.D., 'The Freeing of the Bent Woman and the Restoration of Israel: Luke 13.10-17 as Narrative Theology', *JSNT* 31 (1987), pp. 23-44.

Hare, D.R.A., *Matthew* (Interpretation; Louisville, KY: John Knox Press, 1993).

—*The Son of Man Tradition* (Minneapolis, MN: Fortress Press, 1990).

—*The Theme of Jewish Persecution of Christians in the Gospel according to St Matthew* (SNTSMS, 6; Cambridge: Cambridge University Press, 1967).

Hare, D.R.A., and D.J. Harrington, '"Make Disciples of all the Gentiles" (Mt. 28.19)', *CBQ* 37 (1975), pp. 359-69.

Harnack, A., *Die Chronologie der altchristlichen Literatur bis Eusebius* (Leipzig: Hinrichs, 1897).

Harrington, D.J., *The Gospel of Matthew* (Sacra Pagina, 1; Collegeville, MN: The Liturgical Press, 1991).

—'Sabbath Tensions: Matthew 12.1-14 and other New Testament Texts', in T.C. Eskenazi, *et al.* (eds.), *The Sabbath in Jewish and Christian Traditions* (New York: Crossroad, 1991), pp. 45-56.

Hawkins, J.C., *Horae Synopticae* (Oxford: Clarendon Press, 1909).

Held, H.J., 'Matthew as Interpreter of the Miracle Stories', in G. Bornkamm, G. Barth, and H.J. Held, *Tradition and Interpretation in Matthew* (trans. P. Scott; London: SCM Press, 1963), pp. 165-299.

Henderson, I.H., '*Didache* and Orality in Synoptic Comparison', *JBL* 111 (1992), pp. 283-306.

Hendrickx, H., *The Miracle Stories* (London: Geoffrey Chapman, 1987).

Hengel, M., *Judaism and Hellenism* (2 vols.; trans. J. Bowden; London: SCM Press, 1974).

—*The Zealots: Investigations into the Jewish Freedom Movement in the Period from Herod I until 70 AD* (trans. D. Smith; Edinburgh: T. & T. Clark, 1989).

Hertzberg, H.W., *I & II Samuel* (trans. J.S. Bowden; OTL; London: SCM Press, 1964).

Hicks, J.M., 'The Sabbath Controversy in Matthew: An Exegesis of Matthew 12.1-14', *ResQ* 27 (1984), pp. 79-91.

Higgins, A.J.B., *Jesus and the Son of Man* (London: Lutterworth, 1964).

—'Son of Man—*Forschung* since "The Teaching of Jesus"', in A.J.B. Higgins (ed.), *New Testament Essays* (Manchester: Manchester University Press, 1959), pp. 119-35.

Hill, D., 'The Figure of Jesus in Matthew's Story: a Response to Professor Kingsbury's Literary-critical Probe', *JSNT* 21 (1984), pp. 37-52.

—*The Gospel of Matthew* (NCB; London: Marshall, Morgan & Scott, 1972).

—'On the Use and Meaning of Hosea vi. 6 in Matthew's Gospel', *NTS* 24 (1978), pp. 113-16.

—'The Rejection of Jesus at Nazareth (Luke iv 16-30)', *NovT* 13 (1971), pp. 161-80.

—'Son and Servant: an Essay on Matthean Christology', *JSNT* 6 (1980), pp. 2-16.

Hirsch, E., *Die Frühgeschichte des Evangeliums*, II (Tübingen: Mohr, 1941).

Hirschfeld, H., 'Remarks on the Etymology of Sabbath', *Journal of the Royal Asiatic Society of Great Britain and Ireland* 53 (1896), pp. 353-59.

Hobbs, T.R., *2 Kings* (WBC, 13; Waco, TX: Word Books, 1985).

Hoehner, H., *Herod Antipas* (SNTSMS, 17; Cambridge: Cambridge University Press, 1972).

Hoenig, S.B., 'The Designated Number of Kinds of Labor Prohibited on the Sabbath', *JQR* 68 (1977), pp. 193-208.

Hooker, M., *The Gospel according to St Mark* (BNTC; London: A. & C. Black, 1991).

—*The Son of Man in Mark* (London: SPCK, 1967).

Hoskyns, E.C., 'Jesus, the Messiah', in G.K.A. Bell and A. Deissmann (eds.), *Mysterium Christi* (London: Longmans, Green, 1930), pp. 69-89.

Howell, D.B., *Matthew's Inclusive Story: A Study in the Narrative Rhetoric of the First Gospel* (JSNTSup, 42; Sheffield: JSOT Press, 1990).

Hübner, H., *Das Gesetz in der synoptischen Tradition: Studien zur These einer progressiven Qumranisierung und Judaisierung innerhalb der synoptischen Tradition* (Witten: Luther Verlag, 1973).

Hultgren, A.J., 'The Formation of the Sabbath Pericope in Mark 2.23-28', *JBL* 91 (1972), 38-43.

Hummel, R., *Die Auseinandersetzung zwischen Kirche und Judentum in Matthäusevangelium* (BEvT, 33; Munich: Chr. Kaiser Verlag, 2nd edn, 1966).

Hunter, A.M., 'Crux Criticorum—Matt. XI. 25-30—A Re-appraisal', *NTS* 8 (1962), pp. 241-49.

Ito, A., 'The Question of the Authenticity of the Ban on Swearing (Matthew 5.33-37)', *JSNT* 43 (1991), pp. 5-13.

Jackson, F.J.F., and K. Lake, *The Beginnings of Christianity* (5 vols.; London: MacMillan, 1920–33).

Jefford, C.N., 'Did Ignatius of Antioch Know the *Didache?*', in *idem* (ed.), *The Didache in Context: Essays on its Text, History and Transmission* (NovTSup, 77; Leiden: Brill, 1995) pp. 330-51.

—*The Sayings of Jesus in the Teaching of the Twelve Apostles* (SupVC, 11; Leiden: Brill, 1989).

Jenni, E., *Die theologische Begründung des Sabbatgebotes im Alten Testament* (Theologische Studien, 46; Zollikon-Zürich: Evangelischer Verlag, 1956).

Jeremias, J., *The Eucharistic Words of Jesus* (trans. N. Perrin; London: SCM Press, 2nd edn, 1966).

—*Jerusalem in the Time of Jesus: An Investigation into Economic and Social Conditions during the New Testament Period* (trans. F.H. Cave and C.H. Cave; London: SCM Press, 1969).

—*New Testament Theology. I. The Proclamation of Jesus* (trans. J. Bowden; London: SCM Press, 1971).

—'Παῖς Θεοῦ', *TDNT*, V, pp. 677-717.

Jewett, P.K., *The Lord's Day: A Theological Guide to the Christian Day of Worship* (Grand Rapids: Eerdmans, 1971).

Joly, R., *Le dossier d'Ignace d'Antioche* (Brussels: Editions de l'université, 1979).

Jones, D.R., *Jeremiah* (NCB; London: Marshall Pickering, 1992).

Jones, G.H., *1 and 2 Kings* (2 vols.; NCB; London: Marshall, Morgan & Scott, 1984).

Kaiser, O., *Isaiah 1–12* (trans. J. Bowden; OTL; London: SCM Press, 1983).

Käsemann, E., *Essays on New Testament Themes* (trans. W.J. Montague; SBT, 41; London: SCM Press, 1964).

Kee, H.C., *Miracle in the Early Christian World: A Study in Socio-historical Method* (New Haven: Yale University Press, 1983).

Kertelge, K., 'κύω', *EDNT*, II, pp. 368-69.

Kilpatrick, G.D., *The Origins of the Gospel according to St Matthew* (Oxford: Clarendon Press, 1946).

Kim, S., *The 'Son of Man' as the Son of God* (WUNT, 30; Tübingen: Mohr, 1983).

Kimbrough, S.T., 'The Concept of Sabbath at Qumran', *RevQ* 5 (1962), pp. 484-502.

Kingsbury, J.D., 'Conclusion: Analysis of a Conversation', in D.L. Balch (ed.), *Social History of the Matthean Community: Cross-Disciplinary Approaches* (Minneapolis, MN: Fortress Press, 1991), pp. 259-69.

—*Conflict in Luke: Jesus, Authorities, Disciples* (Minneapolis, MN: Fortress Press, 1991).

—'The Figure of Jesus in Matthew's Story: a Literary-Critical Probe', *JSNT* 21 (1984), pp. 3-36.

—*Matthew as Story* (Philadelphia: Fortress Press, 2nd edn, 1988).

—*Matthew: Proclamation Commentary* (Philadelphia: Fortress Press, 1977).

—*Matthew: Structure, Christology, Kingdom* (Philadelphia: Fortress Press, 1975).

Klein, R.W., *1 Samuel* (WBC, 10; Waco, TX: Word Books, 1983).

Kloppenborg, J.S., *Q Parallels: Synopsis, Critical Notes, and Concordance* (Sonoma, CA: Polebridge, 1988).

Klostermann, E., *Das Markusevangelium* (HNT, 3; Tübingen: Mohr, 1950).

—*Das Matthäusevangelium* (HNT, 4; Tübingen: Mohr, 2nd edn, 1927).

Knibb, M.A., *The Qumran Community* (CCWJCW, 2; Cambridge: Cambridge University Press, 1987).

Knox, W.L., *The Sources of the Synoptic Gospels* (2 vols.; Cambridge: Cambridge University Press, 1957).

Koester, C., 'The Origin and Significance of the Flight to Pella Tradition', *CBQ* 51 (1989), pp. 90-106.

Köhler, W.-D., *Die Rezeption des Matthäusevangeliums in der Zeit vor Irenäus* (WUNT, 2/24; Tübingen: Mohr, 1987).

Köster, H., *Synoptische Überlieferung bei den Apostolischen Vätern* (Berlin: Akademie-Verlag, 1957).

Kraft, R.A., *The Apostolic Fathers: A New Translation and Commentary*. III. *Barnabas and the Didache* (5 vols. ed. R.M. Grant; New York: Thomas, Nelson & Sons, 1965).

—'Some Notes on Sabbath Observance in Early Christianity', *AUSS* 3 (1965), pp. 18-33.

Krentz, E., 'The Extent of Matthew's Prologue', *JBL* 83 (1964), pp. 409-14.

Kruijf, T. De, 'Go Therefore and Make Disciples of All Nations', *Bijdragen* 54 (1993), pp. 19-29.

Kümmel, W.G., *Introduction to the New Testament* (trans. H.C. Kee; London: SCM Press, 2nd edn, 1975).

Kuthirakkattel, S., *The Beginning of Jesus' Ministry according to Mark's Gospel (1,14-3,6); a Redaction Critical Study* (Rome: Editrice Pontificio Istituto Biblico, 1990).

Kutsch, E., 'Sabbat', in K. Galling, *et al.* (ed.), *Die Religion in Geschichte und Gegenwart*, V (Tübingen: Mohr, 3rd edn, 1958), pp. 1258-60.

Lacey, D.R. De, 'The Sabbath/Sunday Question and the Law in the Pauline Corpus', in D.A. Carson (ed.), *From Sabbath to Lord's Day: A Biblical, Historical, and Theological Investigation* (Grand Rapids: Zondervan, 1982), pp. 159-95.

Ladd, G.E., *The Presence of the Future: The Eschatology of Biblical Realism* (Grand Rapids: Eerdmans, 1974).

Lagrange, M.-J., *Evangile selon Saint Matthieu* (Paris: Gabalda, 7th edn, 1948).

Lambrecht, J., 'The Parousia Discourse: Composition and Content in Mt. XXIV-XXV', in M. Dider (ed.), *L'Evangile selon Matthieu: Rédaction et théologie* (Gembloux: Duculot, 1972), pp. 309-42.

—*The Sermon on the Mount: Proclamation and Exhortation* (GNS, 14; Wilmington, DE: Michael Glazier, 1985).

Lategan, B.C., 'Structural Interrelations in Matthew 11-12', *Neotestamentica* 11 (1977), pp. 115-29.

Leaney, A.R.C., *The Gospel according to St Luke* (BNTC; London: A. & C. Black, 2nd edn, 1966).

Lee, F.N., *The Covenantal Sabbath: The Weekly Sabbath Scripturally and Historically Considered* (London: LDOS, 1969).

Levine, E., 'The Sabbath Controversy according to Matthew', *NTS* 22 (1975/76), pp. 480-83.

Lewis, R.B., 'Ignatius and the "Lord's Day"', *AUSS* 6 (1968), pp. 46-59.

Lightfoot, J.B., *The Apostolic Fathers*. Part II: *S. Ignatius, S. Polycarp* (3 vols.; London: Macmillan, 1889).

—*The Apostolic Fathers*. I. *S. Clement of Rome* (2 vols.; London: Macmillan, 1890).

Lincoln, A.T., 'From Sabbath to Lord's Day: A Biblical and Theological Perspective', in Carson (ed.), *Lord's Day*, pp. 343-412.

—'Sabbath, Rest, and Eschatology in the New Testament', in D.A. Carson (ed.), *From Sabbath to Lord's Day: A Biblical, Historical, and Theological Investigation* (Grand Rapids: Zondervan, 1982), pp. 197-220.

Lindars, B., *Jesus Son of Man: A Fresh Examination of the Son of Man Sayings in the Gospels in the Light of Recent Research* (London: SPCK, 1983).

—*New Testament Apologetic: The Doctrinal Significance of the Old Testament Quotations* (London: SCM Press, 1961).

Lindemann, A., 'Der Sabbat ist um des Menschen willen geworden...', *WD* 15 (1979), pp. 79-105.

Ljungmann, H., *Das Gesetz erfüllen: Matth. 5,17ff. und 3,15 untersucht* (Lunds Universitets Årsskrift. NF, 50/6; Lund: Gleerup, 1954).

Lohmeyer, E., *Das Evangelium des Markus* (Kritisch-exegetischer Kommentar über das Neue Testament, 2; Göttingen: Vandenhoeck & Ruprecht, 1953).

—*Das Evangelium des Matthäus* (ed. W. Schmauch; Kritisch-exegetischer Kommentar über das Neue Testament, 1; Göttingen: Vandenhoeck & Ruprecht, 1956).

Lohr, C.H., 'Oral Techniques in the Gospel of Matthew', *CBQ* 23 (1961), pp. 403-35.

Lohse, E., 'Ich aber sage euch', in *idem* (ed.), *Der Ruf Jesu und die Antwort der Gemeinde, Festschrift für Joachim Jeremias* (BZNW, 26; Göttingen: Vandenhoeck & Ruprecht, 1970), pp. 189-203.

—'Jesu Worte über den Sabbat', in W. Eltester (ed.), *Judentum Urchristentum Kirche* (Berlin: Töpelmann, 1960), pp. 79-89.

—'σάββατον', *TDNT*, VII, pp. 1-35.

Loisy, A., *Les Evangiles Synoptiques*, II (Ceffonds: Prés Montier-en-der, 1908).

Luz, U., 'The Disciples in the Gospel according to Matthew', in G.N. Stanton (ed.), *The Interpretation of Matthew* (London: SPCK, 1983), pp. 98-128.

—'Die Erfüllung des Gesetzes bei Matthäus', *ZTK* 75 (1978), pp. 398-435.

—*Das Evangelium nach Matthäus (Mt 8–17)* (EKKNT, 1/2; Zürich and Brauschweig: Benziger Verlag, 1990).

—*Matthew 1–7* (trans. W.C. Linss; Edinburgh: T. & T. Clark, 1990).

—*Matthew in History: Interpretation, Influence, and Effects* (Minneapolis, MN: Fortress Press, 1994).

Maccoby, H., *Early Rabbinic Writings* (CCWJCW, 3; Cambridge: Cambridge University Press, 1988).

McConnell, R.S., 'Law and Prophecy in Matthew's Gospel: The Authority and Use of the Old Testament in the Gospel of St Matthew' (ThD dissertation, Basel, Friedrich Reinhardt Kommissionsverlag, 1969).

McKane, W., *A Critical and Exegetical Commentary on Jeremiah*, I (ICC: Edinburgh: T. & T. Clark, 1986).

M'Neile, A.H., *The Gospel according to St Matthew: The Greek Text with Introduction, Notes, and Indices* (London: Macmillan, 1915).

Maher, M., '"Take my Yoke upon You" (Matt. XI. 29)', *NTS* 22 (1975), pp. 97-103.

Manson, T.W., 'Mark ii. 27-28', in *Coniectanea neotestamentica*, XI (Lund: Gleerup, 1947), pp. 138-46.

—*The Sayings of Jesus* (London: SCM Press, 1949).

—'The Son of Man in Daniel, Enoch, and the Gospels' (1949), in *idem*, *Studies in the Gospels and Epistles* (Manchester: Manchester University Press, 1962), pp. 123-45.

—*The Teaching of Jesus: Studies of its Form and Content* (Cambridge: Cambridge University Press, 1955).

Manson, W., *Jesus the Messiah* (London: Hodder & Stoughton, 1943).

Marshall, I.H., *The Gospel of Luke: A Commentary on the Greek Text* (NIGTC; Exeter: Paternoster, 1978).

—*Luke: Historian and Theologian* (Exeter: Paternoster, 1970).

—*The Origins of New Testament Christology* (Leicester: IVP, 2nd edn, 1990).

—'Son of Man', *DJG*, pp. 775-81.

Mason, S., *Flavius Josephus on the Pharisees* (SPB, 39; Leiden: Brill, 1991).

Massaux, E., *The Influence of the Gospel of Saint Matthew on Christian Literature before Saint Irenaeus* (3 vols.; trans. N.J. Belval and S. Hecht; NGS, 5/1-3; Macon, GA: Mercer University Press, 1990-93).

Matera, F.J., 'The Plot of Matthew's Gospel', *CBQ* 49 (1987), pp. 233-53.

Mays, J.L., *Amos* (OTL; London: SCM Press, 1969).

—*Hosea* (OTL; London: SCM Press, 1969).

Meier, J.P., 'John the Baptist in Matthew's Gospel', *JBL* 99 (1980), pp. 383-405.

—*Law and History in Matthew's Gospel: A Redactional Study of Mt. 5.17-48* (AnBib, 71; Rome: Biblical Institute Press, 1976).

—*Matthew* (Dublin: Veritas, 1980).

—'Nations or Gentiles in Matthew 28.19?', *CBQ* 39 (1977), pp. 94-102.

Meinhold, J., *Sabbat und Sonntag* (Leipzig: Quelle & Meyer, 1909).

Meyer, E., *Ursprung und Anfänge des Christentums* (3 vols.; Stuttgart and Berlin: J.G. Cotta, 1924).

Miller, P.D., 'Luke 4:16-21', *Int* 29 (1975), pp. 417-21.

Mohrlang, R., *Matthew and Paul: A Comparison of Ethical Perspectives* (SNTSMS, 48; Cambridge: Cambridge University Press, 1984).

Montefiore, C.G., *The Synoptic Gospels* (2 vols.; London: Macmillan, 2nd edn, 1927).

Moo, D.J., 'Jesus and the Authority of the Mosaic Law', *JSNT* 20 (1984), pp. 3-49.

Moore, G.F., *Judaism in the First Centuries of the Christian Era: The Age of the Tannaim* (3 vols.; Cambridge, MA: Harvard University Press, 1927–30).

Morris, L. *The Gospel according to Matthew* (Leicester: IVP, 1992).

Moule, C.F.D., 'The Christology of Acts', in L.E. Keck and J.L. Martyn (eds.), *Studies in Luke–Acts* (Philadelphia: Fortress Press, 1966), pp. 159-85

—'Fulfilment-Words in the New Testament: Use and Abuse', *NTS* 14 (1967/68), pp. 293-320.

Mowinckel, S., *Zur Komposition des Buches Jeremia* (Kristiania: Jacob Dybwad, 1914).

Neirynck, F., *Duality in Mark: Contributions to the Study of Markan Redaction* (BETL, 31; Leuven: Leuven University Press, 1972).

—'Jesus and the Sabbath. Some Observations on Mk II,27', in J. Dupont (ed.), *Jésus aux origines de la christologie* (BETL, 40; Leuven: Leuven University Press, 1975), pp. 227-70.

—'Luke 14:1-6: Lukan Composition and Q Saying', in C. Bussmann and W. Radl (eds.), *Der Treue Gottes trauen* (Feiburg: Herder, 1991), pp. 243-63.

Neusner, J., *Jews and Christians: The Myth of a Common Tradition* (London: SCM Press, 1991).

—*Judaism: The Evidence of the Mishnah* (Chicago: University of Chicago Press, 1981).

Neyrey, J.H., 'The Thematic Use of Isaiah 42.1-4 in Matthew 12', *Bib* 63 (1982), pp. 457-73.

Nickelsburg, G.W.E., *Jewish Literature between the Bible and the Mishnah—A Historical and Literary Introduction* (Philadelphia: Fortress Press, 1981).

Niederwimmer, K., 'Der Didachist und seine Quellen', in C.N. Jefford (ed.), *The Didache in Context: Essays on its Text, History and Transmission* (NovTSup, 77; Leiden: Brill, 1995), pp. 15-36.

Nielsen, D., *Die altarabische Mondreligion und die mosaische Überlieferung* (Strassburg: Trübner, 1904).

Nineham, D.E., *The Gospel of St Mark* (Pelican Gospel Commentaries; London: A. & C. Black, 2nd edn, 1968).

Nolland, J., *Luke* (3 vols.; WBC, 35a-c; Dallas: Word Books, 1989–93).

Norden, E., *Agnostos Theos* (Leipzig and Berlin: Teubner, 1913).

North, R., 'The Derivation of Sabbath', *Bib* 36 (1955), pp. 182-201.

Noth, M., *The Chronicler's History* (JSOTSup, 50; Sheffield: JSOT Press, 1987).

—*Exodus* (trans. J. Bowden; OTL; London: SCM Press, 1962).

—*Numbers* (trans. J.D. Martin; OTL; London: SCM 1968).

Orton, D.E., *The Understanding Scribe: Matthew and the Apocalyptic Ideal* (JSNTSup, 25; Sheffield: JSOT Press, 1989).

O'Toole, R.F., 'Some Exegetical Reflections on Luke 13, 10-17', *Bib* 73 (1992), pp. 84-107.

Overman, J.A., *Matthew's Gospel and Formative Judaism: The Social World of the Matthean Community* (Minneapolis, MN: Fortress Press, 1990).

Paget, J.C., *The Epistle of Barnabas* (Tübingen: Mohr, 1994).

Pamment, M., 'The Son of Man in the First Gospel', *NTS* 29 (1983), pp. 116-29.

Patte, D., *The Gospel according to Matthew: A Structural Commentary on Matthew's Faith* (Philadelphia: Fortress Press, 1987).

Paul, S.M., *Amos* (Hermeneia; Minneapolis, MN: Fortress Press, 1991).

Perrin, N., *The Kingdom of God in the Teaching of Jesus* (London: SCM Press, 1963).

—*Rediscovering the Teaching of Jesus* (London: SCM Press, 1967).

Pesch, R., *Das Markusevangelium* (2 vols.; HTKNT, 2/1-2; Freiburg: Herder, 4th edn, 1984).

Pettirsch, F., 'Das Verbot der opera servilia in der Heiligen Schrift und in der altkirchlichen Exegese', *ZKT* 69 (1947), pp. 257-327, 417-44.

Plummer, A., *A Critical and Exegetical Commentary on the Gospel According to S. Luke* (ICC; Edinburgh: T. & T. Clark, 5th edn, 1922).

—*An Exegetical Commentary on the Gospel according to S. Matthew* (London: Robert Scott, 1909).

Powell, M.A., 'The Plot and Subplots of Matthew's Gospel', *NTS* 38 (1992), pp. 187-204.

Primus, J.H., 'Sunday: The Lord's Day as a Sabbath—Protestant Perspectives on the Sabbath', in T.C. Eskenazi, *et al.* (eds.), *The Sabbath in Jewish and Christian Traditions* (New York: Crossroad, 1991), pp. 98-121.

Pryke, E.J., *Redactional Style in the Marcan Gospel: A Study of Syntax and Vocabulary as Guides to Redaction in Mark* (SNTSMS, 33; Cambridge: Cambridge University Press, 1978).

Przybylski, B., *Righteousness in Matthew and his World of Thought* (SNTSMS, 41; Cambridge: Cambridge University Press, 1980).

Quasten, J., *Patrology* (3 vols.; Utrecht: Spectrum, 1950).

Rabin, C., *Qumran Studies* (Oxford: Oxford University Press, 1957).

Rad, G. von, *Deuteronomy* (trans. D. Barton; OTL; London: SCM Press, 1966).

—*Genesis* (trans. J.H. Marks and J. Bowden; OTL; London: SCM Press, 1972).

—*The Problem of the Hexateuch and Other Essays* (trans. E. Dicken; Edinburgh and London: Oliver & Boyd, 1965).

Rawlinson, A.E.J., *The Gospel according to St Mark with Introduction, Commentary and Additional Notes* (Westminster Commentaries; London: Methuen, 1925).

Reicke, B., *New Testament Era: The World of the Bible from 500 BC to AD 100* (trans. D.E. Green; London: A. & C. Black, 1968).

—'Synoptic Prophecies on the Destruction of Jerusalem', in D.E. Aune (ed.), *Studies in New Testament and Early Christian Literature: Essays in Honor of A.P. Wikgren* (Leiden: Brill, 1972), pp. 121-34.

Rendtorff, R., *The Old Testament: An Introduction* (trans. J. Bowden; London: SCM Press, 1985).

Richardson, C.C., *The Christianity of Ignatius of Antioch* (New York: AMS Press, 1967).

Rist, J.M., *On the Independence of Matthew and Mark* (SNTSMS, 32; Cambridge: Cambridge University Press, 1978).

Rist, M., 'Is Matt. 11.25-30 a Primitive Baptismal Hymn?', *Journal of Religion* 15 (1935), pp. 63-77.

Rius-Camp, J., *The Four Authentic Letters of Ignatius, The Martyr* (Rome: Pontificium Institutum Orientalium Studiorum, 1979).

Rivkin, E., *A Hidden Revolution* (Nashville: Abingdon, 1978).

Robinson, G., 'The Idea of Rest in the Old Testament and the Search for the Basic Character of Sabbath', *ZAW* 92 (1980), pp. 32-42.

—*Let Us Be Like the Nations: A Commentary on the Books of 1 and 2 Samuel* (ITC; Grand Rapids: Eerdmans, 1993).

Robinson, J.A.T., *Redating the New Testament* (London: SCM Press, 1976).

Roloff, J., *Das Kerygma und der irdische Jesus: Historische Motive in den Jesus-Erzählungen der Evangelien* (Göttingen: Vandenhoeck & Ruprecht, 1970).

Rordorf, W., 'Does the Didache Contain Jesus Tradition Independently of the Synoptic Gospels?', in H. Wansbrough (ed.), *Jesus and the Oral Gospel Tradition* (JSNTSup, 64; Sheffield: JSOT Press, 1991), pp. 394-423.

—*Sunday: The History of the Day of Rest and Worship in the Earliest Centuries of the Christian Church* (trans. A.A.K. Graham; London: SCM Press, 1968).

Rosenthal, J., 'The Sabbath Laws of the Qumranites or the Damascus Covenanters', *Biblical Research* 6 (1961), pp. 10-17.

Rowland, C., 'A Summary of Sabbath Observance in Judaism at the Beginning of the Christian Era', in D.A. Carson (ed.), *From Sabbath to Lord's Day: A Biblical, Historical, and Theological Investigation* (Grand Rapids: Zondervan, 1982), pp. 43-55.

Rudolph, W., *Jeremia* (HAT; Tübingen: Mohr, 1958).

Saldarini, A.J., *Matthew's Christian-Jewish Community* (Chicago: University of Chicago Press, 1994).

—*Pharisees, Scribes and Sadducees in Palestinian Society* (Edinburgh: T. & T. Clark, 1988).

Sand, A., *Das Evangelium nach Matthäus* (RNT; Regensburg: Verlag Friedrich Pustet, 1986).

—*Das Gesetz und die Propheten: Untersuchungen zur Theologie des Evangeliums nach Matthäus* (Biblische Untersuchungen, 11; Regensburg: Verlag Friedrich Pustet, 1974).

Sanders, E.P., 'Jesus and the Constraint of the Law', *JSNT* 17 (1983), pp. 19-24.

—*Jesus and Judaism* (London: SCM Press, 1985).

—*Jewish Law from Jesus to the Mishnah: Five Studies* (London: SCM Press, 1990).

—*Judaism: Practice and Belief 63 BCE–66 CE* (London: SCM Press, 1992).

Sanders, E.P., and M. Davies, *Studying the Synoptic Gospels* (London: SCM Press, 1989).

Sanders, J.T., *The Jews in Luke–Acts* (London: SCM Press, 1987).

Schlatter, A., *Der Evangelist Matthäus: Seine Sprache, sein Ziel, Seine Selbständigkeit* (Stuttgart: Calwer Verlag, 1959).

Schmid, J., *Das Evangelium nach Matthäus* (RNT; Regensburg: Pustet, 5th edn, 1965).

Schmidt, K.L., *Der Rahmen der Geschichte Jesu* (Berlin: Trowitzsch & Sohn, 1919).

Schmidt, W.H., *Introduction to the Old Testament* (trans. M.J. O'Connell; London: SCM Press, 1984).

Schneider, G., 'συμβούλιον, ου, τό', *EDNT*, III, p. 286.

Schniewind, J., *Das Evangelium nach Matthäus* (NTD, 2; Göttingen: Vandenhoeck & Ruprecht, 12th edn, 1968).

Schoedel, W.R., *Ignatius of Antioch* (Hermeneia; Philadelphia: Fortress Press, 1985).

Schrenk, G., 'ἐντολή', *TDNT*, II, pp. 544-56.

Schürer, E., *The History of the Jewish People in the Age of Jesus Christ* (3 vols.; ed. G. Vermes, F. Millar and M. Goodman; Edinburgh: T. & T. Clark, rev. edn, 1973–87).

Schürmann, H., *Das Lukasevangelium* (2 vols.; HTKNT, 3/1-2; Freiburg: Herder, 1969).

—*Traditionsgeschichtliche Untersuchungen zu den synoptischen Evangelien* (Düsseldorf: Patmos, 1968).

Schweizer, E., *The Good News according to Luke* (trans. D.E. Green; London: SPCK, 1984).

—*The Good News according to Mark* (trans. D.H. Madvig; London: SPCK, 1970).

—*The Good News according to Matthew* (trans. D.E. Green; London: SPCK, 1976).

—'Matthäus 5, 17-20. Anmerkungen zum Gesetzesversändnis des Matthäus', in *idem*, *Neotestamentica* (Zürich: Zwingli Verlag, 1963), pp. 399-406.

—'Matthäus 12,1-8: Der Sabbat—Gebot und Geschenk', in J. Kilunen, *et al.* (eds.), *Glaube und Gerechtigkeit* (Helsinki: Finnischen Exegetischen Gesellschaft, 1983), pp. 169-79.

—'Matthäus 21-25', in *idem, Matthäus und seine Gemeinde* (SBS, 71; Stuttgart: Katholisches Bibelwerk, 1974), pp. 116-25.

—'Matthew's Church', in G.N. Stanton (ed.), *The Interpretation of Matthew* (London: SPCK, 1983), pp. 129-55.

—'Der Menschensohn (Zur eschatologischen Erwartung Jesu)', *ZNW* 50 (1959), pp. 185-209.

—'Noch Einmal Mt 5,17-20', in *idem, Gemeinde*, pp. 78-85.

—'The Son of Man Again', *NTS* 9 (1962/3), pp. 256-61.

Segal, A.F., 'Matthew's Jewish Voice', in D.L. Balch (ed.), *Social History of the Matthean Community: Cross-Disciplinary Approaches* (Minneapolis, MN: Fortress Press, 1991), pp. 3-37.

Sharvit, B., 'The Sabbath of the Judean Desert Sect', *Immanuel* 9 (1979), pp. 42-48.

Shea, W.H., 'The Sabbath in the Epistle of Barnabas', *AUSS* 4 (1966), pp. 149-75.

Sibinga, J. Smit, 'Ignatius and Matthew', *NovT* 8 (1966), pp. 263-83.

Sigal, P., *The Halakah of Jesus of Nazareth according to the Gospel of Matthew* (Lanham, MD: University Press of America, 1986).

Sloan, R.B., *The Favorable Year of the Lord: A Study of the Jubilary Theology in the Gospel of Luke* (Austin, TX: Schola Press, 1977).

Snodgrass, K.R., 'Matthew's Understanding of the Law', *Int* 46 (1992), pp. 368-78.

Soares-Prabhu, G.M., *The Formula Quotations in the Infancy Narrative of Matthew* (AnBib, 63; Rome: Biblical Institute Press, 1976).

Soggin, J.A., *Introduction to the Old Testament* (trans. J. Bowden; London: SCM Press, 1989).

Spier, E., *Der Sabbat* (Das Judentum, 1; Berlin: Institut Kirche und Judentum, 1992).

Stanton, G.N., 'The Communities of Matthew', *Int* 46 (1992), pp. 379-91.

—'The Gospel of Matthew and Judaism', in *idem, A Gospel for a New People: Studies in Matthew* (Edinburgh: T. & T. Clark, 1992), pp. 146-68.

—'Matthew 11.28-30: Comfortable Words?', in *idem, People*, pp. 364-77.

—'The Origin and Purpose of Matthew's Gospel: Matthean Scholarship from 1945 to 1980', *ANRW* II.25.3 (Berlin: de Gruyter, 1985), pp. 1889-1951.

—' "Pray that your Flight may not be in Winter or on a Sabbath": Matthew 24.20', in *idem, People*, pp. 192-206.

—'Redaction Criticism: the End of an Era?', in *idem, People*, pp. 23-53.

—'Synagogue and Church', in *idem, People*, pp. 113-45.

Stendahl, K., *The School of St Matthew, and its Use of the Old Testament* (ASNU, 20; Lund: Gleerup, 2nd edn, 1968).

Stonehouse, N.B., *The Witness of Matthew and Mark to Christ* (London: Tyndale Press, 1944).

Stott, W., 'The Theology of the Christian Sunday in the Early Church' (DPhil thesis, Oxford, 1966).

Strack, H.L., and P. Billerbeck, *Kommentar zum Neuen Testament aus Talmud und Midrasch* (4 vols.; Munich: Beck, 1922–28).

Strack, H.L., and G. Stemberger, *Introduction to the Talmud and Midrash* (trans. M.N.A. Bockmuehl; Edinburgh: T. & T. Clark, 1991).

Strand, K.A., 'Another Look at "Lord's Day" in the Early Church and in Rev. I.10', *NTS* 13 (1967), pp. 174-81.

Strecker, G., *Der Weg der Gerechtigkeit: Untersuchungen zur Theologie des Matthäus* (FRLANT, 82; Göttingen: Vandenhoeck & Ruprecht, 1962).

Streeter, B.H., *The Four Gospels: A Study of Origins* (London: Macmillan, 1924).

Stuart, D., *Hosea–Jonah* (WBC, 31; Waco, TX: Word Books, 1987).

Suggs, M.J., *Wisdom, Christology, and Law in Matthew's Gospel* (Cambridge, MA: Harvard University Press, 1970).

Tannehill, R.C., *The Narrative Unity of Luke–Acts: A Literary Interpretation* (Philadelphia: Fortress Press, 1986).

Taylor, V., *The Formation of the Gospel Tradition* (London: Macmillan, 1935).

—*The Gospel according to St Mark: The Greek Text with Introduction, Notes, and Indexes* (London: Macmillan, 2nd edn, 1966).

—*The Passion Narrative of St Luke* (Cambridge: Cambridge University Press, 1972).

Temple, P.J., 'The Rejection at Nazareth', *CBQ* 17 (1955), pp. 229-42.

Theissen, G., *The Miracle Stories of the Early Christian Tradition* (trans. F. McDonagh; Edinburgh: T. & T. Clark, 1983).

Thompson, J.A., *The Book of Jeremiah* (NICOT; Grand Rapids: Eerdmans, 1980).

Tilborg, S. van, *The Jewish Leaders in Matthew* (Leiden: Brill, 1972).

Tödt, H.E., *The Son of Man in the Synoptic Tradition* (trans. D.M. Barton; London: SCM Press, 1965).

Traub, H., 'οὐρανός', *TDNT*, V, pp. 509-43.

Trevett, C., 'Approaching Matthew from the Second Century: The Under-used Ignatian Correspondence', *JSNT* 20 (1984), pp. 59-67.

—*A Study of Ignatius of Antioch in Syria and Asia* (Lampeter: Edwin Mellen Press, 1992).

Trilling, W., *Das wahre Israel: Studien zur Theologie des Matthäus-Evangeliums* (Munich: Kösel-Verlag, 3rd edn, 1964).

Tuckett, C.M., *Reading the New Testament: Methods of Interpretation* (London: SPCK, 1987).

—'Synoptic Tradition in the Didache', in J.-M. Sevrin (ed.), *The New Testament in Early Christianity / La réception des écrits néo-testamentaires dans le christianisme primitif* (Louvain: Louvain University Press, 1989), pp. 197-230.

Turner, M.M.B., 'The Sabbath, Sunday, and the Law in Luke/Acts', in D.A. Carson (ed.), *From Sabbath to Lord's Day: A Biblical, Historical, and Theological Investigation* (Grand Rapids: Zondervan, 1982), pp. 99-157.

Tyson, J.B., 'Scripture, Torah, and Sabbath in Luke–Acts', in E.P. Sanders (ed.), *Jesus, the Gospel, and the Church* (Macon, GA: Mercer University Press, 1987), pp. 89-104.

VanderKam, J.C., *Textual and Historical Studies in the Book of Jubilees* (Missoula, MT: Scholars Press, 1977).

Verheyden, J., 'The Flight of the Christian to Pella', *ETL* 66 (1990), pp. 368-84.

Vermes, G., *The Dead Sea Scrolls: Qumran in Perspective* (Philadelphia: Fortress Press, 1981).

—*Jesus the Jew* (London: SCM Press, 2nd edn, 1983).

—'The Use of נשׁ בר/נשׁא בר in Jewish Aramaic', in M. Black, *An Aramaic Approach to the Gospels and Acts* (Oxford: Clarendon Press, 3rd edn, 1967), pp. 310-28.

Vokes, F.E., *The Riddle of the Didache* (London: SPCK, 1938).

Walker, R., *Die Heilsgeschichte im ersten Evangelium* (FRLANT, 91; Göttingen: Vandenhoeck & Ruprecht, 1967).

Walter, N., *Der Thoraausleger Aristobulus* (Berlin: Akademie-Verlag, 1964).

Watts, J.D.W., *Isaiah* (2 vols.; WBC, 24-25; Waco, TX: Word Books, 1987).

Weijenborg, R., 'Is Evagrius Ponticus the Author of the *Longer Recension* of the Ignatian Letters?', *Antonianum* 44 (1969), pp. 339-47.

—*Les lettres d'Ignace d'Antioche* (Leiden: Brill, 1969).

Weiss, B., *Das Matthäus-Evangelium* (Göttingen: Vandenhoeck & Ruprecht, 9th edn, 1898).

Weiss, H., 'The Sabbath in the Synoptic Gospels', *JSNT* 38 (1990), pp. 13-27.

Weiss, H.F., 'φαρισαῖος', *TDNT*, IX, pp. 35-48.

Wellhausen, J., *Das Evangelium Marci* (Berlin: Georg Reimer, 2nd edn, 1909).

Wengst, K., *Didache (Apostellehre). Barnabasbrief. Zweiter Klemensbrief. Schrift an Diognet* (Munich and Darmstadt: Wissenschaftliche Buchgesellschaft, 1984).

Wenham, D., 'Jesus and the Law: an Exegesis on Matthew 5.17-20', *Themelios* 4 (1979), pp. 92-96.

Wenham, G., *The Book of Leviticus* (NICOT; Grand Rapids: Eerdmans, 1979).

—*Genesis 1–15* (WBC, 1; Waco, TX: Word Books, 1987).

Westermann, C., *Genesis 1–11* (trans. J.J. Scullion; London: SPCK, 1984).

—*Isaiah 40–66* (trans. D.M.G. Stalker; OTL; London: SCM Press, 1969).

Whybray, R.N., *Isaiah 40–66* (NCB; London: Marshall, Morgan & Scott, 1975).

Wilckens, U., 'σαγία κτλ.', *TDNT*, VII, pp. 496-528.

Wildberger, H., *Isaiah 1–12* (trans. T.H. Trapp; Minneapolis, MN: Fortress Press, 1991).

Wilkinson, J., 'The Case of the Bent Woman in Luke 13:10-17', *EvQ* 49 (1977), pp. 195-205.

Williams, A.L., 'The Date of the Epistle of Barnabas', *JTS* 34 (1933), pp. 337-46.

Williamson, H.G.M., *1 and 2 Chronicles* (NCB; London: Marshall, Morgan & Scott, 1982).

—*Ezra and Nehemiah* (Old Testament Guides; Sheffield: JSOT Press, 1987).

—*Ezra, Nehemiah* (WBC, 16; Waco, TX: Word Books, 1985).

—'The Origins of the Twenty-Four Priestly Courses: a Study of 1 Chronicles xxiii-xxvii', in J.A. Emerton (ed.), *Studies in the Historical Books of the Old Testament* (VTSup, 30; Leiden: Brill, 1979), pp. 251-68.

Williamson, R., *Jews in the Hellenistic World: Philo* (CCWJCW, 1/2; Cambridge: Cambridge University Press, 1989).

Wilson, S.G., *Luke and the Law* (SNTSMS, 50; Cambridge: Cambridge University Press, 1983).

Windisch, H., *Der Barnabasbrief* (Tübingen: Mohr, 1920).

Witherington, B., 'Matt. 5.32 and 19.9—Exception or Exceptional Situation?', *NTS* 31 (1985), pp. 571-75.

Wolff, H.W., *Hosea* (trans. G. Stansell; Hermeneia; Philadelphia: Fortress Press, 1974).

Wolfson, H.A., *Philo: Foundations of Religious Philosophy in Judaism, Christianity, and Islam* (2 vols.; Cambridge, MA: Harvard University Press, 1947).

Wong, E.K.-C., 'The Matthean Understanding of the Sabbath: A Response to G.N. Stanton', *JSNT* 44 (1991), pp. 3-18.

Wrege, H.-T., *Die Überlieferungs-geschichte der Bergpredigt* (WUNT, 9; Tübingen: Mohr, 1968).

Wright, N.T., *Christian Origins and the Question of God*. I. *The New Testament and the People of God* (London: SPCK, 1992).

Yang, Y.E., 'Jesus, Fulfilment and Law in Matthew 5.17-20: A Discussion Focusing on the Eschatological Dimension' (MA dissertation, London Bible College [CNAA], 1992).

Zahavy, T., 'The Sabbath Code of Damascus Document X:14-XI:18: Form Analytical and Redaction Critical Observations', *RevQ* 10 (1981), pp. 589-91.

Zahn, T., *Das Evangelium des Matthäus* (Leipzig: Deicher, 1903).

—*Ignatii et Polycarpi Epistulae, Martyria, Fragmenta* (Leipzig: Hinrichs, 1876).

Zeitlin, S., 'The Book of Jubilees, its Character and Significance', *JQR* 30 (1939/40), pp. 1-30.

Zimmerli, W., *Ezekiel* (2 vols.; trans. J.D. Martin; Hermeneia; Philadelphia: Fortress Press, 1983).

INDEXES

INDEX OF REFERENCES

OLD TESTAMENT

NEW TESTAMENT

QUMRAN

PHILO

Abr.		*Migr. Abr.*		2.249	75
28	75	89–93	76, 78, 97	2.260	78
				2.41	75
Cher.				2.46-51	76
86–90	76	*Mut. Nom.*		2.56	75
87–91	75	260	75	2.58	75
87	76			2.59	75
		Omn. Prob. Lib.		2.60-70	77
Decal.		81–82	78	2.60-62	76
51	75			2.61-64	78
96	75	*Op. Mund.*		2.64	76
98–101	76	89–128	75, 98, 300	2.65	78
		96	75	2.66-70	78, 170
Deus Imm.		100	75	2.86	75
11	75	102	75	66–70	64
		106	75		
Fug.		107	75	*Vit. Cont.*	
173	75	127	75	30–37	78, 99
		128	75		
Hyp.				*Vit. Mos.*	
7.11-16	77			1.207	75
7.20	77	*Somn.*		2.21-22	78, 97
12–13	78	2.123-32	76	2.22	170
		2.123-24	78	2.209	75
Leg. All.				2.210	75
1.15	75	*Spec. Leg.*		2.211-20	97
1.16-18	76	1.168-76	79, 173	2.211-12	77
2.64	76	1.170	75	2.213-20	78
155–58	77	2.214	75	2.218	75
155	77	2.224	75	2.263	75
156	99, 300	2.249-51	78, 97, 98		
158	77				

JOSEPHUS

Ant.			73	14.223-64	74
1.33	73	12.274	71	14.223-40	71
3.91	73	12.276-77	58, 70, 73, 178	14.223-24	71
3.142-43	173	12.277	70	14.226	71
3.143	73	13.12-14	58, 70, 73, 178	14.228-29	71
3.237	73			14.231-32	71
3.255-56	73, 173	13.14	58	14.241-64	72
4.231-39	170	13.251-52	71	14.241-43	72
12.4	57, 58, 70, 73	13.294	89	14.244-46	72
		13.297	171	14.256-58	72
12.5-6	72	13.337	70	14.262-64	72
12.6	70	14.23.202-10	71	14.63-64	70
12.257-59	71	14.23.236-37	71	14.63	59, 70
12.274-75	58, 69,			16.27-30	72, 74

CLASSICAL